SHADES OF MAO

THE POSTHUMOUS CULT OF THE GREAT LEADER

GEREMIE R. BARMÉ

An East Gate Book

M.E. Sharpe

Armonk, New York
London, England

An East Gate Book

Copyright © 1996 by Geremie R. Barmé

Library of Congress Cataloging-in-Publication Data

Barmé, Geremie.
Shades of Mao : the posthumous cult of the great leader /
Geremie R. Barmé.
P.   cm.
"An East gate book."
Includes bibliographical references and index.
ISBN 1-56324-678-3 (alk. paper).
ISBN 1-56324-679-1 (pbk. ; alk. paper).
1. Mao, Tse-tung, 1893–1976.
2. China—Politics and government—1976–   I. Title.
DS778.M3B374   1995
951.05′092—dc20   95-25979
CIP

Printed in the United States of America

The paper used in this publication meets the minimum requirements of American National Standard for Information Sciences—Permanence of Paper for Printed Library Materials,
ANSI Z 39.48-1984.

BM (c)   10   9   8   7   6   5   4   3   2   1
BM (p)   10   9   8   7   6   5   4   3   2   1

SHADES OF MAO

For truly great men
Look to this age alone
　　　　—Mao Zedong

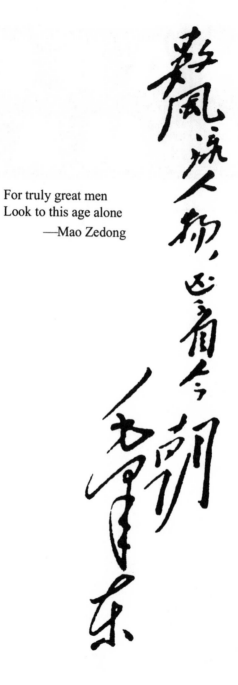

For my mother, Jane Duncan Brown (Roma Glen McNab),
and my brother Scot Barmé

Contents

Acknowledgments

My first contact with the original Mao Cult occurred when I was a high school student in Sydney in 1967. During morning recess one day Samson ("Spock") Voron, a classmate and ham radio enthusiast who delighted in listening to Radio Peking, introduced me to the extraordinary world of *Peking Review* and the glossy glories of *China Pictorial*. As an undergraduate at the Australian National University (ANU) in Canberra my Chinese teacher, Pierre Ryckmans (Simon Leys), revealed the alternative reading of Mao Zedong's poem "Snow," lines from which feature so often in this book.

Then there was the first criticism sessions I was subjected to along with my fellow exchange students at Fudan University in Shanghai in early 1975. It concerned a Mao portrait that had appeared on the front page of the *People's Daily*. It seems that in a distracted moment one of us had used the page in the communal lavatory, and it was not for reading. The Chinese student body, we were told, was outraged.

As a student in China from 1974 to 1977, and then as an editor at *The Seventies Monthly* in Hong Kong from 1977 until mid 1979, I had more to do with the Mao Cult, both pre- and posthumous, than was probably good for me. To an extent, this small volume is a product of an abiding fascination and fixation with the lost world of Chairman Mao.

Anita Chan, my colleague at ANU and general editor of *Chinese Sociology and Anthropology: A Journal of Translations*, urged me to undertake this project and it is through her good offices that some of the material in this book first appeared in that journal. I am also very grateful to Gavan McCormack for pressing me to expand that text into the present volume.

Particular thanks go to Sang Ye, a tireless Mao aficionado who over the years has introduced me to a great deal of Mao arcana, including *Tushu faxing gongzuo wenjian huibian* published for restricted circulation by Xinhua Books in Beijing, the contents of which inspired my work on the fall and rise of the Great Leader. Sang Ye has always been happy to search through his considerable private collection of materials to provide me with obscure information and answer my endless inquires for footnotes in the text. Without his enthusiasm this volume would be far more bland. He has also been kind enough to allow me to quote material from his new series of interviews (see "Musical Chairmen").

Chris Buckley's scholastic (and morbid) interest in Mao has been a great encouragement, and he generously allowed me full access to his own library of recent Mao-related works.

Funding from the Research School of Pacific and Asian Studies of ANU made it possible for me to collect research materials and Mao memorabilia, as well as to revisit Mao's birthplace in Shaoshan in 1992 at the height of the new Mao Cult. I am, as ever, extremely grateful to my colleagues and friends at ANU for their constant interest in and support of my work.

Richard Gordon, Mao groupie and boss at Long Bow in Boston, was crucial in making this book a visual success. The Long Bow Archive provided many of the illustrations in the following pages and Richard and Kimberly Roberts took the time from the more pressing task of making a documentary film to photograph many of these. Long Bow itself indulged and succored me as I finished off this project.

Carma Hinton and Nora Chang, Claire Roberts, as well as John Minford, Jean Hsiung of the Universities Services Centre, Neil Thompson of Qantas, Gloria Davies, Peter Micic, Ruth Waller, Nicholas Jose, Zoë Wang, Susan Lambert, Nancy Berliner, Jonathan Hutt, Y.S. Chan, Tsoi Wing-mui of *Open Magazine*, Wang Youshen, Kam Louie, W.J.F. Jenner, Xu Jilin, Chen Xing, Dai Qing, Zhang Hongtu, Vivienne Tam of East Wind Code in New York, Zhu Dake, Don J. Cohn, Jane Macartney of Reuters, Hannah Fink of *Art and AsiaPacific*, Michael Dutton, Li Kaining, Rebecca Cox, Jean-Philippe Béja of Centre d'Études et d'Information sur la Chine, Liu Qingfeng of *21st Century*, Lionel Bawden, Jon Lee, Jeffrey N. Wasserstrom, Andrew Morris, and Scott Savitt of *Beijing Scene* have all helped me in various ways in my pursuit of the Chairman's shade. Special thanks also go to Fusako McCormack for her assistance with the translation of Zhang Chengzhi's article from Japanese and to Linda Jaivin for her comments on the first draft of the introductory essay.

I am also grateful to Doug Merwin of M.E. Sharpe, who responded enthusiastically to my suggestion that I expand the material I prepared for *Chinese Sociology and Anthropology* into this book, and to Dorothy Lin, my editor at M.E. Sharpe.

SHADES OF MAO

The Irresistible Fall and Rise of Mao Zedong

A Mao for All Seasons

Of the numerous news stories and popular rumors that abounded in China during the months leading up to Mao Zedong's centenary in December 1993, one of the most extraordinary tales issued from Sichuan. It was reported that workers in a local factory believed that Chairman Mao had established an industrial complex in the afterlife, which he was running according to the socialist principles he had espoused before his death. Despairing of the capitalist-style factory management and labor exploitation of the Reform era, and mindful that Mao had often claimed that he would go into the mountains and launch the revolution all over again if China "went revisionist,"[1] a number of workers committed suicide. They hoped to join the Chairman in the netherworld and continue to fight for the revolution under his shade.[2]

Although this story has not attained the status of a Chinese urban myth, it does reflect one facet of the revival of popular interest in Mao Zedong from the late 1980s: a deep dissatisfaction with the status quo and a yearning for the moral power and leadership of the long-dead Chairman.

* * *

This land so rich in beauty
Has made countless heroes bow in homage.

This essay is a much-expanded version of a paper presented at "Mao Craze, Mao Cult? A Symposium on Popular Culture in China Today," 23 April 1994, a workshop organized by the Fairbank Center for East Asian Research, Harvard University. My thanks to the organizers of and participants in that workshop for their encouragement. A shorter version of this book appeared as an issue of *Chinese Sociology and Anthropology: A Journal of Translations* 28, no. 1 (Fall 1995).

> But alas! Qin Shihuang and Han Wudi
> Were lacking in literary grace,
> And Tang Taizong and Song Taizu
> Had little poetry in their souls;
> And Genghis Khan,
> Proud Son of Heaven for a day,
> Knew only shooting eagles, bow outstretched.
> All are past and gone!
> For truly great men
> Look to this age alone.[3]

When Mao's poem "Snow," of which this is the last stanza, was first published in late 1945, a number of observers criticized the writer for indulging in "imperial fantasies." The last lines—"For truly great men/Look to this age alone"—the critics averred, did not refer to "the broad masses of the proletariat," as Communist Party commentators claimed, but to Mao and Mao alone.[4]

The Shanghai writer Li Jie, whose critique of Mao is quoted at length in the present volume, comments on these lines: "Here was the peasant boy listing all of the major father figures of Chinese history, leaving the last and most glorious position, however, for himself" (see "The Mao Phenomenon"; references in parentheses are to material contained in this book). The poem exudes the bravado that Mao's opponents have excoriated for decades; nonetheless, it reflects the kind of self-assertiveness and egomania that continue to beguile those for whom Mao Zedong represents the abiding genius or eidolon of China.

Even before Mao's demise on 9 September 1976, there were those who speculated that in death Mao would "become even more sacred" and be deified in ways only hinted at during his last years.[5] But with the return of Deng Xiaoping to power in the late 1970s and after the protracted negation of Mao's legacy and the Cultural Revolution culminating in 1981, for nearly a decade it seemed that the Chairman had been safely relegated to the ranks of elder revolutionaries. Although Mao had played a pivotal role in the creation of the People's Republic and its first decades, in death he no longer exercised the charismatic power he had enjoyed in life.

From the late 1980s, however, Mainland China witnessed at first a fitful and then a nationwide revival of interest in Mao Zedong. Initially, the phenomenon was called a "search for Mao Zedong,"[6] and according to one commentator it was the fifth of its kind.[7] The official media, ever anxious to employ fashionable "buzzwords" for propagandistic purposes, soon dubbed it a "MaoCraze," the *Mao Zedong re* or simply *Maore*. In this book, the compressed term "MaoCraze" will be used to translate the Chinese expression *Maore*, while Mao Cult indicates the revival of Mao in its myriad forms from the late 1980s as discussed in this introduction and the editorial notes.

This Mao Cult was largely nonofficial and spontaneous. It continued up to the time of the government-orchestrated centenary of Mao's birth in 1993, and it would appear that popular enthusiasm for the Chairman waned in direct proportion to the authorities' promotion of Mao as the founding father of the Party, army, and state. The new Mao Cult was markedly different from the "personality cult" (*geren chongbai* in Chinese or, in post-1976 officialese, *zaoshen yundong*) of the Cultural Revolution.[8] Divested nearly entirely of its original class, ethical, and political dimensions, the new cult flourished throughout the country, prompting propagandists, commentators, and academics to analyze and declaim on the subject in the pages of the Mainland, Hong Kong, and Taiwanese press.

This short volume attempts to digest and elucidate some of that massive body of material with selections taken primarily from Mainland sources. Unfortunately, due to the limited nature of public debate in the Mainland media, in particular because of official strictures on books related to Mao (see "Publish and Perish"), many writers were unable to comment freely on the cult. Within the considerable body of material that did appear, however, diverse views were expressed, often with a frankness that would have been astounding in the not-too-distant past. The following selection is little more than a meager sampling of those materials. Although I have attempted to reflect as broad a range of opinions as possible and touch on the diverse phenomena that constituted the Mao revival, given the vastness of the topic I cannot claim that this book is an exhaustive survey. I can only hope that the present volume may act as an introductory guide to those who wish to delve further into this disturbing yet fascinating realm of Chinese popular culture.

Pulping Mao

During the Cultural Revolution even wedding ceremonies had to be "revolutionized." The newlyweds were invariably presented with copies of *Selected Works of Mao Zedong* or *Quotations from Chairman Mao*.

One couple received sixty-five copies of the Little Red Book and thirty-seven sets of *Selected Works*. When the guests had all left the bride said to her husband:

"What ever are we going to do with this great pile of books? We can't sell them or eat them, nor do we dare burn them. Not even our children or grandchildren will have any use for this many!"

> "Don't worry," the husband replied. "As Chairman Mao has instructed us [in his speech "The Foolish Old Man Who Removed the Mountains"]: 'When your children die you will still have grandchildren, and after them their grandchildren and the grandchildren's grandchildren, and so on for infinity.' We might be faced with an unmovable mountain of books but it will never grow any taller and, volume by volume, the mountain can be shifted."
>
> —Cultural Revolution joke[9]

The public history of the dismantling of the original Mao Cult after 1976 is perhaps best reflected in the fate of the Chairman's most tangible legacies to the nation: his word and his image.

A huge number of unsold and seemingly immutable copies of Mao's works were stockpiled, remaindered, throughout China. They came in all shapes and sizes, from the gaudy plastic-covered "Little Red Book," *Quotations from Chairman Mao*, to traditional clothbound limited-edition versions of the four-volume *Selected Works of Mao Zedong* with extra-large print produced for Mao's myopic coevals. Not only were huge portions of the state publishing budget tied up in this vast mound of Mao-period paper in the late 1970s, but also many acres of floor space in warehouses throughout the country were devoted to storing what was now unpalatable but equally unpulpable political fiction.

One particularly famous storehouse of Mao's works was the "*Bawanba*" (literally, "eighty-eight thousand," the figure denoted the number of square meters of floor space in the building) at Huaqiao Xincun near the Beijing Zoo. In the late 1970s, long after the waning of the Mao Cult but still before the Party had put Mao in his place, *Bawanba* was still spoken of in hushed tones as though it were some sacrosanct repository (although some Beijing people, with their characteristic mordant wit, mocked the fact that it was now nothing more than a mausoleum to the dead letter of Mao's works). It was rumored that in *Bawanba* seemingly endless shelves held neat packages of Mao's works in Chinese, minority, and foreign-language editions preserved in a strictly controlled, air-conditioned and humidified environment. A special detachment of soldiers guarded the building and another group of caretakers methodically worked their way along the shelves, unwrapped the books, and leafed through them to prevent mold and decay, only to repack them once again until the next time they were scheduled for airing. Similar repositories were to be found throughout the country maintaining the written legacy of Mao for possible future use.

Because of the cost of storing the immense print runs of Mao's works and due to the pressing need for warehouse space for the many new titles being produced after the Cultural Revolution, in particular educational texts, by the late 1970s hard decisions regarding the Leader's works had to

be made. These decisions were made by a number of bureaucratic instrumentalities such as the Party's Department of Propaganda, the National
Bureau for Publishing Administration, and Xinhua Books, the major retailer
for books in China, in accordance with Party directives.

Lin Biao, the cult of Mao he sponsored, as well as *Quotations from
Chairman Mao*, which Lin had exploited and even written a preface for,
may have all been defunct from the time of Lin's disappearance in 1971,[10]
but the Little Red Book itself continued to enjoy a shelf life until 1979, as
did many other products of the official Mao Cult. In February of that year
the Department of Propaganda issued instructions to remove from sale all
copies of *Quotations* in Chinese and other languages, along with poster-size
single quotes from Mao and out-of-date Mao portraits emblazoned with the
words "Long live" (*wansui*) or "Eternal life" (*wanshou wujiang*).[11]

As of the day this document, "A Circular Concerning the Withdrawal
from Circulation of *Quotations from Chairman Mao* (12 February 1979),"
was issued by Party Central's Department of Propaganda, all copies and
editions of *Quotations*, in Chinese, minority, and foreign languages, were
banned from sale through the official Xinhua Bookstores and the International Bookstore (*Guoji shudian*). Apart from limited numbers to be held by
province-level Xinhua Bookstores for possible future official use, all other
copies were ordered pulped (*huajiang chuli*) forthwith.

Similarly, all Chinese diplomatic missions, official Chinese residents
overseas, delegations sent abroad, and organizations within China that had
contact with foreigners were to cease immediately distributing or supplying
in any way copies of *Quotations*. In its place, *Selected Works* or individual
tracts by Mao could be provided when necessary. "Foreign friends" who
imported the book for sale in their home countries could wait until they ran
out of stock. This stipulation was probably made because an international
ban on the book would not only have been unenforceable, but also may
have sparked a rush on the now-illicit booklet. No future supplies of the
quotes, however, were to be exported.

This document was circulated on 20 February 1979, to Xinhua Bookstores at the provincial, municipal, and autonomous region levels by the
National Bureau for Publishing Administration.[12] It was followed some two
months later by another circular on how the fiscal losses incurred as a result
of the pulping of this material were to be dealt with. A further notice was
issued by Xinhua Books in June, ordering the pulping to be completed by
September 1979.[13]

Posters of the official portrait that showed Mao in his avuncular or, as
the propagandists would have it, "beatific" old age, however, seem to have
fallen out of favor fairly rapidly. In 1979, internal estimates claimed that

during the Cultural Revolution 2.2 billion portraits of the Chairman had been produced, three for every person in the nation.[14] By the early 1980s, however, there was a critical lack of Mao's votary image—so much so, in fact, that in mid 1981, a member of the county Party committee of Huize in Yunnan Province wrote to the head office of Xinhua Books remarking that a local peasant had bought up ten copies of the official portrait just before Spring Festival, fearful that images of Mao would soon be unavailable. Following the Party's critique of Mao's errors in 1981, the fear among the faithful that there would be a sudden dearth of Mao images must have been so widespread that the head office of Xinhua responded to this letter by instructing bookstores throughout the nation to stock Mao portraits so as always to be ready "to satisfy the needs of Party members and the People."[15]

At about the same time that the comrade from Huize was complaining to Beijing, the Publishing Administration circulated a document from Party Central's Department of Propaganda regarding the proprieties of displaying pictures of Party leaders at meeting places and in public. In the punctilious blather beloved of bureaucrats worldwide, the Department of Propaganda remarked that after many inquiries as to whether it was still appropriate to hang images of leaders in public—especially given the antipersonality cult line that the Party was now pursuing—a number of decisions were made "on the basis of guidelines proposed by various comrades in the central government" that put strict limits on the public hanging of portraits of Party leaders (see "Documenting the Demise").[16]

In January 1983 a new formulation was devised for dealing with the problem of official portraits. By this stage, Hua Guofeng, the interim Party leader handpicked by Mao, had fallen from power and all evidence of his stewardship, including his portrait, as well as all works related to him, songs in praise of his wisdom, and so on, was being obliterated. In the future, the Department of Propaganda instructed, plentiful supplies of official portraits featuring either the Four Dead Great Revolutionaries (Mao, Zhou Enlai, Liu Shaoqi, and Zhu De), or the Six Revolutionaries representing two generations of leaders (Mao, Zhou, Liu, Zhu, as well as Deng Xiaoping and Chen Yun), were to be made available over the Spring Festival period, and Party cells were directed to encourage the masses to buy and hang these pictures in place of Hua Guofeng's portrait.[17]

In 1989, further image consultation resulted in a new move. From April that year Party Central deemed it unnecessary for the portraits of Marx, Engels, Lenin, and Stalin to be displayed in Tiananmen Square on Labor Day (1 May) or National Day (1 October), as previously had been the case. Henceforth, only Mao and Sun Yat-sen were to be seen in public. This decision, the Department of Propaganda pointed out in an internal communiqué, was not to be construed as evincing a change in attitude toward Marxism as such. "Mao Zedong and Mao Thought," the Department reminded its cadres, were, after all, "the concrete manifestation of Marxism in China."[18]

Following the appearance of the new Mao Cult the statistics regarding official portraits show that while officialdom had relegated Mao to history, the masses were creating a new history for the Chairman. In 1989 a mere 370,000 copies of the official portrait of Mao had been printed. In 1990 the number rose dramatically to 22.95 million, of which 19.93 million were sold. In 1991 the number hit 50 million. For the same year the portraits of other leaders (Marx, Engels, Lenin, Stalin, Zhou, Liu Shaoqi, and Zhu De) combined totaled only 2.25 million.[19] In one report published in late 1991, it was claimed that 99.5 percent of households in Changsha County, Hunan, had "invited portraits of Chairman Mao into their homes" (qing Mao zhuxi xiang jinwu).[20]

The fate of Mao's published writings was a more complicated matter. According to secret statistics compiled by the head office of Xinhua Books in June 1979, there were 450 million unsold or remaindered copies of the works of Marx, Engels, Lenin, Stalin, and Mao Zedong in storage, constituting some 24 percent of all remaindered books in China (which ran to a total of 170 million volumes, valued at 1.3 billion yuan). This figure included 8 million sets of Mao's selected works and 2.82 billion copies of speeches and writings in single volumes.

Xinhua Books noted that during the 10 years of the Cultural Revolution more than 40 billion volumes of Mao's works were printed and distributed, constituting, in mid 1979, 8 percent of all unsold books in China. That meant 15 copies of Mao's books for every man, woman, and child in China.[21] Approximately 85 million yuan in interest-free loans had been made available by state banks to produce this revolutionary tide of paper. But due to the new economic strategy that the government launched in 1979, publishers now had to pay interest on the loans, and massive debts were accruing at an alarming rate.

Official Xinhua Bookstore documents conceded that it was unlikely there would be any mass demand for these books in the future and, given the rate at which political books were selling in 1979 (a mere 560,000 volumes in the first half of 1979), remaindered stock would remain stockpiled for decades.[22]

This daunting "mountain of books," as it was called, now took up valuable and much-needed storage space. Its existence hampered the production and distribution of new books, in particular school texts. Furthermore, fluctuating temperatures throughout the year, as well as mold caused by the rainy season, were causing serious deterioration of the laminated covers of the books; volumes were sticking together, binding glue was drying out and cracking, staples were rusting, and pages were yellowing. Such natural attrition had already claimed some 15 to 20 percent of all books.

Emergency measures to deal with the problem were formulated. Complete sets of the writings of Marx, Engels, Lenin, and Stalin, as well as certain editions and Mao's selected works (including single-volume editions, hard- and soft-cover as well as traditional clothbound editions), were to be preserved in toto. Henceforth, 10 to 20 percent of all other editions of Mao's works and single-volume publications were to be kept in storage by local publishing houses. The remainder were to be given away to readers in need (village cultural centers, middle school students, and recently rusticated youths), in accordance with local guidelines. Books that could not even be given away had to be pulped "after a reasonable period had elapsed." All damaged books could be pulped immediately. These regulations also covered editions in minority languages.

The expected losses resulting from this were estimated to be 30 percent of all remaindered books. The loss of possible revenue through gifts would be 24 percent and 32 percent due to pulping respectively. With the agreement of the Ministry of Finance, these losses were to be met by Xinhua Books over a two- to three-year period.

Not surprisingly, many publishers failed to follow these detailed and burdensome directives. In the atmosphere of de-Maoification described above, many localities acted unilaterally in dealing with the Mao opus. In July 1980, for example, it was reported that some bookstores in Shaanxi Province had been pulping more than 90 percent of their political book stock, claiming that they were damaged; others were selling spoiled books to individuals.[23] By early 1982 the decision to pulp Mao had been pursued with such rigor in certain localities that a new crisis in the supply of Mao's works unfolded.

At the time, a number of disgruntled People's Liberation Army (PLA) soldiers stationed in Henan Province complained to the head office of Xinhua Books that local stocks of *Selected Works of Mao Zedong* and famous speeches and writings by Mao, such as "Serve the People" and "In Memory of Norman Bethune," had run out. In response, a document was sent to the provincial office of Xinhua Books in Henan, and a more detailed document was distributed to publishers throughout China stipulating that all of the 43 canonical writings by Mao listed in the Party's 1981 "Decision on Historical Questions" were to be kept in stock for the use of readers and for obligatory political study sessions. It noted that due to the recent unavailability of Mao's works, some comrades had actually been reduced to copying out articles by hand.[24]

While the Mao classics remained inviolable, Volume 5 of *Selected Works*, a tome hastily produced after the Cultural Revolution as part of the power struggle that followed Mao's death, was now found to be seriously flawed. The problem was the book's footnotes. They reflected the politics of the 1970s, and they were completely out of step with the propaganda requirements of the Reform era. In early 1982, a circular issued by the National Publishing Bureau ordered the book withdrawn from sale and pulped.[25]

Mao's works were updated after that, but only following what appeared to be a considerable hiatus. Various articles, speeches, and volumes were produced to provide canonical support for the twists and turns of new Party policies in the 1980s. Then, as the authorities were reaffirming their ideological pedigree in the face of internal dissension and international disorder (in particular the collapse of communism in the West), a second edition of *Selected Works* containing new annotations that expunged "leftist" influences and errors, was published coinciding with the seventieth anniversary of the founding of the Communist Party, on 1 July 1991.[26] On 4 July Party Central issued a circular admonishing Party members and cadres to lead the nation in studying Mao Thought. The official media promotion of the book, not to mention obligatory sales, added to the popular interest already piqued by the new Mao Cult, and by January 1992 10 million sets of the second edition had been sold.[27]

As part of the commemoration of Mao's centenary in 1993, it was announced that a five-volume set of *The Works of Mao Zedong* would be published containing documents not previously included in *Selected Works*, including essays, speeches, telegrams, letters, reports, speeches, directives and so on from 1921 to 1976, arranged by topic.[28]

Similar official Mao-related publishing projects, including the production of deluxe edition coffee-table books,[29] memoirs, collections of essays, and so on, were produced as part of the centenary frenzy of 1993.

Mao Remains: Cold and Hot

In one of the most direct critiques of Mao ever published on the Mainland, the writer Li Jie stated in 1989 that the secret of Mao's political success came from the understanding of the Chinese plight that he shared with the writer Lu Xun (d. 1936). Whereas, Li argued, Lu Xun had used his insight into the weaknesses of the Chinese character to struggle with the burden of tradition and warn his compatriots of its dangers, Mao had manipulated his knowledge of the Chinese to further his political ambitions. The results, as many would agree, were devastating.

A number of writers in this volume claim that Mao was the quintessential representation of China, the embodiment of the nation. There are also those who argue that Mao reconstructed the nation in his image, popularizing his personal traits of suspicion, deviousness, hauteur, manipulation, and power play through mass political movements, eventually infecting the whole country with a Mao malady, the effects of which are still felt today (see, e.g., Wei Jingsheng's essay "Who's Responsible?").[30] Regardless of whether he is regarded as a hero or a monster, Mao the man and the leader still enthralls many Chinese.

There is no way of effectively gauging Mao's shifting popularity in a nation that lacks media openness. One intriguing survey of 1,500 college students carried out by the Beijing-based *University Student* magazine in 1993 found that 65 percent of those questioned knew neither when Mao was born nor when he died. Others were vague about exactly who he was and what he had done.[31] With the collapse of belief in the Party and the cause it represented in the early 1990s, patriots have tended, at least publicly, to uphold the farrago of Mao myths.[32] The results of another survey, by the Chinese Academy of Social Sciences, were published in late 1993 by *Beijing Youth News*, a slick propaganda organ of the Communist Party's Youth League. This survey offered a more layered yet equally unsettling view of popular perceptions of the dead leader. The majority of respondents, regardless of the suffering they might have experienced as a result of his aberrant policies, said they still admired Mao as a great man and leader. Some of the younger people questioned in one poll were even skeptical about the horrors of the past, in particular those of the Cultural Revolution period. They even questioned whether Mao should be blamed for what had happened (see "Galluping Mao"). While the tenor of reports regarding the public standing of Mao in the official media was basically positive, closely reflecting the official verdict on Mao, it would appear that the Party told a very different story to its members in private.

In October 1993 Party Central reportedly distributed for internal reference (i.e., secretly) the results of four nationwide polls conducted by central government offices indicating that the majority of respondents believed that Mao's faults outweighed his achievements and that the new Mao Cult was a social aberration.[33] But in 1994, openly published surveys conducted by *China Youth Daily* in June and October found that Mao had outstripped both Zhou Enlai and Deng Xiaoping as the most popular Chinese leader in recent history.[34] Regardless of these confusing results, at least most Beijing residents knew that Mao was dead, for at one time or another they had trooped past his corpse at the Chairman Mao Memorial Hall in Tiananmen Square.[35]

The post–Cultural Revolution Mao Cult was markedly different from the personality cult of the 1960s. First and foremost, the new Cult was not initiated by the authorities, nor was it ever entirely harnessed by Party propagandists, despite various efforts to "channel" (yindao) it in the Party's favor. Although the Cult certainly bore many traits of a popular folk cult (see "A Place in the Pantheon"), the dimensions of moral revival, sanctity, and the general religiosity and fervor that characterized the earlier Cult were noteworthy for their absence.[36] Moreover, the new Cult was one of a succession of fads that had swept China from the early 1980s (although there were also crazes in the 1970s, such as the popularity of chicken blood remedies during the last years of the decade). The 1980s' fads, symptomatic of the accelerated pace of history, included, as Hua Ming points out in the essay "From Sartre to Mao Zedong," intellectual fashions among university students and cultural figures for Freud, Nietzsche, and Sartre. In the late 1980s one of the most significant mass cults, however, had been that for qigong, China's home grown "naturopathic religion," which dovetailed neatly with the reappearance of Mao Zedong-as-adept, the guru-master of the Chinese nation. There is no doubt that many aspects of the new Mao Cult, in particular the packaging of Mao in the early 1990s, reflected the mercantile fervor of the Reform age that had been initiated in 1978. On this level, the selling of Mao was blatantly mercenary and exploitative. But it is too easy to dismiss, as some writers have, the new Cult as either a cunning political strategy authored by Party leaders facing a legitimacy crisis in the post–4 June period or as yet another example of how Deng Xiaoping's "market socialism" consumed everything, including the Party's revolutionary traditions, as it careened toward some unstated capitalist goal.

Even in the early post–Cultural Revolution period Mao's reincarnation had been deeply problematic. The Party under Deng Xiaoping's guidance,[37] along with the sage intervention of Chen Yun[38] and ideologues such as Hu Qiaomu (one of Mao's leading ideological scribes), Deng Liqun, and many other Party leaders and theoreticians,[39] formulated a means for turning Mao into a malleable icon and thinker whose services could be enlisted for the cause of economic reform and the Open Door.[40] Unlike the Soviet Union's de-Stalinization, China could not jettison Mao without endangering the ideological foundations of both the Party and the nation. Mao was both the Lenin and the Stalin of China,[41] a man whose career was linked inextricably with the history and mythology of the Party, the army, and the People's Republic. Deng and his coevals were aware that to abandon Mao could, in the long run, presage the collapse of the Party itself. As early as 1962 Edgar Snow had remarked: "Mao has . . . become an Institution of such prestige and authority that no one in the Party could raze it without sacrificing a collective vested interest of first importance."[42] Despite the acknowledged disasters of Mao's rule, this remained true even long after his death.

Dismantling the Mao Cult, or what was now dubbed "modern superstition" (*xiandai mixin*), and dealing with Mao's mixed political legacy was a process fraught with danger.[43] The internal debates concerning the Chairman's fate were protracted and cautious for, apart from the need to put Mao in his place, they also involved byzantine power struggles and the ousting of Mao's anointed successor, "the wise leader" Hua Guofeng.[44] But Mao the man was eventually tamed, and Mao Zedong Thought, having been safely reinterpreted as "the crystallization of collective wisdom," was retained as the amorphous ideological basis for Party rule[45] (see Figure 1).

Activists in the Democracy Wall Movement of 1978–79 made the first unofficial assaults on Mao's reputation, and the manner in which the Party was manipulating it to bolster the new orthodoxy.[46] They were soon silenced by the authorities,[47] and in March 1979 a commentator in the *People's Daily* remarked pointedly that China was experiencing a desanctification of Mao, not de-Maoification at all.[48] But the limited cultural flowering that developed in the wake of the political changes emboldened writers and artists to make Mao a target of their work. From the late 1970s, a number of tentative cultural reprisions of Mao appeared, including the sculptures of Wang Keping (e.g., his 1979 "Blind and Silent" and 1980 work "Idol"),[49] the screenplay for *Unrequited Love* by PLA novelist Bai Hua,[50] and an elegiac poem by Sun Jingxuan (see "A Specter Prowls Our Land").

While lip service was paid to the memory of Mao on and around the tenth anniversary of his death in 1986 with the obligatory publication of editorials and memorial essays in the press,[51] as well as with the production of a sanitized *Mao Zedong Reader*,[52] the high tide of economic reform and mooting of political reform ensured that the occasion passed with relatively little fanfare. Interestingly, Mao as a consumer item made his first fleeting appearance at about this time. First, arias from Beijing Model Revolutionary Operas, the cultural staple diet of the Cultural Revolution, were reworked to the garish beat of Mainland-style disco music. Tunes from "The Red Lantern," "Taking Tiger Mountain by Strategy," and "The Red Detachment of Women,"[53] along with a curious selection of songs from popular old Mainland, Japanese, Hong Kong, and Taiwanese films, were produced on cassette and played by radio stations throughout the country. Their release created a nationwide minisensation in 1985–86; it also sparked a heated debate on the merits of reviving what, for many, was nothing less than the Muzak of the Chinese holocaust.[54]

Also at about this time, some fashionable young artists in the nonofficial cultural scene in Beijing began turning up at foreigners' soirées and exhibition openings wearing tailored Mao suits (*Zhongshan zhuang* or *Maoshi fuzhuang*)[55] adorned with discreet Mao badges. By resorting to the *démodé* jackets they proclaimed themselves to be sartorially "revolutionary" in an environment increasingly dominated by *de rigueur* long hair, blue jeans, grimy jackets, and T-shirts.

At the time it was already evident that Mao-period memorabilia had more of a commercial than an ideological significance. From the mid 1980s, the economic reforms had an increasing impact on the publishing industry that made it imperative for publishers to show a profit. Despite the Party's attempts to avoid them, controversial subjects such as the Cultural Revolution became a new source for best-selling books.[56] The relatively open atmosphere of the time also encouraged authors to deal with political topics in a way that had not been permitted since the first wave of anti–Cultural Revolution (and by implication anti-Mao) literature of the late 1970s. Works by writers such as Suo Guoxin, Hu Yuewei, Ye Yonglie, Feng Jicai, Gao Gao and Yan Jiaqi appeared in 1986, and although little of this writing strayed far from Party guidelines, it popularized sensitive issues and helped turn some areas of Party history into a realm ripe for media exploitation.[57] This period of taboo-breaking experimentation was interrupted by the purge of Hu Yaobang in January 1987, but picked up again as the ideological rectification campaign that was launched after Hu's fall faltered. Although the literature that was published on Mao and the Cultural Revolution was deeply flawed and often trite, its appearance presaged the opening up of the way for more serious writing that was beginning to mature in early 1989, on the eve of the disastrous Protest Movement.[58] In 1988, at the height of cultural license, both writers and publishers discovered the untapped potential of Mao Zedong himself and a boom was born that continued well into the 1990s (see "Mao, a Best-Seller" and "All That's Fit to Print").

For many the late 1980s was a time when the reforms had reached an impasse; corruption, nepotism, and economic ineptitude led to widespread disgruntlement, and the Party leadership, its attempts at substantial political reform stymied by infighting, appeared to be increasingly out of touch with everyday realities. Mao, a strong leader who in the popular imagination was above corruption and a romantic unfettered by pettifogging bureaucratic constraints, was for many the symbol of an age of economic stability, egalitarianism, and national pride. Gradually, the image of Mao, long since freed from his stifling holy aura and the odium of his destructive policies, became a "floating sign," a vehicle for nostalgic reinterpretation, unstated opposition to the status quo, and even satire. In one early 1990s' Mainland study of the popularity of Mao among university students, the responses reflected a wide spectrum of opinion. Among other things, the survey found: Mao was popular among people who felt frustrated politically, but also among people with a desire to learn why Mao had been such a political success; there was a nostalgia for a simpler past; there was also a curiosity about previously forbidden information concerning Party leaders and their private lives; and there was a popular longing for a new sage-king, not to mention outright hero worship.[59]

It was also in the late 1980s that artists such as Wang Guangyi, who was then based in Wuhan, began manipulating Mao's image in their works. Wang's clinical framing of a Mao portrait in a grid of red lines was one of the first works of its kind and a "rehearsal" of the Chairman that built on the surreal reprisals of Cultural Revolution culture first undertaken by Wu Shanzhuan in the mid 1980s when he created a work called "Red Humor," an installation of nonsense big character posters.[60] In the literary world, meanwhile, there were moves to reevaluate and even overthrow Mao's cultural canon.[61]

As the Reforms further transformed Chinese society from the mid 1980s, cultural and economic dislocation began to have an increasing impact on the populace. Widespread resentment against the effects of Reform, in particular inflation, corruption, and egregious nepotism within the Party, began mounting to crisis level in 1988. It was also the year in which Mao Zedong initially showed signs of making a popular comeback. The six-part teleseries "River Elegy" featured documentary footage of mass Red Guard adulation for Mao and study sessions from the Cultural Revolution, the first of their kind to be seen on Chinese television for years.[62] Such scenes enthralled younger viewers who had grown up after the Red Guard movement in an age when the religious ecstasy of mass political action was virtually unknown.[63] In 1988 Mao's name also was featured in at least one popular rhymed witticism (*shunkouliu'r*) aimed against the Party leadership and their progeny. It ran: "Chairman Mao's son went to the front line [of the Korean War and died in service]; Zhao Ziyang's kid smuggles color TVs; Deng Xiaoping's son calls for donations [to his foundation for the handicapped]; while the children of the People deal in state bonds." (*Mao zhuxide erzi shang qianxian; Zhao Ziyangde erzi dao caidian; Deng Xiaopingde erzi gao mujuan; Renminde erzi dao dian'r guokuquan*).[64] And it was in a mood partially of playful exasperation and partially sincere protest that some workers and other residents of Beijing decided to carry portraits of Mao into Tiananmen Square during the heady week of the 1989 hunger strike in mid-May. Depending on whom you spoke to at the time, interpretations of Mao's joining the protests varied: He wouldn't have allowed the situation to deteriorate to such an extent without taking action, said one school of thought; he provided moral vision and a sense of self-worth in a way that the new leaders could not, said another.

Yet wit, protests against corruption, and portraits were not the only signs that Chairman Mao had a role to play in the movement. His spirit inveigled itself into the proceedings in a number of ways. The 26 April *People's Daily* editorial declaring that the student protests that erupted after Hu Yaobang's death were instigated by a small handful of plotters intent on overthrowing the Party, immediately revived memories of the official Maoist invective used to denounce the 5 April Tiananmen Square Incident in 1976.

Nor was the rhetoric of the protesters free of hoary political associations. Many of the slogans and much of the speechifying and posturing were also familiar from the Maoist past. Even the language of a key document of the protests, the students' Hunger Strike Declaration, reflected the style of the Chairman. Indeed, some of the lines were an unconscious paraphrase of one of Mao's earliest articles.[65] He also made his presence felt in a more ethereal manner. On the afternoon of 23 May, the massive picture of Mao hanging on Tiananmen Gate was splattered with paint by an errant group of protesters from Hunan.[66] Immediately after this incident a dramatic storm struck the city. Many were convinced that Mao, infuriated with the protests and the desecration of his image, had "manifested his supernatural power" (*xianling*) and struck out at the demonstrators.[67] Among the student leaders, Mao's pervasive influence also made itself felt after this. There were constant purges at the top and endless covert meetings. The general lack of democratic principles, in particular from the time of the hunger strike (mid May) onward, as well as the shrill rhetoric of demagogues such as Chai Ling[68] and the demonizing of opponents in the ranks of the students, teachers, and intellectuals as "traitors," "collaborators," and "capitulationists" who were supposedly engaged in plots and conspiracies to sell the movement out to the government, clearly reflected the political heritage of the long-dead Chairman.

There were other reasons for the reappearance of Mao among workers from the late 1980s (and not only in 1989), as we have indicated in the story referred to in the opening paragraph of this essay. The revival of the Stalin cult in the Brezhnev era may also be instructive in our investigation of the renewed popularity of Mao in the Chinese Reform era. Victor Zaslavsky says of the late 1960s' nostalgia for the days of Stalin:

> The terror increased social mobility, eliminated re-emergent class barriers, and functioned as a socio-psychological mechanism by creating the sensation

of a "negative" equality, or even of protection for individuals against the arbitrariness of local authority. At the end of the 1960s, when various enterprises began massive layoffs of superfluous workers in order to carry out economic reforms, workers often had fond recollections of Stalin's "justice," when factory administrators "lived in fear"—in contrast to this new period, when they could "do as they pleased." . . . With the atomization of the working class and in the absence of any workers' democracy, of the right to association and strike, a strong central power comes to be seen as a guarantee of workers' economic rights against the arbitrariness of local administration.[69]

As for the young, the general mood of helplessness in the 1960s only added to the nostalgia for the past. As Zaslavsky notes in words that adumbrate some of the attitudes that appeared among various strata of China's urban youth in the 1990s: "The young neither fight against communism, argue against it, nor curse it; something much worse has happened to communism: they laugh at it." In the Soviet Union the young—workers, students, and others—were witnessing their society turning into a realm of consumers and found their own lives increasingly meaningless and without goals. Their creativity frustrated and deprived of a positive direction, "the young look[ed] back nostalgically to the period of social revolution inseparably linked with Stalin's name."[70]

There was, however, another level of the abiding reputation of Stalin in the Soviet Union. As the Soviet dissident philosopher Alexander Zinoviev observed, Stalin's rule was the ultimate expression of popular will and the mass personality.[71] He was the embodiment not only of history but of the national spirit as well. To deny him was to negate not only one's own history but also vital facets of the national character. Large numbers of people had participated in the terror that marked Stalin's rule, just as in China the nation had enthusiastically responded to the Great Leap Forward, the Cultural Revolution and the ceaseless political purges that Mao had directed from the early 1950s. To "rediscover" Mao in a period of rapid change and social dislocation was for many also a grounding act of self-affirmation.

In China, the events of 1988 and 1989—natural disasters and economic uncertainty followed by a fear of national collapse, mass protests against corruption and the lack of freedoms followed by the ill-managed government suppression of the 1989 protests, the equivocal response of the Western democracies, and the fall of communism in Eastern Europe—all served to encourage the nascent Mao Cult. As is so often the case when people face economic uncertainty and social anomie, old cultural symbols, cults, practices, and beliefs are spontaneously revived to provide a framework of cohesion and meaning to a threatening world. To many, Mao was representative of an age of certainty and confidence, of cultural and political unity, and, above all, of economic equality and probity.

The Maoist past reflected badly on Deng's present. Yet perhaps it was only with the relative economic freedoms allowed by the reforms that people could afford to indulge in an anodyne wave of pro-Mao nostalgia. Certainly, the new Cult suggested alternatives to the Reformist economic and social order, but it did not offer new or viable political solutions to China's problems. If anything, the Mao Cult looked fondly on strong government, coherent national goals, authority, and power. Mao was, first and foremost, an unwavering patriot who led the nation against foreign imperialism and expelled foreign capital.[72] The formulas of the Mao era also offered simple answers to complex questions: direct collective action over painful individual decisions, reliance on the State rather than a grinding struggle for the self, national pride as opposed to self-doubt. Many could indulge in Mao nostalgia because due to bans on remembering the past they had forgotten its horrors. Unlike Europeans, for example, who are exposed to a continuous media barrage related to World War II, Chinese government censorship of most information on the Great Leap Forward and the Cultural Revolution meant that the populace had not had to deal with unadulterated memory and horror through film, television, newspaper articles, memoirs, and so on. Emotionally, therefore, many people, and in particular the young, could partake in the luxury of a positive nostalgia for the past.

As folk religion flourished outside urban centers from the 1980s, the eclectic nature of Chinese popular beliefs meant that the Chairman could be subsumed within a larger system of faith. Many commentators have noted that Mao has finally found a niche in the traditional Chinese pantheon alongside such martial heroes as Guan Gong, Zhuge Liang, and Liu Bei. The real Cult of Chairman Mao was no longer determined by Party fiat, and the authorities knew it. The old propaganda line "Chairman Mao will forever live in our hearts" (*Mao zhuxi yongyuan huo zai women xinzhong*) had literally come true. But Mao no longer ruled as he once did through Party organizations, overt propaganda, and ceaseless political campaigns. His spirit was more ineffable, perhaps even more omnipresent.

EveryMao

There was something for everyone in the Mao persona. As Edgar Snow wrote in the early 1960s: "What makes him [Mao] formidable is that he is not just a party boss but by many millions of Chinese is quite genuinely regarded as a teacher, statesman, strategist, philosopher, poet laureate, national hero, head of the family, and greatest liberator in history. He is to them Confucius plus Lao-tzu plus Rousseau plus Marx plus Buddha. . . ."[73] In the 1990s, Mao remains a patriotic leader, martial hero, philosopher-king, poet, calligrapher (surrounded as he so often was with the bric-a-brac of the traditional literatus—clothbound books, writing brushes, and ink stones). But he is also widely seen in a positive light as a strong and irascible figure, a wily infighter, a man who was both emperor and oracle, the ultimate Machiavellian manipulator who knew, many would argue, just how to keep the restive Chinese nation in place.[74] Mao consciously played on the contrasting Chinese traditions relating to the sage-emperor and rebel chieftain,[75] as a modern-day itinerant worker (*mangliu*) observes at the end of this volume (see "Musical Chairmen"). As one academic has noted—and it is a remark that remains significant today—the Communist revolution (and we could include here Mao as both an individual and symbol) had "carried through [an] . . . attempt to reconstruct the world in the spirit of inner-worldly transcendence inherent in Confucianism."[76]

For many people Mao represented not only national but also physical potency. Most of the Mao-related jokes current from the early 1980s cheerfully reflected the leader's prowess in bed, and they often used figures like Zhou Enlai or Hua Guofeng as foils. On one level such humor represented a transgression against the august figure of the Leader and allowed a popular invasion of the "forbidden zone" (*jinqu*) relating to the person of Mao. On another level, they were also indicative of a gradual process that has seen Mao become more human, approachable, and, in the new Mao Cult, the familiar of the Chinese masses. Through this process, one often described by Chinese critics as "secularization" (*shisuhua*), Mao has been enlisted in the ranks of the people in contrast and even opposition to the present leaders, who were increasingly perceived of as being sectarian, corrupt, and lackluster.[77] The fascination with the details of Mao's everyday life, as given in the plethora of books published from 1988 (discussed below, and see "All That's Fit to Print"), is also an indication of this process. Despite the Chinese authorities' denunciations of the BBC for broadcasting Dr. Li Zhisui's revelations concerning Mao's sex life in late 1993, one could speculate that popular opinion in China was probably neither particularly outraged nor surprised by the latest proof of the Chairman's talents. If anything, people may well regard Mao's voracious appetites as further evidence of his exceptional stature, superhuman energy, and unequivocal success.

It could also be argued that Mao, the ultimate father-mother official (*fumu guan*), enjoyed such a broad appeal because, to an extent, he was a love object[78] (see the comments on the "young Mao" by the woman taxi driver in "CultRev Relics" and the poem "Dreaming of Chairman Mao" in "Praise Be to Mao"). One could argue that he was also a bisexual or omnisexual figure. Mao's official portrait shows the enigmatic face of a man-woman (or grandfather-grandmother). In poetry, song, and prose he had often been eulogized as a mother/father, and his personality in all of its majesty and pettiness fits in with complex attitudes regarding sexual personae. In his dotage Mao, a bloated colossus supported by young female assistants,[79] often looked like a grand matriarch, time having blurred his features into a fleshy, unisex mask. Li Zhisui's memoirs, *The Private Life of Chairman Mao*, provides numerous fascinating insights into the Chairman's various peccadilloes, not least of which was his irrepressible and, in some cases, bisexual appetite. Not only did he disport himself with a bevy of comely ingenues, it would appear that he was not above lunging at the handsome young men in his guard who put him to bed, or to expect a "massage" from one of their number before retiring.[80]

In this context it is instructive to recall the reaction of the American journalist Agnes Smedley to her first meeting with Mao in Yan'an:

> His hands were as long and sensitive as a woman's. . . . Whatever else he might be he was an aesthete. I was in fact repelled by the feminine in him. An instinctive hostility sprang up inside me, and I became so occupied with trying to master it, that I heard hardly a word of what followed. . . .[81]

The Mao suit only added to the sexual egalitarianism of the Mao image. While in his later years Mao was a wrinkled, green-toothed, slack-jawed old man, the official description of the Chairman was of a vibrant and healthy individual whose features remained unravaged by that mighty sculptor, time. His pictures were airbrushed to perfection and his appearance in documentary footage carefully doctored to present the best possible image so that even in terminal decline official propaganda could claim that he "glowed with health and vigor, and he enjoyed a ruddy complexion" (see "The Sun Never Sets").

In the popular imagination, however, Mao remained above all a martial hero and patriot possessed of the genius of Zhuge Liang, the strategist *par excellence*, and the "style of a great knight-errant" (*daxia qidu*).[82] A number of the selections in the present volume give obvious and undeniable reasons for Mao's rebirth; other, more deep-seated cultural and psychological causes for his rehabilitation are only hinted at. Li Jie goes as far as any in speculating on the "force field" surrounding Mao, and Liu Xiaobo makes important contrasts between Mao and Deng Xiaoping, as does Wang Shan, the author of *China Through the Third Eye*. In selections from a sensationalistic popular magazine such as *True Tales of the Adventures of Mao Zedong* (see "Martial Mao") we also can discern elements of Mao's roughness, callousness, and heroic charisma that make him an attractive martial hero for a population succored on traditional tales of chivalry, violence, and acts of courage (see Figure 2).[83]

In the popular imagination Mao is EveryMao: he is the peasant lad made good; warrior/literatus as well as the philosopher/king. He is an ideal, and his heartlessness in the face of massive suffering is not something his constituents would necessarily find abhorrent. Interestingly, the 1993 survey by researchers at the Chinese Academy of Social Sciences, published in *Beijing Youth News* (see "Galluping Mao"), reveals an abiding admiration for Mao even among his victims.[84] Whether this is the view we would get if there was press freedom and an end of one-party rule in China is a matter for speculation. Indeed, the most fearful thing about the Mao Cult may be that it has become a permanent part of China's cultural landscape, and nothing, be it economic development or political upheaval, can alter this.

The exact origins of the new Mao Cult of the early 1990s are uncertain. In the following pages there are those who argue that the fascination with Mao began among university students in Beijing who were disillusioned with imported intellectual fads from the West (see "From Sartre to Mao Zedong" and "A Typology of the MaoCraze"). Others claim that Mao never really disappeared but was merely resting throughout the 1980s while the people of China got on with the pressing business of economic Reform (see "The Sun Never Sets"). But for many, the post–June 4 popular Mao Cult really began when talismans (commonly called *guawu*, they can be interpreted in traditional terms as *hushenfu*), laminated images of the Chairman hung from the rear-view mirrors of taxis, buses, and trucks, first appeared in South China and gradually spread throughout the country from 1991.

According to a story that was to become one of China's most widely told urban myths, the driver of a vehicle involved in a serious traffic accident in Shenzhen that left a number of people dead survived unscathed because he had a picture of Mao on the dashboard. Another version of the story claims that the accident occurred in Guangzhou and a whole busload of people were protected by Mao's image. Shortly after the tale began spreading, laminated images of Mao appeared in vehicles in cities, towns and villages throughout China. These images were not unlike the St. Christopher medallions popular with European drivers or the Virgin Mary of the Highway images found, for example, in Brazil. Many of them showed Mao in the guise of a temple god or guardian spirit and were said to be capable of deflecting evil (*pixie*).[85] Some people preferred pictures of Mao as a young man, or in a PLA uniform; others favored the official portrait of Mao in his later years. Many of the pictures were placed in gold-colored plastic templelike frames or had red tassels or gold ingots dangling from them, thereby combining aspects of the Mao persona with elements of folk culture and religion (see Figure 3).

It was probably no coincidence that the fad for the talismans originated in the South, where traditional beliefs are generally stronger than in the North; and even more interesting is the fact that Mao supposedly first revealed his supernatural powers in Shenzhen, the laboratory of post-Maoist capitalist reforms (see "Hanging Mao"). Indeed, the vitality of the Cult that spread from the South calls into question just how successful the official de-Maoification of the early 1980s had been. As Maurice Meisner commented at the time: "As Mao's successors in Beijing pursue 'de-Maoification' in the cities, as they seek to replace the personal authority of Mao with the impersonal bureaucratic authority of an authoritarian state, they must ponder the political implications of the persistence of the cult of Mao among the great majority of the people over whom they rule."[86]

An indication of Mao's permanent position in the popular Chinese pantheon came in mid 1995 when it was widely reported that a traditional-style temple devoted to the Chairman had been built in his home province. Mao had literally been enshrined in a temple (the *Sanyuansi*) in Leiyang, Hunan Province. Funded by farmers and pilgrims over a number of years the large temple had halls dedicated to China's revolutionary triumvirate of Mao, Zhou and Zhu De. The images, reminiscent of icons found in traditional temples, were the work of a sculptor from the Buddhist complex at Wutaishan. The standing Mao image was said to be some six meters tall and those of the seated Zhou and Zhu were each approximately 4.5m. At the height of its popularity from late 1994 some 40–50 thousand worshippers visited the temple daily. Party authorities closed it in May 1995 on the grounds that it encouraged superstition.[87]

Mao: The Body Corporate

The first Mao Cult reached its apogee during the early years of the Cultural Revolution, when Mao was hailed as "the Great Teacher, Great Leader, Great Commander, and Great Helmsman"[88] and Red Guards swore to sacrifice themselves and, indeed, murder each other to "protect the Chairman." As in the application of the "leader principle" (*Führerprinzip*) in Hitlerian Germany, Mao was cast as "the sole representative of the people on all levels of political and social life. He claimed to embody the total unity of that people, leaving no room for opposition or criticism. All expressions of the national will were to be his. No representation of different groups, interests, and ideas was allowed to exist alongside him. . . ."[89] In the new Mao Cult, the leader again became a vehicle for the will of the people, a symbolic entity who attracted every shade of dissatisfaction and nostalgia that the people experienced as the effects of the economic Reforms swept over the nation.[90]

In life, Mao's body had been the incarnation of mass will. His appearance—carefully presented in photographs and on film so as to maintain an idealized image—was described in hallowed terms. In the Cultural Revolution, Mao was nothing less than the physical representation of Revolution, History, the Fate of China, and the People's Aspirations;[91] he was the culmination of thousands of years of Chinese civilization, the embodiment of China itself.

In the past, people used Mao's image (the Mao badge and even tattoos) to adorn their bodies;[92] his words (quotations and verbal mannerisms, including his coarseness) acted as a currency with a universal rate of exchange, and his style (in clothes, smoking, posturing) was emulated widely in what was a national expression of an "aestheticization of politics"[93] (see "Mock-Mao and the Heritage Industry" below). As the present-day hagiographers Su Ya and Jia Lusheng wrote in their 1992 book *The Sun Never Sets*: "Unity of thought, unity of will, unity of action: in clenching His fist He smelted the loose sands of China into a lead ingot, melding hundreds of millions of Chinese into one body" (see Figure 4). While Mao was rarely represented in film or theatrical productions before the late 1970s, his symbolic presence was indicated by images of the sun, dawn, mountains, and the sea. The manipulation of such symbols was in many ways similar to filmic conventions developed by Fascist and Stalinist filmmakers who were concerned, to use Susan Sontag's formulation, with "the rebirth of the body and of community, mediated through the worship of an irresistible leader."[94]

Loyalty to Mao, or the wedding of the individual to the totalizing state as represented in the body of Mao, created a relationship that bypassed government and Party structures created to regulate the nation.[95] When people despaired in their own lives they thought of Mao and believed that if only he knew what was happening to them the situation would be set straight (this was also a common refrain in Hitler's Germany and Stalin's Russia). He was the godlike figure who had redeemed the nation in 1949, and unquestioning loyalty to him was seen as the path to self-redemption in the Cultural Revolution. In the 1990s, Mao reincarnated as a figure who was outside temporal and spatial realities, an abiding presence that was beyond the atomized confusion of Reformist China. He represented permanence, value, a historical point of reference and significance.

The body had been a central element of debates regarding national prowess in China for more than a century. Physical discipline and self-strengthening were constantly linked to the issue of China's rejuvenation and progress, and Mao Zedong was an early advocate and practitioner of physical education for revolutionary ends.[96] His penchant for swimming—in particular, ablution as political ritual—assumed national importance from the mid-1950s when the Chairman told the people that: "Swimming is a sport in which the swimmers battle against Nature; you should go into the big rivers and seas to temper yourselves."[97] Then, Mao's personal passion for swimming became the center of a minicult from 1966 when, on 16 July, at the age of 73, he undertook an "heroic" swim of 15 kilometers in the Yangtze.[98] "Fear not fierce wind and waves/I swim as though strolling leisurely in a garden," Mao had written in one of his poems, and the supposedly Olympian feat of strength and vitality displayed in his Yangtze swim was reported as an act with both political and quasi-religious significance. It also marked a new stage in the unfolding of the Cultural Revolution.[99] Thereafter, on 16 July every year for more than a decade, people throughout China took to the water with banners and red flags held high to commemorate Mao's display of revolutionary physical strength and to emulate his spirit by confronting the dangers of untamed nature.[100] The subsequent mystique of swimming was such that at various points in his reformist career Deng Xiaoping, Mao's *de facto* successor, took to the water for the media to emphasize his political longevity.[101]

In death, Mao's body belonged to the nation. Even from the time of his funeral "Mao as a person, with family and friends, was displaced by Mao as a transcendent revolutionary leader without a private domain of his own"[102] (see Figure 5). The Memorial Hall built to house his preserved body was itself a formalistic "embodiment" of China built by workers from throughout the country with materials from every province,[103] the last example of what has been called Mao's "participatory democracy."[104] The Lincoln-like statue of Mao in the entrance chamber of the Memorial Hall has behind it a massive picture of the rivers and mountains of China. In much writing about the dead leader his physical being and spirit have been equated with the landscape of the nation, and in many cases Mao's personal revolutionary history drained places of their own history and made them part of his own (see Figure 6). During the new Mao Cult it was claimed that some tourist spots bore a physical likeness to the Chairman. There was, for example, the "Sun Peak" in Huizhou, Guangdong, which was said to look just like a Mao statue,[105] and at "Mao Zedong Mountain" in Xinjiang the dead leader was regarded as having been "transubstantiated as a geographical feature of the national landscape."[106] The "geospiritual remerging" of the Leader with the land reflected traditional ideas of ancestral return[107] and helped regional travel agencies exploit local geography so they could cash in on the new Cult and China's boom in tourism.

Mao's own corpse, on the other hand, was nothing less than "the biological structure of an historical monument," to use an expression favored by Professor Yuri Denisov, director of the Institute of Biological Structures in

Moscow, the organization entrusted with the preservation of Lenin's body and the embalming of other socialist potentates.[108] Although plans to dispose of Mao's body and remove the Memorial Hall were mooted during the de-Maoification process of 1979–80, the Chairman remained *in situ*, and from the late 1980s his body was often reproduced both in living tissue and in effigy for popular entertainment. The actors Gu Yue and Wang Ying, for example, played Mao in numerous big-budget historical films and multi-episode teleseries made before and during the centenary year of 1993 (see "In a Glass Darkly").[109] In 1994, a wax effigy of the Chairman was modeled for public display in the Great Chinese Wax Works in the Chinese Museum of Revolutionary History on the eastern flank of Tiananmen Square. As one commentator remarked upon seeing the lifelike icon of Mao: "He is the banner of the country, the soul of the people as well as being a Great Man. You enter and empower yourself with some of the energy of this Giant; when you leave you can be a more dignified and upstanding Chinese!"[110]

It is as an incorporeal presence, however, that Mao's influence reached beyond the grave. As Hua Guofeng, the transient Chairman who succeeded Mao (and attempted for a time to both look and write like him [see Figure 7]), said in his speech at the opening ceremony of the Mao Memorial Hall in September 1977: "Chairman Mao will always be with us; he will always be in the hearts of each comrade and friend among us; he will always live in the hearts of the Chinese people and of revolutionary people the world over."[111]

As a revolutionary leader Mao had encouraged people to experience hardship as well as engage in sports and naturopathy—swimming, sunbaths, washing with cold water, physical labor, and so on—in a pseudo-religious regimen for the tempering of both body and spirit. Physical vigor was central to his positivistic and subjective project to remake both the self and the world. While Mao's politics are now as much of a historical curiosity as his corpse, his approach to physicality has played a worthy role in the process whereby the Chinese body has been transformed into the temple of the consumer. In 1990s China, one does glory to one's familial ancestors and pays homage to the memory of Mao and other revolutionary elders not only by engaging in the revolution through productive labor, but also by advancing the reforms through shopping (see the comments of the entrepreneur in "The Sun Never Sets").[112]

While Mao's physical remains were palatially accommodated in a crystalline display case, his political career and works were remodeled to suit the shifting exigencies of Party policy.

In 1979, on the occasion of the thirtieth anniversary of the People's

Republic, Marshal Ye Jianying declared: "What we call Mao Zedong Thought . . . is not the product of Mao Zedong's personal wisdom alone; it is the product of the wisdom of Mao and his comrades-in-arms. . . . It is the crystallization of the collective wisdom of the Chinese Communist Party"[113] (see Figure 8). The conversion of Mao into a corporate body had been completed by the ninetieth anniversary of his birth, in 1983.[114] At that time, not only was his Thought decreed to be the product of collective wisdom, Mao himself was recast as *primus inter pares* within the "older generation of proletarian revolutionaries" (*laoyidai wuchanjieji gemingjia*) who had founded the Party, the PLA, and the People's Republic.[115] It was not until the early 1990s, however, that reports filtered out that Mao Thought was literally the result of a collective effort. In December 1993, the Hong Kong press reported on two documents coauthored by the Central Party School, the Party Document Research Center, and the Party History Research Center that had been presented to the Party's Secretariat in August that year. Both documents, if the Hong Kong claims are correct, confirm what has been suspected and discussed for many years, in particular by Sinologists, that famous works published under the name "Mao Zedong" were the product of other and, in some cases, many hands.[116]

The first of the documents, "Problems Involved in the Collation and Publication of the Works of Mao Zedong," revealed that after five years of intensive work analyzing and collating material in Party archives it was found that of the 470-odd speeches, reports, committee decisions, articles, telegrams, editorials, editorial notes, and directives previously attributed to Mao, more than 250, or nearly half, were neither drafted nor revised by Mao himself. Produced by "comrades in the Center, the Central Secretariat, or workers in the Center" in many cases Mao had merely read sections of the final work and written "I agree" (*tongyi*), "good" (*hao*), or simply signed "Mao Zedong" on them. Of the 120 or so military essays, telegrams, orders, and messages ascribed to Mao from the years prior to 1949, only 12 were actually authored by him. The rest were produced by various Party or army instrumentalities or individuals including Zhu De, Zhou Enlai, Chen Boda, Kang Sheng, and Ren Bishi.[117]

As for the post-1949 Maoist works, it was revealed that many crucial documents and speeches were drafted by Chen Boda, Kang Sheng, Ai Siqi, Yang Xianzhen, Lu Dingyi, Hu Qiaomu, Deng Liqun, and Zhou Rongxin, revised by Liu Shaoqi, Zhou Enlai, and Deng Xiaoping, and merely approved by Mao. Indeed, from 1962, Mao instructed Chen Boda, Kang Sheng, Ai Siqi, Hu Qiaomu, and Deng Liqun to act as the collective authors of Mao Thought. It was even revealed (or at least claimed) that Mao's most famous three essays, the "Three Standard Articles" (*lao sanpian*)—"In

Memory of Norman Bethune," "The Foolish Old Man Who Removed the Mountains," and "Serve the People"[118]—were the work of Hu Qiaomu, Mao's political secretary. Mao himself is supposed only to have made a handful of corrections to Hu's original drafts.[119]

Similarly, there are doubts about the authorship of Mao's two major theoretical works—the "*lianglun*," "On Practice" (*Shijian lun*), and "On Contradiction" (*Maodun lun*). It is claimed that these two pillars of Mao's philosophical contribution to Marxism-Leninism were the result of a collaborative effort between Zhang Wentian, Wang Jiaxiang, and Chen Boda, although Ai Siqi's family had argued for some time that Ai was the real author.[120]

Even if the scribes were inspired by the wave of privatization in China there was little chance they would revolt. The Chinese Copyright Law of 1990 dealt with possible claims by former official ghostwriters by clearly stipulating that the copyright of any work drafted collectively for Party and state leaders, or speeches, articles, and so on written by state employees for the leadership, belonged to the person in whose name that work was produced or published.[121]

Despite these internal revelations, Mao's official status as one of the great twentieth-century masters of Chinese prose remained intact. But just as he was only one sage political leader within the Party collective, so, too, as a writer he was but one of many outstanding talents. In 1994 Mao was "literarily" put in his place by the editors of *A Treasury of Literary Masters of Twentieth-Century China*. Announced in late 1994 by the Hainan Publishing House, this "Treasury" aimed, as a report in *Beijing Book News* put it, to "blow away the nonliterary mists that have clouded literary history in China."[122] A quarter of the multivolume series was devoted to prose writing, and examples of Mao's essays were included. Although, according to the editors of the *Treasury*, the quality of his work justified him being ranked about above Lin Yutang, San Mao, and Feng Zikai, as a literary figure he was obliged to take his place in a line behind Lu Xun, Liang Shiqiu, Zhou Zuoren, Zhu Ziqing, Yu Dafu, and even the contemporary Shaanxi writer Jia Pingwa.[123]

It is Mao's life, however, and the charisma of his personality rather than his writings that continued to appeal to the popular imagination. One of the most prolific popularizers of information on Mao's personal life was the PLA author Quan Yanchi. By producing from the late 1980s a series of best-selling titles such as *Mao on the Way to the Altar*, *Inside and Outside the Vermilion Walls*, and *The Head of the Bodyguards Talks about Mao Zedong*, Quan played a crucial role in revealing the Chairman as a human being, thereby making him more sympathetic, commercializing the Mao industry, and, in the course of doing so, profited handsomely from it. His books, which were written in a cloying and affected prose style that carefully avoided controversial issues, appeared just as the 1988–89 crisis of faith in the future of the Reforms was fueling protests against the status quo and a wave of nostalgia for the past. This was also a period that saw a secularization of dead Party leaders' lives, information about which had previously been treated as a state secret. Only in death, in eternal repose, could the true mien of leaders like them be revealed.

Much of Quan's early work was based on lengthy interviews with members of Mao's inner circle of security guards, in particular Li Yinqiao, a man who also features in Li Zhisui's account of life on the inside. The impressive sales figures of Quan's books encouraged numerous imitators and, according to State Publishing Bureau statistics, by June 1991 the seven best-selling works of reportage related to Mao, of which Quan was the leading author, had sold some 3.67 million copies.[124] As his informants realized the type of money that could be made out of the memoir industry, however, Quan became the object not only of envy but also of litigation, and he found himself embroiled in a bitter public dispute with Li Yinqiao, who accused him of taking unfair commercial advantage of material he had provided.[125]

While the masses were eager to read the easily digested but essentially anodyne writings of authors such as Quan and the much-published Shanghai reportage writer Ye Yonglie, who first came to prominence in the 1980s writing about the victims of Mao's rule, at least one survey claims that it was Chinese translations of Western studies of Mao, in particular Ross Terrill's *Mao: A Biography*, that had a major impact on the young (see "Galluping Mao"). More revealing accounts of the past by Mainland authors such as Li Rui, a onetime secretary of Mao's, or lugubrious but interesting works by Party stalwarts such as Wang Dongxing, the head of Mao's security office, and Bo Yibo, a leading economic planner, however, attracted far less attention.[126] And although there were a number of journals devoted to studies of Mao Thought, they were not widely read.[127] For more than a decade there had been a steady trickle of fascinating and highly controversial material in both restricted circulation and openly available publications that gradually revealed—and continues to reveal—a great deal about the inner history of the Party, Mao, and other leaders. Not surprisingly, much of this work was either too arcane or too limited in scope to attract the attention of the general reader[128] (see Figures 9a, 9b, 9c). That is not to say that some of the more popular essays and books on Mao did not contain new, and in some cases startling information about the Mao period, including such things as Mao's activities in the early stages of the Cultural Revolution and the impact of the Lin Biao Incident on him.[129] Much of the material that appeared in both sources, however, often suffered from serious flaws in terms of use of sources, historical method, veracity, and style, and tended to add to rather than reduce the baggage of traditional Mao mythology.[130] It will take some time, and probably a new political order, before a Chinese insider availing himself or herself of archival material will be in a position to write a book such as Dmitri Volkogonov's *Lenin: A New Biography*.[131]

In early 1993, the flood of books on revolutionary leaders, in particular Mao, led to new regulations being promulgated by the State Press and Publication Administration in concert with the Party Department of Propaganda. Works that "distorted historical facts," it was declared, were no longer to be tolerated and henceforth political biographies had to be "accurate, serious and healthy." The new regulations were announced because, due to economic pressures, media sensationalism and the general ideological malaise numerous unapproved works had been published in 1992—thirty-seven books having been produced by some twenty-seven publishing houses without official permission.[132]

The illicit works included one bizarre volume, *Mao Zedong's Son—Mao Anlong*, a total fabrication published in Inner Mongolia in 1992. This "autobiography" was the handiwork of two writers, one of whom, Ma Jian, was notorious for his pursuit of sensational subject matter. The protagonist of the book, "Mao Anlong," claimed he was the long-lost son of Mao and Yang Kaihui (his "brothers" being Mao Anqing, who died in the Korean War, and Mao Anying, a mentally handicapped charge of the state).[133] "Anlong" tells the tale of his opposition to Mao and how he had been forced by the Chairman into a lifetime of silence and self-sacrifice. This gambit did not get him or his collaborators very far, for shortly after the book appeared "Anlong's" real brother publicly denounced him for having concocted the whole story.

Regardless of the propaganda strictures on Mao publications, the revelations in the library of sanctioned books about the Chairman's "long march to destiny," as Thomas Scharping puts it in an illuminating review of this material in 1994, make for very grim reading indeed. Scharping's tally of the casualties of Mao's irresistible rise based on a reading of twenty-eight of the books published on Mao is sobering:

> . . . eight major secretaries of Mao, among whom three committed suicide, three suffered more than a decade of imprisonment, and one was forgotten for nine years; four designated successors, one dumped in a crematorium (Liu Shaoqi), one crashed in the desert (Lin Biao), one remains in prison

(Wang Hongwen), and one disposed of soon after the Chairman's death (Hua Guofeng); nine other close comrades-in-arms who perished in the Cultural Revolution and dozens who were sent off for prolonged periods of labor reform; three wives divorced or sacrificed for politics, three sons meeting death in war and revolution, one son mentally deranged, one adopted son imprisoned immediately after his benefactor's death, and four daughters dead or missing. And there are other disturbing scenes: General Luo Ruiqing, whose limbs were broken during a failed suicide attempt following his purge, insists on a limping salute to the Chairman; former Party head Li Lisan praises Mao before swallowing an overdose of pills; secretary Tian Jiaying, who, after risking some frank remarks in front of Mao, breaks down before the Chairman and begs forgiveness; writer Ding Ling, banished to a Chinese Siberia, who returns after Mao's death to confirm the greatness of her persecutor....[134]

It is no surprise, then, that the media took advantage of the new Cult and the centenary to shed some light on the fate of Mao's remaining family members, most of whom had lived in relative obscurity since the Chairman's death.[135] Jiang Qing, Mao's widow, had been out of the media spotlight ever since her trial, and she barely featured in any official new works on Mao, except as an ambitious and scheming harpy. Her daughter, Li Na, was interviewed about her father in the press and for the twelve-part CCTV documentary "Mao Zedong" (1993), and Li's sister Li Min occasionally appeared in the media. He Zizhen, the woman Mao left for Jiang Qing, reappeared in public for a while in the early 1980s and produced a volume of memoirs before her death in 1984.[136] But it was the family of Mao Anqing, the second son of his union with Yang Kaihui, that enjoyed greatest media exposure in the 1990s. Anqing was trotted out by Shao Hua, his wife, and their son, Mao Xinyu, on various occasions.[137] This family was also credited with editing a thirty-two-volume book series—*China Has Brought Forth a Mao Zedong*[138]—to mark the centenary, and they are said to have cashed in not only on the books, the production of which took them all over China to collect material, but also by doing product endorsements.[139]

Mock-Mao and the Heritage Industry

The most interesting case of Mao imitation must certainly be that of Mao Xinyu, Mao's grandson mentioned above. As the centenary approached, the gargantuan youth born in 1970 basked for a time in the reflected glory of his parhelion grandparent, and numerous articles about him appeared in the press.[140] Xinyu had come to public attention when, in 1991, he played the role of his grandfather in a Central Beijing Opera Troupe performance of *The Butterfly Longs for the Flower* (*Dielianhua*). Based on Mao's poem about his long-dead second wife Yang Kaihui (Mao Xinyu's grandmother), the opera was staged to commemorate the seventieth anniversary of the founding of the Communist Party. To aid the masquerade, the troupe's makeup artist shaved Xinyu's forehead and made a mole for his chin. "After considerable effort everyone felt the effects were praiseworthy," it was reported. "A special performance of the opera was put on for Party and state leaders at the Great Hall of the People."[141]

According to published accounts, Xinyu was also one of the leading consumers of Mao Cult publications and supporters of the Mao mystique, and he added to his grandfather's Cult by reporting on the frugal personal habits of Mao in a widely acclaimed essay based on a visit to Mao's one-time residence in Fengzeyuan, Zhongnanhai.[142] He also featured prominently in the TV documentary "Mao Zedong," discussing, in one episode, his grandfather's reading habits with the staff of Beijing Library.[143]

The media depictions of Xinyu concentrated on how the revolutionary progeny of the Mao clan was carrying on the family tradition. Xinyu was consistently shown as being the embodiment of modest revolutionary succession. As Mao was supposedly frugal and plain-living, so his grandson is spartan and down-to-earth. In December 1993, on the eve of the Mao centenary, Mao Xinyu was inducted into the Communist Party. Shortly thereafter, Party General Secretary Jiang Zemin met him in Shaoshan on 20 December at a ceremony organized to mark the unveiling of a massive new bronze statue of Mao. When Jiang congratulated him on joining the Party, Xinyu replied: "I will continue to grow under the leadership of the General Secretary."[144] Back in 1989 he had already showed his steadfast support for the Party when his fellow students at the People's University reportedly attempted to get him to lead a group of hunger strikers during the 1989 demonstrations. As he said himself: "I resolutely refused. I'd approve if it was in support of Chairman Mao, but I'd never agree to anything that negates socialism and promotes bourgeois liberalism." He spent 4 June at home studying and learning how to use a Chinese typewriter.[145] As a student of Chinese history, and of the history of his grandfather, he claimed his "heroes" were Qin Shihuang, Genghis Khan, Zhu Yuanzhang (the founder of the Ming dynasty), and, of course, Mao Zedong.[146]

In other ways the exaggerated form of Mao Xinyu is a grotesque incarnation of the Maoist past and the Reformist present. In July 1994, although by then a graduate student in the Party History Department of the Central Party School, Xinyu undertook a traineeship at the Shangri-la Hotel in the northwest of Beijing. After a period working in hotel management he commented perspicaciously: "Granddad was right, theory must be united with practice!" In relation to his investigation of the stock market he remarked:

"Economics is much harder than studying Party history." While he pursued the task of coming to grips with contemporary Chinese realities, however, he also devoted time to writing a history of the Qing dynasty, a project supported by his father, who hoped his son would make a name for himself. The fleshy emanation of Mao's spirit, Xinyu did not fail to keep in touch with the shade of his ancestor. On 1 October, National Day, 1994, he said he was going to Tiananmen "To ask Granddad to give me the strength to meet the challenges of modern society."[147] In mid 1995, Xinyu announced that he would be recording an album of songs in memory of his grandfather to be released in October that year.[148]

As a number of authors in this volume point out, imitating the Mao style has been common in China from the time of the Cultural Revolution, a period during which Mao was the role model for the youth of the nation. Maoist diction and posturing are still evident in China among official hacks, intellectuals who write advice papers for the authorities and even within the business world. High dudgeon is a favorite mode of expression, and it usually takes the form of Maoist diatribes.[149] When the Chinese government expresses outrage in international forums, for example, it generally does so in what could be termed MaoSpeak (see "MaoSpeak"). Some exiled writers and academics realize the abiding influence of this style of language and have made preliminary attempts to analyze it.[150]

One of the first post-1976 examples of the ironical exploitation of the Mao mystique, however, used the language of another, more ancient Chinese orthodoxy. In the early 1980s, the Committee for Cultural Relics Administration in Qufu, Confucius' birthplace in Shandong, produced a new version of *The Analects* (Lunyu), the classical collection of sayings attributed to the Master. The book was designed in the same shape and size as *Quotations from Chairman Mao*. It had a red plastic cover, with the title printed in gold lettering, in imitation of the mini-Maoist bible. The format of the printed text followed that of a traditional Chinese book, but simplified characters were used (see Figure 10). At the time such clever emulations were still rare.

In the 1990s, it was not only Mao's *Little Red Book* that was being copied. During the Cultural Revolution, lines from Mao's poems, or the poems in their entirety, had been carved on every conceivable surface; they were etched onto the minute to the monstrous, from grains of rice to mountain crags and rock faces[151] (see Figure 11). Since then, the calligraphic commemoration of Mao has continued. In 1992 it was reported that Mao's own handwritten version of a portion of the Tang poet Bo Juyi's "Song of Everlasting Sorrow" had been carved onto a massive stone stela and erected at the Xianyou Temple in Zhouzhi County, Shaanxi Province, the place where the poem was composed. The 4-meter-high, 5.28-meter-long stela was placed in a traditional pavilion structure roofed with mock-imperial glazed *liuli* tiles. For reasons not given, Mao reproduced only 224 of the 840 characters of the original poem. Unsigned and not inscribed in any way, this calligraphic jotting was, nonetheless, deemed worthy of reproduction and insinuated into the ancient site of Bo Juyi's composition[152] (see Figure 12).

Although Mao's highly individualistic style of calligraphy continues to be emulated, the quality of the original works is questionable. One of the most perceptive comments on Mao's hand comes from the art historian Pierre Ryckmans, writing as Simon Leys:

> His [Mao's] calligraphy . . . is strikingly original, betraying a flamboyant egotism, to the point of arrogance, if not extravagance; at the same time it shows a total disregard for the formal discipline of the brush, and this contempt for technical requirements condemns his work, however powerful, to remain essentially inarticulate. His poetry, so aptly described by Arthur Waley as "not as bad as Hitler's painting, but not as good as Churchill's," was rather pedantic and pedestrian, managing to combine obscurity with vulgarity; and yet, within the framework of an obsolete form, it remains, in its very awkwardness, remarkably unfettered by conventions.[153]

As the Mao Cult was reaching its height in late 1991, the Shandong artist Zhou Pengfei (b. 1970) put on a major exhibition of his Mao-style (*Maoti*) calligraphy in Beijing, issuing invitations in imitation Mao handwriting.[154] Zhao Yihong, the manager of the Yihong Book Workshop in Chengdu, Sichuan, specialized in book covers using Mao calligraphy, showing particular preference for the word "struggle" (*dou*) as penned by the Chairman in his designs. For imitators and students of Mao's calligraphy by then there were also a number of useful reference books; the most impressive was *The Great Compendium of Mao Zedong's Calligraphy*, which contained 2,362 characters in Mao's hand culled from numerous sources as well as a 16-page selection of Mao's signatures.[155]

Imitation, however, is not necessarily the most sincere form of flattery. In late 1994, the well-known *guohua* (Chinese painting) artist Wu Guanzhong took the major Shanghai art company Duoyunxuan and the Hong Kong Yongcheng Antique Auctioners to court for auctioning a Cultural Revolution–period painting reputedly by him bearing the inscription "Bombard the Headquarters—my big character poster" (*Paoda silingbu— wode yizhang dazibao*) in Mao-style calligraphy.[156] Wu denied that he had done the work, which fetched H.K.$528,000 when sold to a Taiwanese collector in 1993, and was outraged by accusations that he was attempting to profit out of the Mao centenary in such an unscrupulous fashion.[157]

Other, more commercial imitations of Mao include advertisements such as the massive billboard visible near Shanghai Station in December 1991 for wallpaper and interior decorating products that featured the line "*Yu gong yi shan*"—the title of Mao's famous homily "The Foolish Old Man Who Removed the Mountains"—followed by words to the effect that if you used their product you, too, could move beautiful mountain scenery into your own living room. In 1992 the Changsha Advertising Company in Hunan maintained a massive billboard featuring Mao's calligraphic inscription "Learn from Comrade Lei Feng" to promote itself (see Figure 13), and for years the Beijing tourist authorities have used a line from Mao's poetry—*budao Changcheng fei haohan* (If you don't make it to the Great Wall you're not a real man)—to sell tours to the Great Wall. But the exploitation of Mao's image in advertising was officially banned with the promulgation of China's advertising law in October 1994.[158]

Mao's poetry, also the subject of controversy, inspired such imitators as Chen Mingyuan, a man jailed after 4 June as a dissident. In the 1960s Chen authored numerous poems in the classical style, and in the early years of the Cultural Revolution a collection of these were produced in book form in the belief that they were actually by Mao. Chen's attempts to clear up this misunderstanding in both the 1960s and 1980s led to seemingly endless political persecution.[159]

Reprisals and marketing of Mao have been particularly successful in the free port of Hong Kong. David Tang, founder of the China Club, an upmarket retreat for the well heeled, has played with Cultural Revolution fashion and Mao kitsch in the décor of the club and the uniforms of its workers. In early 1995 he opened Shanghai Tang, a department store on Pedder Street in Central District that specialized in stylish and pricey nostalgia goods inspired by Old Shanghai and the formerly revolutionary China.[160]

From the mid 1960s, local authorities made many attempts to evoke the cachet of Mao. But, as we have noted, by the early 1980s Mao had become both a political and an economic burden. Internal documents and circulars similar to those referred to in "Pulping Mao" above were also issued to organizations outside the publishing industry that were still promoting the defunct Mao Cult.

In 1979 an internal *Guangming Daily* report published in the limited-circulation publication *Propaganda Trends* commented on attempts to commemorate an inspection tour Mao had made of Wuhu in Anhui Province in 1958. During the tour Mao had spent the night in Building No. 2 of the Tieshan Guesthouse. In the Cultural Revolution, Mao's rooms in the guesthouse were closed to the public and converted into a museum. By the time this tardy consecration took place, however, none of the original bedding, books, or other everyday trivia that Mao had used during his visit could be found, so simulacra were provided.

Being withdrawn from public use at a time of increased local and international tourism, and hardly a site worthy of revolutionary adulation, in 1979 the two hotel rooms represented nothing more than lost revenue: More than 5,000 *yuan* were forfeited annually to maintain the suite's cult status. As the report observed: "Comrade Mao Zedong was always in favor of frugality. Since there is a Chairman Mao Memorial Hall in Beijing and museums in places where Chairman Mao spent considerable periods of time like Shaoshan, Jinggangshan, Zunyi, and Yan'an, surely such minor commemorative rooms are not really necessary."[161]

The first boom in "Mao tourism" during the 1960s had seen the conversion of numerous other places Mao had been, the rooms in which he had worked or slept, and even the paths on which he had walked, turned into commemorative spots with plaques or cenotaphs recording details of the historic visitation.[162] Although revolutionary fervor was dying down in the late 1970s and official attempts were being made to bring an end to Mao worship, organizations throughout the country were gradually realizing the commercial potential of the revolutionary sites that came under their jurisdiction. Some places were already charging foreign travelers exorbitant rates for rooms they claimed had been built for or lived in by Mao. A Department of Propaganda notice was circulated in 1979 warning that the exploitation of Mao's name was not only improper but it also gave foreigners entirely the wrong impression.[163] Despite such official interdictions, however, the "Chairman Mao slept here" ploy was often used to attract visitors and became an excuse to charge high prices. From the late 1980s, the largest Mao tourist trap in China was his hometown in Hunan.

Shaoshanchong (now Shaoshan City), Mao Zedong's birthplace, or "the place where the Red Sun rose," as the Cultural Revolution hosanna put it, was a small town of some 1,500 inhabitants. At the height of the Mao revival in the early 1990s it became a major profit center.

Shaoshan had originally been a district in Xiangtan County, Hunan. During the Cultural Revolution it was promoted to the status of Special District and put directly under provincial control, in recognition of its unimpeachable revolutionary pedigree. In 1980, as Mao's status fell, so did that of his birthplace, and Shaoshan was reduced once more to being a district in Xiangtan. The bloated bureaucracy of the township was also cut back and, in what became a major scandal, a local budget surplus of 1.4 million *yuan* was covertly distributed among these employees in lieu of severance pay. The scandal was duly reported in the *People's Daily*,[164] and an odium clung to the township throughout the decade.[165] With the Chairman's revival in the 1990s, however, such economic freewheeling seemed to be more prescient than reprehensible.

"May you make a fortune out of Chairman Mao!" (*fa Mao zhuxide cai!*), according to one report, became the usual greeting in Shaoshan as the new Mao Cult attracted tourists in numbers not seen for nearly a quarter of a century.[166] In the early 1990s some 3,000 visitors arrived daily, and in 1992 alone more than 1.2 million people trekked to Shaoshan to see the Mao family home and the many sites associated with Mao's childhood.[167] This came after a low in the mid 1980s, when only 50,000 to 60,000 visitors were visiting the town annually.[168] While the numbers of tourists in the 1990s could hardly compare with the mass of pilgrims who inundated Shaoshan in the mid 1960s—60,000 a day, most of whom traveled by foot—nonetheless, the new influx caused a major economic shift in the district, and many locals abandoned traditional agricultural production in favor of the hospitality industry. Of the population of 1,500, more than 780, or 52 percent, were soon engaged in the catering business or selling Mao trinkets at stalls lining the approaches to Mao's house[169] (see Figure 14).

With Shaoshan awash in tourist dollars, sex workers also saw a dramatic increase in their takings. Many of these prostitutes were reportedly Hunan women who, having failed to make the grade in the highly competitive environment of Guangdong (in particular the Special Economic Zones of Shenzhen and Zhuhai), returned home to ply their trade. When I visited Shaoshan in mid 1992 after an absence of some seventeen years, I was accosted by young girls whose general come-on line was as simple as it was direct: "Wanna screw?" (*dadong bu?* literally, "wanna poke the hole?"), they asked.

Hotels and restaurants throughout the township sported names that exulted in the Mao surname. Dozens of local houses were converted into eateries and pensions. The earliest and most famous of them was the Mao Family Restaurant (see Figure 15).

Situated on a hillock overlooking the Mao homestead, the Mao Family Restaurant (*Maojia fandian*) was run by Tang Ruiren, a distant relative of Mao Zedong himself. Before opening her restaurant in 1984, "Granny Tang's" main claim to fame was that she had been photographed with Mao and a number of other local peasants in 1959.[170] Customers would be greeted and have a Mao badge pinned on the clothing. Tang would then encourage them to order the most expensive items on the menu: spicy and greasy dishes she claimed were "Chairman Mao's favorites"[171] (see Figure 16). Along with the bill at the end of the meal, diners would be presented with autographed copies of the photograph in which Tang, in the flush of youth, appears standing near Mao.[172] To avail herself better of the opportunities presented by the Mao revival and its international curiosity value, Tang also learned enough English, Japanese, and Russian to entertain foreign diners.[173]

Tang's history reflects the dizzying progress of Party policy over the years. As a young and energetic relative of Mao, she had led the local peasants to "get organized" and established the first agricultural cooperative in Xiangtan County. In all subsequent campaigns she was a tireless activist. Guilty at first about exploiting the Mao name for her own profit—and she's done well out of it, as a picture of her taken in Beijing with other "outstanding model entrepreneurs" and Premier Li Peng testifies—Tang gradually managed to reconcile a revolutionary past with her pecuniary present. Already in her sixties when the Mao Family Restaurant took off, Tang literally made a million out of the Chairman's legacy and, in the centenary year, she opened a branch of her restaurant in Beijing.[174]

Throughout Shaoshan, other locals who ran restaurants, hotels, or stalls mostly named after Mao or members of his family displayed pictures showing them with Mao or relatives of theirs photographed with the Chairman. Every gimmick was used to exploit the image, and their range of Mao wares is discussed below in "Modern Mao Artifacts and Multi-media Mao."

Shaoshan also benefited from official largesse during the years leading to the Mao centenary. Among other things, a new highway between the provincial capital of Changsha and the town was built, as was a spacious guesthouse, presumably constructed to accommodate foreign tourists and the Chinese dignitaries who are obliged to make the pilgrimage to the birthplace, and a new "forest of stelae" (beilin) on Shaofeng Peak in which the leader's poems were engraved on one hundred tombstonelike stone blocks.[175]

Other major construction projects in Shaoshan linked to the centenary were: the building of a 10.1-meter-tall bronze Mao statue[176] designed by Liu Kaiqu (the man responsible for the bas-reliefs on the Monument to the People's Heroes in Beijing); a Revolutionary Martyrs' Park to commemorate the 148 people from the town who died for the revolution, including six of Mao's relatives; and a Mao Zedong artifact storehouse and library. The latter was planned as the largest center for the study of and research into Mao Zedong Thought in the world.[177] The family home, gaudily repainted clan temple (see Figure 17), and the often reorganized Mao museum, which among other things features the cream-color, Soviet-built Gaz limousine Mao had used during his 1959 visit and a replica of his Zhongnanhai residence, were all open to visitors.[178] Another favorite spot on the Shaoshan tourist map was the guesthouse at Dishuidong outside the town, where Mao lived during his mid 1966 secret sojourn in the early phase of the Cultural Revolution.[179] In 1992 it was particularly memorable for the one souvenir that was sold there: reproductions of a U.S.$100 bill printed on cloth on which the image of Mao had replaced that of Franklin. At the time, nearly a year before the New Year's paintings featuring Mao and money appeared, this simple tea towel–size cloth eloquently expressed the Chairman's re-formist reincarnation (see Figure 18).

Not everyone in Shaoshan, however, was willing to cash in on the Mao Cult. Mao's aged cousin, Mao Zelian, was scornful of the mercenary revival of the flagging spirits of the Leader. "Chairman Mao had no love for private business, and he would despise those who now make money from his name . . . ," he said. "Chairman Mao's idea was to make the country rich, while Deng's idea is to allow a few people to get rich. It's all gone wrong."[180]

In early December 1993, a reporter for *Beijing Review*, the English-lan-guage propaganda weekly produced by the Foreign Languages Press, com-mented dourly on the threat, not of the Mao Cult, but of the depredations of the "M-Cult," or Money Cult, that had overwhelmed the nation, including Shaoshan.[181]

As the Mao Cult of the early 1990s faded and Shaoshan became just another quaint destination on the tourist map, one writer did formulate a means for keeping the spirit of Mao's politics alive in the context of China's turbulent economic upheaval. In August 1994 a journalist writing for the Hong Kong *Eastern Express* suggested a new form of "politico-tain-ment." It offered a spoof vision of what a "Maoland" theme park in Shaoshan would look like. Youthful park attendants, it was suggested, could dress as Red Guards and carry the *Little Red Book*, messy visitors could be struggled, and there would be a Cultural Revolution roller coaster that would hurtle passengers around as though they were experiencing a political purge. There could even be a "Haunted Politburo," featuring the ghosts of leaders airbrushed out of history.[182] Even though "Maoland" waits to be built, real Maoist theme places already exist. One of these is Linying County in Henan, a revived socialist collective-cum-corporation that has become wealthy pursuing semi–Cultural Revolution policies.[183]

Modern Mao Artifacts and Multi-Media Mao

The nature of nostalgia is that it relies on collective memories, fantasies and imagined pasts. Physical artifacts—originals or simulacra—are often the very things that elicit a nostalgic mood, a mood that can be tempered by any number of emotions, from the sublime to the ridiculous. In China objects embarrassingly derided as the by-products of a national psychosis just a few years ago were during the early 1990s recycled or remodeled for circulation to play a role in the new socialist market economy.

Flea markets and "antiques stores" in China's major cities had been selling genuine Cultural Revolution Mao knick-knacks at generally affordable, although highly inflated Reform era, prices for years (see Figure 19). However, true lovers of kitsch/camp/trash have generally been disappointed by the lack of imagination displayed in the meager array of newly manufactured Mao artifacts. This probably is because by the early 1990s the economic reforms had still failed to produce a sufficient surfeit of goods, leisure, and laxity that would allow Mainland Chinese (unlike people in Hong Kong and Taiwan) to realize John Waters' dictum on kitsch: "In order to acquire bad taste one must first have very, very good taste."[184] Nonetheless, there are those of us who regard the new Cult as a deification of Mao as Chairman Camp,[185] and we await anxiously for items such as "Mao in a snowstorm" and crystal sarcophagus soup tureens to be produced. We hanker after exhibitions of the Chairman's preserved viscera and crave the marketing of Mao shrouds in the tradition of the Turin hoax. To date, major tourist options have also been overlooked, such as the renting of Mao's suite in Zhongnanhai to the new rich of China so that billionaire entrepreneurs can entertain peasant wenches in the Dragon Bed and play at being Chairman for a night. Surely there is also a market for Holy Revolutionary Relics.[186] Before the rich possibilities of this nascent market are realized, however, it would be best if we consider the more mundane, contemporary artifacts that became available from the late 1980s:

Mao badges or buttons, those ubiquitous symbols of that bygone age, were recycled by the ton, and new badge factories went on line to satisfy increased consumer demand.

The first Mao badges appeared in Yan'an in late 1948, made by university students using old toothpaste tubes.[187] The object of passionate devotion during the Cultural Revolution, the badges were often used as a means to establish revolutionary credentials and camaraderie. Many people built up large private collections, including the sycophantic Zhou Enlai, although he was also one of the first to criticize the excesses of Mao-mania when, in March 1969, he said: "More than 700 million copies of *Quotations* are in circulation, as well as 2.2 billion Chairman Mao badges. People are indulging in feudalism and a bourgeois style. What we want is frugality."[188]

Mao's own criticism of the badges came in a discussion held with student leaders in April that year when he made his famous remark "Give me back my airplanes (*huan wo feiji*). It would be far more useful," he continued, "to make airplanes to protect the nation out of the metal being expended in the production of Mao badges."[189]

The renewed interest in Mao badges in the 1990s was symptomatic of the Mao Cult, and the new rate of exchange had nothing to do with revolutionary credentials and everything to do with commerce. Prior to the Mao revival, the Shaoshan Mao Badge Factory had been churning out a line of undistinguished and nonrevolutionary chotchky; then, in the early 1990s, it was retooled and converted back to badge production. And there was, for example, "Mao Badge City," which I visited in Wuhan in May 1992. A few rooms in a ramshackle building near the chinoiserie-cement Huanghe Pavilion housed a collection of Cultural Revolution–period Mao trash carelessly arranged on the walls and in display cases for the diversion of tourists on their way to or from the pavilion. Fairy lights and badges arranged in heart shapes added to the attraction,[190] and hopeful shop assistants masquerading as museum guides attempted to hawk pieces of the tawdry collection.

A number of semicommercial Mao badge exhibitions were also held in 1992–93 in Beijing, Shaoshan (in the Mao clan temple), and cities such as Wuhan. One display of 10,000 badges was put on in Beijing in mid 1993, while major permanent collections of badges were established in Sichuan, Guangdong, and Xi'an. At last, after years of rejection, obsessive collectors finally had a chance to display their massive hoardings (some number in the tens of thousands) and "badge experts" like Zhou Jihou from Guizhou were able to publish books such as *The Ninth Wonder of the World: The Mystery of the Mao Badge,*[191] which tells the history of the badges and discusses the new fad for them. A Mao Badge Research Society and a magazine titled *Research Papers on Collecting* [Mao badges] were also founded and, for a time, badges were a viable currency once more (see "CultRev Relics").

The calendar boom that developed in China from the 1980s also served as a popular medium for a revival of Mao's image. Whereas movie and song stars, foreign beauties and beaux, girls in a state of semiundress or striking poses with the accouterments of modernization (mobile phones, motorcycles, cars, and so on) generally featured in the annual rash of calendars, during the Mao boom from 1992 to 1994 the Chairman's calligraphy or picture decorated many of the new calendars. A few even featured Mao badge collections with each month devoted to a different display of badges made variously from metal, porcelain, plastic, or bamboo (see Figures 20a, 20b). Then, in 1994, cellophane traditional-style New Year's paintings (*nianhua*) appeared bearing images of Mao (see Figure 21), or Mao and his cohorts (Zhou, Liu, and Zhu) as they appear on the 100 *yuan* Chinese bank note, surrounded by time-honored symbols of longevity (pine trees and herons [Figure 22]) or good fortune (money, gold bullion, fat babies, fish, and the like [Figure 23]). These were the most gaudy mass-produced (dare we say "kitsch"?) items of the new cult.

At the ill-kempt temple stalls that choked the exit at the south end of the Chairman Mao Memorial Hall in Tiananmen visitors who had been herded by the remains could also pick up such items as "Lucky cigarettes" (*Jili xiangyan*), the packet of which featured a picture of the Mao-as-Abe-Lincoln statue inside the hall. Also available were Mao cigarette lighters that noisily chimed "The East Is Red" (see Figure 24) or "Jingle Bells," imitation ivory Mao Memorial Hall chopsticks, tacky shopping bags, cuff links, barometers, glow-in-the-dark busts, Mao lighters, diamond-studded Mao watches, pocket watches with Mao holograms and a plethora of Mao-inspired postage stamps (see Figure 25).

In Shaoshan, Mao brooches, tie clips, watches, badges, and pendants with spectral holograms of the leader's head could be purchased (see Figures 26, 27), while in various parts of the country shoppers could pick up numerous other novelty items, such as Mao yo-yos containing a computer chip that enabled it to chortle the words of "The East Is Red," and T-shirts with fawning slogans such as "I Love Chairman Mao" or "I Like to Study His Books Most" (see Figures 28, 29); or slightly more ironical statements such as "A spark can start a prairie fire" (*xingxing zhi huo keyi liao yuan*), or clever and pointed distortions of famous Mao quotes such as "I don't fear hardship, I'm not scared of dying, nor am I afraid of you" (*yi bupa ku, er bupa si, ye bupa ni*),[192] and even a type of shirt with a caricature of Mao held up by a worker-peasant-soldier trinity bearing the logo "assures safety and exorcises evil" (*baoan pixie*).[193]

In late 1993 fashionable purveyors of wannabe po-mo (postmodern) culture in Beijing even produced a pastiche calender for 1994–95 featuring both Mao and Deng in cut-up collage[194] (see Figures 30a, 30b, 30c). Those with more traditional tastes in representations of the Great Leader, however, could obtain a series of Cultural Revolution–style Mao matchbox covers (*huochaihe*) at the Baihua Bookstore in Beijing, opposite the China Art Gallery between Wangfujing and Shatan'r, which specializes in art books[195] (see Figure 31).

Through books, comics, films, television and music the Older Generation of Revolutionary Leaders, as Mao and his coevals are known, have become part of the audiovisual repertoire of mass pop culture. In the early 1990s, a popular interlude at any major celebration held by a wealthy work unit in the capital or on television would be to welcome some of the actors who play the Older Revolutionaries to do a turn.[196] As I have written elsewhere, "Doing their patter in heavy local accents and done up in a modern version of opera masks (*lianpu*)—Mao with his brush-backed hair and mole, Lin bald and myopic, Zhou bushy-browed and face drawn—they act as comics or compères, talking heads who add a touch of class to an evening's entertainment."[197] At least these dead leaders have a status to live up to and the stature to appear in stage productions. It is hard to imagine that 1990s Chinese politicians, the gray bureaucrats of Reform, will ever achieve such a reputation unless, of course, an ironical, popular penchant for retro "nonpersonality cults" springs up in the years to come.

Numerous teleseries and documentaries related to Mao's life were produced in the lead-up to the centenary. Some of them included rare archival footage, as in the case of the hagiographic twelve-part TV documentary "Mao Zedong (1893–1993)," which screened in December 1993.[198] Then there were TV programs such as the Mao quiz show called "The Sun and Truth," with its competing teams parroting Mao quotes and giving publication details, dates, place and so on.[199] Other programs, such as the successful 1990 multiepisode TV soap "Aspirations," used Mao or rather Mao-period nostalgia to highlight the worldly cynicism of the Deng era. "Aspirations" contrasted the human closeness of the past (despite the attendant horrors of the Cultural Revolution period) with the heartless materialism of the present.[200] The 1992 sitcom "The Editors" treated Maoist diction and style with playful irreverence,[201] and in the popular 1993 series "A Beijing Man in New York," Mao appeared as the patron saint of struggling entrepreneurs. In episode 9, the protagonist Wang Qiming launches into an impassioned soliloquy before starting up his knitwear sweatshop. Imitating the tone and delivery of a Party secretary, he satirizes the Party and authoritarian rule while still affirming that for things to be run effectively you have to have a transparently bad person in control. It's better to be up front about how bad you are, he argues, than to pretend to be good. Wang concludes his speech with an admonition to a roomful of imaginary workers to "abandon your illusions," a reference to the title of a famous article Mao wrote criticizing the United States in 1949, and get to work.[202]

After a hiatus of three decades, Mao reappeared on both stage and screen in the early 1980s.[203] The veteran PLA actor Gu Yue came to specialize in the mature Mao (see "In a Glass Darkly"), while Wang Ying of the Central Experimental Theater Company concentrated on playing the handsome young Mao.[204] With the enormous popular success of such character actors, it soon seemed that everyone wanted a Mao of their own, and places as far flung as Inner Mongolia found Chairman look-alikes to perform at local benefits and shows.[205]

While official biopics have been common in China for years, starting in the early 1990s, Mao also featured one way or another in many non- or semiofficial films, such as Shi Jian and Chen Jue's *Tiananmen* (1991),[206] Wu Wenguang's *My 1966* (1993), a droning documentary about ex–Red Guards, Chen Kaige's epic *Farewell My Concubine* (1993), and Zhang Yuan's *The Square* (1994). In Tian Zhuangzhuang's *Blue Kite* (1993), one of the most brooding historical films made in China, Mao did not play an on-screen role, but his presence is felt throughout the film. In 1995 Chen Kaige planned a new project titled *To Kill a King*, a film about the assassination attempt on Emperor Qin Shihuang, to whom Mao had compared himself (see "The Mao Phenomenon"). The screenplay of *To Kill a King* was the work of the ex-army writer Wang Peigong, the author of *WM*,[207] the controversial 1985 play about the Cultural Revolution, and an activist jailed for his support of the 1989 student demonstrations who, like Bai Hua and so many others of his generation, was bedeviled by a fascination with Mao.[208]

Theater productions have featured Mao for many years, although in the centenary year attempts were made to depict the Leader as something of a tragic hero. In late 1993, for example, the PLA staged a work titled *The Sun Never Sets*. Set in January 1976, shortly after Zhou Enlai's death, it shows Mao as a solitary figure, fearful of death, superstitious, and wary of the karmic punishment that awaits him. He receives news that a massive meteorite has fallen in the Northeast of China and sees it as an omen of his imminent demise. Despite these more human touches, Zhu Shimao, a noted actor and the producer of the play, averred that "Mao was a god," and in the production the Chairman spouts quotations about hard work, thrifty living, and sacrificing personal interest in the service of the state even as death approaches. Some critics, not surprisingly, saw the play as a veiled criticism of the corrupt values rife in contemporary China.[209]

Although John Adams and Alice Goodman's opera *Nixon in China* appeared in the West in 1987, the first traditional Chinese opera featuring Mao was not staged in Mainland China until 1994. *Mao Zedong in 1960*, a *pingju*-style opera created in Mudan, Heilongjiang Province, and featuring an aria-singing Chairman, premièred in Beijing in November 1994. The story reflects, to quote official propaganda, "how a Great Man dealt with everyday life while also confronted with the ever-changing complexities of international politics, the natural disasters faced by China, and the confusion experienced by both the Party and the People."[210] To date, no overtly critical stage representation of Mao has appeared.[211]

At the same time as a second spate of state-sanctioned iconoclasm aimed at removing the remaining public statues of Mao Zedong saw the demolition of Mao monoliths at such symbolic sites as the entrance to Beijing University in 1988,[212] artists such as Wang Guangyi, as we have noted above, began including reworked images of Mao in their paintings. The humorous use and abuse of Mao in Mainland works did, to an extent, reflect what Li Xianting (see "The Imprisoned Heart") called a "Mao obsession." As Li remarks, it was a fixation "that still haunted the popular psyche," combining "both a nostalgia for the simpler, less corrupt, and more self-assured period of Mao's rule with a desire to appropriate Mao Zedong, the paramount God of the past, in ventures satirizing life and politics in contemporary China." Practical political considerations, however, as well as the vagaries of the marketplace, meant that few of these works were openly iconoclastic, questioning, or even much more than comely pop trivia. All too often they displayed the tired tropes of po-mo, playing on the Chairman's image with all the resources that appropriation and pastiche could muster while rarely reflecting any of the true cultural complexity of the popular Mao Cult, or the residual social and cultural aftershocks of the original Cult.

Avant-garde Mao art, like so much of nonofficial Mainland culture after 1989 indulged itself more in consumer irony than in social critique (see Figure 32). As I have commented on such tendencies elsewhere: "When . . . irony itself is commodified and used 'to grease the wheels of commerce, not . . . to resist its insidious effects,'[213] the cultural significance of market-oriented dissent becomes deeply disturbing."[214] The most threatening thing about the Shanghai artist Yu Youhan's noted floral-patterned Maos, for example, is that they could be easily mass-produced as bedspreads or curtains.[215] And many other artists have used Mao as a decoration, cultural wallpaper, in their work, rather than as a subject for serious depiction. Such playfulness does indeed have a liberating dimension, and this is evident in the work of Beijing artists such as Liu Wei, himself a product of the Cultural Revolution, whose paintings present the indulgent yet equally unsettlingly distorted vision of Mao, not unlike the image you'd get if you looked at the Chairman through a fish tank.[216] Zhu Wei, another Beijing artist (and former PLA soldier) whose work was exhibited in Hong Kong in 1994,[217] used Mao, his writings, and his poetry in the winsome, bloated literati fantasies of his *Beijing Story* series[218] (see Figure 33). Numerous other painters have also had a brush with Mao, including Yan Peiming and Yu Hong[219] and their works safely adorn the walls of expat collectors in China and of connoisseurs in Hong Kong and Taiwan, and can be found on display in museums and art spaces throughout the world. The Mainland has yet to produce a group like St. Petersburg's "necrorealists," however—artists who have made much of the corpses and deaths of Lenin, Stalin, and Hitler.[220] Liu Dahong, a Shanghai-based painter, has gone as far as any other Mainland artist to date in reworking Mao within the context of traditional subject matter to achieve a more layered and complex vision. This is particularly true of the four paintings *Mao for All Seasons* and in *The Honeymoon*, a colorful tableau showing the Great Leader lecturing a gathering of Party heroes in what can be construed as a satire on Mao's cultural policies.[221] Liu's later scroll painting *The Butterfly Longs for the Flower* shows

Mao as an aged emperor surrounded by his phantasmagoric court.[222] However, none of the Mainland artists mentioned here have matched the nuanced approach of the late 1980s *Chairmen Mao Series* by the New York–based painter Zhang Hongtu (Hong Tu Zhang)[223] (see Figure 34). Zhang's work, playful and deeply earnest, was used in dress, jacket, and T-shirt designs by Vivienne Tam of East Wind Code in late 1994[224] and enjoyed a commodified success in a way that was as provocative and even more commercial than his Mainland counterparts[225] (see Figure 35).

From 1987, the Beijing rock-pop singer Cui Jian recycled the detritus of Maoist culture to help create his own bad-boy image and, at the time, his wonderfully baneful renditions of old Party favorites such as "Nanniwan" outraged the authorities.[226] By the early 1990s, however, rearranged and revamped Party hymns were commonplace, and numerous wannabe rock stars invariably produced their own versions of songs such as "The East Is Red."[227] Now that everyone was "playing" (*wan'r*) with Party tradition there was nothing particularly risqué about the music; repackaged revolutionary rock was just another part of the cultural landscape[228] (see Figure 36a, 36b). Mao was also very popular among the stylishly naughty boys and girls of the Beijing rock demimonde, so much so that pro-Mao machismo was endemic to the scene.[229] As happened so often during the Mao revival, the Chairman was manipulated by diverse groups with totally conflicting interests, even achieving a new popularity with the urban subculture while still maintaining his status as an authoritarian figure.

At roughly the same time (1990–91), the Party began to orchestrate a response to the latest invasion of Canto Pop from Hong Kong-Taiwan by commissioning karaoke-versions of pro-socialist patriotic favorites for use in bars and clubs throughout the country[230] (see Figures 37, 38, 39). Many of the MTVs produced—on videotape as well as laser disk—were risible, and some contained young male students longing for the Chairman in what I can only describe as "homoerotica with Chinese characteristics."[231] This trend for revamped revolutionary songs, sparked to a great extent by the paucity of new popular Mainland music following the boom year of 1988,[232] led to the production and success of "The Red Sun" tape in late 1991 (see "Let the Red Sun Shine In" [Figure 40]),[233] as well as of its numerous imitators[234] (see Figures 41, 42, 43).

While Mao has been part of the designer-wallpaper of the China Club in Hong Kong for some years, he generally enjoyed a more exalted public status on the Mainland—that is, until the Beijing Hard Rock Café opened on 16 April 1994, when he was joined by members of the older generation of revolutionary rebels from the West. Linda Jaivin described the scene as follows:

England's Fab Four and China's Great One come together, right now, over me. On the ceiling dome of Beijing's new Hard Rock Café, the Beatles, Chuck Berry, and other venerable ancestors of rock pose like tourists in front of Beijing's Temple of Heaven and Tiananmen Gate. Mao gazes down from his perch on Tiananmen at posters of the Sex Pistols, Chinese bartenders mixing cocktails under a sign that reads 'Love All, Serve All,' Westerners scoffing burgers, and local DJs downing draught beers. It's hard to tell if he's still smiling.[235]

Mao More Than Ever

In fact, the new Mao Cult shared a number of features in common with the cult of Elvis, "the King," spirit guide of the Hard Rock chain. In *Dead Elvis: A Chronicle of a Cultural Obsession*, Greil Marcus described the Elvis cult in terms that strike a familiar chord as we contemplate the abiding popularity of Chairman Mao in China:

> When he died, the event was a kind of explosion that went off silently, in minds and hearts; out of that explosion came many fragments, edging slowly into the light, taking shape, changing shape again and again as the years went on. No one, I think, could have predicted the ubiquity, the playfulness, the perversity, the terror, and the fun of this, of Elvis Presley's second life: a great, common conversation, sometimes, a conversation between specters and fans, made out of songs, art works, books, movies, dreams; sometimes more than anything cultural noise, the glossolalia of money, advertisements, tabloid headlines, bestsellers, urban legends, nightclub japes. In either form it was—is—a story that needed no authoritative voice, no narrator, a story that flourishes precisely because it is free of any such thing, a story that told itself.[236]

In some ways the popular and "ironic" rehearsals of Mao and Mao-era styles are typical of what, in 1994, the now defunct London journal *The Modern Review* termed the "art of revival."[237] As critics writing for *TMR*, which specialized in "low brow culture for highbrows," state: ". . . although revivals don't offer convincing reconstructions of the past, preferring re-arrangements, the way one period re-arranges another certainly offers a telling impression of the revivalist age."[238] This was certainly true of the new Mao Cult of the early 1990s. Economic reform and ideological decay had freed Mao from the carefully-cultivated persona fostered by Party propaganda.

Another aspect of the Mao Cult was that it capitalized on China's new teeny-bopper and youth culture market—that is, the buying power of the young. Many consumers of Mao products were adolescents or people in their early twenties who were unfamiliar with the Mao era. Unconcerned with the burdens of the past, they could indulge their curiosity and be playful in their approach to Mao memorabilia. Young people often regarded Mao not as a unique Great Leader but as a homebred luminary who deserved a position in the galaxy of Hong Kong and Taiwan pop stars popular on the Mainland. Some of these fans, or "star-chasers" (*zhuixingzu*) as they were called in Chinese, indulged in necrolatry, lavished attention on Mao for a time, enjoyed the Cultural Revolution songs that had been revived from 1991, and read books related to him and his role in modern Chinese history. Mao was such a complex and overwhelming figure that his star shone bright while other Mainland icons lost what luster they still enjoyed. There was an unbridgeable gap between those who had lived through the Mao years and those who had not; the Cult provided a common ground and a hazy realm of consensus in a society in which the generation gap was increasingly making its impact felt. Young converts to the new Mao Cult also found in it a perfect way to express adolescent rebelliousness and romantic idealism. Here was a politically safe idol that could be used to annoy the authorities, upset parents, and irritate teachers. But after a while even this attraction palled; Mao was not really an up-to-date or hip figure, and his dress sense, and that hairstyle!

Not all adolescents were impressed by tales of Red Guard devotion to him. Rebuked for her infatuation with contemporary pop singers by an ex–Red Guard, one teenage girl chided: "You have your idol, I have mine. Why does there only have to be one sun in the sky? Like, you're so lacking in imagination!"[239] For the young, especially middle school students, fashions and styles were now being set by Hong Kong and Taiwan singers, crooners of Canto Pop. By 1993–94, the fans might have accepted Mao but they were still more involved with their own (mostly offshore) teen idols, referred to by the Mainland media with the generic expression the "Four Great Devarāja" (*sida tianwang*).[240] At about this time Mainland propagandists attempted to "obliterate the star chasers" (*mie zhuixingzu*)[241] by limiting performances by non-Mainland singers and promoting local songs. These efforts, however, did little to undermine the popularity of the offshore stars and tended only to encourage Mainland singers to emulate more closely Hong Kong and Taiwan icons.[242]

Mao's stellar fate was not only problematic among the young. In 1993, as part of the centenary activities, a satellite was launched with a payload consisting of a Mao medallion made of 18K gold and embedded with forty-four diamonds. The "8341" satellite, named after Mao's guard corps, went missing only days after the launch. It was originally expected to be recovered a week after liftoff, but the reappearance of "8341" was now calculated to occur sometime in March/April 1996, more than two years late. The delay was expected only to add to the value of the cargo, and plans were soon afoot to auction the gold Mao medallion once it was recovered.[243] (For the significance of the name "8341," see "Mao, a Best-Seller.")

More so than any of the other short-lived fads, cults and fashions China experienced from the late 1970s, the Mao Cult revealed to a fearful extent the paucity of the cultural resources of Mainland China. Reading the selections in this book, one could claim that the Cult was a manifestation of how an age-old living folk tradition had finally co-opted Mao Zedong, the ultimate icon of communism, and converted him into a native god. Similarly, one could cheerfully observe that the "ironic" inversions of Mao in pop art, music, and mass culture indicated a further rejection or devaluing of ideology. It could also be claimed that the revivalists have used Mao creatively, that they have not become slaves to the past but have proved they could "enslave the past and transform it into a vehicle for the expression of their own tastes."[244] To an extent, all of these views are valid. The Mao Cult came at the end of a decade of fads that represented the voracious consumption and rejection of both nativist and foreign cultural "quick fixes" to the dilemmas China faced as a nation that had lost both its value system and its sense of purpose (apart from a crude economic imperative).[245] In this context, the Mao Cult reflects a state of anxiety and a real sense of cultural emptiness, or what Svetlana Boym termed a "totalitarian nostalgia."[246] After the heritage of communism has been worked through, variously commercialized, lampooned, and sanctified, what's next?

This study of the waxing and waning of Chairman Mao's posthumous cult was written at a time when Deng Xiaoping, the man who was neither Mao's chosen successor nor close comrade-in-arms, was approaching his own apotheosis. While the corporeal Deng lingered at death's door, his achievements were being commemorated with gold-plated badges, Deng quiz shows on TV, and the production of a CD-ROM which would provide easy, interactive hi-tech access to his published works.[247] It may be too early to say whether Mao's shoes were figuratively too big for Deng, but we do know that Deng was so impressed with the cloth shoes (*qiancengdi buxie*) especially handmade for Mao's corpse that he ordered a pair of leather-soled shoes from the same cobbler for himself.[248] On 5 April 1995 it was reported that a Beijing publisher of traditional-style books was offering Chinese speculators a limited clothbound edition of Deng works, and it is probably only a matter of time before the entire body of works is engraved on grains of rice or slivers of jade. For those with a taste for the gargantuan, on the other hand, there was already a calligraphic scroll of the diminutive man's works measuring 4 kilometers (2.4 miles) in length.[249]

While irony was a major element of the Mao revival in the realm of nonofficial culture, the greatest irony was perhaps reserved for Deng Xiaoping himself. Intimately involved in attempts to limit the personality cult of

Mao from the 1950s, in particular from the time of the Eighth Party Congress in 1956 and the engineer of the demystification and ultimate subjugation of Mao for the sake of the Reformist agenda, in his last years Deng was increasingly perceived of as being an autocrat whose style of rule was not, in essence, very much different from that of Mao Zedong.[250] Narrow and unfair though such an evaluation may be, Deng lived long enough to witness the decline of his own prestige and the mass-based popular rebirth of Mao Zedong. The man he had so assiduously worked to reinvent was given a new lease on life just as Deng was losing a grip on his own. Deng had been able to shunt aside and move beyond the festering abscess of the Cultural Revolution and deny the legacy of Maoist extremism without ever really finding an effective treatment for the ills of Chinese political life.[251] The opponents of the Reforms, fearful of the ideological laxity that thrived because of them, tried manipulating the Mao legacy in their own favor.[252] Supporters of Reform, however, responded by manufacturing a lame cult of the "Grand Architect of Reform" (zong shejishi)—the preferred sobriquet used for Deng following the Party's Fourteenth Congress in October 1992, when it was announced that forthwith the Party was "to be armed with Deng Xiaoping's theory on building socialism with Chinese characteristics."[253] Not surprisingly, this did not enjoy the mass appeal, or playful commercial possibilities, of the Mao revival.

Even on the cusp of Mao's centenary year it was obvious that it was Deng's Thought, not Mao's, that was being hailed by the official media as the nation's guiding light. In early 1993, a sycophantic tome on Deng was published by the Central Party School,[254] and later in the year, the third volume of *Selected Works of Deng Xiaoping* appeared amid nationwide clamor just as the Mao celebrations were getting under way.[255] Deng Thought was commended as representing and developing the kernel of the best of Mao.[256] On one level the centenary was being used to mark the symbolic end of Mao's official career in China. From the pronouncements made at the time (see "Sparing Mao a Thought" and "The Last Ten-Thousand Words") it was evident that the authorities who were now basking in the radiance of Deng's utilitarianism no longer felt that they were in Mao's shade (see Figure 44).

Perhaps in the future in China the Mao revival itself can be revived. Mao, at least, will continue to be a figure whose varied legacy can be drawn on, reworked, modified, and exploited to suit the exigencies of the day. This is something Mao had perceived, albeit in narrow political terms, in the famous letter he wrote to Jiang Qing in July 1966 (see "Chairman Mao Graffiti"). In it Mao speculated on his posthumous fate:

I predict that if there is an anti-Communist right-wing coup in China they won't have a day of peace; it may even be very short-lived. That's because the Revolutionaries who represent the interests of over 90 percent of the people won't tolerate it. Then the Rightists may well use what I have said to keep in power for a time, but the Leftists will organize themselves around other things I have said and overthrow them.

Rightists and Leftists—not to mention activists on all points along the political spectrum—have been engaged in a tussle over the legacy of Mao ever since. In 1993, Party Central reportedly received some 3,500 letters a month opposing any commemoration of Mao, while others lobbied for a full re-evaluation of Mao and a thoroughgoing denunciation of his years of misrule at a future Party Congress.[257]

But so far had the pendulum swung in Mao's favor that some "revisionists," such as the leading Party historian Hu Sheng, attempted at the time of the centenary a further positive reassessment of Mao's record. In a lengthy defense of Mao published in the *People's Daily*, Hu argued that the devastation wrought by the Chairman's "experimentation" (*tansuo*)—a clinical code word for the murderous policies initiated from the 1950s[258]— seen in context was unavoidable as China struggled to break free of the Soviet economic model.[259] Furthermore, Hu claimed, it was Mao's refusal to be at the beck and call of the Soviets that laid the basis for the success of the Reforms and helped China weather the storm of 1989 and survive the collapse of communism in the Soviet Union and the Eastern Bloc.[260]

Even without Hu's benediction, there were those who construed the 1990s popular "reversal of the verdict" on Mao as a kind of validation of their heinous acts, as well as the cowardice and complicity of which they had been guilty in the past. The Chairman's renewed credibility was a relief from the burden of history. As the Marquis de Custine had remarked about Russia more than 150 years ago: "Sovereigns and subjects become intoxi-cated together at the cup of tyranny. . . . Tyranny is the handiwork of nations, not the masterpiece of a single man."[261] The Party's pronounce-ments in the early 1980s on the Cultural Revolution and the purges that had preceded it had effectively banned public discussion of the past; there had been no opportunity for people to debate seriously the issues of historical responsibility or even to be apprised of the scale and extent of the depreda-tions of Mao's rule. Thoughtful critics had been silenced long ago or were reduced to publishing in the overseas Chinese press. By the 1990s, people— past victims, their persecutors, as well as the innocent who had not experi-enced the grinding horror of the past—could participate in the new Mao Cult because its moral dimensions and ramifications were, for the most part, still unclear. For many middle-aged and young Chinese the Mao era was surrounded by a beguiling aura, appearing in retrospect as a time of greater simplicity, purity, and idealism (see "A Star Reflects on the Sun").

At the other end of the political spectrum commentators such as the dissidents Wei Jingsheng and Liu Xiaobo argued that the Maoist political legacy remained both vital and malignant (see "Who's Responsible?" and "The Specter of Mao Zedong"). But such opinions, though perhaps widely held, have only found a forum in the overseas Chinese press. When surveying China's political and intellectual life over the past two decades, including the baleful outcome of the 1989 Protest Movement from which extremists in both camps profited, as well as the continued repression of dissident opinion in China, we are reminded of Ryszard Kapuscinski's observation on Iran: "A dictatorship . . . leaves behind itself an empty, sour field on which the tree of thought won't grow quickly. It is not always the best people who emerge from hiding, from the corners and cracks of that farmed-out field, but often those who have proven themselves strongest. . . ."[262] It is to these figures in particular that the spirit of Mao has the greatest attraction.

In the vacuum created by officially enforced silence, a multiplicity of interpretations and uses of Mao have arisen, from the bizarre to the traditional. The entrepreneurial passion that possessed the nation led some people to interpret the abiding spirit of Mao Zedong and Mao Thought to be a talent for unprincipled manipulation and ruthless ambition. But the masses of dispossessed peasants and workers were also armed with Mao Thought in their own struggle against the new order. For them Mao represented hope. A popular saying held: "[The military strategist] Zhuge Liang was the embodiment of Chinese wisdom, the Monkey King Sun Wukong, the soul of courage, and Mao Zedong the spirit of rebellion."[263] The itinerant worker (*mangliu*) whose words end this volume expresses just such a view when he predicts that China's future leaders will come not from an urban or military elite, or a new middle class, but from the ranks of the dissatisfied and restive rural populace, as has been the case in the past (see "Musical Chairmen").

Contestation over the memory and legacy of Mao is sure to continue, and now, with the help of local compradors, the representatives of international capital also have been invited to the party.

In late 1993, the chichi Beijing eatery Maxim's organized a Mao birthday buffet for two hundred. The printed invitations bore the slogan "Long live Chairman Mao!" and patrons were requested to wear Mao suits. The restaurant was decked out with pictures of the Chairman and Cultural Revolution wall posters for the occasion. While the food was standard haute cuisine, an excerpt from *The White-Haired Girl*, one of the showcase productions of the Cultural Revolution, was staged as the evening's entertainment.[264]

Maxim's celebration of the event was very much in the spirit of the public, nonofficial use of Mao, of those who, to use the popular necrophagous expression, "eat Mao" (*chi Mao*). The event was also typical of the cynical collaboration between Dengist bureaucracy and Western investors who, when required to, readily slip into socialist drag.

While Mao was being "eaten" everywhere from Maxim's to the faddish Cultural Revolution revival restaurants around Beijing, more serious attempts to ingest his spirit were being made by young cultural conservatives. Among their number were the "new leftists" (*xin zuoyi* or *zuopai*)[265] such as Wu Qin, who was one of the organizers of a major symposium on socialism in the international scene in Beijing in mid 1994.[266] Educated in the United States, Wu was one of a younger group of thinkers armed with the ideological weapons of Western new leftism. It is younger scholars like these perhaps who were best suited to carry out an effective critique of the social, political, and economic chaos of Deng's China. Indeed, such intellectual activists may, in the long run, have something in common with late–Cultural Revolution critics of Maoist socialism such as the Li Yizhe group in Guangzhou.[267] Although the figure of Mao is only one of their rallying points, many aspects of his Cult as revealed in the following pages are recognized as having a value in debates concerning China.[268]

The shade of Mao Zedong continues to cast a long shadow over Chinese life. Although the MaoCraze of the early 1990s has faded, replaced, for example, by such things as a passing fashion for late-Qing heroes like Zeng Guofan,[269] some discussions of Mao and his legacy have continued in the public arena. Wang Shan's *China Through the Third Eye*, a controversial best-seller in China in the summer of 1994, took as its central theme a comparison between the Mao and the Deng eras, often expressing sympathy if not outright support for Maoist policies.[270] One of the constant refrains of the book was that the Chinese have failed to understand and appreciate Mao fully![271] Meanwhile, outside China the publication of Li Zhisui's magisterial memoir in late 1994 elicited a new wave of debate about the Chairman, and his place in the nation's history, among overseas Chinese, especially within the dissident diaspora,[272] and the Chinese version of the book was much sought after on the Mainland. Committed intellectuals continue to debate the heritage of Mao,[273] and many are concerned that the Mao heritage, reformulated by an ideologically bankrupt Party in terms of a crude nationalism, may be a dangerous factor in China's future.[274] To paraphrase William Bouwsma, however, Mao, much like water and electricity, is now a public utility.[275]

Long ago Mao's person achieved the status of national myth, and in his posthumous rebirth his history, as presented in the Chinese media, fits in neatly with what Bruce Chatwin called "the Hero Cycle" (a cycle that Elvis also fulfills). Mao weathered numerous setbacks, trials, and tribulations, including the agonies of the failure of his own policies, and in death he has come out victorious. As Chatwin wrote in *Songlines*:

> Every mythology has its version of the "Hero on his Road to Trials," in which a young man, too, receives a "call." He travels to a distant country where some giant or monster threatens to destroy the population. In a super-human battle, he overcomes the Power of Darkness, proves his manhood, and receives his reward: a wife, treasure, land, fame.
>
> These he enjoys into late middle age when, once again, the clouds darken. Again, restlessness stirs him. Again he leaves: either like Beowulf to die in combat or, as the blind Tiresias prophesies for Odysseus, to set off for some mysterious destination, and vanish. . . .
>
> Each section of the myth—like a link in a behavioural chain—will correspond to one of the classic Ages of Man. Each Age opens with some fresh barrier to be scaled or ordeal to be endured. The status of the Hero will rise in proportion as to how much of this assault course he completes—or is seen to complete.

The Hero Cycle, Chatwin remarks, "is a story of 'fitness' in the Darwinian sense: a blueprint for genetic 'success'."[276] An appreciation of the Hero Cycle may also help us understand the reasons for the abiding charisma of Mao Zedong and the relevance of his persona and mythological status in China in the future.

Chinese cultural history, like that of many nations, is rich in examples of objects, symbols, and individuals who have been "lost and refound, overvalued, devalued, then revalued."[277] The battle for China's past, over Mao's reputation and the history of the Communist Party, will continue in both the public forum and among archivists and scholars in and outside China. One day Chinese readers will gain access to that unfolding past.[278] In the meantime, Chairman Mao has entered the stream of Chinese history as man, icon, and myth, and there is little doubt that the Cult of the early 1990s is only the first of the revivals he will experience in what promises to be a long and successful posthumous career[279] (see Figures 45a, 45b).

May–June 1995
Canberra–Sydney–Boston

Notes

1. See, for example, Mao's comments at the 1959 Plenum in Stuart R. Schram, ed., *Mao Tse-tung Unrehearsed*, p. 139.

2. This story was related to me by Sang Ye, who read a report of it in the Chinese press. Unable to locate the original source, I record it here for the reader's information. In a similar vein, old workers retrenched in Shanghai in 1987 reportedly went to a restaurant, got drunk, and returned home, each cradling a portrait of Mao in their arms.

See *Shanghai wenhua yishu bao*, 24 March 1989, quoted in Zheng Youxian, "Shixi 'Mao Zedongre' xingcheng he fazhande yuanyin," p. 20.

3. See Mao Zedong, "Xue—Qinyuanchun," in *Mao zhuxi shici (zhushi)*, p. 90. For this English translation, see "Snow—to the tune of *Qin yuan chun*," February 1936 in Mao Tse-tung, *Poems*, pp. 23–24. Although the poem was dated 1936, Jerome Ch'en in *Mao and the Chinese Revolution*, pp. 340–41, argues that the poem was most likely written in 1944–45.

4. See Tang Wan'er, "Chongqing Dagongbao pi Mao yiwen—Mao Zedong yongxueci fengbo," pp. 53–54.

5. See Ninian Smart, *Mao*, pp. 92–94; and Reinhard Bendix, "Reflections on Charismatic Leadership," *Asian Survey* 7, no. 7 (1967), pp. 349–51, quoted in Stuart R. Schram, "Party Leader or True Ruler? Foundations and Significance of Mao Zedong's Personal Power," in S. R. Schram, ed., *Foundations and Limits of State Power in China*, pp. 243–44.

6. *Xunzhao Mao Zedong*. This also happened to be the title of one of the earliest books on the then-nascent Mao revival. See Wu Fangze et al., *Xunzhao Mao Zedong*.

7. See Zhang Xixian, "Lüelun Zhongguo jin xiandaishishangde wuci xunzhao Mao Zedong," pp. 89–95. Zhang lists five periods during which the Chinese have "searched for Mao Zedong." They are: (1) on the eve of the Zunyi Congress in 1935; (2) at the outbreak of the war with Japan; (3) on the founding of the People's Republic; (4) during the Cultural Revolution; and (5) following 4 June 1989.

8. See "The Cult of Mao Tse-tung" in Maurice Meisner, *Marxism, Maoism and Utopianism*, pp. 155–83. For a bibliography of works related to the first Mao Cult, see pp. 248–49.

9. "Jiehunde geming liwu" in Cheng Shi, Shan Chuan, et al., eds., *Wenge xiaoliao ji*, p. 13.

10. For a short history of *Quotations from Chairman Mao*, see Zhongguo Mao Zedong sixiang lilun yu shijian yanjiuhui lishihui, ed., *Mao Zedong sixiang cidian*, pp. 589–90; and Ma Linchuan, *"Mao zhuxi yulu* tanyuan," pp. 50–52.

11. "Zhongyang xuanchuanbu wenjian, Zhongxuanfa [1979] 5 hao: Guanyu tingzhi faxing *Mao zhuxi yulu* de tongzhi, 1979 nian 2 yue 12 ri," reprinted in *Tushu faxing gongzuo wenjian huibian (1979)*, pp. 9–10.

12. Guojia chuban shiye guanliju, "Zhuanfa Zhongxuanbu guanyu tingzhi faxing *Mao zhuxi yulu* de tongzhi, (79) chubanzi di 83 hao, 1979 nian 2 yue 20 ri," *Tushu faxing gongzuo wenjian huibian (1979)*, p. 8. In the early 1990s, one artist formulated an innovative way of recycling a portion of the Mao heritage. In his 1993–94 work "Post-Testament" (*Houyue*) the Beijing/New York artist Xu Bing used high-quality, acid-free "political document paper" (*zhengwen zhi*) manufactured prior to the Cultural Revolution for the express purpose of printing foreign-language editions of Mao's *Selected Works* and poetry. Xu found a cache of this paper in the warehouse of the Beijing Foreign Languages Press and was able to acquire an amount of it for his own work: hand-bound volumes containing a nonsense text.

13. See, respectively, Zhonghua renmin gongheguo caizhengbu, guojia chuban shiye guanliju, "Guanyu *Mao zhuxi yulu* deng tingshou sunshi fudande tongzhi, (79) chuhuizi di 14 hao/(79) caishizi di 87 hao, 1979 nian 4 yue 9 ri," *Tushu faxing gongzuo wenjian huibian (1979)*, pp. 11–12; and Xinhua shudian zongdian, "Guanyu guanche tingzhi faxing *Mao zhuxi yulu* tongzhide jidian yijian, (79) zongzi di 93 hao, 1979 nian 6 yue 16 ri," *Tushu faxing gongzuo wenjian huibian (1979)*, pp. 13–14.

14. See Su Ya and Jia Lusheng, *Buluode taiyang*, p. 29.

15. See Zhao Darong, "Haishi yinggai yinfa Mao zhuxi huaxiang, 1981 nian 8 yue 13 ri," *Tushu faxing gongzuo wenjian huibian (1981)*, pp. 8–9; and Xinhua shudian

zongdian, "Mao zhuxi biaozhun xiang, Xinhua shudian menshibu bixu jingchang youshou, (81) zongzi di 201 hao, 1981 nian 10 yue 7 ri," *Tushu faxing gongzuo wenjian huibian (1981)*, p. 7.

16. See Guojia chuban shiye guanliju and Zhongyang xuanchuanbu, "Guanyu zai huichang he gonggong changsuo gua lingxiu xiang wentide tongzhi, Zhongxuanfa [1981] 13 hao, 1981 nian 7 yue 29 ri," *Tushu faxing gongzuo wenjian huibian (1981)*, pp. 10–11.

17. Zhongyang xuanchuanbu bangongting, ed., *Dangde xuanchuan gongzuo wenjian xuanbian (1983–1987)*, p. 1126.

18. See Zhongxuanbu, ed., "Zhongyang xuanchuanbu guanyu jieri qijian Tiananmen guangchang xuangua weirenxiangde qingkuang tongzhi, Zhongxuan fawen [1989] 5 hao," p. 1867.

19. Hou Dangsheng, *Mao Zedong xiangzhang fengyunlu*, pp. 123–24.

20. See *Zhongguo funü bao*, 17 December 1991, quoted in Zhou Jihou, *Mao Zedong xiangzhang zhi mi—shijie dijiu da qiguan*, p. 232. To "invite" a portrait or statue into one's dwelling was an expression traditionally used in Daoist and Buddhist practice.

21. From figures given in Su Ya and Jia Lusheng, *Buluode taiyang*, p. 29.

22. This and the following information come from Guojia chuban shiye guanliju dangzu, "Guanyu jiejue Ma Lie zhuzuo, Mao zhuxi zhuzuo jiya wentide qingshi baogao, 1979 nian 12 yue 7 ri," *Tushu faxing gongzuo wenjian huibian (1979)*, pp. 6–9.

23. Xinhua shudian zongdian, "Qing dui chuli jiyade Ma Lie zhuzuo, Mao zhuxi zhuzuo qingquang jinxing yici jiancha, (80) zongzi di 154 hao, 1980 nian 7 yue 29 ri," *Tushu faxing gongzuo wenjian huibian (1980)*, p. 10.

24. Xinhua shudian zongdian, "Qing renzhen zhua yixia Mao zhuxi zhuzuode gongying gongzuo, (82) zongyezi di 23 hao, 1982 nian 3 yue 30 ri," *Tushu faxing gongzuo wenjian huibian (1982)*, p. 73; and Xinhua shudian zongdian, "Guanyu renzhen zuohao Mao zhuxi zhuzuo faxing gongzuode tongzhi, (82) zongzi di 66 hao, 1982 nian 3 yue 30 ri," *Tushu faxing gongzuo wenjian huibian (1982)*, pp. 74–75.

25. Guojia chuban shiye guanliju, "Guanyu *Mao Zedong xuanji* diwujuan tingshou wentide tongzhi, Guojia chubanju wenjian, (82) chubanzi di 241 hao, 1982 nian 4 yue 10 ri," *Tushu faxing gongzuo wenjian huibian (1982)*, p. 76.

26. See the editorial "Jianchi Mao Zedong sixiang, fazhan Mao Zedong sixiang" and Cheng Ying, "Dalu wenhua xuanchuande sanzhuang fenzheng," p. 38.

27. Liu Jintian and Wu Xiaomei, *Mao Zedong xuanji chubande qianqian houhou*, p. 171.

28. Xinhua News Agency, 6 September, 1993, "Jing Zhonggong zhongyang pizhun *Mao Zedong wenji* niannei chuban."

29. These included volumes of photographs of Mao at various stages in his career. One of the most extraordinary of these books, however, is a collection of photographs of Mao memorabilia from Zhongnanhai. See Zhongnanhai huace bianji weiyuanhui, ed., *Pingfan yu weida—Mao Zedong Zhongnanhai yiwu yishi*. The contents of this book are discussed below.

30. Adam Hochschild in *The Unquiet Ghost*, p. 66, describes in similar terms the impact of Stalin's personality on the citizens of the Soviet empire.

31. Jan Wong, "Around Mao's Centennial," quoting from the magazine *Daxuesheng*.

32. In this context, see Hochschild, *The Unquiet Ghost*, pp. 58–59.

33. The surveys were conducted by the Party Department of Propaganda, the Central Policy Research Office, the Academy of Social Sciences, and the State Education Commission. See Luo Bing, "Jinian Mao mingshou zao feiyi," pp. 8–10.

34. Chan Wai-fong, "Mao Outstrips Deng in Popularity Poll." In a 1988 survey,

Zhou had received 49.7 percent of the vote to Mao's 10 percent. In the 1994 survey, Mao got 40.1 percent to Zhou's 26.6 percent. Deng scored merely 9.6 percent, up from the 9.2 percent he got in 1988.

35. In May 1995 it was reported that there was a village of exiles living in the mountain wilds of Shaanxi who had no contact with the outside world. When one of them was asked what he wanted to know about current events, he said: "Who's Chairman Mao these days?" See "Heihu buluo."

36. In regard to the original Cult, see, for example, Robert W. Rinden, "The Cult of Mao Tse-tung," and George Urban, ed., *The Miracles of Chairman Mao*. For a comparison of the two Cults, see Zhou Qun and Yao Xinrong, "Xinjiu Mao Zedong chongbai," pp. 36–43. For a useful comparison of the Stalin and Hitler cults, see Moshe Lewin, *Russia/USSR/Russia*, pp. 209–29 and 241–44.

37. See Deng Xiaoping, "Dui qicao 'Guanyu jianguo yilai dangde ruogan lishi wentide jueyi' de yijian," *Deng Xiaoping wenxuan (1975–1982)*, pp. 255–74.

38. As the official Xinhua News Agency eulogy for Chen said: "Comrade Chen Yun vigorously supported Comrade Deng Xiaoping's idea of scientifically establishing Comrade Mao Zedong's historical position and of upholding and developing Mao Zedong Thought. He repeatedly stressed: Comrade Mao Zedong's merits are primary and his errors are secondary. Comrade Mao Zedong made a unique contribution; that is, he trained a generation of cadres, including ourselves." See Xinhua News Agency, "Eulogy on the Glorious Life of Chen Yun."

39. See, for example, speeches made by Chen Yun and Peng Zhen in Zhonggong zhongyang wenxian yanjiushi zonghezu, ed., *Lao yidai gemingjia lun dangshi yu dangshi yanjiu*, pp. 191–94 and 229–30.

40. See Hu Qiaomu, *Hu Qiaomu wenji*, vol. 2, pp. 130–87; and Deng Liqun, "Xuexi 'Guanyu jianguo yilai dangde ruogan lishi wentide jueyi' de wenti he huida," pp. 162–74.

41. The Lenin/Stalin dichotomy remained an important element of both Soviet and Western "revisionist" views of Soviet history until quite recently. With the opening of the Soviet archives and work of such writers as Richard Pipes and Dmitri Volkogonov, however, Lenin can be more clearly seen, as the historian Steven Miner puts it, as "the progenitor of modern revolutionary violence and radical, bloody social change . . . [who] gave the world a blueprint for the ideology-based terror state." See Steven Merritt Miner, "Revelations, Secrets, Gossip and Lies," p. 20.

42. Edgar Snow, *The Other Side of the River*, p. 151.

43. See, for example, Li Honglin, *Lilun fengyun*, pp. 39–57; Tao Kai et al., *Zouchu xiandai mixin—guanyu zhenli biaozhun wentide dabianlun*, pp. 3–98; Wu Jiangguo et al., eds., *Dangdai Zhongguo yishi xingtai fengyunlu*, pp. 477–97; and Michael Schoenhals, "The 1978 Truth Criterion Controversy," pp. 243–68.

44. For a study of this process, see Helmut Martin, *Cult & Canon: The Origins and Development of State Maoism*, pp. 50–139; and Laszlo Ladany, *The Communist Party of China and Marxism, 1921–1985*, pp. 386–440.

45. There is a large body of material on this subject. Some relevant quotations from Deng and Party Central are included in the present volume. See also Hu Qiaomu, *Hu Qiaomu wenji*, vol. 2, pp. 130–186; Zhongyang xuanchuanbu bangongting, ed., *Dangde xuanchuan gongzuo huiyi gaikuang he wenxian (1951–1992)*, pp. 328–36, 357–64, and 367–70; and Zhonggong zhongyang wenxian yanjiushi, *Guanyu jianguo yilai dangde ruogan lishi wentide jueyi, zhushiben (xiuding)*, pp. 500–578; also Susanne Weigelin-Schwiedrzik, "Party Historiography," in Jonathan Unger, ed., *Using the Past to Serve the Present*, pp. 151–73.

46. See James D. Seymour, ed., *The Fifth Modernization*, pp. 196–98 and 204–5.

47. See Martin, *Cult & Canon*, pp. 113–15 and 127–29.

48. Dong Tai, "Dui 'wailun' de jingyan jiaoxun."

49. See Joan Lebold Cohen, *The New Chinese Painting, 1949–1986*, pp. 60 and 63.

50. See Deng Xiaoping, "Guanyu fandui cuowu sixiang qingxiang wenti," *Deng Xiaoping wenxuan (1975–1982)*, p. 337. Also, Jonathan D. Spence, "Film and Politics: Bai Hua's *Bitter Love*," in Spence, *Chinese Roundabout*, pp. 276–92. In an essay on the Mao centenary, Bai Hua, writing for a Hong Kong magazine, said that the scene in *Unrequited Love* most widely condemned in 1981 had been one showing the protagonist as a youth asking a Buddhist abbot why the face of the Buddha in his temple was so dark. He is told that worshippers had burned so much incense to the Buddha that his features had turned black. See Bai Hua, "Bainian gudu—Mao Zedong bainian mingchen ji," pp. 50–52.

51. See, for example, "Mao Zedong Still Fresh in Memory," pp. 15–18; and Wang Zhen, "Mao Zedong sixiang shi dangde baoguide jingshen caifu—Mao Zedong tongzhi shishi shi zhounian ganyan," in Zhonggong zhongyang wenxian yanjiushi zonghezu, ed., *Lao yidai gemingjia lun dangshi yu dangshi yanjiu*, pp. 265–71.

52. *Mao Zedong zhuzuo xuandu*, edited by the Zhonggong zhongyang wenxian bianji weiyuanhui and published by Renmin chubanshe, the book was released on 9 September 1986.

53. *Hongdengji, Zhiqu Weihushan*, and *Hongse niangzi jun*, respectively.

54. The cassette was called *Huanying qisheng: yingshi yinxiang dalianzou*. See Bai Jieming, "Yangbanxide zai jueqi," pp. 144–45. See also note 3 in "Let the Red Sun Shine In" in this volume.

55. The Chinese term *Maoshi fuzhuang* is a translation of the English expression "Mao suit." The common term for such jackets is *Zhongshan zhuang*, or "[Sun] Yat-sen suit." They are an imitation of old Japanese college uniforms, which, in turn, were inspired by a German original.

56. For details, see Barmé, "History for the Masses" in Unger, ed., *Using the Past to Serve the Present*, pp. 266–76. For the Party's Department of Propaganda ban on Cultural Revolution books see Zhongyang xuanchuanbu bangongting, ed., *Dangde xuanchuan gongzuo wenjian xuanbian (1988–1992)*, pp. 1796–97.

57. Barmé, "History for the Masses," pp. 271–73.

58. Ibid., pp. 275–76. Of this literature, Dai Qing's work on Wang Shiwei and Chu Anping, and her collaboration with Wang Donglin, who wrote about Mao Zedong's relationship with the "last Confucian," Liang Shuming, is particularly noteworthy. See Dai Qing, *Xiandai Zhongguo zhishifenzi qun* and Barmé, "Using the Past to Save the Present," pp. 141–81, esp. pp. 162–63 and p. 168, n. 149.

59. See Fang Lixiong et al., *Zhongguoren zenmele?!*, pp. 128–31.

60. See Lü Peng and Yi Dan, *Zhongguo xiandai yishu shi*, pp. 166–68 and 295–98, respectively.

61. For details, see Barmé, "History for the Masses," pp. 267–69.

62. Such footage appears in most of the episodes of the series.

63. See Barmé and Linda Jaivin, eds., *New Ghosts, Old Dreams*, pp. 160–61.

64. For a shorter verion of this *shunkouliu'r* see Elizabeth J. Perry, "Casting a Chinese 'Democracy' Movement: The Roles of Students, Workers, and Entrepreneurs," in Jeffrey N. Wasserstrom and Elizabeth J. Perry, eds., *Popular Protest and Political Culture in Modern China*, pp. 33–34, 80, and n. 28; and Joseph W. Esherick, "Xi'an Spring," in Jonathan Unger, ed., *The Pro-Democracy Protests in China*, p. 79.

65. The 13 May declaration reads in part: "The nation is our nation, the people are our people, the government our government. If we do not cry out, who will? If we do not act, who will?" See Wu Mouren et al., eds., *Bajiu Zhongguo minyun jishi*, p. 190;

also Han Minzhu, ed., *Cries for Democracy*, p. 200. In 1919 Mao had said in an essay published in issue 4 of *Xiangjiang pinglun*: "The world is our world, the nation is our nation, the society is our society. If we do not speak out, who will? If we do not act, who will?" See "Zhonghua minzhongde dalianhede xingshi" in Stuart R. Schram, ed., *Mao's Road to Power*, for a translation of this article. This lines quoted above were also very popular with Red Guards during the Cultural Revolution. Mao discouraged their use because he claimed he could not recall having written them. See "1967 nian 2 yue 21 ri Zhang Chunqiao zai Shanghai qunzhong dahuishangde jianghua" in *Ziliao xuanbian*, a Red Guard publication without a date or place of publication.

66. See Dierdre L. Nickerson, "Ge Xiaoguang," p. 74; Deng Wei, "Letters: Mao Thought"; and "Tiananmenshangde Mao Zedong." Ge's painting and touching up of the Mao portrait features in the opening sequence of the eight-part documentary "Tiananmen," directed by Shi Jian and Chen Jue; see "Modern Mao Artifacts and Multimedia Mao" below. For details on the fate of the perpetrators of this incident, see Asia Watch, ed., *Detained in China and Tibet*, pp. 101–2. In response to the Italian journalist Oriana Fallaci's question about the Mao portrait on Tiananmen in August 1980, Deng had the following to say: "Mao Thought led the revolution to victory in the past. Both now and in the future it should be seen as a precious resource for both the Party and the Chinese nation. Therefore, Chairman Mao's portrait will hang forever on Tiananmen and act as the symbol of our country. We must honour Chairman Mao as the founder of our Party and our state. Furthermore, we must persevere with Mao Thought." See Deng Xiaoping,"Da Yidali jizhe Aolin'aina Falaqi wen, 1980 nian 8 yue," *Deng Xiaoping wenxuan (1975–1982)*, p. 303.

67. See, for example, Luo Fu, "Mao Zedong xianshengde gushi," pp. 18–19. From late 1995, it was widely believed in Beijing that Mao had "manifested his supernatural power" once more by killing Dr. Li Zhisui, who died suddenly in February 1995, in revenge for publishing his memoirs about the Chairman.

68. Chai's numerous recorded speeches in the Square are evidence of this, as is the chilling interview she gave to the American reporter Philip Cunningham on 28 May 1989. For highlights of this interview, see the documentary film "The Gate of Heavenly Peace." For evidence of Chai's Mao-like political style, see also *Huigu yu fansi*, 230.

69. Victor Zaslavsky, *The Neo-Stalinist State*, p. 12.

70. Ibid., pp. 15–16.

71. See Alexander Zinoviev, *Stalin et Stalinisme*. Zinoviev's work is referred to in Simon Leys, "Is There Life After Mao?" in *The Burning Forest*, pp. 166–67.

72. See Edward Friedman, "Democracy and 'Mao Fever,' " pp. 90–91.

73. Quoted in Jerome Ch'en, ed., *Mao*, p. 131.

74. Ironically, one of the most evocative fictional depictions of Mao as mastermind can be found in the Albanian novelist Ismail Kadare's *The Concert: A Novel*, written in Albanian and translated from the French of Jusuf Vrioni by Barbara Bray, pp. 25–39, 79–90, 181, 311–12, 323.

75. Schram, "Party Leader or True Ruler?," p. 235 and n. 84.

76. See Shmuel Eisenstadt, "Innerweltliche Transzendenz und die Strukturierung der Welt. Max Webers Studie über China und die Gestalt der chinesischen Zivilisation," quoted in Schram, "Party Leader or True Ruler?," p. 228. In this context, see also Thomas A. Metzger, *Escape from Predicament*, pp. 121 and 233, also quoted in Schram, pp. 226 and 228.

77. As the government's campaign against corruption widened in 1995, many people seemed unimpressed by all the storm and fury. One typical comment was: "All the Beijing officials are corrupt. Chairman Mao wasn't a good man, but at least he knew how to deal with corruption." Graham Hutchings, "China's Anger with Leaders Bursts Out."

78. See Mayfair Mei-hui Yang, *Gifts, Favors, and Banquets*, pp. 257–58.

79. For the memoirs of the two most prominent of Mao's "personal secretaries," or *shenghuo mishu* as they were commonly referred to, see Zhang Yufeng, *Mao Zedong yishi*, and Meng Jinyun's recollections as published in Guo Jinrong, *Mao Zedongde huanghun suiyue*.

80. Zhisui Li, *The Private Life of Chairman Mao*, pp. 358–59.

81. Quoted in Simon Leys, "Aspects of Mao Tse-tung (1893–1976)," *Broken Images*, p. 64.

82. See also "Mao Zedong zui chongbaide xiake shi shei?" pp. 54–57, in which the three martial heroes the young Mao admired most are listed. They were Yuan Yuan (1635–1704), Li Gong (1659–1733), and Tan Sitong (1865–1898).

83. Li Zhisui also notes that, in his last years, Mao particularly enjoyed watching kung fu movies from Hong Kong. Li, *The Private Life of Chairman Mao*, p. 574.

84. See the chapter "The Stalin in Us" in Hochschild, *The Unquiet Ghost*, pp. 115–27.

85. See "Chairman Mao as Pop Art" in Orville Schell, *Mandate of Heaven*, pp. 281–82 and 284. In 1987, the life of a Fujian woman was reportedly saved by a Mao portrait. Suffering from a "fox-cat curse," the woman was fearful that her vital essence would be sucked out by a rampant "fox-cat spirit" (*hulimao*). On the advice of friends she hung a Mao portrait on her front door. Mao's image was presumably so powerful that the spirit did not dare enter the house, and the woman was saved from certain death. See Liu Xuesong, "Mao Zedong shaoxiang ke 'baoan pixie' ma?" pp. 96–97.

86. Meisner, "The Cult of Mao Tse-tung," p. 179.

87. See Reuter News Service, "Chinese Officials Ponder Temple to Mao Tsetung," and Zeng Ni, "Zhongguo Hunan jiancheng shouzuo Mao Zedong shenmiao, gedi xiangke dapi yongshi rida wuwan ren."

88. The "Four Greats," or *sige weida*. Mao rejected these accolades and on 18 December 1970, remarked to Edgar Snow that the personality cult had gone too far.

89. Karl Dietrich Bracher, *The German Dictatorship*, p. 424.

90. For a comparison of the first Mao Cult to the those of Mussolini, Hitler, and Stalin, see Leonard Schapiro and John Wilson Lewis, "The Roles of the Monolithic Party Under the Totalitarian Leader," in John Wilson Lewis, ed., *Party Leadership and Revolutionary Power in China*, pp. 114–15, quoted in Meisner, "The Cult of Mao Tse-tung," pp. 172–73.

91. Zhang Hongtu's "Bilingual Chart of Acupuncture Points and Meridians" in his *Chairmen Mao Series* is a representation of Mao's body as a chart/map of the political history of post-1949 China. See Barmé and Jaivin, eds., *New Ghosts, Old Dreams*, p. 384.

92. See Yang, *Gifts, Favors, and Banquets*, pp. 249–50 and 260–61.

93. The term comes from Walter Benjamin's observation of fascism. See Simonetta Falasca-Zamponi, "The Aestheticization of Politics: A Study of Power in Mussolini's Fascist Italy," Ph.D. diss., University of California at Berkeley, referred to in Yang, *Gifts, Favors, and Banquets*, p. 250.

94. From Sontag's 1974 essay on Leni Riefenstahl, quoted in J. Hoberman, "The Fascist Guns in the West," p. 68.

95. Yang, *Gifts, Favors, and Banquets*, pp. 264–65. In this context, see also Kenneth Dean and Brian Massumi, *First and Last Emperors*, in particular the conclusion.

96. See, for example, "Tiyu zhi yanjiu," partially translated in Stuart R. Schram, *The Political Thought of Mao Tse-tung*, pp. 152–60. This and other works related to early twentieth-century Chinese attitudes to physical education can be found in Andrew Morris, "Mastery Without Enmity."

97. "Chairman Mao Swims in the Yangtse," p. 4. See also page 2 of this article for Mao's poem "Swimming—to the Tune of 'Die lian hua.' "

98. As a propaganda report of the time put it: "The Yangtse was in spate; its current was swift and the rolling waves pounded the shores. Swimming in the vast river, Chairman Mao sometimes made his way through the turbulent waters by side-stroking and sometimes he floated on his back, looking at the blue sky. The news of Chairman Mao's swim in the Yangtse stirred all hearts and brought immense inspiration and strength to everybody." See "Chairman Mao Swims in the Yangtse," pp. 3–4.

99. For more on Mao's 16 July swim, see Li, *The Private Life of Chairman Mao*, p. 463; and Lucian W. Pye, *Mao Tse-tung: The Man in the Leader*, pp. 72–73. The tenth episode (*Dao zhongliu jishui*) of the twelve-part China Central Television documentary "Mao Zedong" (broadcast in December 1993) is devoted to Mao's aquatic feats and features footage of his particular chaise-longue swimming style. In the Mainland press, Mao's swimming is still described in the most reverent terms. See, for example, a report on the young girls who were called to accompany Mao on his Wuhan swims, Xiao Fan, "Tamen wei Mao zhuxi hengdu Changjiang baobiao."

100. For a typical example of the ritual that was repeated in rivers and lakes throughout China, see "Proletarian revolutionaries in Peking cross Kunming Lake [of the Summer Palace] in celebration of the anniversary of our great leader Chairman Mao's swim in the Yangtse a year ago," the front cover illustration of *China Pictorial* 9 (1967). To this day, the swimming costume Mao wore on that occasion—a "Mao suit" worthy of the name—has been preserved and is on display in Zhongnanhai. See Zhongnanhai huace bianji weiyuanhui, ed., *Pingfan yu weida*, p. 133.

101. A scene showing the octogenarian Deng swimming is used in the title sequence of the 1990 four-part propaganda television documentary "On the Road" (*Shijixing*). See Barmé, " 'Road' versus 'River,' " p. 32. As the crooner Liu Huan sings the line "You are a banner, having fallen and risen, you emerged victorious/ You gave us the Truth," Deng is shown bobbing up and down in the water, doing the breaststroke. In 1993 Premier Li Peng made a similar, although far less photogenic, gesture when he appeared in his swimsuit supposedly enjoying sun and surf as a sign of his political resilience. The former Party secretary Zhao Ziyang, purged in 1989, preferred to use the golf course—the internationally recognized leisure-time arena for power politicians and CEOs—to display his vigor.

102. See Frederic Wakeman, Jr., "Mao's Remains," p. 263. See also Rudolf G. Wagner, "Reading the Chairman Mao Memorial Hall in Peking: The Tribulations of the Implied Pilgrim," pp. 378–423.

103. Wakeman, "Mao's Remains," p. 281; and A.P. Cheater, "Death Ritual as Political Trickster in the People's Republic of China," pp. 85–94.

104. See David E. Apter and Tony Saich, *Revolutionary Discourse in Mao's Republic*, p. 313.

105. Cai Yongmei, "Maorede shangpinhua," pp. 63–64.

106. Ann Anagnost, "The Nationscape," p. 601 and n. 31.

107. See Mark Elvin, "Tales of *Shen* and *Xin*," p. 259. By having his ashes scattered after his death, Zhou Enlai achieved a "geospiritual return" with greater effect. Zhou was the first leader whose ashes were scattered after being cremated at the Babaoshan Revolutionary Crematorium and Columbarium. His cremation is also noted for being the longest (three hours) and producing the finest-quality ash. For these details, see Li Weihai, *Weiren shenhoushi—Babaoshan geming gongmu jishi*, pp. 266–67.

108. See Simon Sebag Montefiore, "History in a Pickle," p. 5. For details of the preservation of Mao's remains, see also Li, *The Private Life of Chairman Mao*, pp. 16–25; and Lincoln Kaye, "Mummy Dearest," p. 17. From the 1980s, reports on the state of Mao's preserved remains became something of an annual event. Over the years

it has variously been claimed that Mao's corpse was shinking, bloating, or changing color. In 1995 the authorities denied reports that the Mao mummy was turning green. See Hamish McIlwraith, "Raise the Red Emperor."

109. For details, see "Modern Mao Artifacts and Multi-media Mao" below.

110. See "Suzao weiren," p. 4. This was not the first waxwork of Mao made for display in Tiananmen. See Li, *The Private Life of Chairman Mao*, pp. 23–24.

111. Quoted in Wakeman, "Mao's Remains," p. 284.

112. In his *Dialectic of the Chinese Revolution: From Utopianism to Hedonism*, Ci Jiwei offers an analysis of this journey from revolution to consumption and notes the bizarre corollary between the two.

113. See *Renmin ribao*, 30 September 1979, quoted in "Mao's Thoughts, Not Mao's," p. 2.

114. "Mao Zedong sixiang yongfang guangmang."

115. Wakeman, "Mao's Remains," p. 287.

116. Luo Bing, "Mao Zedong zhuzuo duo daibi," pp. 11–12. In this context, see also Michael Schoenhals, "Ghost-Writers: Expressing 'The Will of the Authorities'," in *Doing Things with Words in Chinese Politics*, pp. 55–77 and 114–15.

117. Luo Bing, "Mao Zedong zhuzuo duo daibi."

118. Also called the "Three Most Read Articles," or the "Three Old Favorites." For an example of the canonization of these three essays, see "Long Live the 'Three Most Read Articles'!"

119. Luo Bing, "Mao Zedong zhuzuo duo daibi." In 1992 it was widely rumored in Beijing that Hu was attempting to verify his authorship of many of Mao's works. Officially published materials, however, make no mention of this, and Hu's memoirs relating to Mao are limited to his pre-1949 work. See Hu Qiaomu, *Hu Qiaomu huiyi Mao Zedong*. The most detailed official account of the evolution of *Selected Works* is Liu Jintian and Wu Xiaomei, *Mao Zedong xuanji chubande qianqian houhou*.

120. Luo Bing, "Mao Zedong zhuzuo duo daibi," pp. 11–12; and Schoenhals, "Ghost-Writers," pp. 55–77 and 114–15.

121. See "The Copyright Law of the People's Republic of China" (7 September 1990). See Zhang Peilin, ed., *Banquanxue anli*, p. 20.

122. "Jiannan chuan shiji, shui ling bainian fengsao? *Ershi shiji Zhongguo wenxue dashi wenku* wei 20 shiji Zhongguo wenxue dashi chongding zuoci."

123. Ibid.

124. Zhou Jihou, *Mao Zedong xiangzhang zhi mi—shijie dijiu da qiguan*, p. 233.

125. "Li Yinqiao yu Quan Yanchi fenzhengde yuanqi"; and Zhang Shulin, "Mao Zedong re, rechu yichang lianhuan guansi," pp. 26–30. Li produced his own sycophantic memoir in 1991. See Li Yinqiao, *Zai Mao Zedong shenbian shiwu nian*.

126. Li Rui's account of the 1959 Lushan meeting (*Lushan huiyi shilu*) and another book on Mao's youth and old age (*Mao Zedongde zaonian yu wannian*) are particularly noteworthy. See also, Wang Dongxing, *Wang Dongxing riji*; and Bo Yibo, *Ruogan zhongda juece ji shijiande huigu*.

127. These include *Mao Zedong sixiang yanjiu* (began publication in December 1983); *Mao Zedong sixiang yanjiu tongxun* (March 1986); *Mao Zedong junshi sixiang yanjiu* (May 1986); and *Mao Zedong zhexue sixiang yanjiu* (1982). A number of Mao Thought research associations established from the early 1980s also produced their own restricted-circulation publications.

128. A personal favorite is a fascinating essay that discusses the classical Chinese texts (histories, poetry, and so on) Mao ordered in annotated large-print, limited editions for his personal reading in the early 1970s. See Liu Xiuming, "Cong yinzhi 'daziben' guji kan Mao Zedong wanniande sixiang he xintai," pp. 22–33. Liu was one of the

scholars appointed to annotate these reprints and in this essay speculates on Mao's state of mind at the time. Other intriguing books and essays in this vein comment at length on Mao's penchant for classical histories and literature, and a few tentatively reflect on the issue of how his political style was affected by traditional statecraft. See, for example, Gong Yuzhi, Pang Xianzhi and Shi Zhongquan, eds., *Mao Zedongde dushu shenghuo*; Li Rui, *Mao Zedong zaonian dushu shenghuo*; and Sun Baoyi, *Mao Zedongde dushu shengya*.

129. For details, see Zhu Yuan, "Mao Zedong zhenxiang qiaoqiao baoguang—dalu Maorezhongde zhongyao zixun xuan," pp. 52–55; and Guan Weixun, *Wo suo renshide Ye Qun*, which portrays Lin as a victim of Mao's machinations. For an example of a Western academic work that utilized recent Mainland material, see Frederick C. Teiwes and Warren Sun, *The Tragedy of Lin Biao*.

130. In this context, see Thomas Scharping's useful observations on the new Mao books in the review essay "The Man, the Myth, the Message—New Trends in Mao-Literature from China," p. 169.

131. See Dmitri Volkogonov, *Lenin: A New Biography*. Volkogonov was a onetime Stalinist and colonel general and deputy head of the Political Administration of the Armed Forces who, availing himself of previously restricted archival material, produced a major and damning study of Lenin. See David Remnick, *Lenin's Tomb*, pp. 400–411; and Robert Conquest, "The Somber Monster," pp. 8–12.

132. Xinhua News Agency, "False Biographies Are Now Forbidden."

133. See A Yin and Ma Jian, *Mao Zedong zhi zi: Mao Anlong*. For the Hong Kong edition, see *Wo shi Mao Zedongde erzi*.

134. Scharping, "The Man, the Myth, the Message," pp. 178–79.

135. Li Yanchun, "Mao's Family Members Brought Out of the Shadow," pp. 20–22. See also Scharping, "The Man, the Myth, the Message," pp. 169–70.

136. Wang Xingjuan, *He Zizhende lu*.

137. See, in particular, the eleventh episode (*Lingxiu jiafeng*) of the CCTV documentary "Mao Zedong." For other pictures of this family, see Zhongguo zhaopian dang'anguan and Beijing Hangkong hangtian daxue, eds., *Huainian*, pp. 125, 128, 133, 135, 136, 138, 139, and 142.

138. Cheng Tong, "Zhongguo chulege Mao Zedong"; and Wei Wei, "Women, qidaizhe . . . ," p. 3. A picture of the obese Mao Xinyu at a book signing for the series can be found in *Beijing qingnian bao*, 6 September 1994.

139. Cai Yongmei, "Maorede shangpinhua," p. 64.

140. See, for example, the lengthy report by one of the editors of *China Has Brought Forth a Mao Zedong*, Zhao Zhichao, "Yingmian zoulai Mao Xinyu," *Qingnian yuebao*, pt. 1, pp. 11–13, and pt. 2, pp. 14–16. Mao's other grandchildren, the children of Li Min and Li Na, enjoyed scant public attention.

141. Zhao Zhichao, "Yingmian zoulai Mao Xinyu," pt. 1, p. 12. For more examples of Mao Xinyu's Mao-mania, see Zhao Zhichao, "Yingmian zoulai Mao Xinyu," pt. 2, p. 14, et passim. Mao's poem "Dielianhua: da Li Shuyi" is dated 11 May 1957.

142. Mao Xinyu, "Tashi xunchang baixing jia," referred to in Zhao Zhichao, "Yingmian zoulai Mao Xinyu," pt. 1, p. 12. Mao lived in the Juxiang Study of the Fengzeyuan complex until 1968, thereafter moving to the "Swimming Pool," also in Zhongnanhai.

143. See the opening sequence of the fifth episode (*Shushan youlu*) of "Mao Zedong."

144. Li Yanchun, "Yeye bainian danchen sunzi zhuangzhong xuanshi: Mao Xinyu guangrong rudang." This article is accompanied by a winsome picture of the bloated Mao Xinyu making a pledge before the Party flag and dressed in what appears to be aluminum foil.

145. Zhao Zhichao, "Yingmian zoulai Mao Xinyu," pt. 2, p. 16.

146. Ibid., pt. 1, p. 11.

147. "Mao Xinyu zouchu shufang rongru shehui."

148. "Buzuo shengyi dang gexing; Maosun dasuan chu changpian."

149. For an example of this from a "democratically minded" dissident, see "Mini-Mao" and also the use of Maoist slogans by the prostitute in "Are You Ready?" in Sang Ye's volume of interviews with Chinese in Australia, *The Year the Dragon Came.* For a stunning example of Maoist-style rhetoric from a leading group of exiled Chinese dissidents, see Chai Ling, "Qing zunzhong lishi"; Ruan Ming, "Zenyang 'chonggu' lishi?"; Bai Meng, "Tiananmen shenpan"; and Ni Yuxian, "Cong fouding Chai Ling dao fouding Minyun," pp. 31–49.

150. See Li Tuo, "Resisting Writing," in Liu Kang and Xiaobing Tang, eds., *Politics, Ideology and Literary Discourse in Modern China*, pp. 273–77; and Mengke's work, referred to in Jianying Zha, *China Pop*, p. 46.

151. See Richard C. Kraus, *Brushes with Power*, pp. 65–74.

152. "Zhouzhi luocheng Mao Zedong shoushu 'Changhenge' beilang."

153. Leys, "Aspects of Mao Tse-tung," p. 63. For recent and glowing Mainland appraisals of the "Mao hand" see Li Shuting, *Mao Zedong shufa yishu* and Wang Hebin, *Xingcao shusheng Mao Zedong*; also Liu Tao, "Mao Zedong yu shufa," pp. 59–61.

154. Sponsored by Wu Shuqing, the post–4 June president of Beijing University, Zhou's calligraphy was exhibited at the Chinese Painting Research Academy (*Zhongguohua yanjiuyuan*) on the Third Ring Road in northwest Beijing.

155. Wang Yue and Li Guijun, eds., *Mao Zedong moji dazidian.*

156. "*Paoda silingbu—wode diyi zhang dazibao*" was the title of Mao's "big character poster" written on 5 August 1966 in support of the student rebels led by Nie Yuanzi of Beijing University. Its publication led to heightened attacks on and the overthrow of the "Liu Shaoqi and Deng Xiaoping Bourgeois Headquarters." See "Fabiao paoda silingbu"; *Mao Zedong sixiang wansui* in Okura henshū keikaku, ed., *Mao zhuxi wenxuan, Mao Zedong sixiang wansui*, p. 36; and Zhongguo Mao Zedong sixiang lilun yu shijian yanjiuhui lishihui, ed., *Mao Zedong sixiang cidian*, p. 593.

157. Jiang Hui, "Wu Guanzhong zhuanggao Duoyunxuan," pp. 54–55; Wu Guanzhong, "Huangjin wanliang fu guansi," pp. 57–63; and Zhai Mowen, "Wu Guanzhong jiahua susongan zhuizong."

158. See article 7, item 2 of "Zhonghua renmin gongheguo guanggaofa (1994 nian 10 yue 27 ri dibajie quanguo renmin daibiao dahui changwu weiyuanhui dishici huiyi tongguo)." The law went into effect on 1 February 1995.

159. See Lu Ding, *Hongdong quanguode "weizao Mao zhuxi shici" yuanan*; and Chen Mingyuan, *Jiehou shicun—Chen Mingyuan shixuan.*

160. Tang was also the patron of Johnson Chang, the curator of Hanart TZ, the Hong Kong-Taipei gallery that introduced much post-'89, in particular ironic Mao, art to overseas audiences.

161. "Zhezhong 'jinianshi' yinggai quxiao," pp. 135–36.

162. In relation to this, see Anagnost's remarks in "The Nationscape," pp. 600–601.

163. "Duiwai jieshao yao zhuyi yige wenti," pp. 258–59.

164. See *Renmin ribao*, 3 May 1981.

165. See "Mao's Birth Place" in "Signs of Disintegration," p. 5; and Su Ya and Jia Lusheng, *Buluode taiyang*, pp. 166–67.

166. Guo Weijian, "Jinri Shaoshan 'ganhai' mang," p. 24.

167. Ibid.

168. For one of the earliest articles on the revival of Mao in Hunan in late 1989 and early 1990 see Andrew Higgins, "Maoists Emerge from the Closet."

169. Guo Wenjian, "Jinri Shaoshan 'ganhai' mang," p. 24.

170. For a picture of Tang and her husband holding up the photograph in front of Mao's birthplace, see William Lindesay, *Marching with Mao*, opposite p. 96.

171. Going one step farther, Hong Kong entrepreneurs invited a chef whose Changsha teacher had once made a meal for the Chairman in 1964 to create a "Chairman Mao banquet" for the territory's gourmands. See Cheng Lai, "Mao zhuxi taocan." In Nanchang, Jiangxi Province, one restaurant called its "red cooked meat" dish (*hongshaorou*), "Runzhi Brain-Enrichment Food" (*Runzhi bunaoshan*) in honor of Mao, whose *zi* was "Runzhi." See Li Yong, "Zouguo yige lunhui zhan zai weiren shenhou."

172. The Shanghai artist Yu Youhan's floral reinterpretation of this photograph is used as the cover image of Jochen Noth et al., eds., *China Avant-Garde*, and is reproduced on p. 180 of the text.

173. Yu Xuejun, "Xiaoxiang xunji Mao Zedong," p. 4.

174. Guo Weijian, "Jinri Shaoshan 'ganhai' mang," p. 24; and Jan Wong, "Around Mao's Centennial."

175. The dimensions of the main slab, on which the poem Mao wrote upon returning to Shaoshan in 1959 was carved, reflected significant dates in Mao's life. It was 12.26 meters tall, a measurement that denoted Mao's birthday on 26 December; 9.9 meters wide, marking Mao's demise on 9 September; and 0.83 meters thick, indicating the age at which Mao died. See Yi Jun, "Furongguolide 'Mao Zedong re,' " p. 46. During the Cultural Revolution, the mathematics of Mao statues generally reflected a similarly esoteric code.

176. At the unveiling of this, Mao Xinyu had his happy encounter with Jiang Zemin.

177. Yi Jun, "Furongguolide 'Mao Zedong re ,' " pp. 45–46.

178. For more details on how the Party refurbished the corporate image of Mao, see "Shishi qiushide xuanchuan Mao Zedong tongzhi," pp. 92–95.

179. For illustrations, see Lin Jianhui and Dai Chixian, "Shaoshan jixing," pp. 22–27. See also Schell, *Mandate of Heaven*, p. 283.

180. Uli Schmetzer, "Cashing in on Mao's Name in Hunan Shaoshan."

181. See Li Haibo, "A Journey Back to Mao's Birthplace," p. 22.

182. See "Fun in the Magic Kingdom of Mao."

183. See Lincoln Kaye, "Against the Grain."

184. Peter Ward, *Kitsch in Sync*, p. 6. Or, as Susan Sontag put it in her "Notes on Camp": "It is beautiful *because* it is awful." See Sontag, *Against Interpretation*, p. 293. For a layered argument on the significance of kitsch and camp in relation to modernism and how revolutionary kitsch can exploit the avant-garde, see Matei Calinescu, *Five Faces of Modernity*, pp. 225–64.

185. This is a term I have often used in describing the new Mao. See, for example, Linda Jaivin, "Mao's Bigger—and Better—Than Ever." Since Christopher Isherwood and Susan Sontag's meditations on camp, there has been a renewed interest in the subject in the 1990s. In the present context I would choose to use Philip Core's succinct definition of the term: "Camp is a lie that tells the truth." See Philip Core, *Camp*, p. 9. Another useful description of the term is that camp revels in "a taste for the bizarre, the extreme and the perverse for their own sake." See Laurence Marks, "Watching a Pile of Popcorn," p. 49. But, to paraphrase Waters, it is also a form of aesthetic indulgence in the most extreme examples of kitsch that indicates superior taste. A thorough study of revolutionary Chinese camp is simply screaming cut to be done, and it is unfortunate that the topic is outside the purview of the present book. While I see Mao in the 1990s as something of a camp image, the future perhaps belongs to his widow. Jiang Qing may one day be a viable camp icon among, say, the gay sybarites of Shanghai and she could eventually find her rightful place amidst the likes of Butterfly Woo (Hu Die), Lily Lee (Li Lili), Ruan Lingyu, Zhou Xuan, and other 1930s stars and starlets.

186. As mentioned above, a glossy album of some of Mao's personal effects, mostly selected because they exhibited the frugality of their owner, was produced in 1993. This book contains pictures of such diverse objects as Mao's 1950s Zhongnanhai gate pass, items of clothing (Mao jackets, caps, overcoats, shoes, slippers, socks, scarf, pajamas, belt), bedding (pillows, quilts, bed), thermos flasks, teacups, sewing kit, TV, writing implements, telephone, a special humidor made for handmade cigars, sleeping pills, water bottles, combs, glasses, Beijing opera records, a mah-jongg set, Ping-Pong table, rackets, and balls. See Zhongnanhai huace bianji weiyuanhui, ed., *Pingfan yu weida.*

187. Zhou Jihou, "Mao Zedong xiangzhang xingshuailu."

188. "Zhou Enlai 1969 nian 3 yue zai quanguo jihua gongzuo huiyi jianghua," in Li Ping, *Wengezhongde Zhou Enlai.*

189. See Qijibu 519 Bingtuan, *519 zhanbao.*

190. Opened in April 1992, "Mao Badge City" was also a major commercial dealer in badges. See Zhou Jihou, *Mao Zedong xiangzhang zhi mi—shijie dijiu da qiguan*, p. 268.

191. Ibid.

192. See Sang Ye, "Zai Beijingde yitian." This last slogan had been popularized by Mao during a movement enjoining the nation to learn from the PLA martyr Wang Jie in the 1960s. Regarding these T-shirts, see Barmé, "Culture at Large," p. 15.

193. See Liu Xuesong, "Mao Zedong shaoxiang ke 'baoan pixie' ma?," p. 96, and p. 97 for an illustration of the T-shirt.

194. Produced for the 1993 centenary, the calendar features Mao for the twelve months of 1994 and Deng for 1995. See "Huainian Mao Zedong ganji Deng Xiaoping 1994–1995," designed by Wang Wangwang, text written by Sun Jin.

195. It should be noted in the context of contemporary Mao artifacts that the present essay was written with the aid of a "Mao's Pad" mouse pad. Produced by China Books and Periodicals in San Francisco, the "Mao's Pad" is a red foam rubber pad festooned in black with a portrait of the young (Edgar Snow) Mao framed by seven Mao quotes. These include old favorites such as: "Who are our enemies? Who are our friends?" (from "Analysis of the Classes in Chinese Society"); "Don't wait until problems pile up and cause a lot of trouble before trying to solve them" (from "Contract on a Seasonal Basis"); and "You can't solve a problem? Well, get down and investigate the present facts and its past history!" (from "Oppose Book Worship"). My thanks to Naomi Jaivin for sponsoring my "Mao's Pad."

196. See, for example, Yin Zhao, "Weinisi yingzhan zuijia nü yanyuan Gong Li rongyao xiangei Shandong xiangqin."

197. See Barmé, "The Greying of Chinese Culture," ch. 13.

198. "Mao Zedong" was produced by China Central Television (CCTV) in cooperation with the CPC Central Documentary Research Office, the Political Department of the People's Armed Police, the China Film Archives, Zhongnanhai Xiyuan Publishing House, and Liaoning People's Publishing House. The Central News and Documentary Studio released another major documentary, "Zhongguo chulege Mao Zedong," at about the same time.

199. See Schell, *Mandate of Heaven*, p. 284.

200. See the TV series "*Kewang*"; and Zheng Wanlong and Li Xiaoming, *Kewang*; also, Jianying Zha, *China Pop*, pp. 25–55.

201. "Bianjibude gushi" was the work of Wang Shuo, Feng Xiaogang, et al. See Wang, Feng, et al., *Bianjibude gushi—youmo dianshi gushi*, 2 vols., esp. Feng's "Shei zhu chenfu" in *Bianjibude gushi (renjian xijuji)*, pp. 1–55.

202. See "Beijingren zai Niuyue," episode 17, and Mao Zedong, "Abandon

Illusions and Prepare to Fight" (Diudiao huanxiang, zhunbei douzheng), 14 August 1949, in Mao Zedong, *Mao Zedong xuanji (yijuan ben)*, pp. 1372–79.

203. Mao was first represented on the stage in 1951. Yu Shizhi of the People's Theater Company in Beijing appeared that year as Mao in Li Bozhao's (Yang Shangkun's wife) opera *The Long March* (*Changzheng*). See Xu Min, "Banyan Mao Zedongde diyi ren—fang Yu Shizhi," pp. 4–5.

204. For details of Gu Yue's career, see Guo Xiangxing, "Yingtan 'Mao Zedong' dengtanji—Gu Yue chudeng yingtan quwen," pp. 22–24. For Wang Ying see Yun Fei, "Cong 'Kaitian pidi' dao 'Qiushou qiyi'—ji qingnian Mao Zedong banyanzhe Wang Ying," pp. 8–9. In her doctoral thesis, "Recasting the Middle Kingdom: A Leadership Myth in Reel Life—Mao Zedong in Propaganda Movies in Contemporary China 1981–1993," Angela Lee Barron plans to deal with the work of both actors at length. For a comment on varied responses on post-1989 Mao movies, see Paul G. Pickowicz, "Velvet Prisons and the Political Economy of Chinese Film-making," p. 220.

205. For details of Yin Hairong, the "Gu Yue of Inner Mongolia," see Huangye Xianzi, "Neimenggu chulege 'Mao Zedong,' " p. 33.

206. The eight-part documentary "Tiananmen" was directed by Shi Jian and Chen Jue and produced by The Structure, Wave, Youth, Cinema Experimental Group in Beijing in 1991. Made for CCTV, it was not broadcast on the Mainland.

207. For a partial translation of *WM*, see "Urbling Winter" in Barmé and Minford, *Seeds of Fire*, pp. 105–17. The Chinese title of *To Kill a King* was *Ci Qin*.

208. In Western popular cinema Mao has made a memorable, if fleeting appearance. There is Gregory Peck's Ping-Pong game with Mao in *The Chairman* (1969) and the anarcho-surreal appearance of Mao in the extraordinary French documentary "Peking Duck Soup" (see Leys, *Broken Images*, pp. 67–73). Mao also features in the Ping-Pong scene in *Forrest Gump* (1994).

209. See Cheng Jin, "Banren banshen, beiguan zimin—Mao Zedong wannian shenghuoju 'Buluode taiyang' zai Shenzhen shouyan," pp. 82–83.

210. Yi, "Xiandai pingju *Mao Zedong zai 1960* jinwan shangyan."

211. In the 1980s, writers such as Bai Hua used historical plays to make oblique criticisms of Mao (see his "The Golden Lance of the King of Wu," for example), but nothing as direct as the Soviet playwright Mikhail Shatrov's still relatively mild 1988 play "Onwards . . . Onwards . . . Onwards" appeared. In Shatrov's play Stalin's ghost cries: "Leave me in peace," to which comes the reply: "If you only knew how little we want to have to talk about you. The problem is that whatever we turn to today, we find ourselves looking at you." See Hochschild, *The Unquiet Ghost*, p. 4, and Remnick, *Lenin's Tomb*, pp. 70–72. Similarly, the figure of Stalin haunts Tengiz Abuladze's 1980s film *Repentance*. See Denise J. Youngblood, "*Repentance*: Stalinist Terror and the Realism of Surrealism," pp. 139–54.

212. See Barmé, "Critics Now Chip Away at China's Concrete Eyesores," p. 54. Other Mao statues have remained, in particular the coffee-fudge Mao in Shenyang, and the Lincoln-Mao in the entrance hall of the Mausoleum in Tiananmen Square. In mid 1995, state workers, enraged by efforts to close down unprofitable factories in the heavy-industry city of Shenyang, reportedly tried to immolate the Mao statue with gasoline as a protest against the "capitalist" authorities. See Patrick E. Tyler, "With Deng's Influence Waning, Privatizing of China's State Industries Stalls." In regard to the relative immutability and extratemporality of such statues, see Mikhail Yampolsky, "The Shadow of Monuments: Notes on Iconoclasm and Time," pp. 93–112.

213. Toby Young, "The End of Irony?," p. 6.

214. Barmé, "Soft Porn, Packaged Dissent, and Nationalism," p. 273.

215. Orville Schell comments on Yu's *The Age of Mao Zedong Series* paintings by saying that they are "centered around silhouettes of Mao outlandishly filled in with chintz and paisley-like patterns as if Laura Ashley had designed a special line in Mao suits." See Schell, *Mandate of Heaven*, pp. 289–90. In conversation with another artist during a trip to New York, Yu Youhan was horrified by any suggestion that his Maos could be used in designing clothes.

216. See Valerie C. Doran, ed., *China's New Art, post-1989 (with a retrospective from 1979–1989)*, pp. 10–17, 76, and 82.

217. For Zhu Wei's work see *Zhu Wei: The Story of Beijing*. The cover of this handsome volume is made from red plastic in the style of Mao's *Quotations*. Plum Blossoms (International), the publisher of the book, also produced a New Year's card using a red pencil sketch of Mao as Santa Claus.

218. The Beijing-based critic Jia Fangzhou calls Zhu's work "the 'Red Rock 'n' Roll' of Chinese *gongbi*" painting. See *Zhu Wei*, p. 11. For Zhu's representations of Mao see pp. 51, 73, 85, 95, 101, and 111.

219. See Noth et al., eds., *China Avant-Garde*, pp. 169 and 175, respectively. In the early-1990s collage "Missing Bamboo," Wu Shanzhuan, creator of "Red Humor" (*Hongse youmo*) in the mid 1980s, replaced Mao's official portrait at a Party congress with the picture of a Panda bear. See Julia F. Andrews and Gao Minglu, *Fragmented Memory: The Chinese Avant-Garde in Exile*, pp. 34–5. While the artist Li Shan created "homo-neurotic" works using Mao's image, during 1992–94, Feng Mengbo, the Beijing "video game artist," used Mao and other Party icons in his faux computer-generated paintings. See "Feng Mengbo," in Li Xianting and Shan Fan, *Der Abschied von der Ideologie: Neue Kunst aus China*, pp. 25–27.

220. See Nancy Condee and Vladimir Padunov, "Pair-a-Dice Lost: The Socialist Gamble, Market Determinism, and Compulsory Postmodernism," p. 89.

221. See Don J. Cohn, ed., *Liu Da Hong, Paintings 1986–92*, pp. 150–59 and 136–39.

222. *Die lian hua* is in the Schoeni Collection, Hong Kong.

223. See Barmé and Jaivin, *New Ghosts, Old Dreams*, pp. xxv–xxvi, 76, 93, 133, 384, 404, and 409. Zhang Hongtu exhibited his Mao *œuvre*, "Material Mao," at the Bronx Museum of the Arts, October 13, 1995–January 14, 1996. See Lydia Yee, *Zhang Hongtu: Material Mao*. One of Zhang's images also was featured on the cover of a collection of contemporary Chinese fiction; see Howard Goldblatt, ed., *Chairman Mao Would Not Be Amused: Fiction from Today's China*.

224. Tam and Zhang joined forces as the result of an introduction from Danny Yung (Rong Nianzeng), director of Zuni Icosahedron, a Hong Kong avant-garde theater group. The T-shirts included Ow Mao (Mao with a bee on his nose), Holy Mao (Mao in a cleric's dog collar), Mao So Young (Mao in pigtails with a gingham dress and Peter Pan collar), Miss Mao (Mao with baby pink lipstick), Psycho Mao (Mao with novelty dark glasses), and Sado Mao (a bare-chested Mao). Tam also produced a T-shirt with Mao wearing an AIDS ribbon for the Macy's Passport Fashion Show, a charity benefit for AIDS sufferers in San Francisco in September 1995. Tam's designs were also used by Zuni in their production "2 or 3 Things . . . of No Significance, Hong Kong 1995," which played on a number of Maoist themes and the looming issue of 1997. See Danny Yung, "Zuni Performance Worsening Day by Day," and *Zuni Daily News*, 20–21 January 1995.

225. Tam released her line of Mao-wear at a spring fashion show in New York in late 1994. By early 1995, her Mao T-shirts and dresses were available in stores from Hong Kong to the United States. See "Quanshen fa 'Mao' "; Charlotte Bevan, "Making a Mint out of Mao"; *People*, May 1995; and Victoria Eng, "Vivienne Tam," pp. 52–

53. The Mao line was particularly controversial in Hong Kong, where some manufacturers with Mainland business connections refused to produce Tam's work. See Fionnuala McHugh, "How Cool Is Mao?," pp. 22, 24, and 26. Tam first used Mao's image and calligraphy in designs she produced in Hong Kong in the early 1980s. The Mainland designer Liang Yuming created a line of revolutionary drag in 1993. He staged a fashion show called "The Revolutionary Era—the Red Star Mao Zedong." All the pure woolen clothing worn by the forty women models was oversized, reminiscent of David Byrne in his "Stop Making Sense" days but without the flare. Looking like children playing at being grown-up soldiers and revolutionaries, the models strutted the stage in Liang's tent-like creations sporting massive army caps with five-pointed stars on them. The musical accompaniment to the show consisted of a rock version of "Singing Praises to the Motherland" and singing by the Choir of the Shanghai Orchestra. It was all part of the opening ceremony of the Sichuan local competitions for the Seventh National Athletics meet in 1993. The Sichuan-based writer Mou Qun praised the affair for being a "post-modern masterpiece." See Mou, "Dangxiade chaoyue yu yiyide shengxian—jian ping Liang Mingyu 'Hongxing Mao Zedong xilie.' "

226. For details of Cui Jian's complex ideological stance, see Andrew F. Jones, *Like a Knife*, pp. 115–43, at p. 140.

227. See, for example, the cassette "The East Is Rocking" (*Dongfang yaogun*), a tape of rock-Party songs produced by Zhongguo kangyi yinxiang chubanshe and released in 1993. The rock version of "The East Is Red" on this tape was recorded by the Beijing singer Qin Yong.

228. Mainland revolutionary music also featured in late 1980s and 1990s Hong Kong cinema, in particular the comic kung fu movies of Tsui Hark (Xu Ke).

229. In this context, see Matei Mihalca's comments on the folksinger Zhang Guangtian, "The Pied Piper of Peking," pp. 54–55.

230. See Xu Weicheng, "'Zhonghua dajia chang (kala OK) jinku' xu," pp. 286–87.

231. See Barmé, "The Greying of Chinese Culture."

232. See the comments by the Beijing-based music critic Jin Zhaojun, "Zai huishou huangran ru meng zai huishou wo xin yijiu—wo dui yindai 'Hong taiyang—Mao Zedong songge' de sikao," and Jin, "Zhi wei na gulaode cunzhuang, hai changzhe guoqude geyao—wo dui 'Hong taiyang—Mao Zedong songge xin jiezou lianchang' de zai sikao."

233. See also Fang Zhou, "Huannian hu? Zichao hu?—toushi dalu 'Hong taiyang' yinyuedai changxiao shehui xinli," pp. 73–74. There was a large body of material to choose from, dating back as far as the early 1950s. See Stuart Schram, "Party Leader or True Ruler?," p. 214, n. 26, where he refers to *Mao Zedong songge*, Beijing: Wanye shudian, 1951, and *Zhongguo chulege Mao Zedong*, Beijing: Renmin wenxue chubanshe, 1951.

234. Revolutionary songs were still being made into popular karaoke tapes in 1994. Pirated videotapes containing music from the 1993 documentary "Mao Zedong" led to litigation over copyright infringement. See Er Yi, "Daxing lishi jilupian 'Mao Zedong' lüzao daoban."

235. Linda Jaivin, "Love All, Serve the People," p. 28.

236. From Greil Marcus, *Dead Elvis*, pp. xii–xiv. Another passage describes the career of the living Elvis as follows:

> Birth in desperate rural poverty, a move to the city, a first record on a local label, unprecedented national and international fame, scandal, adulation; the transformation of a strange and threatening outsider into a respectable citizen who served his country

without complaint, years spent dutifully making formulaic movies and unexciting music, marriage, fatherhood, a quiet life behind the walls of his mansion; then a stunning return, loud and vibrant; and then a slow, seemingly irresistible decline: divorce, endless tours as lifeless as his old films, news replaced by rumors of terrible things, and finally early death [pp. viii–ix]. . . .

See also Jon Katz, "Why Elvis Matters," pp. 100–105; and Paul M. Sammon, *The King Is Dead*, for an anthology of stories inspired by dead Elvis that can be read in tandem with the present book. Wayne Koestenbaum concentrates on another major American symbol, Jacqueline Kennedy Onassis, in *Jackie Under My Skin*; Koestenbaum reveals how far the fetishization of an icon can be taken. See, in particular, "Jackie's Death," pp. 3–14. In the June 1995 promotional music video for "HIStory, Past, Present and Future, Book I," Michael Jackson used a huge statue of himself and mass parade scenes—consisting of the serried ranks of the Czech army—in a conscious emulation of the totalitarian style to affirm his iconic status. The booklet that accompanies the CD set features a testimonial by Jackie O. See also Stanley Crouch's comments on Jackson in regard to Hitler, Stalin, and Mao in "Hooked: Michael Jackson, Moby Dick of Pop," p. 20.

237. The editors of *TMR* also referred to comments made by Robert J. Thompson, an associate professor of television at Syracuse University, to *The New York Times* that are noteworthy in relation to the kitsch and ironic aspects of the Mao revival. Thompson proposed "four rules governing the revival of crass products of the past. First, they must strike the reviving generation as especially and patently crap. Second, they must have been appreciated the first time around, with no awareness of this feebleness, by middle to lowbrow consumers. They are thus in a position to be revived in subsequent years by a clever bunch of ironists, perhaps of a socio-economic class superior to that of the first consumers. Third, the successfully revived product will carry several 'markers' of the period which produced it." (Thompson's fourth rule is that revivals must always be spontaneous.) See "The Art of Revival" in *The Revival Handbook*, p. 8.

238. "Revive, Adapt, Improve . . . ," *The Revival Handbook*, p. 12.

239. Tang Can, "Qingchun ouxiangde bianqian: Cong Mao Zedong dao 'Sida tianwang,' " p. 15.

240. The Four Devarāja were the Hong Kong singers: Aaron Kwok (Guo Fucheng); Leon Lai (Li Ming); Andy Lau (Liu Dehua); and Jackey Cheung (Zhang Xueyou). Other popular H.K.-Taiwan singers included Tong Ange, Wang Jie, Zhao Chuan, Tan Yonglin, Deng Lijun (d. May 1995), Liu Jialing, Kuang Meiyun, and Weng Qianyu. Mainland favorites were Cui Jian, Cai Guoqing, Xie Xiaodong, Mao Ning, Wei Wei, Mao Amin, Hang Tianqi, Cheng Lin, Na Ying, and Ai Jing.

241. For a typical reaction to Hong Kong-Taiwan performers who were generally spoken of as being commercial carpetbaggers, see Guo Tianyun, "Zhengshi zhuixingzu."

242. See Tang Can, "Qingchun ouxiangde bianqian," pp. 14–15; Zhou Yongsheng, "Dangdai qingshaonian yingxiong chongbai yiqing qingxiang tantao—jianlun 'zhuixing' xianxiang," pp. 10–15; and Xu Fei, "Yu sanbai xuesheng tong 'kan' gexing yu gemi," pp. 12–16. Equally, attempts made in the Mainland media to "talk up" Party-approved heroic models by depicting them as though they were H.K./Taiwan stars were risible and unconvincing. See Yu Tian, " 'Chaoxingzu—baozhuangshu' de qishi," p. 21.

243. "Shizong weixing jiang 'za' xiang nali?"

244. "Revive, Adapt, Improve. . . . " in *The Revival Handbook*, p. 12.

245. See Stuart R. Schram, "Mao Zedong a Hundred Years on," p. 136.

246. Svetlana Boym, *Common Places*, pp. 247 and 283ff.

247. "Speculation Rife as Deng Believed Dying."

248. Liu Yida et al., " 'Jinzhaopai' qidai qiangjiu—Laizi Jingcheng laozihaode baogao zhi er."

249. "Collectible Edition of Deng's Writings Planned."

250. See "The Specter of Mao Zedong" below.

251. See Leys, "Is There Life After Mao?" p. 167.

252. Their number reportedly included Song Renqiong, Deng Liqun, and Song Ping. In 1993, for example, they were said to have petitioned Party Central to launch a national campaign to encourage the study of Mao's works. See Cai Yongmei, "Maorede shangpinhua," p. 64.

253. Or, as the formula runs in Chinese: *yi Deng Xiaoping jianshe you Zhongguo tese shehuizhuyide lilun wuzhuang quandang.*

254. Zong Jun, *Zong shejishi.*

255. See Deng Xiaoping, *Deng Xiaoping wenxuan*, vol. 3. See also Bao Zunxin's observations on the significance of this publication, "Huidao Mao Zedong, haishi chaoyue Mao Zedong—cong *Deng Xiaoping wenxuan* disan juan chuban tanqi," pp. 16–18. Various study materials were produced in 1993 and 1995 to "consolidate the banner of Deng Xiaoping" further. See "Gonggu Jiang hexin, gaoju Deng Xiaoping qizhi." And in 1995 Deng Thought was officially endorsed as the ideological font of Party wisdom.

256. See, for example, Xing Bensi, "Shehuizhuyiguanshangde zhongda tupo—du *Deng Xiaoping wenxuan* disan juan," pp. 5–14.

257. See Luo Bing, "Jinian Mao mingshou zao feiyi," p. 10. Deng set the stage for a possible future re-reevaluation of Mao by the Party as early as December 1978 when he said in regard to the major issues of Party history and Mao that "it is impossible and unnecessary for [these questions] to be resolved to our complete satisfaction. We must consider the broader issues, we can afford to be sketchy; it is impossible to clear up every detail, and unnecessary." See Deng, "Jiefang sixiang, shi shi qiu shi, tuanjie yizhi xiangqian kan," *Deng Xiaoping wenxuan (1975–1982)*, pp. 137–38.

258. Some of the details of such "experimentation" appear in official histories such as Hu Sheng, ed., *Zhongguo gongchandangde qishi nian*, p. 486 et passim.

259. A far more balanced assessment of Mao's significance in this context can be found in Schram, "Mao Zedong a Hundred Years on," pp. 139–40.

260. See Hu Sheng, "Mao Zedong yisheng suozuode liangjian dashi," and an expansion of his argument in Hu Sheng, "Dui 'Mao Zedong yisheng suozuode liangjian dashi' de jidian shuoming," pp. 1–5. For a fiery critique of Hu Sheng's argument by a leading veteran Party analyst and writer see Wang Ruoshui, "Mao Zedong wanniande daolu—ping Hu Sheng wei Mao Zedong kaituo zuize," pp. 36–38.

261. Quoted in Hochschild, *The Unquiet Ghost*, p. 123.

262. Ibid., p. 191.

263. *Zhongguo zhihuide huashen shi Zhuge Liang, yonggande huashen shi Sun Wukong, er fankang jingshende huashen ze shi Mao Zedong.*

264. Wong, "Around Mao's Centennial."

265. See Yang Ping, "Lüelun 'xin zuoyi' de chuxian"; and Xiao Gongqin, "Gaige zhuanxingqi Zhongguo zhishifenzide xintai yu leixing fenhua."

266. Wu Qin was editor-in-chief of *Keji yu fazhan: Zhongguo fazhan (zhuankan)*, which began publication in early 1994. See Shao Yanfeng, "Shehuizhuyi shi guoqu geng shi weilai, shoudu xuezhe yantao 'shehuizhuyi zai dangdai shijie.' "

267. See Anita Chan, Stanley Rosen, and Jonathan Unger, *On Socialist Democracy and the Chinese Legal System.*

268. See, for example, Barmé, "Soft Porn, Packaged Dissent, and Nationalism," pp. 273–75.

269. From the early 1990s there was renewed interest among intellectuals and the

reading public in the late-Qing reforms (*xinzheng*). See Yang Ping, "*Zeng Guofan xianxiangde qishi*"; and Lu Jia, "Wan-Qing zhengzhire ranshao quan Zhongguo."

270. See Wang Shan (alias Luoyiningge'er), *Disan zhi yanjing kan Zhongguo*, chs. 2–4.

271. This is the line taken by Liu Yazhou in *Guangchang: ouxiangde shentan* (see "The Mysterious Circle of Mao Zedong" below); and Wang Shan, *Disan zhi yanjing kan Zhongguo*, pp. 45, 46, 49–50, 53–54ff. Yang Ping quotes two such passages in an article that accompanied an excerpt from the book in *Beijing qingnian bao*: "History has only showered love on the Chinese in one respect: it has given them the unadulterated figures of Mao Zedong and Deng Xiaoping"; and "Take advantage of this opportunity and never abandon Mao Zedong or Deng Xiaoping." See Yang Ping, "Disan zhong yanguang—ping *Disan zhi yanjing kan Zhongguo*."

272. Numerous articles on and reviews of Li's memoirs appeared in the non-Mainland Chinese press and particularly in Hong Kong journals such as *Kaifang zazhi, Zhengming, Jiushi niandai yuekan*, and *Mingbao yuekan* in 1994–95. The historical and academic value of Li's book is a highly contentious issue, as a number of Western academics have pointed out—see, for example, Jeffrey N. Wasserstrom, "Mao Matters: A Review Essay"; also Frederick C. Teiwes, "Seeking the Historical Mao," *The China Quarterly*, March 1996; and essays on Li's memoirs by Lucian Pye, Anne Thurston, Barmé, et al, in *The China Journal*, no. 35, January 1996. The Chinese authorities have been cautious about denouncing the book, although one major refutation of Li's portrayal of Zhou Enlai has been made by Zhou's doctor Zhang Puchang. See Zhang Fan, "Zhongnanhai taiyi shouci pengji Li Zhisui," *Hualian shibao*, 26 May 1995. The China Study Group, coordinated by C.H. Hua and C.Y. Tung in New York, undertook a comparison of the Chinese and English texts of this book and noted numerous discrepancies between the two. See "*Mao Zedong siren yisheng huiyilu yishu* neirong zhenshixingde yanjiu baogao zhaiyao" (manuscript version, 1995); also Hua Junxiong and Dong Qingyuan, "*Guyanyu Mao Zedong siren yisheng huiyilu* yishude gongkaixin." This study group also distributed "A Protest Against Random House's Fraudulent Memoirs of Mao's Physician, by Mao Zedong's Staff and Others" (in Chinese "Ruhua fangongde choue biaoyan—women dui Li Zhisui jiqi 'huiyilu' de kanfa") dated 22 July 1995, Beijing (manuscript version). This was a classic MaoSpeak-style denunciation of Li's book signed by 135 people including Wang Dongxing, Wang Hebin (another of Mao's doctors), and what amounts to a Who's Who of Party conservatives. For a more prosaic Mainland account of Mao's relations with his doctors, see Cao Wedong, *Hong bingli*.

273. See, for example, the conversation between Li Zehou and Liu Zaifu, "Mao Zedong beiju pingshuo," serialized in *Mingbao yuekan* in Hong Kong from early 1995.

274. See Barmé, "To Screw Foreigners Is Patriotic."

275. See William Bouwsma, *A Usable Past* (1990), quoted in Peter J. Fowler, *The Past in Contemporary Society Then, Now*, p. 136.

276. These quotations from Bruce Chatwin's *Songlines* appear in "The Starn Twins: Christ (Stretched)," pp. 58–59. See also Apter and Saich, *Revolutionary Discourse in Mao's Republic*, p. 307, on the "cosmocratic evolution" of Mao, involving an Odysseus-like early career and his conversion in Yan'an into a Socratic figure. It is interesting to note here that Mike Tyson, U.S. boxer and convicted rapist, remarked shortly after his release from jail in 1995 that he was so impressed by Mao's writings that he had an image of the Chairman tatooed on his arm. "I like Mao's persistence, his perseverance. . . . He had more guts than anybody in the world," Tyson was quoted as saying in Las Vegas on the eve of his comeback. The boxer also claimed to be partial to Aristotle and Voltaire, and his arm also bears a tatoo of Arthur Ashe. From an AP story reported in

Register-Guard, Eugene, Oregon, July 28, 1995; also reported in the Chinese *Shijie ribao*, 28 July 1995. My thanks to Richard Kraus for this gem.

277. Camille Paglia, "Introduction," *The Revival Handbook*, p. 1, quoting from her essay "Junk Bonds and Corporate Raiders." Paglia's introduction is reprinted as "The Artistic Dynamics of 'Revival' " in her *Vamps & Tramps*, pp. 341–43.

278. In regard to this process in the case of the Soviet Union, see Stephen Wheatcroft, "Unleashing the Energy of History, Mentioning the Unmentionable and Reconstructing Soviet Historical Awareness: Moscow 1987," *Australian Slavonic and East European Studies* 1, no. 1 (1987), referred to in Unger, *Using the Past to Serve the Present*, p. 270, n. 31; and David Remnick, *Lenin's Tomb*, pp. 30–35, 36–41, 60–69, and 398–411.

279. The cult of Napoleon, for example, has flourished for more than 150 years. See Pieter Geyl, *Napoleon For and Against*, trans. Olive Renier; and Karl Marx, "The Eighteenth Brumaire of Louis Bonaparte," in Marx and Engels, *Selected Works*, vol. 1, pp. 221–311. Nancy N. Chen, who has done work with Chinese mental patients, tells me that while the mentally ill in the West may suffer from Napoleonic delusions of grandeur, in China some patients believe themselves to be Mao Zedong. Similarly, Mao is reported to appear as a spirit guide in shamanistic rituals.

Illustrations

Unless otherwise captioned, all photographs were taken by Richard Gordon.

Figure 1. The Six Worthies: (from right to left) Deng Xiaoping, Liu Shaoqi, Mao Zedong, Zhu De, Zhou Enlai, and Chen Yun. Oil painting by Liu Xiqi.

Figure 2. Pulp magazine cover:
True Tales of the Adventures of Mao Zedong
Commemorating the Centenary of Mao Zedong's Birth:
Revealed for the First Time Ever: The Dramas Surrounding the Early History of the
People's Leader—Major Depictions of the Extraordinary Secrets of this Great Man's Life
Mao Zedong Loses Control Over the Army
Mao Zedong Causes an Uproar at Xinhua Gate
Mao Zedong was a Casual Laborer
Mao Zedong Established "The Republic of Hunan"
Originally Mao Wanted to Be a Policeman
Mao Zedong Gives a Loutish Soldier a Knuckle Sandwich
(Published in Sichuan, November 1993)

Figure 3. Mao talisman: Purchased at Jinshan Temple, Zhenjiang, Jiangsu in 1992. This talisman bears a portrait of an elderly Mao in military garb housed in a temple frame with the words "May [we] come and go in safety" under it. The character *fu*, "good fortune," hangs from the superstructure with a tassel and bells attached to it. On the reverse side the words "May the winds fill your sails" are printed in black on an auspicious red background.

Figure 4. "Chairman Mao Is the Sun in Our Hearts Which Will Never Set." Propaganda painting by Gu Gang circa 1977.

Figure 5. "Eternal Glory to the Great Leader and Great Teacher Chairman Mao Zedong": Mao's Funeral, Tiananmen Square, September 1976.

Figure 6. Entrance Chamber, Chairman Mao Memorial Hall, Beijing. Behind a Lincoln-like statue of Mao is a massive picture of the rivers and mountains of China created by the artist Huang Yongyu, the man on whose life story Bai Hua based his scenario "Unrequited Love." The painting is entitled "This land so rich in beauty," the first line of Mao's poem "Snow." This picture was produced on the cover of *Giant of a Generation*, an illustrated set of propaganda materials.

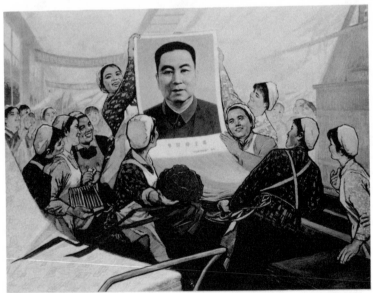

Figure 7. "The Loom Links Us to Beijing; the Weavers Are Joined to Chairman Hua by the Heartstrings." Watercolor by Chen Mingjun and Wu Ziqiang.

Figure 8. "The Light of China." Oil Painting by Hou Rong, He Duojun, Wu Huamin, Cheng Guoying, Fan Huaizhang, and Zeng Tingzhong.

84

Figure 9a. Pulp magazines devoted to Mao: Three magazines typical of the kind of publications produced for mass readership around the time of the centenary and available at book stalls throughout the country.

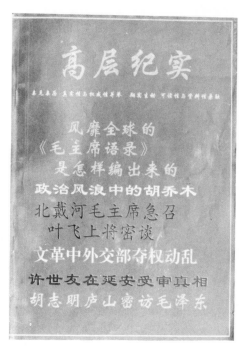

Figure 9b. Pulp magazine cover: *True Tales from the Top* (Eyewitness accounts—true and authoritative—fully detailed—readable and reliable)

How Did they Edit *Quotations from Chairman Mao*, the Book That Took the World by Storm?

The Political Storms Weathered by Hu Qiaomu

Chairman Mao Calls Major General Ye Fei to Beidaihe for Secret Talks

The Turmoil Surrounding the Seizing of Power in the Ministry of Foreign Affairs during the CultRev

The Truth About Xu Shiyou being Investigated in Yan'an

Ho Chi Minh's Secret Visit to See Mao Zedong at Lushan

(Hualing Publishers, October 1993)

Figure 9c. Pulp magazine cover: *Morningstar Lily*
Mao Zedong During the Military Defeat of August . . .

Text of Deng Xiaoping's Speech on the Question of Hong Kong Published in Full

All the Details of the Americans Taken Hostage by Iran

The Life-and-Death Love of the Sister of Sheng Shicai, "King of Xinjiang"

Mao Zedong Invited Him to Swim the Yangtse

The Secret of How Lin Biao Found Favor Revealed

(Huhehaote, September 1993)

Figure 10. *The Analects*, by Confucius. Published by the Cultural Relics Administration of Qufu County, Confucius' birthplace in Shandong, this red-plastic covered version of the Master's sayings was produced in imitation of Mao's "Little Red Book" in the early 1980s.

Figure 11. Invitation to Zhou Pengfei's 1991 exhibition of imitation-Mao calligraphy (gold lettering on a red background).

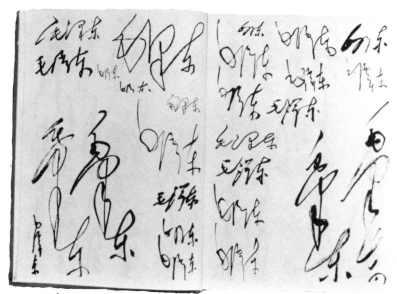

Figure 12. Mao Zedong: A selection of the Chairman's signatures from *The Great Compendium of Mao Zedong's Calligraphy*.

Figure 13. "Learn from Comrade Lei Feng": Mao's 5 March 1963 calligraphic inscription for the PLA's red samaritan along with a dog (Bassett)-eared image of the revolutionary martyr used for promotional purposes by the Changsha Municipal Advertising Company. (Author's photograph, Changsha, June 1992)

Figure 14. Stalls selling Mao trinkets and memorabilia along the approach to Mao's birthplace. (Author's photograph, Shaoshan, June 1992)

Figure 15. Being shaken down by Tang Ruiren, proprietor of the "Mao Family Restaurant" (the name of which features in the background) situated opposite Mao's birthplace in Shaoshan, Hunan. (Author's photograph, Shaoshan, June 1992)

Figure 16. A waitress at the helm of the "Mao Family Restaurant" with Mao's childhood home visible in the background. (Author's photograph, Shaoshan, June 1992)

Figure 17. The restored Mao Clan Temple in Shaoshan, Hunan. (Author's photograph, Shaoshan, June 1992)

Figure 18. $1000 Mao: From Dishuidong, Shaoshan, Hunan, 1992 (dimensions: 17" by 9 1/2"). This US$1–1000 bill sold at Mao's 1966 hideaway outside Shaoshan features a computer-generated image of the Chairman. Printed in blue on white cloth, with Mao in spectral black, the note bears a red seal inscribed with the words "[Mao's] Former Residence in Shaoshan" (*Shaoshan guju*). (Courtesy of Sang Ye)

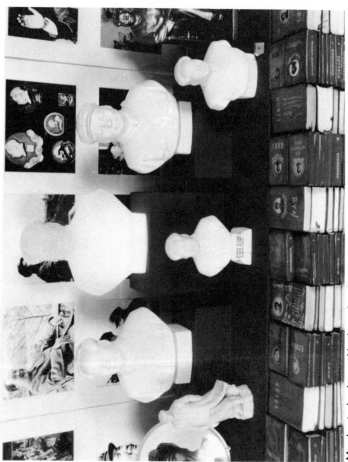

Figure 19. Mao busts, books, and badges: A portion of Sang Ye's private collection of CultRev relics acquired from recycling stations, garbage tips, markets, and private dealers during the late 1980s and early 1990s. (A display at the exhibition "Propaganda and People: Mao and the Cultural Revolution 1966–1976," Powerhouse Museum, Sydney, July 1992-February 1994. Photograph by Sue Stafford)

Figure 20a. "Classic" Cultural Revolution-period Mao badges from the 1994 calendar "365 Red Suns" produced in Anhui Province.

Figure 20b. Porcelain Mao badges from the 1994 calendar "365 Red Suns."

Figure 21. 1994 New Year's Painting: A picture of Mao on celluloid surrounded by symbols of good fortune, the spring and longevity framed by a couplet extolling the chairman's superhuman abilities. The legend at the top reads: "May good fortune nourish ten thousand generations."

Figure 22. 1994 New Year's Painting: The ¥100 note featuring the Four Worthies (Mao, Zhou Enlai, Liu Shaoqi, and Zhu De) with traditional symbols of prosperity and good health (jinseng, peonies, and money), and auspicious sayings. The legend at the top reads: "May you make a fortune."

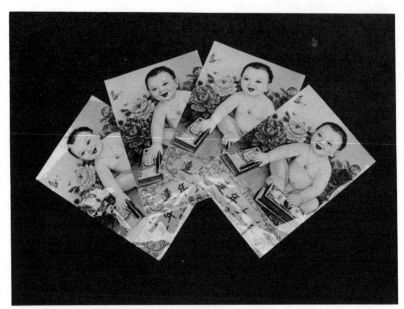

Figure 23. 1994 New Year's Painting: A chubby baby fondling piles of Chinese money (with Mao's image on it) and U.S. dollars.

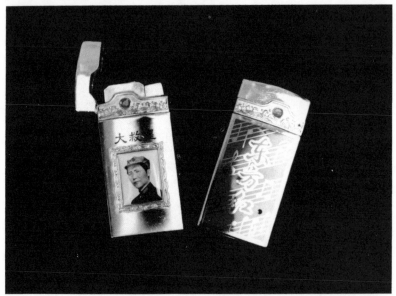

Figure 24. Cigarette lighter featuring the young Mao. When opened the lighter plays "The East Is Red," China's Mao anthem. The Chinese legend over Mao's image reads "The Great Savior." The trimming above this shows a red sun rising from a turbulent sea. Such lighters were popular for a time in 1992–1993.

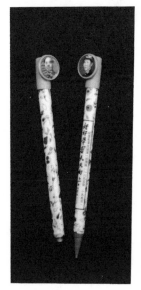

Figure 25. Mao refillable pencils: Produced for the 1993 centenary these pencils for school children feature both the young and the old Mao. They carry the inscription "Study hard and you'll improve every day" in the Chairman's hand (see note 8 in "Galluping Mao: A 1993 Opinion Poll"). (Courtesy of Nancy Berliner)

Figure 26: Assorted Mao accessories: Brooches with rhinestones, a pendant in the shape of a heart, a tie pin, a centenary fountain pen reading "The Great Teacher," and a mini Mao badge. These objects were purchased in Shaoshan, June 1992.

Figure 27. A tea cup with a Cultural Revolution-style picture of Mao's childhood house in Shaoshan. Purchased in Shaoshan, June 1992.

Figure 28. Three Mao T-shirts. The legends on the shirts read (from left to right): "I love reading Chairman Mao's works"; "Sun in our hearts"; "Dad and mom might be dear to me but no one is as dear as Chairman Mao." These shirts were purchased by the author in Beijing, Shanghai, and Changsha, 1992–1993.

Figure 29. Mao T-shirt: The Chairman in a halo of hearts.

Figure 30a. Image from the calendar "Remember Mao Zedong and Be Grateful to Deng Xiaoping 1994–1995," designed by Wang Wangwang, captions by the literary critic Sun Jin. Produced in Shenzhen, 1993.

January-February, 1994: "For truly great men/ Look to this age alone." These words from Mao's poem "Snow" are reproduced below the image of Mao on a sun-baked landscape with a commentary by Sun Jin that reads: "This arid yellow earth has nurtured 5,000 years of culture. Countless heroes have come this way, leaving in their wake evidence of very different aspirations. Because the Great Man succored by this land had his feet firmly planted on the ground he could travel forth without hindrance. His achievements are reflected in all things, for he created a new nation."

Figure 30b. Image from "Remember Mao Zedong and Be Grateful to Deng Xiaoping 1994–1995."

May-June, 1994: This picture is inscribed with a line from Mao's 1929 poem "The Warlords Clash" that reads: "Showering misery through the land." The collage features Chiang Kai-shek, Jiang Qing and Lin Biao, authors of some of China's greatest miseries. Sun Jin's commentary, which opens with a play on a famous PLA slogan, reads: "It is I who has been violated. If none violate me I will still respond. If it is all but word games then how should we understand the term humanity? All surfaces are equally illuminated by the sun; page after page is turned. When history invades everyday life, perspective transforms some people into part of the mottled wallpaper of existence."

Figure 30c. Image from "Remember Mao Zedong and Be Grateful to Deng Xiaoping 1994–1995."

November-December, 1994: "Today the autumn wind still sighs, But the world has changed!" These lines come from Mao's 1954 poem "Beidaihe." Sun Jin's commentary, referring to two famous photographs of Mao (one with children sporting red bandanas, the other of him in a crowd of smiling visitors from the Third World) on which this collage is based, reads: "A youth tied a red bandana around his neck; people of different races smiled in his presence. He, however, deeply questioned all of this: 'How many of them are true believers?' He was no different from anyone else; he didn't enjoy seeing the masses all wearing the same expression."

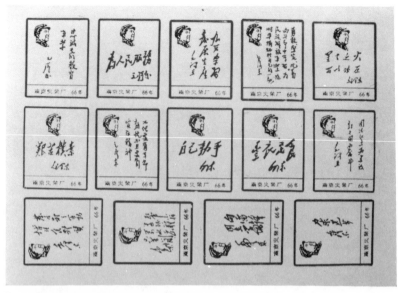

Figure 31. Matchbox covers with Mao quotes, reprints of Cultural Revolution originals.

Figure 32. "Eternal Effulgence." Painting by the Hangzhou artist Geng Jianyi. The portrait of Mao-as-the-sun has been replaced by a picture of China's other national symbol, the panda bear. (Courtesy of Li Xianting)

Figure 33. Santa Mao: A 1994 Christmas card by the Beijing artist Zhu Wei designed for his Hong Kong dealer. (Courtesy Carma Hinton and Richard Gordon)

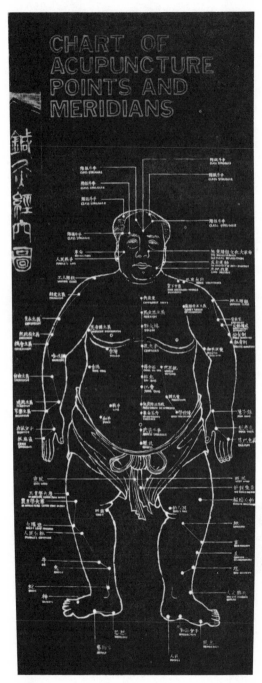

Figure 34. "Chart of Acupuncture Points and Meridians": the Physiology of a Revolutionary. Painting by Zhang Hongtu.

Figure 35. Baby Mao: sequined T-shirt by Vivienne Tam. Based on a painting by Zhang Hongtu which was in turn inspired by the Mao quote: "The masses are the real heroes, while we ourselves are often childish and ignorant." (Courtesy of Vivienne Tam)

Figure 36a. "The East Is Rocking": Revolutionary songs rearranged to pop music in Beijing.

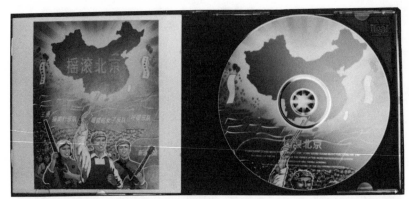

Figure 36b. "Rocking Beijing": A 1994 Mainland/Hong Kong CD collection of Beijing rock music. Cover design by Frankie Fan.

Figure 37. Mao karaoke video cassettes produced to cash in both on the centenary and the karaoke craze of the early 1990s.

Figure 38. "Classical Revolutionary Songs (I)": Cover illustration of a karaoke video cassette produced in Guangdong, purchased in Beijing in early 1993.

Figure 39. "OK2: The Red Sun to a New Beat": Cover illustration of a karaoke video cassette produced in Fujian, purchased in Beijing in early 1993.

Figure 40. A CD-version of "The Red Sun" compilation that sold by the million in 1992.

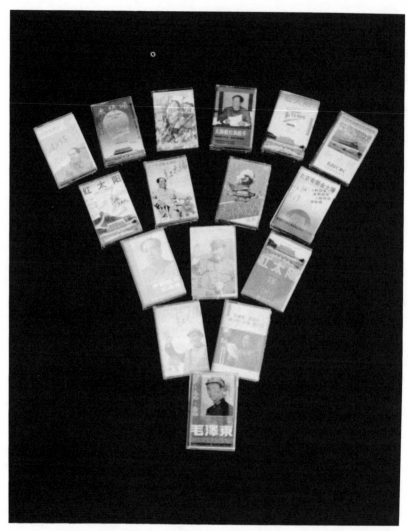

Figure 41. Music cassettes: A selection of 16 cassettes produced in 1992–1993 during "The Red Sun Craze."

Figure 42. "The People Cannot Forget Mao Zedong": Back cover of a music cassette produced for the centenary featuring Mao in the Cultural Revolution.

Figure 43. "Mao Zedong's Poems Set to Music": A CD collection of Mao's poems produced by the China Record Company in Guangzhou in 1992.

Figure 44. Deng Xiaoping: "Facing the Future." Oil painting by Chen Jiwu.

Figure 45a. "May you make a fortune": 1995 Year of the Pig greeting card by the Hong Kong-based pop singer/composer Lo Ta-yu (Luo Dayou), cover image. The card features the official portrait of Mao with the traditional greeting "May you make a fortune" over it. On either side an intentionally corrupted version of the opening lines of the Taoist *Daodejing* are printed. The original reads: "The Way that can be spoken of is not the Eternal Way" (*dao ke dao fei chang dao*). In this version the word "Way" (*dao*) has been replaced by "cock" or "prick" (*diao*).

Figure 45b. "May you make a fortune": 1995 Year of the Pig greeting card by Lo Ta-yu. Inside the card is a pop-up cutout of Mao flanked by two lines taken from the poem "Snow." The original lines read: "This land so rich in beauty/ Has made countless heroes bow in homage. . . . All are past and gone!/ For truly great men/ Look to this age alone." This version reads: "This land so rich in beauty/ Enticing Mao to swing his prick left and right. . . . All are past and gone!/ For truly great men/ Bow in His direction." In the bottom right-hand corner are the words "Greetings from Lo Ta-yu for 1995, a fat Year of the Pig."

A Note on the Translations

- Most of the translations are excerpts from longer articles, books or texts. The titles are, generally, my own formulations and the arrangement is roughly chronological.
- Most selections are prefaced by an editorial comment in italics.
- The annotations are my own and are aimed at elucidating some of the more important, as well as the arcane, expressions of late-socialist Chinese prose.
- Sources are given at the end of the book.
- Mainland Chinese typographical conventions, especially the irksome habits of Communist typesetting, are not necessarily adhered to in the translations. For example, in Mainland texts the expression the Cultural Revolution is invariably isolated within the embrace of inverted commas, an indication of official disdain. This is also true in the case of such unhappy expressions as the Gang of Four and in the use of other buzz words like "craze" (*re*), "phenomenon" (*xianxiang*) and so on, when a somewhat negative gloss is being implied. Whereas Mao will always be referred to as Chairman Mao, Comrade Mao Zedong or Mao Zedong in the Mainland texts, the translations may use these terms or, for the sake of brevity, simply the unadorned surname Mao.
- Capital letters are used in the case of some expressions (Great Leader, etc.) not only for emphasis but to convey something of the awkwardness and mild absurdity of such dated formulations in contemporary Mainland prose. Capitals are also employed occasionally in the case of the third person singular pronoun (He, Him, His) when the pseudo-religious tone of the original calls for it.
- Except for a few passages quoted from Chinese propaganda-in-translation sources like *Beijing Review*, all translations are my own or, in a few cases, a collaborative effort as indicated in the Sources. The style of translation depends very much on the original text. When a piece is littered with officialese—MaoSpeak (or *Xinhua wenti*, New China NewSpeak, as it is called in Chinese), the translation attempts to convey this both in spirit and letter. If a work is somewhat more ambitious and fluent in style, the translation attempts to reflect that. If the original is patently absurd, an effort is made to maintain a concomitant flavor of the surreal in English.

Mao on Mao

Mao Zedong

In 1972, U.S. President Richard Nixon and Secretary of State Henry Kissinger were received by Mao Zedong at the Chairman's residence in Zhongnanhai, Central Beijing.[1]

Kissinger remarked that he had assigned Mao's writings to his classes at Harvard. Indulging in characteristic self-deprecation, Mao said, "These writings of mine aren't anything. There is nothing instructive in what I wrote." I said, "The Chairman's writings moved a nation and have changed the world." Mao, however, replied, "I haven't been able to change it. I've only been able to change a few places in the vicinity of Peking."

Notes

1. See He Di, "The Most Respected Enemy: Mao Zedong's Perception of the United States," pp. 144–45 and n. 3.

The Mysterious Circle of Mao Zedong

Liu Yazhou

The following passage concludes the book The Square—Altar for an Idol *by Liu Yazhou, which was published in Hong Kong in early 1990. The then 37-year-old novelist was the son-in-law of Li Xiannian, China's former State President and Chairman of the National People's Political Consultative Conference.*

Another popular explanation for the "mysterious circle of Mao Zedong" mentioned below is that the dying Chairman was trying to tell those around him to work together, and not purge each other after he was gone. As was the case for most of Mao's sanguine admonitions, it was assiduously ignored.

An ideal antidote to this sanctimonious writing is the gruesomely comic description of Mao's death and the battle to preserve his "biological structure," as the Soviets called the corpses of socialist potentates, given by Zhisui Li in The Private Life of Chairman Mao.[1]

It was three days before his death and Mao Zedong could no longer talk. He put his thumb and forefinger together to form a circle, and showed the doctors and nurses. Then, afraid they hadn't understood, he lifted his arm with great effort and traced a circle in the air.

But what did it mean? Was this some mysterious cipher? A prophesy? In the last days of his life, he bequeathed a riddle in the shape of a circle to his empire.

The doctors panicked. Hua Guofeng, Wang Dongxing, and the rest rushed to his bedside. They tried to work out what he meant, like children playing a guessing game. Jiang Qing came as well, but not even she knew what her husband's gesture signified. . . .

I don't understand what he meant either. No one will ever know for sure. But if you ask me, I'd say that he was describing his own history.

History is circular.

Everything is circular.

Isn't that so?

He began in Tiananmen Square and that's where he ended up. He had traveled in a big circle.

He returned to Tiananmen Square, never to leave again. He became the Square's resident in perpetuity, its only resident. . . .

The largest tomb in the modern world was erected on Tiananmen Square. But it's not really a tomb. It's a spacious and resplendent villa. It has a white marble armchair inside. You can see it when you enter the main hall. There's a bed, too, and that's where you'll find him. The place is air-conditioned, and has an elevator too. In the morning, the elevator takes him up to the hall where he works, and at night it lowers him to the depths where he sleeps.

Mao Zedong presides over Tiananmen Square. He is forever observing his people; and the people forever watch him, ever mindful of his Thought. No matter how you look at it, he is immutable.

Mao Zedong, male, from Xiangtan County, Hunan Province, 1.78 meters tall, born of a rich peasant family.

Notes

1. See Zhisui Li, *The Private Life of Chairman Mao*, pp. 3–30.

Deng Xiaoping: Mao in Short

Deng Xiaoping

When the leaders of the Communist Party were deliberating the official appraisal of the Mao years in 1980, Deng Xiaoping made a number of gnomic pronouncements which determined the tenor of the final Central Committee document on Mao's "errors" and post-1949 Chinese history.[1]

The banner of Mao Zedong Thought can never be discarded. To throw it away would be nothing less than to negate the glorious history of our Party.... It would be ill-advised to say too much about Comrade Mao Zedong's errors. To say too much would be to blacken Comrade Mao, and that would blacken the country itself. That would go against history.

25 October 1980

Notes

1. See also Gong Yuzhi, "Deng Xiaoping lun Mao Zedong."

The Party on Mao

Central Committee of the Communist Party of China

This extract is taken from the official 1981 Party ruling on post-1949 Chinese history and Mao's role in it. The formulations in this document—drafted by Hu Qiaomu under the aegis of Deng Xiaoping—remain the Party's last word on the Chairman. The following passages are taken from the official Chinese translation.

All the successes in these ten years [1956–1966] were achieved under the collective leadership of the Central Committee of the Party headed by Comrade Mao Zedong. Likewise, responsibility for the errors committed in the work of this period rested with the same collective leadership. Although Comrade Mao Zedong must be held chiefly responsible, we cannot lay the blame on him alone for all those errors. During this period, his theoretical and practical mistakes concerning class struggle in a socialist society became increasingly serious, his personal arbitrariness gradually undermined democratic centralism in Party life and the personality cult grew graver and graver. The Central Committee of the Party failed to rectify these mistakes in good time. Careerists like Lin Biao, Jiang Qing, and Kang Sheng, harboring ulterior motives, made use of these errors and inflated them. This led to the inauguration of the Cultural Revolution. . . .

Chief responsibility for the grave Left error of the Cultural Revolution, an error comprehensive in magnitude and protracted in duration, does indeed lie with Comrade Mao Zedong. But after all it was the error of a great proletarian revolutionary. Comrade Mao Zedong paid constant attention to overcoming shortcomings in the life of the Party and state. In his later years, however, far from making a correct analysis of many problems, he confused right and wrong and the people with the enemy during the Cultural Revolution. While making serious mistakes, he repeatedly urged the whole Party to study the works of Marx, Engels, and Lenin conscientiously and imagined that his theory and practice were Marxist and that they were essential for the consolidation of the dictatorship of the proletariat. Herein lies his tragedy. . . .

Comrade Mao Zedong's prestige reached a peak and he began to get arrogant at the very time when the Party was confronted with the new task of shifting the focus of its work to socialist construction, a task for which the utmost caution was required. He gradually divorced himself from practice and from the masses, acted more and more arbitrarily and subjectively, and increasingly put himself above the Central Committee of the Party. The result was a steady weakening and even undermining of the principle of collective leadership and democratic centralism in the political life of the Party and the country. This state of affairs took shape only gradually and the Central Committee of the Party should be held partly responsible. From the Marxist viewpoint, this complex phenomenon was the product of given historical conditions. Blaming this on only one person or on only a handful of people will not provide a deep lesson for the whole Party or enable it to find practical ways to change the situation. . . .

Comrade Mao Zedong was a great Marxist and a great proletarian revolutionary, strategist, and theorist. It is true that he made gross mistakes during the Cultural Revolution, but if we judge his activities as a whole, his contributions to the Chinese revolution far outweigh his mistakes. His merits are primary and his errors secondary. He rendered indelible meritorious service in founding and building up our Party and the Chinese People's Liberation Army, in winning victory for the cause of liberation of the Chinese people, in founding the People's Republic of China, and in advancing our socialist cause. He made major contributions to the liberation of the oppressed nations of the world and to the progress of mankind.

A Specter Prowls Our Land

Sun Jingxuan

In the late 1970s and early 1980s, during the nationwide reaction against Mao's rule and the Cultural Revolution, a number of powerful attacks were made on the Mao cult. These included the following poem by Sun Jingxuan.

Begun in 1979, Sun published this poem in early 1981. After the Party launched a purge of the arts, he was obliged to write a self-criticism in which he said: "In exposing and criticizing feudalism [a code word for Mao, the personality cult and autocracy in general], my viewpoint was totally incompatible with the ideology of the proletariat. Although I sought in this poem to oppose feudalism, I was in fact promulgating and advocating bourgeois liberalism and human rights. . . ."

> Those who do not remember the past are condemned to relive it.
> —*George Santayana*[1]

Oh my brothers! Have you seen
The specter prowling our land?

Brothers! Do not call
Our land fair, our skies bright,
While this specter,
    like a gust of wind,
    like a wisp of smoke,
Prowls unencumbered o'er our land:
Swaggers into peasant's hut,
Struts into herdsman's yurt;
Issues orders, revels in pride,
Like Great Caesar of Ancient Rome,
Grasps the destiny of us all;
And any thing we have is granted by its spectral whim.

Brothers! Have you seen
The specter prowling our land?

In this century, this Nuclear Age,
To talk of specters seems absurd
But it's the truth—the terrible and tragic truth!
This specter,
    like a gust of wind,
    like a wisp of smoke,
Prowls unencumbered o'er our land;
Trails like a shadow,
Clutches with invisible claws,
Silently sucks blood and marrow,
Dictates every action, controls every thought;
Tramples on dignity,
Destroys the quest for beauty, the yearning for love.
The slightest hint
And you are locked away for years
    in some dark and gloomy prison-cell!
This specter decrees death,
posthumous humiliation,
Or tolerates a life of vexatious vegetation.
You are, then, spectral slave and spectral subject,
Without the right to cry out in protest.

Brothers! Have you seen
The specter prowling our land?

You may not recognize him,
    though he stands before your eyes,
For like a conjurer,
    master of never-ending transformation,
One moment in dragon-robe of gold brocade
He clasps the dragon-headed scepter,
The next in courtier's gown
He swaggers through the palace halls;
And now—behold—a fresh veneer!
The latest fashion! And yet
No mask, no costume, no disguise
Can hide the coiled dragon
    branded on his naked rump.

Ah China! Ancient and mysterious land!
Ancient as your Great Wall,
   mysterious as your hieroglyphs,
Wooden plough, spinning wheel,
   water mill, rattan basket,
Innumerable tombs, pagodas, temples,
Palaces, sacred objects and ancestral shrines.
These ancient mysteries have spawned
   legends innumerable
Have made you an abode for gods,
   a haunt for ghosts. . . .
And I, son of a northern peasant,
Was born amidst terror,
   raised in piety. . . .
Childhood! Wretched childhood!
The bleak and dreary village, the tumbledown hovel;
Wrapped in tattered cotton padding,
Curled on the ice-cold earthern *kang*,
I stared blankly at the smoke-black wall
And its icons:
God of
   WAR majesty on tiger-skin throne;
Goddess of
   PITY on lotus-seat afloat the sea;
And OLD LONGEVITY
(Though I was never the least impressed by his benevolence). [2]
On the altar stood the Tablet, inscribed
   HEAVEN
   EARTH
   LIEGE
   PARENTS
   TEACHER
Loftiest representation of divinity (said Mother)
And when she stuck the joss-sticks in the burner (the usual three)
I knelt at a distance,
   not daring even to lift my head and watch.
At night I dreamt,
   smokey haze-filled dreams
      of Hell and Heaven. . . .
Such was my childhood,
My infant head stuffed with graven images.

I believed these gods to be
    omnipresent, omnipotent:
Even the old locust-tree outside my home
    breathed a divine aura.
In time of famine, I knelt beneath the blazing sun,
Closed my eyes, clasped my hands, and prayed to the almighty gods.
But for all my piety and supplication
Life continued hard and wretched,
    Mother Earth remained desolate. . . .

Ancient China! A loathsome specter
Prowls the desolation of your land. . . .

I shall never forget the heady night
When the misty moon shone on the threshing-floor
And we first learned to sing the Internationale.
"No more gods!" we vowed, "No more emperors!"
The song quickened our hearts,
Taught us the worth and strength of man,
Became our cry, our banner.
Barefoot, spear in hand,
    we roamed the plains and mountains of China.
That song gave us strength to bear the hunger,
to fight from the Changbai Mountains in the north,
    the Taihang Range in the west,
Down to south of the Yellow and Yangtze rivers.
Knowing that song, that cry, that oath,
We could hold aloft a new sun,
    in hands and arms that still dripped blood.

The decaying palaces, the dark temples
    crumbled, crashed to the ground
And the Red Flag waved in the bright skies of China;
Like children we wept tears of joy,
Forgot the hardships and sorrows of the past.
But how brief were the days of cheer!
Reality came, dragging with it bitter disenchantment:
We had thought ourselves masters of our fate,
That we could now live happy and free on our land,
But now we found ourselves mere "screws"[3]
Driven tight into some machine;

Numbers on a statistical chart,
Pieces on a Go board—black and white.
Flesh and blood and thinking mind we had
But could not wreak feeling, will or thought.
Oh misery! We were abstractions!
Our bounden duty to raise our hands and clap. . . .
Willingly we forgave errors:
After all, a revolution is no stroll down the street.
A cleansing tide is bound to damage
    ships and homes.
Perhaps this childish goodwill
lies at the root of our misfortune. . . .
But even we are human,
Even we can think,
And in the end we saw:
Our sweat and blood, given for the Great Edifice of Socialism,
had built a cathedral of fear. . . .

Brothers! While we lay deep in slumber
A specter prowled our land.

I cannot forget that year of frenzy
When I went back to my village,
    ancient crossing on the Yellow River,
That once cradled the young revolution,
Suckled it
    like some simple-hearted peasant nurse.
After thirty years, I returned:
The old place was sure to have changed, I thought.
Yes, there were great changes—
The old men of my youth were now laid in their graves,
The youngsters were old greybeards;
A loudspeaker high in a tree
Blared hysteria from dawn till dusk.
In every home I entered, gone were the gods—
    door gods,
    wealth gods,
    kitchen gods;
A new icon had taken their place.
The guerrilla-leader had aged,
His face was lined with grief.
From dull despondent eyes he apologized:

"After these thirty years,
  I owe you a good drink.
But my vegetable garden has been flooded
  by the Red Sea,
My little plot of onion and garlic washed away!"
That night I lay awake, brooding,
My heart heavy with an immeasurable grief.
What could I say to these country folk
  who had nursed us?
I felt such shame, for the promises
  of thirty years past.
What could I say?
Had we overthrown the Three Great Mountains[4]
only to build a new Temple?
Had we toppled Wealth and Mercy
only to hang a new icon in their shrine?

China! Ancient, mysterious China!
Home of gods,
  cradle of myths, hotbed of tyranny;
In your innumerable temples and palaces
In your countless emperors' tombs,
The specters come, the specters go,
  inhabit this man's corpse, that man's soul.
Your vast domain breeds feudalism.
They argue that land in peasant's hands
  breeds capitalism:
False! Tyranny is too well entrenched:
No new class can strike root
  in the feudal fortress.
Which of us has even set eyes on capitalism—
Premature, infant, strangled in the cradle?
China, like a huge dragon, gobbles all in its path,
Like a huge vat, dyes all the same colour.
Have you not seen the lions of Africa,
  the lions of America,
Fierce kings of the jungle?
When they enter our dragon's lair
    they become mere guard-dogs,
    rings through their pug nostrils,
    standing guard at yamen and palace gate. . . .

Ah China! My beloved China!
You need fresh blood, air,
Wind, rain, sun;
You need to change your putrid soil!
Ah China! do not fear
    jeans, long hair,
    Taiwanese love-songs
    Indian love ballads;
Fear the specter from within the ancient fortress,
Prowling our land.

Notes

1. These words were placed by William Shirer at the beginning of his classic study of Nazism, *The Rise and Fall of the Third Reich*, the translation of which has been very popular with Chinese readers. They also stand at the entrance to the Dachau concentration camp museum.

2. These gods of War, Pity and Longevity are Guan Gong, Guanyin and Laoshouxing, traditionally worshipped throughout China. During the original Mao Cult, Mao as martial figure, as the leader who served the people and as the symbol of Chinese strength and continuity, subsumed or was subsumed by all three gods.

3. Lei Feng, the Party's model martyr, spoke of wanting to be but a screw in the machinery of the revolution. He was extolled for what was called his "screw spirit" (*luosiding jingshen*).

4. The *sanzuo dashan* of feudalism, imperialism and bureaucrat-capitalism.

Documenting the Demise

Central Department of Propaganda

Mao Zedong's official fall from grace was a gradual process that unfolded during secretive consultations, Politburo meetings and Party plenums. Its progress was marked, among other things, by the issuing of documents by Party Central and its Department of Propaganda. The Department, with branches at provincial and municipal level throughout the nation, was in charge of the implementation of Party rulings on Mao.

These communications—droning documents that reveal the gimlet eye to detail beloved by all bureaucrats—were issued secretly (or "internally"). However, in terms of their practical impact—the removal of slogans, books, statues, and so on—they limned the public face of de-Maoification.

The following Department of Propaganda documents are taken from a four-volume restricted-circulation selection of materials published by the CPC Central Party School in 1994.

Central Department of Propaganda Circular on Not Using Bold Type to Print Quotations from Marx, Engels, Lenin, Stalin and Chairman Mao in Newspapers, Periodicals, Books, and Documents in the Future (23 March 1978)

Bold type had been employed for quotations from Mao and the Marxist classics during the Cultural Revolution. Deployed very much in the way some po-mo academics use quotes from French philosophers and theoreticians, bold quotes from the works of leaders deified in the Party pantheon prefaced books, magazines, and were scattered throughout news stories, articles and reports, thereby adding validity and authority to the texts they decorated. The elimination of bold-font quotes was a major break with CultRev-style propaganda.

In accordance with a directive from Party Central, bold type is no longer to be used when citing quotations from Marx, Engels, Lenin, Stalin and Chairman Mao in newspapers, periodicals, books and documents.

Central Department of Propaganda Request for Instructions Concerning the Disposal of Extant Objects Related to "Loyalty" (28 July 1978)
(This document has been approved by the Centre)

"Loyalty" (zhong) is a code word for all matters related to the personality cult of Mao Zedong that thrived during the early years of the Cultural Revolution.

According to a report received from the General Political Department [of the People's Liberation Army] dated 19 July, during the course of clearing out its warehouses the Army has come across large stocks of objects related to "loyalty." These include [Mao] statues made of aluminum, plaster of paris, porcelain and other materials, as well as badges. According to incomplete statistics from five departments in the Kunming Military Region alone, they have in excess of 2,300 kilograms of Chairman Mao badges, ten metal moulds [for the production of "loyalty" products], 720 plastic statues [of the Chairman], 100 plaster and porcelain statues, 250 portraits on tinplate, 550 on plywood, as well as 6,000 quotation badges made from perspex. Some of these are of inferior quality and the images thereon substandard, others have warped or are soiled, some are half made, and a considerable number of them feature inscriptions by Lin Biao. This is not merely an Army matter, it is a problem that exists throughout the society at large.

In order to dispose appropriately of statues and badges that detract from the glorious image of Our Great Leader and Teacher Chairman Mao, we suggest the following:

1. Units and organizations that have large stores of badges, statues, embroidered images, paintings and quotation badges similar to those described in the above, regardless of whether they are fully- or only partially-complete, should hand them over to their political departments for disposal. All objects that are: i. crudely made and substandard; ii. are warped or damaged; or, iii. marked with inscriptions by Lin Biao, are to be destroyed. The metal, paper and chemical materials remaining should be recycled by local factories. In the case of porcelain and plaster works these should be broken up and buried in suitable locations.

2. The disposal of these statuettes and badges is an extremely serious business. The relevant Party committees involved should strengthen ideo-

logical and political work during the disposal process and be sure to explain to the workers involved in carrying out this task its objectives and frame of reference so as to avoid any misunderstandings.

If these suggestions are found practicable, we propose to send notification to the Propaganda Department of the General Political Department, as well as to the Departments of Propaganda of all provinces, municipalities and autonomous regions for reference and action.

Central Department of Propaganda Circular Concerning the Withdrawal from Circulation of *Quotations from Chairman Mao* (12 February 1979)

A request has recently been received from the State Publishing Bureau inquiring how best to dispose of the huge number of *Quotations from Chairman Mao*, single-sheet quotations of Chairman Mao and portraits of the Chairman with the legends "Long live Chairman Mao" and "Eternal life to Chairman Mao" that exist. It is the Department's considered opinion that:

1. *Quotations from Chairman Mao* was produced by Lin Biao in an attempt to amass political capital. In it Mao Zedong Thought is taken out of context and distorted. Since its publication this book has had a widespread and pernicious influence. To eliminate the impact of Lin Biao and the "Gang of Four" the Xinhua and Guoji [International] Bookstores will halt all sales of *Quotations* in Chinese, minority and foreign languages forthwith. All remaining copies, apart from a small number to be kept by provincial Xinhua Bookstores for future use by the relevant organizations, are to be pulped.

Single-sheet quotations from Chairman Mao are to be dealt with in a similar manner and pulped.

2. Our embassies overseas and diplomatic staff, delegations visiting foreign countries and units working with foreigners are no longer to provide copies of *Quotations* in any language. If foreigners request this book they should be provided with *Selected Works of Mao Zedong* or single volumes of Chairman Mao's writings.

As for bookstores run by foreign friends that still have stocks of *Quotations* it is advisable to let them dispose of that stock. We will no longer replenish supplies.

3. Portraits of Chairman Mao which carry outdated legends like "Long live Chairman Mao" and "Eternal life to Chairman Mao," or which are yellowed and damaged, are to be withdrawn from sale and pulped.

Central Department of Propaganda Circular Concerning the Disposal of Quotation Signboards and Slogans (6 September 1979)

From 1979 onwards, the Hong Kong Chinese press and the foreign media speculated about the fate of Mao whenever prominent political slogans were repainted or removed in Beijing. The large slogan signboards at the Chang'an-Dongdan, Chang'an-Wangfujing and Chang'an-Xidan intersections in the centre of the city, and the billboards on the eastern flank of the Ministry of Public Security near Tiananmen and the west side of the Great Hall of the People were under constant obvervation.

This Department of Propaganda circular marked the beginning of the end of Mao slogans in the streets of Chinese cities. The process took some years to complete.

Recently, we have received a number of letters from various regions and departments as well as the masses reporting that some slogan boards and slogan pylons, slogans on walls and buildings, certain bas reliefs and statues erected in the streets and squares in large and medium cities throughout the nation, and also in county townships, organizations, schools, mines, factories, villages and pastoral areas often contain incorrect sentiments and are obviously outmoded; others have been seriously eroded by the elements and are in a state of disrepair. All of the above have a negative political impact. Furthermore, many people have voiced their criticisms of this type of propaganda. These reports are quite timely and the method of dealing with this matter is as follows:

1. A thorough cleaning up of signboards, slogan pylons, slogans, bas reliefs and statues in public places throughout the country is to be made. An investigation is to be carried out prior to the upcoming National Day [1 October]. In the first instance, units open to foreigners, tourist spots and areas where there are a lot of people are to be cleaned up. Those [slogans, etc.] that are erroneous, outdated or in ill-repair are to be removed. Slogans on prominent signboards that are in keeping with the spirit of the Third Plenum of the Eleventh Party Congress can, where appropriate, be retained;[1]

2. In realizing the Four Modernizations it is necessary that propaganda be effective. In the future, no matter whether it is in the cities or in villages, in units that are open to foreigners, tourist spots or residential areas it is important that propaganda is carried out in a clean and ordered atmosphere, one in which environmental work and beautification have taken place and less formalistic propaganda is carried out; and,

3. Implementing the above decision is an extremely serious business. It

is imperative that various erroneous attitudes be negated and that people liberate their thinking. Goals should be pursued with an attitude that is informed by Marxism-Leninism and Mao Zedong Thought. It is important that careful ideological work is carried out among the masses before taking action so as to avoid unnecessary confusion and rumour-mongering.[2]

Central Department of Propaganda Circular Concerning Eliminating Out-of-date Slogans (2 June 1980)

Since the Department of Propaganda issued its "Circular Concerning the Disposal of Quotation Signboards and Slogans" (Department of Propaganda document no. 14 [1979]) and the suggestion that slogans be dealt with was published in issues 6 and 11 of *Propaganda Trends*,[3] propaganda organs throughout the country have become mindful of this issue and have taken steps to deal with the problem. As a result, the situation has seen some improvement. However, some places have not made a concerted effort in this area and, although slogans have been painted over, with the passing of time the paint has worn off and the original slogans have reappeared. As the spirit of the Third and Fifth Plenums [of the Eleventh Party Congress] has possessed the hearts and minds of the people, passé and incorrect slogans have become increasingly repugnant to the masses. If they are not cleaned away they will seriously interfere with efforts to encourage stability and unity and further the construction of the Four Modernizations. The masses have recently been writing to the Department voicing their extreme displeasure with the situation.

The wiping out of all old slogans is a task that will brook no further delay. The Propaganda Departments in Party Committees throughout the country and in all organs and units should give this task top priority. It is necessary to take practical, effective and immediate measures to ensure this decision is implemented. A thorough investigation of the situation must be launched forthwith. All old and out-of-date slogans that do not conform with the spirit of the Third, Fourth and Fifth Plenums or with the propaganda guidelines formulated by this Department, regardless of whether they occur in urban centres, townships or villages, must be eliminated immediately and no trace of them is to be left. This task is to be completed before September this year. Inappropriate slogans dating from before the "Cultural Revolution," out-of-date slogans from the post–"Gang of Four" purge,[4] as well as temporary posters put up on the occasion of greeting or farewelling [Party leaders, groups, etc.] are also to be eliminated. As for problematic slogans or historically inaccurate images of a more permanent nature that have been carved (or built) into walls and buildings, or included in sculptures and statues, these too must be replaced with all speed. In cases where this is not feasible for either practical or economic reasons, they can remain *in situ* for the time being but only with the permission of relevant Party Committees above county level. However, positive and effective steps to deal with the problem should be considered.

We hereby reiterate that: in the future all propaganda work must be centred around the Four Modernizations, be practicable and effective. The posting of massive slogans and other kinds of formalism are not to be encouraged.

CPC Central Office Circular Concerning the Problem of Statues of Comrade Mao Zedong (6 November 1980)

Recently, controversy concerning statues of Comrade Mao Zedong has erupted in a number of places. The Secretariat of Party Central has discussed this issue and we herewith communicate the Centre's guidelines on the subject:

In the directives relating to Party Central's policy on "cutting back on propagating individuals" of 30 July this year, it was noted that excessive numbers of portraits of Comrade Mao Zedong are on display and it was recommended that these could gradually be reduced (but not all taken down at once) to an appropriate level.[5] In those directives no concomitant remarks were made about pre-existing steel and concrete statues or other durable sculptures. The Centre acknowledges this oversight. Such statues can be found throughout the country and although fairly common they are by no means numerous. Whereas preserving them will have no harmful effect, to eliminate them would prove quite difficult; there is absolutely no need to destroy them all in concert. On the contrary, it would be a disservice to the people of China if a few statues of Comrade Mao Zedong and monuments of historical significance were not left standing. Presently, controversy concerning such statues has arisen in a number of places (like Fudan University in Shanghai and Mengjin in Henan).[6] It is the wish of the Centre that no statues be destroyed in places where such debates have occurred. It is also hoped that those in favour of destroying the statues can be persuaded to renege so that opposing factions will not develop among the masses. In the case of other influential commemorative structures, if there is a need to close, demolish or remodel them, it is imperative that full explanations are made and persuasive propaganda is used to convince the masses of the necessity to do so.

Central Department of Propaganda Circular Concerning the Hanging of Portraits of Leaders in Public Places (29 July 1981)

Recently this Department has received numerous letters and telephone enquiries asking whether portraits of leaders can be displayed at meetings or hung in public in the future. In accordance with the relevant stipulations of Central Party documents Nos. 59 and 79 (1980) and in the spirit of the relevant speeches made by responsible comrades in the Centre, we hereby issue the following circular:

1. Henceforth, no official portraits will be displayed during meetings;

2. Portraits of Chairman Mao can be hung in public places but with due regard for moderation and dignity, and so as not to offend international sensibilities. Note that excessive numbers of portraits should not be hung, yet it is inappropriate to ban the display of portraits altogether;

3. No portraits of living central Party leaders are to be hung either during meetings or in public; and,

4. It is entirely up to the individuals as to whether they hang portraits of living or dead leading comrades in their homes or in private. It is forbidden for Party, state or army organizations at any level to interfere with individual preference in any way.

Notes

1. The Party's Third Plenum in December 1978 initiated the economy-oriented policies of the Reform era.

2. Among other things, this refers to rumours that the removal of Maoist slogans was a sign that Mao and his political legacy were being abandoned.

3. *Xuanchuan dongtai*, a restricted circulation reference journal devoted to propaganda issues.

4. Literally, "the movement to uncover, criticize and investigate [the crimes of the Gang of Four]" of 1976–77. In Chinese, *jiepicha yundong*.

5. Item 4 of that document reads:

> There are too many portraits of Chairman Mao, quotations from his writings and poems on display in public places. It is politically undignified and offensive to international sensibilities. Henceforth, they are to be reduced to an appropriate level ... Chairman Mao badges are to be recycled as far as possible so as to avoid an excessive waste of metals.

See "Zhonggong zhongyang guanyu jianchi 'shao xuanchuan geren' de jige wentide zhishi, Zhongfa [1980] 59 hao, 1980 nian 7 yue 30 ri," in Zhongyang xuanchuan bu bangongting, ed., *Dangde xuanchuan gongzuo wenjian xuanbian (1976–1992)*, vol. 2, p. 706.

6. The statue of Mao at the entrance of Fudan University was maintained and, throughout the 1980s, a calligraphic inscription by Lin Biao, Mao's one-time close comrade-in-arms and chosen successor, although painted over, could still be discerned on the plaque at the base of the statue. Mengjin is a county seat north of Luoyang, Henan Province. The Mao statue there was demolished without prior consultation resulting in a public furor.

Mao, a Best-Seller

Gao Jiangbo

Following the short-lived resurgence of interest in Cultural Revolution cul-
ture and history during the mid 1980s, a new phase of (relative) publishing
freedom in the late 1980s led to a boom in the Mao industry. Many popular
works related to Mao's life and the more controversial aspects of Commu-
nist Party history were produced.

The tabloid press had proved to be extremely popular as soon as it was
allowed to develop in 1984–85. Now, cashing in on general interest in
scandal and mudracking, and spurred on by the imperatives of economic
rationalism, publishing houses throughout the country vied with each other
to exploit the nascent Mao Cult. The ideologically correct, like the author of
this article which was published in a straitlaced publishing trade paper in
April 1989, were disturbed by the lawlessness of the industry. In the stilted
prose of an official out of touch with everyday reality, Gao calls for clear
guidelines and policies in the hope that the publishing anarchy could be
quelled. Although some contentious works were banned after 4 June 1989,
consumer demand and weakened Party control meant that politically incor-
rect works continued to appear in the 1990s.

Since the second half of last year [1988], there has been a marked increase in the publication of biographies and works of reportage related to
Party and state leaders. This has created something of a publishing phenomenon and there is every indication that it will continue to develop. The
volume of book sales indicates that there is a considerable market for such
publications. Similarly, the media and public have noted this development
and people are studying it. Some of these studies are particularly outspoken
about certain aspects of the phenomenon. The main events in the lives of
Party and state leaders are invariably linked to major incidents in Party
history. For this reason, the material dealt with in such biographies is of a
highly sensitive nature and therefore requires serious analysis.

Periodicals (including periodicals produced as books)[1] have featured in the present publishing frenzy, and publishers are in competition to produce works of reportage on the lives of the nation's leaders. The lion's share of these depict the life and activities of Comrade Mao Zedong. I believe that the MaoCraze that has developed in our periodicals has come about for a number of reasons.

In the past, specific historical factors meant that very few biographical works related to Party and state leaders could appear.[2] With the gradual deepening of Reform and the approaching fortieth anniversary of the founding of the People's Republic of China [in 1989], people are given to reflecting on our journey through history in the hope that some lessons can be drawn from the past. Many people, specialists and general readers alike, are therefore anxious to gain a deeper and more concrete understanding of our leaders, both past and present. Because of Comrade Mao Zedong's unique role in the Chinese revolution it is understandable that he is the focus of such attention. At the same time, interest in Mao Zedong reflects a deep reverence for the achievements of Older Revolutionaries in general, their outstanding political morals and frugal lifestyle. This public interest has been further piqued by the fact that because political life in China was not sufficiently open to public scrutiny, our leaders have, in both their political and private lives, worked under a cloak of mystery. The publications that have appeared recently, therefore, make it possible for readers to appreciate the amazing foresight and superhuman efforts that our Great Leader made in his public life, as well as allowing them to gain an insider's understanding of the everyday pleasures and sorrows he experienced, including details of his relationship with his children. This, if anything, has brought our Leader closer to us. Some works have also revealed thrilling and titillating episodes in the Chairman's career, thereby satisfying a kind of popular voyeurism. . . .

The above analysis shows that the MaoCraze in publishing has developed for a number of complex reasons and in response to a specific public need. The majority of works published in journals objectively introduce the revolutionary achievements of Comrade Mao Zedong, and evaluate various historical personages in a balanced and truthful fashion, thereby helping readers gain an accurate understanding of our Revolutionary Leaders and major historical incidents. However, we must point out the shortcomings of these publications, some of which are quite grave. From my own reading, I would classify the problem areas in the following way:

1. Distortions of history that occur because of the evaluation of major incidents in Party history or the misrepresentation of historical figures on the basis of biased or erroneous views. . . .

2. The smearing and depreciation of Comrade Mao Zedong's image.

Some works make a point of dwelling on the details of Mao Zedong's early married life. They put words into the mouths of some Red Army soldiers to make the point that Zhou Enlai was a true gentleman whereas Mao was "a lascivious lord of the manor." The point here is not the accuracy of such information but that we do not see what possible relevance excessive attention to these matters can have for the reader. Admittedly, writers should not avoid the truth just because the subject is a deeply revered individual; however, to describe the private life of a Great Leader respected by the entire nation in such a fashion is not a mark of courage, but an act of egregious vilification.

There are also works that negate entirely the political struggles that occurred after 1949, including the Suppression of Counterrevolutionaries, as well as the Three-Anti and the Five-Anti Campaigns.[3] They even claim that during these movements Mao himself made "tens of millions of enemies" and, to prevent any of these people from plotting against him as well as to protect his Chairman's throne, he began to study the history of court intrigue, becoming increasingly paranoid and secretive in his movements. In the hands of such writers, our Revolutionary Leader ends up looking like a feudal emperor imprisoned in solitary splendor.

3. The sensational revelation of the so-called behind-the-scenes story of major internal Party struggles through which writers speculate on and distort the motives and psychology of key political figures.

In limning Mao's life many works also dwell on internal Party struggles and in so doing touch on many Central Leaders who have either passed away or who are still in positions of authority. Since their sources are unreliable these accounts are often contradictory and analytically inconsistent. This makes it extremely difficult for readers to distinguish fact from fiction and leads to considerable confusion.

Works, for example, that describe the Lushan Meeting[4] quote verbatim the debate between Mao and Peng Dehuai, including all the swearing. Various versions of this exchange exist. There are also a number of mutually contradictory evaluations of this historical episode and of the people involved. How are readers expected to judge any of this for themselves?

Then there are the works that speculate on the motives of historical figures and indulge in barefaced distortions. There are those who claim that the real reason Mao did not retain his position as State President [in 1959] was that he wanted to let Liu Shaoqi clean up the mess he had created with the Great Leap Forward in 1958. Then there are works that claim that when, in 1965, Mao repeatedly let it be known that he would "soon be meeting his Maker," he was only saying this to gauge Liu Shaoqi's attitude and give himself time to initiate the Cultural Revolution. Such subjective speculations are baseless and serve only to confuse the reader.

4. The contents of such works are often vulgar and absurd. They also at times propagate feudal superstition.

China's feudal emperors often spoke of themselves as "True Dragons and Sons of Heaven," and these new writings regularly describe our Revolutionary Leaders in such terms. One work says that China has had three Sons of Heaven since 1949: Mao Zedong, Hua Guofeng, and Hu Yaobang. Other works are even more absurd and ridden with superstition. One, for example, has an old man claim that Mao was a true Son of Heaven since he lived eighty-three years and ruled as emperor for forty-one of those. And this is no isolated instance, for in another work it is claimed that, in 1949, Mao Zedong asked a Daoist priest to tell his fortune. The priest supposedly gave him a prediction, a piece of paper with the four numbers "8341" written on it. People note that Mao lived eighty-three years and was Chairman of the Party for forty-one years.[5]

Then there are works that analyze the *dramatis personæ* [of Chinese politics] on the basis of physiognomy. They say that Mao "had a majestic and large mouth and ears with thick lobes just like Milo Buddha," therefore he was "preternaturally clever and enlightened" for which he "won the support of others and achieved respect and honor." It is shocking to read works that depict a Revolutionary Leader in such a patently absurd and superstitious fashion.

The responsibility for such writings lies not only with their authors but also with the publishers themselves. Some writers follow neither the spirit nor the letter of Party Central's official evaluation of Comrade Mao and Party history. Instead they rely on fantasy and imagination. Other authors simply do not take their work seriously and make little effort to collect historical documentation or undertake the meticulous research required. Their efforts are cursory in the extreme and rely on whatever they have on hand to manufacture works of fiction. Other writers garner all manner of material, including politically biased information, from the Hong Kong and Taiwan press. There is even a small number of writers who simply throw together whatever rumors they happen to have heard. . . .

As for publishers, there are two other problems deserving our attention: the Party leadership of some periodical publishers have a very underdeveloped concept of Party discipline. They blatantly ignore the relevant regulations and act exactly as they see fit, producing works that distort Party history and sully the image of Mao Zedong without having made any attempt to subject them to a rigorous editorial process. Furthermore, some publishers place fiscal gain over quality, fossick around for manuscripts and publish books without a thought as to their actual worth. It is no surprise, then, that the errors outlined in the above are so common.

The MaoCraze in periodical publications is evidence of the popularity of such works among readers. Be that as it may, in terms of the publishing industry, things are far from satisfactory. At present, an ever-increasing volume of such material is being produced and the situation is becoming quite grave. The result is widespread concern among readers everywhere. It is necessary for the relevant authorities to formulate coherent policies with clear guidelines for the publication of biographies and works of reportage related to the lives of Party and state leaders so that publishers can be adequately supervised in the future.

Notes

1. Due to the restrictions on the number of new journals and periodicals that could appear, for both economic and political reasons, publishers often produced journals in the guise of books, using state-allocated "book numbers" (*shuhao*) to do so.

2. "Specific historical factors" is a delightful circumlocution that disguises the fact that the reasons were entirely political.

3. *Zhenya fangeming yundong* and the *Sanfan, wufan yundong*. The Suppression was launched in mid 1950 and aimed at the "elimination of all bandits, special agents, local tyrants and other counter-revolutionaries that harm the People." It continued into 1951. The Three-Anti Movement was launched in early 1952 and was aimed at "opposing corruption, waste and bureaucracy inside the Party and State organs." The Five-Anti Movement was initiated in 1952 "to oppose bribery, tax evasion, theft of state property, cheating on government contracts and stealing economic information for the purposes of speculation."

4. The Party's Lushan Meeting of 1959 was one during which Peng Dehuai criticized Mao and the Great Leap Forward. This led to Peng's fall from power.

5. Many works have also pointed out that the Central Committee Security Force was called "Unit 8341" and it is widely believed that Mao so named his "praetorian guard" after having his fortune told.

The Mao Phenomenon:
A Survivor's Critique

Li Jie

*Li Jie, a Shanghai-based cultural critic, wrote a lengthy study of Mao
Zedong in early 1989 from which the following excerpts are taken. This
idiosyncratic but thought-provoking article was published in* A Hundred
Schools *(Baijia), a controversial Anhui journal banned following 4 June
1989. Li Jie's critique was daring even for the pre–4 June era of outspo-
kenness.*

*Readers familiar with the work of the U.S.-based academic Lung-kee Sun,
author of* The 'Deep Structure' of Chinese Culture *(Zhongguo wenhuade
"shenceng jiegou") which had such an impact in China in the early to mid
1980s, may see something of Sun's style here. Psychoanalytic and cultural
anaylsis of Mao was a feature of important early Western studies by academics like Richard H. Solomon and Lucian W. Pye.[1] Perhaps the only
comparable critique of Mao by a younger Mainland writer was published in
Hong Kong by Liu Xiaobo, one of Li Jie's bêtes noires, in late 1988.[2] Both
Li and Liu's writings on Mao are suffused with the venomous anger—not to
mention the overweening self-importance—of ill-tempered and unfilial sons
resentful of a patriarch whose influence lives on beyond the grave. Or, as Li
Jie puts it: "It is obvious that the Chinese father complex is not one that
leads to patricide but merely to jealousy of the father figure."*

*This excerpt from Li Jie is followed by two denunciations published in
the post–89 purge. It is also instructive to read Li Jie in juxtaposition to He
Xin's pro-Mao palaver. Interestingly, Li Jie's highly negative evaluation of
the contemporary Chinese character is essentially the same as that made by
He Xin elsewhere.[3]*

Although the Mao Zedong phenomenon is a historical fact it is not
merely a historical phenomenon, it is also a cultural phenomenon as well as
being a phenomenon with psychological, linguistic, political, and even eco-

nomic, military, literary, philosophical, as well as physiological and anthropological dimensions. Our understanding of it also depends on how far a study of the phenomenon goes. I merely want to make the point here that the Mao phenomenon is one with a very broad and rich ambit. Yet I feel that it is up to others to define and explicate its contents and ramifications more thoroughly. I can thereby save myself some effort and say that, for me, the study of the phenomenon of Mao Zedong is no more than an academic exercise that may or may not interest others.

For a nation like China, one that has already put so much work into creating *The Dream of the Red Chamber* studies and Lu Xun studies,[4] it would be woeful if we fail to develop "Mao studies." It is quite possible that the establishment of Mao studies will be of the greatest significance and value to the Chinese and to Chinese history. Naturally, this will not merely be limited to its scientific relevance.

In terms of both scale and time, the Chinese have already put a great deal into the study of Mao's *Selected Works*. But just how many people can really say they understand Mao Zedong? And that goes for people who knew Mao personally. Rather than blaming this ignorance on low IQs, I would say it has more to do with the linguistic fog that Mao shrouded himself in, both intentionally and unintentionally. His works, pronouncements, thought, and action created a veritable magnetic field that drew countless Chinese in; once inside this field of attraction, no one could really unravel the mysteries of it. No matter how learned or capable a person was, as soon as that person entered this force field, he or she was blinded as to its true significance. It was as though the individual had entered a mysterious cave. Mao has mesmerized many scholars who have attempted to study him. . . . To understand Mao, therefore, we have to break free of the force field, only then can we develop a scientific and rational attitude toward Mao; only then can we regain our awareness and innate sensitivity. There are many ways of breaking free of the Mao force field. In this study I employ two methods that are presently very popular although little applied to Mao: modern psychology and comparative cultural studies. These two methods will allow me to make Mao into a Chinese once more, albeit a very rare type of Chinese. He suffers many of the particular deficiences of the Chinese. These are things that no non-Chinese specialist could understand even after a lifetime of work. Only with the aid of a Chinese who has experienced Chinese reality can an outside observer adequately explain and analyze this "Chinese ugliness." I am just such a Chinese. . . .

There is a perfect symmetry between the structure of the Chinese family and the style of Chinese politics. The "emperor's art," as it is called, is divided into the Way of the Hegemon and the Way of the King, the two are mutually complementary. In the family, the father and mother serve a similar role, complementing each other: the father rules with an iron fist and the mother through kindness; the former is the unyielding *yang*, the latter the passive *yin*. The father is tough and resolute, the mother moderate and mild. The parallels between the family and the government are particularly obvious in post-1949 politics with Mao Zedong playing the father to Zhou Enlai's mother. It was as though this particular political marriage was made in heaven. . . .

Because of the symmetry between the family and political life, the Chinese obsession with rejecting the father and loving the mother has acquired a particular cultural significance. Despite the fact that it can at times pair off into a relationship like that between Mao and Zhou, in general, the father-mother relationship is like the two sides of a coin. In China, father-hating often expresses itself in terms of the peasant rebellion [against the father/emperor]. Such rebelliousness is completely irrational and seeks only its own gratification, the negation and overthrowing of everything. It relies on personal whim as its sole standard for the evaluation of good and evil. Superficially, such rebels appear to be individually rejecting, as they do, all authority and always ready to be iconoclastic. In reality, they are, without exception, worshippers of the very things they wish to oppose and overthrow. Following every rebellion, victorious rebels invariably re-create what they had set out to destroy. It's all like a rehearsal of Ah Q's revolution. The successful Ah Q simply replaces [his overlord] Master Zhao. The defeated Master Zhao then becomes another Ah Q.[5] The revolution fails, therefore, to eliminate either Ah Q or Master Zhao. It is obvious that the Chinese father complex is not one that leads to patricide but merely to jealousy of the father figure. This most often expresses itself in a desire to rebel and replace the father.

If we are to say that Mao Zedong was China's greatest rebel then we must also admit that he was the most typical of all Chinese father-haters, or a man jealous of his father. At about the same time as he was speaking with Edgar Snow [in the 1930s about his unhappy relationship with his father], Mao penned that famous poem:

> But alas! Qin Shihuang and Han Wudi
> Were lacking in literary grace,
> And Tang Taizong and Song Taizu
> Had little poetry in their souls;
> And Genghis Khan,
> Proud Son of Heaven for a day,
> Knew only shooting eagles, bow outstretched.
> All are past and gone!

For truly great men
Look to this age alone.[6]

The tone is self-confident and heroic, certainly, but it also reveals a deep admiration and jealousy. Here was the peasant boy listing all of the major father figures of Chinese history, leaving the last and most glorious position, however, for himself. There is a grand boldness of vision all right, but behind that vision lurks an ugly cultural pettiness. Grand or petty, it is a typical example of the Chinese obsession with the father. . . .

This obsession is, at its root, an expression of a mother-complex. The Chinese hate the father who takes the form of ruling emperor, but they cleave to the idea of the mother lode, an autocratic system and feudal culture, a nurturing womb for the emperor. . . . The Chinese yearn for the earth just as, in political-psychological terms, they yearn for the ruler. The Motherland is always depicted in the most ravishing, feminine terms. Similarly, for the Chinese, a good emperor is a caring, beneficent and warm figure, not a cold, serious, distant, and harsh ruler. Although the emperor is a father figure, the Chinese invariably idealize him so he becomes a mother-substitute. . . .

The secret of Mao's success lies in the fact that he created a belief system for the masses and launched a grand enterprise. The victorious Mao combined the elements of Sage-ruler (based on a belief system) with that of the political hero (realized through his autocracy). He reached a pinnacle of success unprecedented in the thousands of years of Chinese history. The power of belief cannot be underestimated. Qin Shihuang, Han Wudi, Tang Taizu, and Song Taizu all enjoyed periods of ultimate power,[7] but which of them became a popular god? Mao's success was, primarily, the success of the masses' belief in him. . . .

The greatest secret of Mao Zedong's success lies in the understanding of the Chinese that he shared with Lu Xun.[8] Whereas Lu Xun used his insight to criticize the Chinese, Mao utilized the weaknesses of the Chinese to further his own Mao-style revolution. . . .

The decade-long Cultural Revolution is often described as a period during which Chinese killed Chinese, or Communists fought Communists. It would be more precise, however, to say that it was a mêlée in which Mao Zedong became entangled with Mao Zedong. This is because, by 1966, the Chinese could only think Mao Zedong Thought; they had suffered a complete stupefaction of their own thought processes. Hundreds of millions of people were turned into clones of Mao himself. They all believed they belonged to Mao, regardless of whether they were rebelling against the authorities or protecting the powerholders, regardless of whether they declared themselves to be revolutionaries or were branded counterrevolutionaries. They all believed there was only one Mao and they belonged to him. Even today there are probably many people who still do not realize that in his later years Mao was schizophrenic. Mao was, on the one hand, ordering them to rebel while, at the same time, he called on them to protect the proletarian Motherland. It was nothing less than a black comedy. . . .

During those years, anyone who had a modicum of power as a rebel leader would turn into a mini-Mao. The way they talked, their enunciation, speech patterns, and even grammar were all *à la* Mao. The most convincing evidence of this was the use of Mao quotes by both sides as a weapon during every debate and bloody skirmish. They all cried, "We swear an oath to protect Chairman Mao with our lives." The Chinese were not fighting with one another; two Mao Zedong's were locked in mortal combat. . . .

It is a truism to say that you get the government you deserve. The collective stupidity of the Chinese meant that they got, and they deserved nothing more than to get, a ruler like Mao Zedong. Here we should point out that the Mao Cult in the Cultural Revolution was not a metaphysical phenomenon, as it is understood in Western religious history. It was not simply a spiritual phenomenon, a religious haven for those who were in crisis. Rather, it was a practical political and ethical choice, a form of emotional hysteria resulting from the collapse of rationalism. Chinese feudalism had finally reached an apogee; in the Mao Cult a perfect symmetry was achieved between politics, ethics, morals, and psychology. If we take Qin Shihuang to be the progenitor of this style of feudal culture, then Mao Zedong is its historical conclusion. He marks the completion of a perfect historical cycle. Mao Zedong used the most extreme methods to bring to an end this form of historical extremism.

Of course, once he had reached this point Mao imploded in on himself. . . .

The cultural ramifications of the personality split Mao suffered in his last years have only been fully realized in the 1980s. Mao came to embody the moral and political icon (sage-emperor) so dear to the hearts of the Chinese. The moment that the living icon Mao and the worship of him came to an end, the Chinese lost all cultural coherence. The Chinese of the 1980s are a discombobulated people. Their icon has crumbled and with it their psychological linchpin has disappeared. Extreme mental imbalance has either turned them into unprincipled louts or forced them to search for a new spiritual goal. With the death of the tyrannical father his ignorant progeny survive as a dark and brooding mass. They have no self-confidence and readily abandon any vestige of self-respect. What others possess they lack entirely; their very existence is little different from that of most primitive animals. Their sole criterion for thought and action is a passive response to external material stimulation plus a crude need to gratify the senses. . . .

Mao's philosophy of struggle cast the Chinese into the abyss of feudalism and now forces them to reascend the peak of humanism. Mao could destroy the Chinese, but he can also save them; the path they choose is entirely up to the Chinese themselves.

Sadly, in the 1980s, the Chinese seem to have forgotten the historical lessons Mao taught us (or perhaps we have not even bothered considering them). Most people are too busy struggling for power, making money, or fleeing the country with their families to care. Few have the time to consider the desperate need we have to change the cultural and psychological state of China today. Mao may have made us all enact his philosophy of political struggle, but his is a rare and important historical legacy.

. . . Mao Zedong conquered the Chinese and their society. To what extent they understand this and can overcome it is hard to say. It is entirely up to the Chinese themselves, for they have to use their intelligence and talents to start from where Mao left off: with the Cultural Revolution. The situation is similar to that of Western culture following World War II when new things had to grow out from the rubble left by Hitler. . . .

Mao was a very rare revolutionary leader. We can compare the significance of Mao Zedong in Chinese history to the importance of Hitler in world history. It is a creative thing. In a sense, modernism would not have come about without Hitler. Similarly, Mao created the conditions for modernism and postmodernism in China. . . .

Of course, Mao Zedong left other indelible impressions on the life of the Chinese. In both the villages and cities of China in the 1980s, Mao's shadow can be seen everywhere. Whenever you see a shop assistant rudely ask a customer what he wants; whenever a concierge shouts at a visitor; whenever a policeman lectures in an imperious manner someone who has violated traffic regulations; whenever an official makes a report in front of a microphone in a droning monotone . . . you can always make out the shadow of Mao in the background. People may have learned nothing of Mao's "art of struggle" but they all know the rude and arbitrary style he would adopt when he was out of sorts. To use an expression current in the Cultural Revolution, they all "can give attitude just like a Revolutionary Rebel." . . .

Mao Zedong has left us with many riddles. Some are obvious like the abiding need the Chinese have for the mother-fixation as expressed in terms of the culture of small farm production. But it is more layered and complex than that. There is, in particular, a need for self-awakening and self-reconstruction. The Chinese, in particular Chinese intellectuals, still probably have not realized that they have more than a basic right to exist. They also have the right to live as human beings. Whenever this right is abused, they should arouse themselves in self-defense. It is a defense that should not come in the form of carnivalesque mass movements; rather, it should find expression in independent activities such as finding recourse in the law [when you are wronged]. Only when the Chinese have learned their right to such a life and their need to protect it will the Mao Zedong era truly draw to an end. Only then will China's feudal history be over.

The phenomenon of Mao Zedong has not disappeared; on the contrary, its covert influence continues to inveigle itself into the society and the soul of every Chinese. . . . Regardless of whether we view it historically or in terms of our present predicament, we should think of the Mao phenomenon not as a beginning but as a full-stop.

January–10 February 1989, Shanghai-Guiyang

Notes

1. See Richard H. Solomon, *Mao's Revolution and the Chinese Political Culture*; and Lucian W. Pye, *Mao Tse-tung: The Man in the Leader.*

2. See Liu Xiaobo, "Hunshi mowang Mao Zedong," 11; and Barmé and Jaivin, eds., *New Ghosts, Old Dreams*, p. xxvi, for a quotation from Liu's article.

3. See, for example, He Xin quoted in Barmé and Jaivin, eds., *New Ghosts, Old Dreams*, p. 213.

4. *The Dream of the Red Chamber* studies (*Hongloumeng xue*, or simply *Hongxue*) refers to the academic and journalistic industry devoted to the dissection of the famous mid-Qing novel *The Dream of the Red Chamber* (or *The Story of the Stone*) written by Cao Xueqin and Gao E, a book regarded as depicting a microcosmic Chinese world. Lu Xun studies (*Lu Xun xue* or *Luxue*) have made a major cultural industry out of the analysis of the writer Lu Xun (d. 1936). Both are sponsored by the state.

5. This is a reference to Lu Xun's fictional tale "The True Story of Ah Q" (*A Q zhengzhuan*) published in the early 1920s.

6. Mao Zedong, "Snow," see Mao Tsetung, *Poems*, pp. 23–24.

7. Qin Shihuang, Han Wudi, Tang Taizu and Song Gaozu were prominent rulers of the Qin, Han, Tang and Song dynasties respectively.

8. For more on Mao and Lu Xun, see "Chairman Mao Graffiti" below.

Crazed Critics: Two Views of Li Jie

Ying Congying and Meng Fei

I

"The Mao Phenomenon" is a pernicious work that launches an open and reckless attack on Mao Zedong Thought, as well as Comrade Mao's achievements, while also indulging in character assassination. At one point, the author, a "famous young critic," compares Comrade Mao Zedong to Qin Shihuang[1] and plays on this theme in the most incoherent language. He says: "If we take Qin Shihuang to be the progenitor of this style of feudal culture, then Mao Zedong is its historical conclusion. He marks the completion of a perfect historical cycle. Mao Zedong used the most extreme methods to bring an end to this form of historical extremism." Then he likens Comrade Mao to Adolf Hitler, the leader of international Fascism, and makes the wild claim that: "We can compare the significance of Mao Zedong in Chinese history to the importance of Hitler in world history."

At the end of a process of absurd reduction and extrapolation this "critic" declares that Mao Zedong was a schizophrenic and, in his last years, "mentally unbalanced." As proof the author cites Mao Zedong's strategy to "entice" all of China's intellectuals into a trap so he could "eliminate" them. The fact that Mao never wore a Western-style suit is presented as evidence that he "despised" "leading intellectuals and institutions of higher learning."

The article moves from its attack on Mao Zedong to a denunciation of the Party, the People, as well as Socialism. The author fulminates that: "The phenomenon of Mao Zedong has not disappeared; on the contrary, its covert influence continues to inveigle itself into the society and the soul of every Chinese." He vilifies the whole Chinese nation when he claims that Chinese people are suffering from "collective imbecility."

Can any Chinese citizen possessed of normal powers of judgement remain unmoved when they read these vicious slanders against Comrade Mao Zedong, the Communist Party of China, Socialism and the Chinese People?

—*Ying Congying, March 1991*

II

It is accepted wisdom that after the Chinese walked out of the mists of the personality cult Mao once more became a man. He is no longer a god. The author of "The Mao Phenomenon," however, applies his "perspicacity and sensitivity" in an attempt "to make Mao into a Chinese once more." This is hardly a creative endeavour worthy of comment.

When one has plodded through this article what manifests itself in the mind's eye is certainly not the image of an endearing and lovable Chinese. What we are presented with is "a violent father," a Qin Shihuang-esque autocrat, "a genius of strife," a master of internal attrition, a "political leader drunk on power," a "willful child," "a peasant boy spoilt by mass adulation," an abnormal individual who was "mentally unstable." . . .

But enough of all that! We can't tolerate quoting any more of this stuff. No matter what people say, Mao Zedong is a Proletarian Revolutionary Leader who, in the final analysis, deserves the respect of the whole nation and should be a source of pride. Are all of these deprecations, satirical slurs, slanders and attacks typical of the "scientific attitude" of a serious scholar?

At the very outset, the author makes it more than clear that he thinks the "Mao phenomenon" is nothing more than an "academic exercise." The reader hardly need bother picking up the political subtext of the author's argument, however, since the text is strewn with provocative expressions like those quoted in the above. Rather than claiming this to be academic research, let's call it what it really is: an expression of political disgruntlement.

—*Meng Fei, April 1991*

Note

1. Mao once made the comparison to Qin Shihuang himself. "So what's the big deal about Qin Shihuang? He only buried 460 Confucians alive; well, we've buried 46,000. . . . We're a hundred times greater than Qin Shihuang." At the time the comparison was regarded as risible, although both Lin Biao's followers and the Li Yizhe group in Guangzhou were to make the same comparison, for somewhat different reasons, in the 1970s. See Mao Zedong, "Zai bada erci huiyishangde jianghua, di yici jiang hua (1958 nian 5 yue 8 ri)," in *Mao Zedong tongzhi shi dangdai zui weidade Makesi-Lieningzhuyizhe,* p. 195.

From Sartre to Mao Zedong

Hua Ming

Published in the People's Daily *in early 1990, this article is typical of the positive interpretation that the authorities gave the Mao Cult as it developed from mid 1989.*

The "Sartre craze" first swept Beijing University in 1979, and over the following ten years, along with the "fad for Freud" and the "vogue for Nietzsche," it swelled and subsided, leaving everyone quite dizzy. Cool reflection reveals that below the surface of these crazes was a cargo cult for all manner of foreign import. But university campuses are places that are forever trying to come up with something different. And as we enter the 1990s, a new message is emanating from them.

Now, university students are "Mao-crazy."

—On 26 December [Mao's birthday] 1989, more than ten universities in the capital organized a "rediscover Mao Zedong" seminar at the Chairman Mao Memorial Hall in Tiananmen Square;

—Mao Xinyu, Chairman Mao's grandson, an undergraduate in the History Department of the Chinese People's University, is increasingly popular with his fellow students, who crowd around to hear his stories about his granddad;

—Whether it's at schools in the capital like Beijing University, the People's University, Beijing Normal University, China Youth Political College, or in the border regions like Jishou University, or Luzhou Medical College in the southwest.... Mao Zedong's philosophical writings and poems have been exhumed from under layers of dust, and are once more attracting attention. Books like *A Biography of Mao Zedong* and *Mao Zedong's Family History* are particularly popular.

—Shaoshan, Mao Zedong's birthplace, an unpopular destination for so many years, hosted more than 1.8 million visitors in 1989, 70 percent of whom were young people, and the majority of those were middle school and university students;

—At Beijing University students are organizing themselves into special groups for the study of Marxism-Leninism and Mao Zedong's writings.

What are we to make of the new craze? Everyone is talking about it. Most people are of the opinion that university students have now found the answers to China's problems in the treasury of Mao Zedong Thought. To build a new China one has to understand China's national characteristics. . . . This writer believes this is the root cause of the MaoCraze.

What was the greatest lesson taught to us by the disturbance in the spring and summer of 1989? Intense and profound reflection has led university students to the conclusion that Western remedies cannot provide cures for China's ills. . . . Over the past century of change . . . when it comes to understanding the realities of China, no one can compare to Mao Zedong; and no one has achieved such successes. Mao Zedong's call to "adapt the universal theory of Marxism to the practical situation of China," together with Deng Xiaoping's formulation to "build socialism with Chinese characteristics," represent the crystallization of the living essence of Mao Zedong Thought. Following last year's [1989] disturbance, university students have spoken of "searching for Mao Zedong, and being ashamed of [their] attitude to Deng Xiaoping." This is a sign of their determination to discard all Western philosophy and political thought and soberly confront the realities of China.

Over the past decade, a generation of young Chinese intellectuals have traveled the path from Sartre to Mao Zedong. It has been a tortuous journey and much time has been spent in deep thought, but they have now found the road that leads from vacuousness to relative maturity.

Permanently on Heat: An Interview with Comrade Deng Liqun

Deng Liqun, or Little Deng (Xiao Deng) *as he was called to distinguish him from Old Deng* (Lao Deng), *Deng Xiaoping, was a leading ideological watchdog from the late 1970s. He honed his political skills as a disciple of Chen Boda, a prominent Party "ghost writer" and ideological hack, during the Yan'an purges of the early 1940s. By the early 1990s, Little Deng played the role of token Maoist in Party Central, one of his concerns being to concoct an official history of the People's Republic. In 1994, he was involved in the founding and publication of the very PC journal,* Research Into Contemporary Chinese History (Dangdai Zhongguoshi yanjiu). *Deng's was the voice of ideological rectitude and stability. His comically stilted language exudes a certain nostalgic charm for those familiar with the heyday of the wooden language of Chinese Communism. This interview first appeared in the December 1991 issue of* Zhongliu, *a magazine established by ideological revanchists following the 1989 purge.*

Question: As a social phenomenon the MaoCraze has been the center of both Chinese and international attention, study, and analysis for some time. ... As an Older Comrade who has worked for many years at the front line of ideological and theoretical work, you have devoted considerable energy to discussing this issue.[1] In your comments you have expressed the concern typical of Older Comrades in developments among the young and have evinced your keen interest in the fate of socialism. It is not surprising, then, that so many young people are deeply impressed with your stance. Many of our readers hope that you will take advantage of this forum to discuss your views at length.

Answer: During the high tide of Bourgeois Liberalization a few years ago [from 1987 to 1989] there was a tendency to negate, undervalue, vilify, and attack Comrade Mao Zedong and Mao Zedong Thought, and under this guise these attacks aimed at denigrating Comrade Deng Xiaoping, as well as other members of the Older Generation of Revolutionaries. Things came to a head when it became fashionable to act in this way. Similarly, a general ambience called the "three belief crisis"[2] developed in the society.

Following the political turbulence that occurred in Beijing in 1989, particularly after the setbacks suffered in Eastern Europe and the disintegration of the Soviet Union, there has been an unprecedented international wave of anticommunism. Some have even declared that "communism is dead." It is noteworthy that given this situation China is experiencing a MaoCraze, particularly among sensitive young intellectuals. It is a Craze that is, if anything, becoming more pronounced. It is a remarkable development not only for socialism in China but also in terms of the history of the communist movement. It is out-of-the-ordinary and worthy of reflection and study. It calls for a Marxist interpretation.

Q: I recall that at a symposium of young intellectuals organized by the Beijing magazine *University Student* in January 1990, a number of young people spoke up about this and attempted their own analysis of it. At that meeting Xin Ming, a research student at Beijing University (and the author of the article "Discovering Mao Zedong"[3]), responded to a question about what had led to the MaoCraze by quoting from a poem by the Chairman to the effect that "Today, a miasmal mist once more rising, / We hail Sun Wukung, the wonder-worker."[4] And, when replying to a question related to how he saw the setbacks suffered by socialism in Eastern Europe, he used another line from Mao: "Plum blossoms welcome the whirling snow; / Small wonder flies freeze and perish."[5] Such thoughtful explanations fascinated other participants and were subsequently commented on and repeated by many people in public speeches and articles.

A: Such responses and explanations [like that of Xin Ming] are indeed very descriptive as well as being quite *à propos* and fairly incisive. What is more significant is that a young person should formulate such responses. It is also evidence that the MaoCraze is no longer being seen in a superficial way, simply in terms of the Craze itself, but that there are those who are analyzing it from a broader and deeper historical perspective that attempts a rational and theoretical level of analysis. Indeed, with the unprecedented international wave of revisionist thought, coupled with the tide of Bourgeois Liberalism in China, we have indeed seen "a miasmal mist once more rising." This is the historical root-cause of the MaoCraze we have been witnessing of late.

Regardless of whether we see the MaoCraze in terms of a social phenomenon or we look at it in an attempt to understand and explain it, we are all faced with the fact that it has been continually developing and evolving.

We must realize that the younger generation lacks personal experience of Comrade Mao Zedong and his revolutionary achievements. This is not just because, unlike people of my generation, they were not able to engage in revolutionary struggle with Chairman Mao themselves. Nor is it simply because for some time now we have neglected adequate and effective ideological education. More importantly, it is because the miasma of Bourgeois Liberalization, in particular this desire to negate, undermine, and vilify Comrade Mao, has polluted many young minds, infecting them with mistaken ideas, corrupting the facts and leading them to erroneous conclusions. The effects of this have been deleterious in the extreme. Their age and limited experience have made it impossible for younger people to resist this canker. It is only natural, therefore, that for them it is necessary to go through a period of "searching" and "discovery" before they can find the true mien of the Chairman, come to a realization of his historical position and influence, understand his theories, thought, and practice while also appreciating the evaluation of him that is to be found in [the Party Central document] "Resolution on Certain Questions in the History of Our Party Since the Founding of the People's Republic of China."[6] The number of articles and books written on such subjects in recent years is proof of this search.

The political turbulence of 1989 was followed almost immediately by the setbacks suffered by some socialist nations in Eastern Europe. This was a massive blow that has led to the low tide of the international communist movement. Many people, particularly young people, were deeply shocked and unsettled by these developments. Numbers of our young people found themselves in a state of ideological dysfunction, confusion, and frustration. What is fascinating about this is that these extraordinary events and cruel realities have given them an overwhelming desire to reconsider and explain to themselves what has happened. This historical opportunity has led to the present MaoCraze.

Q: It is quite true to say that faced with the recent complex and unsettling developments both in China and overseas, many young people are questioning everything. There are those who, having found themselves at the crossroads, have undertaken this present journey of discovery.

A: As I have previously said, the majority of young people who have undertaken this journey of discovery have avoided simplistic value judgments and ready-made conclusions. Although our Party produced its "Resolution on Certain Questions in the History of Our Party" way back in 1981, in which it formulated a correct evaluation of Comrade Mao, it was an evaluation that for quite a period was ignored and even negated by people in their political practice. For the young, who do not have a mature historical perspective, this presented a number of practical problems. This present journey of discovery had its origins in the publication of the memoirs of the Older Revolutionaries as well as booklets based on the recollections of Mao Zedong's staff. The publication of a mass of material like *Mao Zedong's Guard Remembers* and *Mao Zedong Quits the Altar* elicited an enthusiastic response from younger readers and they became best-sellers. This was the first phase of the present MaoCraze.

Quan Yanchi produced a number of books based on interviews with the Chairman's staff which, despite certain deficiencies and controversial points, have served a positive historical function.[7] These firsthand materials contradicted those who were plotting to denigrate the Chairman. He certainly was not a god, but nor was he a heartless "devil." Rather Mao Zedong was a living, breathing man, an all too human man who also happened to be very personable. These books also reveal him to be a man of extraordinary character and intelligence, a revolutionary who selflessly devoted his whole life to the enterprise of the People's Revolution. For example, in the early 1960s, during the years that natural disasters coupled with human error produced a period of hunger among the broad masses,[8] Comrade Mao and his whole family shared the sufferings of the people by refusing to eat meat. Their diet was so bad that they developed dropsy. Such facts have deeply moved millions of readers. For the majority of Chinese this was a real "discovery." Such facts have confounded the efforts of all those people who have tried to depict Comrade Mao as a heartless "emperor."

Q: These works, as well as the films, teleseries, and plays based on them have repeatedly achieved mass popularity and have elicited an unprecedented response from the younger generation. Such films as "The Majestic Kunlun Mountains," "The Founding of the People's Republic," "Mao Zedong and His Sons," "Mao Zedong and the People of His Hometown," "A New Beginning" (as well as fictional works like "A Red Ribbon Around the Earth") have presented audiences with a multifaceted and realistic image of Comrade Mao. All of this has certainly had a cumulative effect on the MaoCraze. . . .

Over recent years China has seen many crazes come and go. These include the Freud Craze, the Sartre Craze, and the Modernism Craze. Will the MaoCraze go the same way and simply peter out?

A: There is simply no comparison. Those other theories were the product of particular phases in the development of capitalist society in the West. They lack a solid basis in Chinese reality. For all the efforts made by some to disseminate these ideas as part of a new fashion, they have failed to take root since they provide no solution to China's historical predicament. The MaoCraze is quite different. Mao Zedong Thought is the product of Chinese social and historical reality. Mao Zedong both lived Chinese history and changed it, and he will continue to influence it. For this reason, the MaoCraze will not disappear with the passing of time or lose its historical power or significance. The study of Comrade Mao Zedong, his age, and his thought is now an eternal element of Chinese history.

Notes

1. For Deng's earlier comments on the Cult, see Deng Liqun, "Zhengque renshi shehuizhuyide maodun, zhangwo chuli maodunde zhudongquan"; and *Deng, "Guanyu Wuchanjieji gemingjia fengfan congshu bianzhuan gongzuode jidian yijian."*
2. The "three belief crisis" (*sanxin weiji*) dating from the early 1980s was: a crisis of belief (*xinren*) in the leadership of the Communist Party; a crisis of belief (*xinxin*) in the socialist system; and a crisis of belief (*xinyang*) in the Communist ideal.
3. See Xin Ming, "Faxian Mao Zedong," pp. 18–21. This article is typical of the exhibitionist fawning of a young apparatchik on the make. Xin Ming's glib use of a few lines of Mao's poetry to formulate a response to major international events is also representative of the hack literati tradition on the Mainland. See also Xin Ming's comments on how the MaoCraze did not constitute a rejection of Reform but rather could help the Party "perfect" its new policies in "Guanyu 'Mao Zedongre' de sikao yu tantao—Beijing daxue bufen shisheng zuotanhui fayan," pp. 19–35, at p. 27.
4. Mao Zedong, "He Guo Moruo tongzhi," *Mao zhuxi shici*, p. 173. For this English translation, see "Reply to Comrade Kuo Mo-jo—a *lü shih*," 17 November 1961, Mao Tsetung, *Poems*, p. 41.
5. Mao Zedong, "Dong yun," *Mao zhuxi shici*, p. 185; this English translation is taken from Mao Tsetung, *Poems*, p. 45.
6. For some relevant passages from this document, see "The Party on Mao" in this volume.
7. Quan Yanchi (b. 1945), a PLA writer and author of numerous reportage (*jishi wenxue*) studies of Mao's life. For details, see "Mao: the Body Corporate"; and Tian Hao, "Ta shenwenle 'lingxiure'."
8. This so-called "period of difficulty" or *kunnan shiqi*, as the Chinese euphemism puts it, was a result of the economic disaster created by Mao's utopian policies in the Great Leap Forward. The "period of hunger" Deng Liqun speaks of left millions dead.

A Fan from Way Back

He Xin

The conservative yet generally perspicacious writer He Xin, a Beijing-based critic and sometime adviser to the Chinese government, writes and speaks with the diction of updated Maoism. He is the Jeremiah of the Reform period, a man whose opinions annoy people regardless of their position on the political spectrum.[1]

Given the political sensitivity of the subject, it is not surprising that the following comments made in 1991 are not typical of He Xin's usually muscular style of exposition. Although expressed in the overblown, self-important diction characteristic of Beijing's intellectual strategists (zhishi zonghengjia), his comments do not stray from the Party line. He Xin's pro-Mao sentiments are shared by a range of intellectuals and writers who cannot be simply classified as "Maoists" or "conservatives." Perhaps "proto-nationalist" would be a more accurate tag.

Question: How do you see the MaoCraze and the Mao Zedong Thought Craze of recent years? (Tass Agency)

Answer: Let me say right at the start that Mao Zedong is one of the people I've most admired throughout my life.

In my opinion, three people have determined the fate of China in the twentieth century. The first was Sun Yat-sen, the second Mao, and the third Deng Xiaoping. Mao Zedong initiated a new era. He was a man who not only inherited from the past, he also bequeathed a legacy to the future.

In my view, Mao's greatness lies not only in the fact that he was a politician but that he was also a strategist and a thinker. He is undoubtedly an Historical Hero for the following three reasons: In the first place, he was a Revolutionary Hero born into a lowly family who brought about a political miracle. Second, he was a Patriotic Hero who led the Chinese people to wipe clean the slate of national humiliations suffered over a century. Third, he was a World-class Hero in the league of Stalin, Roosevelt, and Churchill and, like them, he changed the international political and economic balance of power and had a massive influence on world history in the second half of the twentieth century.

I believe there are three main aspects to Mao Zedong Thought. The first is its clarity. Mao was never a person to indulge in flowery rhetoric. His language was forthright, direct, concise, and to the point. He never acted the sophist or played word games. Second, Mao Thought was uniquely Chinese. Mao saw the world and analyzed problems on the basis of the practical realities of China. He was never divorced from Chinese realities. Third, Mao Thought is practicable. In his view, if a theory, no matter how high-and-mighty sounding, had no practical validity, then it was meaningless.

In my personal opinion, Mao Zedong's errors were primarily in the economic sphere. A second error occurred because he often attempted to deal with problems that were not, given China's immediate historical context, ripe for resolution. His economic theories were rudimentary and it would appear that he lacked a relatively in-depth understanding of the way an economy functions. In terms of his economic aims, he was often impatient and ignored reality, preferring instead to pursue his own ideals. Nonetheless, if you make a study of Mao's economic thinking today you will often be startled by his extraordinary historical perspicacity and his strong intuition. He was outstanding, a man who was ahead of his time, and far superior to the general mass of humanity. (Take, for example, the two volumes of notes he made on the basis of his reading in economic theory.)

During the Mao era, especially during the Cultural Revolution, I was struggled and jailed. But even then my belief in him never wavered. I still respect him.

I believe that all future, meaningful Chinese moves toward modernization will have to start off from the historical base provided by Mao Zedong. You cannot overthrow that basis. If the legacy of Mao Zedong was obliterated, then China too would be finished.

As for the spontaneous MaoCraze that has appeared in China over recent years, allow me to make two points:

In the first place, today the Chinese are rediscovering patriotism. Mao Zedong is the symbolic figure who led China to achieve international recognition and historical respect in the twentieth century; second, having experienced many new social phenomena in the 1980s the Chinese people have come to appreciate the prescience of Mao Zedong's historical predictions. They have thereby discovered the relevance and significance of some of his theories.

Note

1. For more on He Xin, see his "A Word of Advice to the Politburo" and "A Letter from Beijing."

A Typology of the MaoCraze

Zhang Weihong

*This excerpt is from a restricted-circulation "sociology" publication pro-
duced in Shanghai. It offers a relatively objective and, presumably for the
authorities, sobering overview of the Mao Cult among university students in
the early 1990s.*

Following the Beijing storm of 1989, all books related to Mao Zedong
suddenly disappeared from the libraries at Beijing and Qinghua universities
[having been borrowed by students]. Now, on the bookshelves of some
university students, one can find a recent addition of *Selected Works of Mao
Zedong*, which sits alongside the usual array of works by Sartre, Freud, and
Nietzsche.

A considerable number of students began searching out biographies of
Mao like *Mao Zedong Quits the Altar, Mao Zedong Approaches Divinity,
The Tears of the Leader, A Biography of Mao Zedong, Inside and Outside
the Palace Walls, History in the Palm of His Hand, The Latter Half of Mao
Zedong's Life, His Guards Discuss Mao Zedong, Mao Zedong and His
Secretary Tian Jiaying*. These and many other biographies are best-selling
books, and students have been among their most enthusiastic readers.

On 26 December 1989, on the ninety-sixth anniversary of Mao Zedong's
birth, some students at Beijing, Qinghua, Chinese People's, and Beijing
Normal universities spontaneously organized a trip to the Chairman Mao
Memorial Hall to commemorate this historical giant. A MaoCraze born at
the university campuses of Beijing quickly spread to schools throughout the
nation. At Nankai University and other tertiary institutions in Tianjin, students organized their own Mao Zedong Study Groups. University and middle school students in the Northeast led the way in reviving the wearing of
Mao badges, which had not been seen for years. In Guangdong, Mao
badges were soon selling for as much as 20 *yuan* each. . . .

Although the MaoCraze has been particularly evident at tertiary institutions throughout China, it has never completely surplanted the "TDK Craze" (or TOEFL, Dance, and Kiss Craze) among young people who want to "go overseas, dance, and make love."

The MaoCraze of the 1980s and 1990s is no simple rehearsal of the Movement to Study Mao's Works that we saw in the 1950s and 1960s. The most obvious difference being that, in the past, Mao enthusiasts saw Mao as a god; in the present craze, Mao is regarded as a human being. The Mao enthusiasts of the past were basically of the "protect and respect" type. . . . In the 1980s and 1990s the typology of Mao enthusiasts is far more complex. . . .

Based on my own investigations, observation, and analysis, I would say that university students involved in the present MaoCraze can be divided into two groups: the theoretical-analytical type and the performance-art type. The former have engaged in a relatively systematic and in-depth study of Mao's life and writings, the latter browse through Mao books and enjoy raving on about Mao and thereby reveal a range of political sentiments. The theoretical-analytical group can be further broken down into those who support Mao, those who oppose him, and the pragmatists. The performance-art type can be subdivided into those who respect Mao and those who ridicule him.

The theoretical-analytical pro-Mao type. After achieving an in-depth understanding of Mao, these individuals come to appreciate Mao's character and personality. "He was neither an affected and self-important 'god', nor was he one of those political mediocrities who knew what he should do but could never muster enough courage to act." Second, they affirm his place in history. Third, they recognize the theoretical value of Mao Zedong Thought. In particular, they admire Mao's line that "everything should be done first and foremost for the People." These students are working hard at becoming the young bloods who will invigorate the Communist Party that Mao Zedong created. They want to struggle for the rest of their lives for the cause of socialism in China. This group forms the core of all Mao Study Groups.

The theoretical-analytical oppositionists. These individuals are particularly interested in studying the errors Mao made during peacetime and the erroneous statements he made in his later years. Of course, they do not ignore what he said and did in his younger years either. They are the opposite of the group described above since, first and foremost, they want to negate the personal worth of Mao. They also have a frightening capacity for unearthing historical material. For example, by delving into official publications they have discovered that although Yang Kaihui [Mao's much-praised first wife] was arrested on 24 October 1930 and executed on 14 November of that year, Mao married He Zizhen some two years earlier, in September 1928.[1]

Most oppositionists have availed themselves of the famous contemporary Taiwan writer Li Ao's works, which can be found in the humanities collections at major university libraries.[2] Li Ao has published more than a hundred books, many of which have been banned by the Taiwanese authorities. His work on Sun Yat-sen, Chiang Kai-shek, and Nationalist [KMT] history is meticulous, his ultimate aim being to undermine the KMT itself. In his *Researches into Sun Yat-sen*, Li Ao declared: "Everyone on both sides of the Taiwan Straits snaps to attention in the presence of Sun. Well I, Li Ao, am issuing the order for everyone to stand at ease." Oppositionist students find that they share a lot in common with Li Ao's style and, like him, study the minutiæ of Party history, Mao, and Mao's writings. Their ultimate aim is, when the time is right, to produce a "thoroughgoing theory" that will overturn Mao Zedong Thought and destroy communism. They despise and oppose the Party's Leadership, the Socialist Path, and the Proletarian Dictatorship as first formulated by Mao Zedong. Although the pro-Mao group and oppositionists are completely different, their energy and devotion to their research is strikingly similar.

The theoretical-analytical pragmatists. The aim of these individuals is, in their own words, to study Mao Zedong so they "can cut through the excess flab and get to the meat of the subject." A typical example of their attitude was evident in July 1989, after the PLA tanks occupied Tiananmen Square. They started studying Mao Zedong's essay "On Protracted Warfare" and declared that "we must embrace the spirit of the Anti-Japanese War and utilize the strategy and tactics of the Eighth Route Army, the Guerrillas, and the People in their struggle against the Jap devils to oppose the. . . . "[3] As the deputy secretary of the Beijing Municipal Communist Youth League commented: "The 'Craze to Find Mao Zedong' does, on one level, reflect a kind of nostalgia, an attraction to the rebelliousness of the past, and a fascination with power politics."

The pragmatists are particularly interested in Maoist strategies like how the weak can take advantage of the strong and defeat them and the confident manner with which he formulated military maneuvers. The pragmatists invariably think they are experienced and world-wise. Since they are regarded by their elders as immature and malleable, they are even more determined to get a hold on Mao Zedong. Some of them are quite hubristic and declare: "Just as Marx overthrew Hegel, so too will we discard Mao Zedong Thought."

The reverential performance-art type. They are involved in the Craze but are too busy with their studies to spend time researching Mao Thought. They rely instead on the indoctrination they have received over the years and believe that Mao Thought is a shining achievement and that the Party is a glorious organization. They have all read some of Mao's works and have been moved by Mao's prose. Although they lack the solid theoretical base of the pro-Maoists found among the theoretical-analytical type, they are devoted to the Party and its leader, enthusiastically stating that they will always maintain unity with the Party. Of all the people involved in the MaoCraze they appear the most stable.

The irreverent performance-art type. Some time ago there was a shooting incident at an art exhibition in Beijing which left a deep impression on this type of student. That exhibition featured many strange forms of "performance art," one included a couple who fired a gun at their own art work resulting in their detention by the police. They claimed that by shooting at their installation they had completed a work of "performance art."[4]

The irreverent types of Mao fan will bedeck themselves with Mao badges pinned at odd angles, enjoy reworking "The East Is Red," a traditional paean for Mao, with frenetic rock music while singing it as though it were a dirge. Or they will sing the moving and sentimental [Yan'an period revolutionary song] "Nanniwan" in a stentorian fashion. They express their rejection of society and its values in various romantic ways. . . . They are particularly active participants in the fad, but their enthusiasm will wane as suddenly as it waxed. . . .

From the above it is evident that, in the first place, the MaoCraze of the late 1980s was an indication that China's university students were gradually leaving behind the "crisis of belief" that had been evident before. Secondly, people were moving out of the crisis in different ways and going in different directions. Thirdly, the new belief systems that are being established are mutually unrelated.

Notes

1. The sources given in the text are: *Mao Zedong yiwenlu*, pp. 37–43 and 57–60, originally published in *Zhongyang dangshi shijian renwu lu*, Shanghai: Shanghai renmin chubanshe, and *Mingren zhuanji* magazine, 1987: 5.

2. Li Ao (b. 1935) moved to Taiwan with his family in 1948. A student of the historian Hu Shi, Li has been the most acerbic and prolific critic of Taiwan political life since the 1960s. Some of his works were published on the Mainland from 1989.

3. Presumably, the author's sense of political decorum led him to expunge the words "Communist Party" here.

4. The "shooting incident" occurred in February 1989 at the "Modern Chinese Art" exhibition held at the China Art Gallery. Tang Song and Xiao Lu, both students of the Zhejiang Art Academy, shot two rounds of ammunition at their own work, a sculpture entitled "Dialogue," which featured a pair of telephone booths. The artists were detained for a short time by the police and the exhibition was closed down. See Barmé and Jaivin, *New Ghosts, Old Dreams*, pp. 279–83.

The Sun Never Sets

Su Ya and Jia Lusheng

Better known for works of reportage that border on the controversial—like
White Cat Black Cat—An Insight into the State of the Reforms,[1] *Su Ya and
Jia Lusheng authored one of the most sycophantic contributions to the
MaoCraze.* The Sun Never Sets *is a volume of reportage devoted to Mao
published in early 1992. In it the writers plumb depths of tastelessness
rarely fathomed even by official propagandists. While less hysterical than
Cultural Revolution paeans to Mao, the authors' adulation for the Leader
would be familiar to the formulators of the* Führerprinzip *in Nazi Germany
or the Kim Il-song/Kim Jong-il cults in North Korea.*

*Much of the book is worth quoting, however, due to limitations of
space, only a number of short selections have been made for the
reader's delectation.*

A Corpse That's Like a Constellation

Isn't China just like an ancient architect?

The Great Wall, the Epang Palace,[2] the Forbidden City, the Ming
Tombs, the Temple of Confucius, the Dunhuang Caves. Centuries of work
and artistic endeavour have resulted in a uniquely Chinese building style, an
insignia of our own.

Opposite Tiananmen, the Gate of Heavenly Peace, stands a grave and
powerful structure—

The Chairman Mao Memorial Hall!

The materials used in its construction are nothing out of the ordinary:

There is marble and granite—the skeletons of our mountain ranges;

Pine and dragon spruce—the limbs of our forests;

And the warmth of our own furnaces—steel and concrete. . . .

Add to that the talent, workmanship, sweat, faith, respect, longing and concern of a massive nation, combine them all into a seamless whole and then this stellar structure shines brilliantly.

The most important thing is its location: Tiananmen Square, the bosom of the People.

This is the final resting place for the wisest and strongest soul that China has seen in her recent history; an abode for the body of a Great Man who saved his nation from disasters unknown anywhere else or at any other time in history.

The People have built this tomb in their heart, in Tiananmen, for this is the place where they entrust their hopes and aspirations, where they go for comfort and consolation.

No one will ever forget that terrible day: 9 September 1976.

On that night a massive star fell from the heavens of the East.

It was the greatest funeral in the 5,000 years of Chinese history.

Everyone, from babes in swaddling clothes to old people with walking sticks, judges and convicts, thinkers and illiterates, wore black armbands as a sign of mourning.

Dark clouds shrouded the land.

In the silence that enveloped the nation all that could be heard was crying and funeral music, an expression of collective grief for the life that had left that Great Body.

Amidst the dirges that issued from hoarse throats the whole nation bowed thrice solemnly and the coffin was closed tight.

But the People's hearts have not thereby been sealed.

Fifteen years have passed and still columns of mourners pass by His coffin every day. In those fifteen years over 67 million people have come to view His remains. It is like a dream. People who never had a chance to see him when he called out "Long Live the People"[3] can find satisfaction in viewing His remains today, even if only for an instant. . . .

He lies preternaturally still, His body covered with the red flag of the Party. The powerful hammer and sharp sickle, insignia of struggle and symbols of belief, are now forever branded on His chest.

No more need He do battle with the tempests of life. The gravid storm clouds and the unpredictable tides have receded now.

History makes Great Leaders the subject for research because they rule over a whole age and their rule shakes the very earth. For History Mao Zedong possesses a charisma that surpasses that of Qin Shihuang, Emperor Wu of the Han, as well as the founders of the Tang, Song, Ming and Yuan dynasties.[4]

Who can deny it?

He started out as a humble student and went on to create a philosophical system. He founded a political party and developed a powerful armed force. After 28 years, He overthrew the old power structure and sent shockwaves through the world by turning the "Sick Man of Asia" into a force to be reckoned with. These are unique achievements in the annals of Chinese history.

Look! History has its gaze fixed firmly on the body of Mao Zedong, this Great Man. History looks out from the eyes of every mourner and the gaze of the People creates the line of vision of History itself.

First and foremost they see the mole that is so perfectly positioned on that broad chin of His. And from it issues a series of mysterious questions: are the extraordinary talents of the Leader the mere product of nature? Why was He the one to establish the Republic? How did a peasant's son from an isolated mountain village become the shimmering Big Dipper in our firmament?[5] Fate decreed Him to be the Generalissimo, the Subduer, the Liberator. How did a young boy who studied at a local school develop such a wise soul? Was He really a genius?[6] When the Age chooses a genius is it inevitable or accidental?

But the Leader is the Leader, it's as simple as that. It is a status that can only be bestowed by Time itself.

Mao Zedong's existence is answer enough to all of these questions.

It is in a state of calm reflection that we must recognize that we have a responsibility to learn from the mysteries of the Leader. It is a responsibility that everyone living in China today shares in common. As we become aware of the material nature of His body, its mystery evaporates. The difference between the earth, mountains, forests, lakes and seas lies entirely in their unique makeup. Perhaps, in the same way, the makeup of the Leader's soul is different from that of normal people.

He had an oriental face inherited from His parents. Everything about it was big: it was broad, the eyebrows bushy, eyes large. His nose was prominent, His lips thick and He had big ear lobes. He had a massive forehead, too, it was like the door to a treasurehouse; it is as though the energies of the whole race were stored in that one skull. Perhaps He needed a powerful body to hold high that massive head.

The stature of that body is equivalent to the significance He had on the scales of social reality.

He maintained the equilibrium of an age. Without the Leader the People would have been incomplete. Without Him the great mansion of socialism would have collapsed.

Although He went through so much, none of His suffering marked His face with wrinkles. Its skin was smooth and, when He was alive, it "glowed with health and vigour, and he enjoyed a ruddy complexion."[7] He shone with the light of energy. In the crystal sarcophagus His face has lost the sheen of life and appears more solemn. He is majestic and aloof.

He was an awesome Commander-in-Chief who subdued an age of restlessness through will-power alone. The raging torrents of the Yellow River and the Yangtze coursed through His veins. His massive chest rose like a great mountain. No force on earth could withstand Him; none could control Him. He was the enactor of His own will; it was like lightning or a tempest, both majestic and terrifying. He deployed it as a warrior would wield a weapon.

He was a Lord of Destruction: swinging a shovel in His hands he buried Old China in an instant.

He was a Master of Creation: using the methods that eliminated reactionaries He established a new order.

Unity of thought, unity of will, unity of action: in clenching His fist he smelted the loose sands of China[8] into a lead ingot, melding hundreds of millions of Chinese into one body.

That profound gaze of His could see through everything.[9] Nothing could escape His vision, not even the most subtle changes deep in the hearts of men. Therefore, He was able to discover all plots, starting with Zhang Guotao[10] and right up to the time of Lin Biao and the "Gang of Four."

In His speech He combined the talents of both lawyer and judge. The Hunanese accent sounded particularly powerful and moving when it issued from His lips. He used it to advocate causes throughout His life: for the "movement of the riffraff,"[11] for a boat on the horizon, the morning sun and a baby,[12] for democracy, freedom and dictatorship, in defence of the "Three Red Banners,"[13] in inner party struggles, and so on and so forth. When speaking in favour of something every word would touch His listeners. His unshakable faith made it possible for Him to turn the tide in His favour. He delighted in contradictions, and in the face of conflict He would act as the arbiter of truth, settling the fate of the universe with unflinching certainty. But His arguments and decisions were never simplistic; they were like the sun that shines into every nook and cranny of society. The brilliant effulgence of His Thought lit up the souls of all Chinese. . . .

Mao Zedong, the man who once stood on the rostrum of Tiananmen, now lies in front of it. The sun no longer shines on Him, and the holy aura that once surrounded Him has faded.

Those who come to see Him experience many different emotions: some are sorrowful, others thoughtful, and there are those who are moved. But none are as delighted as they were in the past to see Him. A transmogrification has occurred: in the past He was respected as a god, today He is revered as a man.

People, therefore, can appreciate His weaknesses and inadequacies. Indeed, He is like the sun that shines down on a brooding, dark land but, because He is the sun, He leaves a penumbra around the objects He illuminates.

For someone to cast a shadow that is the same shape as their body is a type of good fortune.

Transmigration: What If Mao Zedong Came Back. . . .[14]

Strange thoughts often occur to a person who is lost in soulful reflection: "What would it be like if Mao Zedong really did come back?"

What a ridiculous idea!

But when a university student questioned a number of people no one thought he was being silly for he had introduced himself by saying: "I am a time-traveller searching for Mao Zedong in my spaceship, 'The Explorer.' "

You could tell from his thick volume of research notes that everyone had responded to his absurd question with the utmost seriousness.

It was as though we too are driven by a mysterious force that begs us to meditate on the prospect of Mao's return.

If he came back would everyone still support His authority? Would they still cry out "Long Live Chairman Mao!"? What would he think of China today? Could His genius formulate answers to the problems of modernization? Would He want to revise His Thought? Which of His past policies would He continue to pursue?

People are willing to take this ridiculous hypothesis seriously because it raises a number of sensitive and practical issues. It forces people to compare the past with the present. It undermines superficial harmony and reveals the tension between sentiment and rationality. It forces people to be honest and practical, as opposed to hypocritical and fashionable. Praise and well-intentioned criticism are thereby placed on an equal footing. The penetrating clarity of traffic lights always confronts people mesmerized by flashy displays of neon street signs. . . .

Very well, then, let us look into the logbook of "The Explorer" and see what representatives of various groups of people have said:

A retired cadre replied emotionally as he stared at the portrait of Chairman Mao on his wall:

"I followed Chairman Mao into battle and took part in national construction after 1949. I suffered quite a lot during the CultRev although I was only following the Chairman's instructions. But my life is inextricably linked with the name Mao Zedong. If He were still alive I would follow His orders. I often dream of Chairman Mao. Sooner or later I will go to see Him in the afterlife. If I let Him down now how could I ever face Him?"

A theoretician who stood in the front ranks in the struggle against Bourgeois Liberalization said, tired though obviously delighted with victory:[15]

"Chairman Mao would be deeply relieved to know that we have undertaken the present struggle against Bourgeois Liberalization. The Chairman was always on the alert when it came to the corrosive influence of bourgeois thought. He never ceased His fight against it and never showed any pity."

After slight hesitation one intellectual said:

"There's no denying the fact that intellectuals are much better off now than they used to be. But . . . Chairman Mao was never against knowledge as such, although He laid greater emphasis on transforming intellectuals than using them. This was understandable. Intellectuals from the old society were deficient in many respects and if they weren't kept in check there would have been trouble. Most intellectuals today were trained in New China, when the Chairman was alive. He would have approved of them."

One entrepreneur, the first 10,000 *yuan* businessman in his district, wasn't that comfortable with the question:

"There's no denying the fact that people are better off than they used to be. And the private economy is developing. I don't know why, even among people who've made a bundle, there's a lot of nostalgia for the days of Chairman Mao. Would He approve of 10,000 *yuan* households? I wouldn't dare speculate, but I do know He'd be happy that the standard of living has improved."

A youngster of primary-school age (in sixth grade, sincere and devoid of all signs of crass acquisitiveness) responded:

"My parents and grandparents, as well as my aunts, uncles and teachers often tell me stories about Granddad Mao. They're great! He was a real hero. I'd love to have met Him so He could tell me how He led the Red Army in the War. I've been to the Memorial Hall to see Granddad Mao. I don't know why but I cried. He was lying there all still in that crystal case. It was really sad."

This evidence makes it impossible for us to make any definite claims. . . .

There's an absurd yet heartfelt popular myth: Mao Zedong has reincarnated. . . .

It is easy to understand the sincere and well-meaning people who want

Mao to live forever. In life people prayed that He would live 10,000 years; after He died, they hoped He would be reborn.

But do people realize that Chairman Mao hasn't left us at all? Rather, when He died, He entered our very souls and has merely been enjoying a rest there. After His life-long labours He deserved a respite. Anyway, everyone was so busy with carrying out Reform He didn't want to distract us.

But this rebirth of History has taken place in response to our present needs, a response to a feeling of dependency.

Mao Zedong exists today not as a physical reality for long ago He was transmogrified into a spiritual force, a belief, an ideal.

It's a simple principle: He exists, but only if you believe in Him.

If you have faith in Mao Zedong then He will live in your heart forever.

Notes

1. Su Ya and Jia Lusheng, *Baimao heimao—Zhongguo gaige xianzhuang toushi*.

2. *Epang gong* was built by Qin Shihuang.

3. Mao offered the masses of adoring supporters who lined the Yangtse to greet him on his famous 1966 swim the response: "Long Live the People!" (*renmin wansui!*). See the editorial "Genzhe Mao zhuxi zai dafeng dalangzhong qianjin."

4. These are the historical figures listed derisively by Mao in his poem "Snow."

5. The Big Dipper or Northern Dipper (*Beidouxing*), a group of stars in Ursa Major, represents the God of Longevity and is a traditional object of veneration. Other stars are said to revolve around it.

6. A *tiancai*. Lin Biao claimed that Mao was a genius, a status from which Mao himself resiled.

7. In Chinese *shencai yiyi, hongguang manmian*. This standard propaganda formulation was used to describe Mao in his declining years.

8. In the past the Chinese were spoken of as being like a "plate of loose sand" (*yi pan sansha*) that could never be formed into a whole.

9. "To see through everything," or *dongcha yiqie*, was commonly used in the Cultural Revolution to describe Mao's supposedly uncanny ability to uncover plots against himself and, in the same token, the Party.

10. Zhang Guotao (1897–1979), a Party leader who split with his fellows over the route of the Long March in 1936, established his own Central Committee. In 1938, he sided with the KMT and was purged from the Communist Party.

11. The "movement of the riffraff" (*pizi yundong*) was the Hunan peasant movement Mao wrote about in 1927. See "Report on the Hunan Peasant Movement" (*Hunan nongmin yundong kaocha baogao*), *Mao Zedong xuanji, yijuanben*, p. 18.

12. This is a reference to Mao's debate with the early Communist Party leader Chen Duxiu and others who doubted the speed with which a revolutionary movement could develop in China. Mao claimed that a revolutionary high tide would soon be upon them and that it was approaching, like the mast of a ship visible on the horizon of the sea, like the morning sun seen from a mountain peak, or like a baby anxious to be born. See Mao's 1930 letter, "A Spark Can Start a Prairie Fire" (*Xingxing zhi huo, keyi liao yuan*), *Mao Zedong xuanji*, p. 103.

13. The "Three Red Banners" (*sanmian hongqi*) were: the General Line, the Great Leap Forward and the People's Communes propounded by Mao in 1958. The General Line initiated a mass movement urging people "to work energetically, struggle against all odds and build socialism faster, better and more economically." The Great Leap Forward attempted an overnight realization of industrialization and the People's Communes saw the reorganization of the nation's agriculture along socialist lines. These policies resulted in economic catastrophe and millions of deaths. After 1978 the Three Banners were rejected as being the result of impractical "leftist" errors on Mao's part.

14. A question asked often since 1976. For a satirical response to this question by Xiao Tong (Yau Ma Tei), a Beijing writer based in Hong Kong, see "Maosoleum," in Barmé and Minford, eds., *Seeds of Fire*, pp. 189–92.

15. The purge of Bourgeois Liberalization referred to here was launched after the Beijing Massacre of 1989. See "Permanently on Heat" above.

A Star Reflects on the Sun

Liu Xiaoqing

Liu Xiaoqing is an actress from Sichuan. Although her fame was eclipsed in the early 1990s by Gong Li, director Zhang Yimou's leading lady, Liu remained one of China's most popular performers. She was also remarkable for her brash and outspoken personality—something with which few of her rivals could compete, and she was denounced during the 1983 Anti-Spiritual Pollution Campaign for producing an autobiography entitled I Did It My Way (Wode lu). *Among her numerous screen roles her portrayal of the Empress Dowager Ci Xi in Tian Zhuangzhuang's film "Li Lianying" (1990) was, perhaps, most noteworthy.*

Liu's memoir, from which this excerpt is taken, was written at the height of the Mao Cult. Its sentiment was shared by many of Liu's generation as they looked back on a youth spent in the thrall of Cultural Revolution zealotry. Regardless of the horrors of those years—and there is no dearth of material concerning the devastation wrought by Mao's rule—for many his was an age of passion, excitement and social engagement. Maoism was suffused with religiosity and it catered to young idealists who yearned for sincerity and altruism, things unknown and unthinkable in Deng Xiaoping's China. This memoir shows that Liu's longing for a lost moment of "beauty" had grown more intense with the passage of time and stronger in the atmosphere of the cynicism that enveloped the People's Republic now that it was bereft of anything other than a faith in economic might. It also reveals a level of objectification of Mao that brings to mind the German book Love Letters to Adolf Hitler.[1]

I have only seen Mao Zedong twice. On the first occasion he was standing, the second time he was flat on his back. The first time he was on Tiananmen Gate to review the Red Guards who, like me, had traveled to Beijing to see him. The second time was at the Chairman Mao Memorial Hall where I lined up to view his body.

Everyone says that you never forget your first love. I cannot really say that I ever had a first love, for in my childhood and youth the man I loved and admired most of all was Mao Zedong. I gave him everything I had: my purest love, as well as all my longing and hopes. He was an idol I worshipped with all my heart.

Chairman Mao, you were my first object of desire!

The first song I learned to sing was "The East Is Red." I knew what Chairman Mao looked like from the time I could recognize my parents. When I was a Red Guard I could recite all his quotations word perfect. My brain was armed with Mao Zedong Thought. During the unprecedented Cultural Revolution I used Chairman Mao's words as my weapon to fight opponents. My prodigious memory and quick tongue always meant that my "enemies" would retreat in defeat.

If I ever had any problems I would search Chairman Mao's writings for an answer. When we lost one of our chicks I looked for help in his works. When, not long after, the chick reappeared, I knew it was due to the intercession of our Great, Wise, and Correct Chairman Mao.

When, as a child, I played games with my friends, our pledge of honor was: "I swear by Chairman Mao." If someone said that, even if they prefaced it by claiming that they had just come from Mars, we would believe it without question. Naturally, no one ever took this oath lightly.

I worshipped and loved Chairman Mao so utterly that there was absolutely nothing extraneous or impure in my feelings for him. When I grew a bit older and learned the secret of how men and women made babies, I had the most shocking realization: "Could Chairman Mao possibly do that as well?" Of course, I immediately banished these sacrilegious thoughts from my head. . . .[2]

Then Chairman Mao set the revolutionary blaze of the Cultural Revolution alight. It also ignited our youthful enthusiasm. We were like moths drawn to a flame, and we threw ourselves into the inferno *en masse*. We were in a frenzy and utilized every ounce of energy at our disposal.

We would have given anything to protect Chairman Mao, including our very lives. Our love for the Chairman consumed us body and soul. If anyone had dared to try and harm our beloved Chairman, we would have pounced on him, bitten his hand off, gouged out his eyes, screamed in his ears until he was deaf, spat on him until he drowned in a lake of spittle, and would have happily died in the effort just like [the revolutionary martyr] Dong Cunrui.

On 18 August 1966, Chairman Mao reviewed the Red Guards for the first time. I was too young to become a Red Guard, but I spent all my time dreaming of joining the organization that was sworn to protect Chairman Mao. After making extraordinary efforts, I was finally allowed to take part in a peripheral grouping called the "Red Brigade." They gave me a red armband too. It was like a dream come true. Although it was not the same as the Red Guards, the difference was only one word. I put on the armband so that the word "Brigade" was hidden under my arm. I stuck out my chest and, just like a real Red Guard, strutted around the school yard incredibly proud of myself.

Soon after that, Chairman Mao called on the Red Guards to travel around China on Revolutionary Link-ups. Our group of Red Brigade members decided to respond to Chairman Mao's call too. Without a penny to our names, and each carrying a yellow-green PLA knapsack that we had all done our darndest to get a hold of (including some who had dyed their own bags), we set out. I had cut off my beloved pigtails so I looked like the revolutionary Sister Jiang.[3] At the train station, we fought our way past all the people who tried to persuade us to "return to the classroom and continue the revolution there." Pushing them aside with determined urgency we boarded the train. With a great clamor the train moved out of the station. We were in very high spirits, our hearts throbbing with revolutionary ardor. Then one of my classmates asked: "Where are we going?" I was stunned and asked the others: "Where's this train headed?" We took out a map of China and put our heads together and, doing our best to put to use the elementary geography we had just learned in class, we scrutinized the map and finally worked out that we were on the Baocheng line. There would be a change of locomotive at Baoji and the train would then head for Beijing.

Beijing! The city where Chairman Mao lived! We went wild.

Over the next few days, we were so excited about going to Beijing that we did not sleep a wink. But where would Chairman Mao be? Would we be able to see him? We all stood atop the "Gold Mountain of Beijing" which we had dreamed of for so long, tormented by these questions.

We imitated the Red Guards of Beijing scrupulously, literally aping their every move. When we got on a bus we would take out *Quotations from Chairman Mao* and start reading in really loud voices. "Revolution is not a tea party. It is not like writing an essay, painting, or embroidering flowers, . . . revolution is an act of violence, it is the violent overthrow of one class by another." We did our best to make our heavily accented Sichuan voices sound as much like Beijing dialect as we could. We read one quotation after another right to the end of the trip. . . .

I will never forget 31 August 1966. On that day I joined all the Red Guards who had come from throughout China to be in Beijing to see him, to see Chairman Mao, the leader we dreamed of and thought of twenty-four hours a day.

A few days earlier we had been told by the Revolutionary Committee of the Agricultural Museum [, our billet,] that some Central leaders would see us on August 31. When we heard this, everyone exploded in excitement. Speculation was rife: Which leader or leaders would be there? Would Chairman Mao come? The result of our group deliberations was that Chairman Mao was sure to be too busy to come. Since we were not from Beijing, there was even less reason for him to see us. But there was a small and adamant group who were sure that Chairman Mao would appear. Naturally, I wanted to believe them. Truth, after all, is often the prerogative of the minority.

It was 6:00 A.M., August 31. We all woke with a start. Although we were all at the age when it is impossible to wake up in the morning, everyone had been really excited the night before. People had woken at the slightest noise and looked around to see that nothing was going on, before drifting off to sleep again. But this time it was for real. We all got dressed in record time and, armed with the food and water we had set aside the night before, ran into the courtyard.

Once assembled, we climbed into our bus and were driven to Tiananmen Square. We lined up and sat in ranks; the Square was turned into a massive sea of green. We waited wide-eyed and expectant. Morning broke slowly, and we saw the majestic outline of Tiananmen Gate. As the sun rose, we began to get hot. But we waited and waited. Our eyes were popping out of our heads. The sweat trickled down our brows and into our eyes. Everyone was constantly wiping the sweat away with their hands. We took out our food and water and started chatting as we ate. Some people nodded off to sleep, heads cushioned on their knees. As a person nodded, his or her head might slip off the knee and they'd awake with a shock, look around, and then nod off again. This happened repeatedly. Some people simply lay down to sleep, using their caps and satchels as a pillow. I stood up and looked out over the Square, a massive expanse occupied by an army of battle-weary Red Guards. I sat down and was overcome by drowsiness myself and, despite my best efforts to keep awake, I was exhausted and fell asleep.

Suddenly drums could be heard, a weak sound at first that grew louder. After the drum roll, all the loudspeakers on the Square resounded with the opening chords of "The East Is Red," followed by the tumultuous sound of the orchestral arrangement of the song. The very earth shook with the volume of the sound. Everyone jumped to their feet. My heart was in my throat; I could feel my pulse around my lips, in my head and neck. The eyes of a million Red Guards were riveted on Tiananmen Gate.

The leaders of Party Central had appeared! But who was behind them? It was Chairman Mao himself!! Everyone threw down their hats, satchels, bread, water flasks, and began shouting as we surged toward Tiananmen. All those acres of green-clad bodies that had been sitting passively only a moment before turned into a solid wave of human flesh, like a wall of football players. We all shouted "Long Live Chairman Mao!" At first it was an uncoordinated cry, but slowly the chant issued forth in unison. The love that tens of thousands of Red Guards felt for their leader burst forth like lava flowing from Mount Vesuvius. It was a torrent, an explosion of liquid steel. Without a second thought, I joined in and tears streamed from my eyes. I hated the people in front of me who blocked my line of vision and kept Chairman Mao from me. I resented the fact that I was nearsighted, that at this most precious moment I could not see the Chairman clearly. I begged a Red Guard in front of me to lend me his telescope. He was staring into it looking intently at the rostrum on the Gate. Tears had flowed down his cheeks to the corners of his mouth and were dripping onto his clothes. His face was ecstatic. I pleaded with him to let me have one, quick look. "Just for a minute or even only a second. I'll give it back immediately, I swear. I swear by Chairman Mao." He finally gave in and handed me the telescope. I put it up to my eye as quickly as possible but I could not find the Chairman anywhere. What was wrong? He wasn't there. Then suddenly the human wave surged in my direction and I was thrown to the ground. I was held down by a mass of hysterical Red Guards. I pressed down with both my arms to keep myself from being crushed, still the breath was squashed out of me. I struggled for all I was worth, but I could feel my strength being sapped away. I could not keep myself up and my face was being forced against the ground, my cheek crushed downward. I could hear my bones creaking, but I could not scream out because the breath had been knocked out of me. I was afraid I would die without ever having seen Chairman Mao. What a wasted life! But my instinct for self-preservation took over and I started fighting my way out, regardless of the cost. Miraculously, the crowd in front of me parted and a wide road appeared. In that instant I saw Chairman Mao. He was in an open limousine that was moving slowly in our direction. He was like a statue, as tall as the heavens. He was dressed in military uniform, and he waved at us. Tens of thousands of eyes turned toward us, saw our faces, our bodies, and saw into our hearts. I went limp, but I was held up by the mass of other Red Guards. I felt warm all over; I was drunk with happiness. My tears soaked the front of my army-green uniform. I forgot everything, my studies, my future. Life seemed so unimportant, irrelevant. Nothing could compare with this instant, because I had seen him!

I did nonetheless have one major regret. I did not get a chance to shake Chairman Mao's hand. How I wished I could have become a spirit or a martial arts expert and flown over the crowd to sit next to Chairman Mao! But I couldn't. The people who shook Chairman Mao's hand that day were our heroes. We all rushed up to them so we could hold them by the hand, reluctant to let go. We nearly tore them to pieces.

Even today, whenever I hear "The East Is Red," that incredibly familiar tune, my heart beats faster. It is because that moment was so profound, so exciting and happy. I have only felt like that once in my whole life. I am sure I will never, ever feel like that again. . . .

Some years later, I went to Beijing with my mother. One day, we visited the Chairman Mao Memorial Hall. Over the years people have ceaselessly gone to see the Chairman's corpse. Our line was like a coiled dragon that wound around the center of the Square.

We entered the stately and solemn foyer of the Mausoleum. The stream of people made a slow circumambulation. This was the second time I had seen Chairman Mao. He was the undying idol of my heart, the man who possessed and ruled me throughout my adolescence and youth. If the truth be told, I had lived solely for him for two decades.

Mao Zedong was lying there so still and quiet, at repose in his crystal sarcophagus. The flag of the People's Republic was draped over his body, his face had a peaceful expression on it. I experienced a strange cocktail of emotions: bitter, sweet, sour, and hot. I could not take my eyes off him, my leader.

In my mind's eye, I saw him make the announcement: "The People's Republic of China is hereby established. The people of China have stood up!"

I saw him dressed in a military uniform waving a cap in his hand as he said: "Long live the People!"

I saw him in his limousine driving toward the hysterical Red Guards.

I saw him standing there with that expression on his face that I was so familiar with from all the photographs, extending his massive hand in my direction. . . .

I could not help reaching out for his hand in return, just as I had so many times before in my dreams. But there was nothing there. The Chairman was still lying there, and we inched forward with the rest of the crowd. We moved past the bier that was surrounded by fresh flowers and made our way slowly to the exit.

I bid farewell to Chairman Mao. I bid farewell also to twenty years of my life, the most precious, enthusiastic, and impressionable time of my youth.

We walked out into Tiananmen Square, which was bathed in bright sunlight, in the direction of Tiananmen Gate where we could see [the portrait of] Chairman Mao, although Chairman Mao was not there himself.

Even now the songs I most often sing, the songs I am most familiar with, that I can sing from beginning to end, are ones written in praise of Chairman Mao. The works I can still recite by heart are Chairman Mao's poems. And I still quote Chairman Mao at the drop of a hat. I know and hold it to be true that Mao Zedong will live on in my heart forever.

This year I am in Shenzhen for Spring Festival. During the holiday I happened to take taxis a number of times. None of the taxis had the usual talismans for good fortune hanging from their rear-view mirrors. What hung there instead was Chairman Mao's portrait. I asked the drivers about it and they all said that they hung the Chairman because he could ward off evil.

Dear Chairman Mao, people throughout China miss you.[4]

6 February 1992, Shenzhen

Notes

1. See Stephen Kinzer, " 'Love Letters' to Hitler, a Book and Play Shocking to Germans."
2. Subsequent to the publication of Li Zhisui's memoirs in 1994, one Beijing-based writer questioned whether Liu Xiaoqing had re-evaluated her innocent view of the Chairman. See Xue Yu, "Zhide pengMaozhe renzhen yidu," p. 39.
3. "Sister Jiang" (*Jiangjie*) is a pre-1966 opera about the Sichuan revolutionary martyr Jiang Zhuyun. It is based on the novel *Red Crag* (Hongyan).
4. Liu was far from being the only screen personality to express such sentiments. Jiang Wen, her actor-boyfriend and one of China's leading actors, made his directorial debut in the summer of 1995 with a CultRev nostalgia film "Under the Radiant Sun" (*Yangguang canlande rizi*). Mao Zedong is prominent *in absentia* in this highly popular movie, one that was based on the 1991 Wang Shuo story "Wild Beasts" (*Dongwu xiongmeng*). See, for example, Sandrine Chenivesse, "For Us, Mao Was a First Love."

In a Glass Darkly: An Interview with Gu Yue

*The search for Mao look-alikes (*texing yanyuan *in Chinese), clones who could play the Great Leader in theater and film productions, began in the late 1970s. Not only did these actors have to look like Mao, they had, above all, to be politically reliable.[1] The foremost of their number was Gu Yue, a PLA actor personally selected by Marshal Ye Jianying for the role. He made a career playing Mao and by 1993 had been the Chairman in over 30 films and teleseries.*

In 1992, Gu Yue was told he could not do product endorsements in his Mao persona, but that did not stop him from trying to make up for lost income. In August 1993, Gu went to the flood-stricken Heze district in Shandong with a number of other performers to put on a "charity concert" for the peasants. Chinese press reports claim that he demanded and got an appearance fee of 20,000 yuan. According to outraged journalists, all Gu had to do for this not inconsiderable sum was to come out on the stage and salute the amassed comrades. In his defense Gu Yue argued that playing Mao had deprived him of a normal life and that by all rights he should have had the rank of general, but in 1993 he was still only a divisional commander. Furthermore, he claimed, he was often exploited by the entertainment industry; while he earned relatively little others were making a fortune out of his appearances.

His critics commented that for actors who played Mao to be paid for public appearances was not only injurious to the image of the Chairman but undermined the curiosity value of the performer. One recommended solution to the problem of low pay was that Gu Yue should be placed under state "protection" and given special privileges so he could maintain the mystique of Mao.[2]

In answering the following questions posed by a Hong Kong reporter, Gu Yue is fairly circumspect, although something of the afflatus of Chairman Mao does seem to make its way through the verbiage.

Question: Does the MaoCraze in China have anything to do with your extremely successful portrayal of Mao on the screen?

Answer: The Craze for our Leader, for Mao Zedong, has developed because, as the quality of our material civilization has improved, people have a greater interest in spiritual civilization. People think fondly of the achievements of Chairman Mao. There are those who say, on the other hand, that my successful representation of Chairman Mao has inculcated a renewed sentiment for him, that Mao has benefited from his association with me. But only others can say that; it would not be suitable for me to claim such a thing. What I can say is that I have been the beneficiary of Chairman Mao.

Q: Some people claim that the MaoCraze is a mass expression of dissatisfaction with Deng's policies, policies that encourage people to think only of money. What do you think?

A: I disagree. Deng's open door and reform policies are entirely in keeping with Mao Zedong Thought. Ping-Pong diplomacy and the establishment of diplomatic relations between China and the United States, as well as China and Japan, were all policies initiated by Chairman Mao and implemented by Premier Zhou Enlai. If there hadn't been a thaw in Sino-U.S. relations, the Open Door and Reform would not have been possible.

Q: Mao's errors have been clearly explicated in Party Central documents; yet, in your films, you avoid all question of Mao's mistakes. For example, the way Mao treated Liu Shaoqi.

A: None of the films I've worked on have touched on these questions. None have dealt directly with the Cultural Revolution. I can hardly be blamed if it's not in the script. If, in the future, the script calls for it, then I'll do what is required of me.

Q: What did you think when, as you were working on developing your Mao character, you came across his dark side?

A: Mmm. Nobody's perfect after all, and Mao Zedong is no exception to that. Mistakes and errors were inevitable given the long and protracted struggles in which he was involved. The Party Central line on this at the present time is quite correct. I wouldn't speculate on how he'll be seen in the future. I do feel, however, that Comrade Deng Xiaoping has been magnanimous in the way he has dealt with this matter. Despite the numerous attacks made on him personally, Deng has not treated Mao Zedong in a vengeful fashion. Western journalists often ask me what I think of Mao's errors. Once in Ji'nan [the capital of Shandong Province] I responded to an American journalist with a question of my own: What do you think of the statue of Venus? Her arms may be broken but she's still beautiful. I see Mao Zedong in the same way. Flawed beauty is more alluring.

Q: The MaoCraze in China leads one to reflect on the Soviet Union. They not only negated Stalin, now they've even dumped Lenin. Do you think that one day China will act like this?

A: If we support the Four Basic Principles as formulated by Deng Xiaoping, China will not change.[3] If, however, we abandon those principles, China will naturally go the way of the Soviet Union.

Q: Will China abandon the Four Basic Principles after the generation of Older Revolutionaries has died?

A: That's just what the prognosticators of Western imperialism are hoping for. It depends entirely on the next generation of leaders.

Q: If there is a change, Mao will be the first to get it. Are you prepared for that possibility?

A: One can understand that some people hold fears for China becoming like the Soviet Union after our Older Revolutionaries pass away. But the Soviet Union didn't change overnight and we are presently taking precautions.

Q: A report in Sing Pao[4] today claims that Mao's daughter thinks of you as her father. Is that true?

A: Not exactly. When I was filming *The Final Conflict* at Xibaipo, Li Na [Mao and Jiang Qing's daughter] happened to make a trip there. She had lived there with Mao when she was seven. She asked to see me. I recall that we met in a conference room. She held me by the hand, and said: "Your hand's big and soft just like my father's." She's only a little younger than me, but she's had a hard life. After her father died, her mother [Jiang Qing] had certain difficulties.[5] Li Na must have been deeply disturbed and affected by all of that. When I was seeing them off she ran over, hugged me, and burst into tears. I was taken completely by surprise. I realized that there were no words that could express what she was feeling at that moment. I cried too. Everyone present became tearful. Finally I said to her: "I understand."

Q: Have you met all of Mao's family?

A: I see Li Min [the other of Mao's daughters] and her husband, Kong Linghua. Since first meeting them in 1984, she always invites me to spend December 26 [Mao's birthday] at their house. I invariably meet a number of old comrades who knew Mao very well there. So, if I'm free, I go every year and, through her, I've met Mao's secretaries, doctors, nurses, and personal guards. They all remember Chairman Mao with great affection and it has been a valuable learning experience for me. Through them, I've also been able to find out a great deal about the Chairman's private life. I've also met Mao Anqing and his wife.

Q: Have you ever met Zhang Yufeng?[6]

A: Someone told me she was in the same theater when I went to see a performance of some description, but I did not search her out.

Q: There's a rumor that she had a child by Mao. Is that true?

A: As far as I know it's just that, a rumor. Someone wrote about it in a book, and a leader in the Central government remarked that if such gossip persists legal action can be taken for defamation. I believe people who have a grudge against the Chairman made the story up. If it were really true, there's no way it could be kept a secret these days. So many people hate him, and there's been all this material pointing out his errors that you can't tell me you could keep a thing like that secret.[7] Zhang Yufeng is presently a Section Head in the Ministry of Rail Transportation.

Q: Lin Biao and Liu Shaoqi rarely make an appearance in the films about Party leaders. Is this intentional?

A: No. From what I understand there is a central plan for the production of such films. Initially, we are making films about the historical events everyone can agree on, like *The Final Conflict* and *The Three Great Campaigns*, and various periods before the Cultural Revolution. A lot of water has passed under the bridge and people can reflect on the past more calmly. It will be easier to make such films from now on.

Q: Are there deliberate attempts to emphasize Deng Xiaoping's role?

A: No. It is a matter of historical fact. *The Final Conflict* is about a period during which Liu Bocheng and Deng Xiaoping were equally important but, after Liberation, Liu didn't play as major a role as Deng. In the same token, Liu Shaoqi doesn't have a large role in *The Final Conflict*, and that's a matter of historical fact too.

Q: What do you know about Jiang Qing?

A: She really was an ambitious woman. I've read some things that show she didn't start out that way. But she revealed a typically feminine kind of jealousy from the time she became an actress. The moment she got into power she wanted revenge. I've been told that when she and Mao were married, Zhou Enlai proposed that she be kept out of politics. As a result her political ambitions were frustrated for years and she harbored a grudge against the Premier. She had a real lust for power.

Q: Do you have access to classified material?

A: Only limited access. For example, I've read top-secret military telegrams related to the Three Great Campaigns (now stored in the Academy of Military Science).[8] Mao Zedong directed the campaigns by telegram and there are more than 400 telegrams in the files, of which he composed 360.[9] I made reams of notes as background research.

Q: What does Deng think of your acting?

A: Every time I've seen him he's praised my work. I've met the state leaders on various national holidays.

Q: Who's in charge of films related to Party leaders? Is the funding particularly good?

A: Li Ruihuan [then the Politburo leader in charge of ideological matters] is the highest authority. All the films are vetted by "The Steering Committee on Major Revolutionary Historical Themes" which is chaired by Ding Qiao [a former government minister in charge of cinema]. Wang Renzhi [then head of the Department of Propaganda] and Ai Zhisheng [then head of the Ministry of Film and Television] are also involved. Budgets for revolutionary epics are pretty big, but they're based on box office projections. It really depends on the film.

Q: Mao films are so predominantly political, do you think there's any chance they can reach an international audience?

A: I believe there are great possibilities. There's a well-known American director by the name of Oliver Stone who wants to make a film about Mao Zedong. If he wants to find an actor in China for the role I'm confident that I can do it since I've played Mao [in all stages of his life] from youth to old age. If Stone wants me, I'll do my utmost for the role. Mao Zedong is, after all, a national hero. *Gandhi* made it internationally, so there is no reason Mao can't do the same.[10] As long as you have a good script and the film is performed and filmed well, there's a real chance of success. *The Final Conflict* could be an international war epic.

Q: But such films have a hard time even making it to Taiwan.

A: That goes without saying. But people on both sides of the Strait want an accurate portrayal of history. We no longer present a caricature of Chiang Kai-shek in our films; we try to be as convincing as possible.

Q: How do you compare your work to Soviet films about Party leaders?

A: Our films are an advance on the style of filmmaking developed from 1928 by Soviet directors like Eisenstein. I'm particularly impressed by the work of the actor who portrayed Lenin as a great yet also ordinary man.

Q: As you're such a successful Mainland film star, do you make much more than other actors?

A: Let me be frank. Although I'm politically advantaged in that I've often been given audiences with Central leaders, something unheard of for most actors, financially I'm at a distinct disadvantage. I can't negotiate my own terms. According to the regulations of the Ministry of Film and Television, an actor on loan [to another studio] should receive four times their usual wage. But all that money goes to their film studio, in my case, the 1 August Studio. I don't make any extra money. My monthly wage is about three hundred *yuan*. Many other famous actors can get seven or eight times their basic wage when they work for another studio, but I do it for nothing. At most, I get an extra living allowance. To play a leader you have to be prepared to make some sacrifices. What can I do about it? If you play a hero, you have to act the hero in real life. If I haggled about such things, I could damage Mao's image.

Q: Has there been any adverse effect on your family life?

A: No. My wife and I still make more than most people. We do okay. But, of course, we can't compare to movie stars overseas.

Notes

1. See "Zhongyang xuanchuanbu zhuanfa wenhuabu dangzu 'Guanyu xiju, dianying fanying weida lingxiu Mao zhuxi he Zhou zonglide guanghui xingxiangde qingshi baogao' (Zhongxuanfa [1978] 2 hao)," Zhongyang xuanchuanbu bangongting, ed., *Dangde xuanchuan gongzuo wenjian xuanbian (1976–1982)*, vol. 2, p. 607.

2. See the chapter "Mingxing chuchangjia" in Yin Jindi, *Zhongguo wenhua getihu dasaomiao*, pp. 260–61 and 253 respectively.

3. The Four Basic Principles are: to support the leadership of the Communist Party; to support Marxism-Leninism and Mao Zedong Thought; to support the dictatorship of the proletariat; and to support the socialist path.

4. *Sing Pao* (Xingbao) is a Hong Kong–based daily newspaper.

5. That is, Jiang was sentenced to life imprisonment for her "counterrevolutionary" crimes.

6. Zhang Yufeng was Mao's chief "personal secretary" (*shenghuo mishu*) during the Cultural Revolution. She enjoyed such a privileged position that she was even shown walking in front of the Chairman in official photographs. See, for example, issues of *The Liberation Army Pictorial* (Jiefangjun huabao) from the early years of the Cultural Revolution. Not surprisingly, Zhang sank into relative obscurity after the Chairman's demise, although from the late 1980s, like so many others (including Meng Jinyun, another of her ilk), she attempted to cash in on the Mao Cult. See also Zhisui Li, *The Private Life of Chairman Mao* for details of Zhang's relationship with Mao.

7. Li Zhisui claims that Mao was impotent by this time and incapable of fathering a child.

8. The Three Great Campaigns were the Liao-Shen, Huaihai and Ping-Jin Campaigns launched by the PLA against the Nationalist army from September 1948 to early 1949.

9. From what has been said in the introduction in regard to Mao's authorship of such documents, this may now be a fairly contentious claim.

10. In 1995, it was widely rumored that Oliver Stone was still interested in Mao, but was thinking of doing a screen version of Li Zhisui's bedside memoirs.

Draco Volans est in Coelo

Jiang Shui and Tie Zhu

This is the preface from a volume entitled Mao Zedong's Military Philoso-phy and Modern Business Warfare. *The Chinese title translates literally as "Can the dragon ever be bound?" I have chosen to use a Latin heading, "Flying dragon in the heavens," which is taken from the early eighteenth-century Latin translation of Qian, "The Creative," the first hexagram in the* Book of Changes.[1]

The ill-lettered and cliché-ridden prose of this essay is typical of much popular writing on the Mainland today. Bereft of the ideological standards of yesteryear yet incapable of clear and concise thought, the authors could easily be taken to be writing a parody if they were not pursuing their subject with such dogged earnestness.

There's a common saying that people in different professions are sepa-rated by a vast abyss. It would appear that warfare and doing business have absolutely nothing to do with each other. So why do we talk about them in the same breath in this book?

Let's answer with another saying that "stones from another hill may be used to polish the jade of this one" [that is, the advice of others can help overcome one's shortcomings]. Round-about methods can invariably awaken people to the realities of a situation that would otherwise appear insoluble.

There are those in China who have enjoyed marked success in applying the lessons of [classical works like] *The Military Strategies of Sunzi* and *The Romance of the Three Kingdoms* to the business world.[2] Mao Zedong's Military Philosophy is steeped in the wisdom of the past and the present, covering both Chinese and foreign knowledge. It is effulgent with all the brilliance of human understanding, and its validity has been proven time and again in practice. It is a great pity that because of a period when *Quotations from Chairman Mao* were vulgarized and abused [i.e., during the

Cultural Revolution] the true worth of the Chairman's genius is now ignored. There are readers who are hopeful of applying military strategy to their business practices. But if you only have an average education, especially if you have a limited knowledge of classical Chinese and history, why should you discard what is so close at hand [i.e., Mao Thought] and search for answers in the distant past?

Mao Zedong once made a brilliant exposition of the relationship between warfare and business:

> It often happens that only by loss can loss be avoided; this is the principle of "Give in order to take." If what we lose is territory and what we gain is victory over the enemy, plus recovery and also expansion of our territory, then it is a paying proposition. In a business transaction, if a buyer does not "lose" some money, he cannot obtain goods; if a seller does not "lose" some goods, he cannot obtain money. The losses incurred in a revolutionary movement involve destruction, and what is gained is construction of a progressive character. Sleep and rest involve loss of time, but energy is gained for tomorrow's work. If any fool does not understand this and refuses to sleep, he will have no energy the next day, and that is a losing proposition.[3]

History has shown the unparalleled astuteness of Mao Zedong's Military Philosophy. Despite being equipped by the Americans, Chiang Kai-shek's eight-million-strong army was to learn this lesson for it was defeated in a glorious victory for the homespun troops of Mao Zedong within the space of three short years. Apart from various objective reasons stemming from Chinese history and the progress of world history, it cannot be denied that Mao Zedong's Military Philosophy played a decisive role in that victory.

It is with regret, however, that we must note that in the 1960s and 1970s Mao quotes were generally vulgarized, and this led to a tendency for people "to throw the baby out with the bath water" in the 1980s. Quite a number of people, including some high-level cadres, came to believe that Mao Zedong Thought was no longer valid for the task of construction in China today. They felt Mao had no role to play in the economic tasks posed by the Open Door and Reform policies. Such attitudes were the result of ignorance and prejudice, while the proponents of Mao's works insisted that people study Mao in the same old dogmatic fashion.

Mao Zedong's military philosophy spans all ages and nations. It can be scientifically applied to military strategy as well as providing analogies for a range of areas, in particular ever changing social realities. The essence of Mao Zedong Thought is not to be superstitious about anything, nor dogmatic; all problems should be analyzed in concrete terms and a solution should be found in a practical and realistic manner. There are limitless possibilities for the application of Mao's Military Thought in the economic realm today as we enliven the local economy and open up to the outside world. The problem is simple: do we want to set out on this Long March of 25,000 *li* and head north to fight a war of resistance?[4]

Perhaps we will need a few more years before we can free ourselves entirely from the shadow of the Cultural Revolution. Then we will be able to perceive clearly the true value of Mao Thought. We look forward to the advent of business people who will apply Mao Thought to the realm of the economy, just as we hope that theoreticians versed in this area will appear.

It is in this spirit that we humbly offer this meager volume to those noble individuals engaged in the commodity economy. We cast forth this brick in the hope that it will elicit comments of jade.

9 September 1991

Notes

1. See Jean-Baptiste Regis, Joseph de Mailla & Pierre de Tartre, S.J., trans., "De Explicatione Textuum Libri *Y-King*, Caput Primum: *Kien*: Coelum," in *Y-King*, from John Minford & Joseph Lau, eds., *Classical Chinese Literature, Vol. 1: From Antiquity to the T'ang.*

2. *Sunzi bingfa* and *Sanguo yanyi*. Both works have been trawled by writers and publishers in Japan, China, Taiwan, Hong Kong, Thailand and the U.S. to provide today's merchants with ancient strategies that can be applied to modern business.

3. This quotation is from Mao Zedong, "Zhongguo geming zhanzheng he zhanlüe wenti," *Mao Zedong xuanji*, vol. 1, p. 195. For the English text, see *Selected Works of Mao Tse-tung*, vol. 1, p. 221. The curious use of this quotation is itself an example of how Mao's words can be so easily taken out of context.

4. These are two clichés that originate in the Communist Party's struggles with the Nationalists and the Japanese.

Let the Red Sun Shine In

During the winter of 1991–92, The Red Sun: Odes to Mao Zedong Sung to a New Beat, *a rearrangement and recording of Cultural Revolution songs, was released on cassette tape and immediately became a nationwide bestseller. Over one million copies of the tape were sold in the space of a few months and some 14 million copies were reportedly sold by 1993. Needless to say, CD, karaoke and laser disk versions of this collection and other similar compilations were soon marketed.*

For those familiar with the near-ecstatic qualities of the original songs, dithyrambic outpourings for the quasi-religious figure of the Great Leader, the new versions are limp, mushy and kitsch. As Xu Jilin points out below, they reflect perfectly the tenor of the times.

In the following round-table discussion, a group of Shanghai academics and writers known as active cultural critics, reflect on the significance of what was called "The Red Sun Craze" and comment on what they think the modern classics should be ("The Magic Flute" with electronic synthesizers).

Time: Afternoon, 20 January 1992
Place: The Conference Room of *China Youth News*, Shanghai
Participants:
Xu Jilin: Researcher in the Cultural Institute of the Huadong Chemical Industries Institute
    He Ping: Editor, *The Shanghai Cultural Almanac*
    Yan Bofei: Researcher in the Philosophy Institute of the Shanghai Academy of Social Sciences
    Yang Jianguo: Reporter, *Shanghai Culture and Arts News*

Yang Jianguo: The overwhelming popularity of *The Red Sun* dating from late last year [winter 1991] has taken music publishers, distributors, and the media by surprise. When the Shanghai Branch of the China Record Company produced this tape, they estimated that the market could absorb about seventy to eighty thousand copies but the overwhelming public response has been quite unexpected. The Shanghai Music Bookstore ordered a thousand copies but sold out within two days. By the time Mao Zedong's birthday came around on December 26, there was no stock left in the city. Over the New Year holiday, nine families living in the Cao-Yang New Village all played the tape at full volume, and the whole building became a massive loudspeaker.

Sales outside Shanghai have also been remarkable. The Wangfujing Bookstore in Beijing ordered two thousand tapes but because of a clerical error received only two hundred. There was a rush on them and they were sold out in little over an hour. They had to send an urgent telex for more. A private entrepreneur from Hunan came to Shanghai and ordered five thousand copies of the tape and paid for them on the spot in cash. Asked whether he could be sure they would sell, he retorted: "No worries, Hunan is the Red Province of China."[1]

In early January [1992], the China Record Company "guesstimated" that they could sell 300,000 copies of the tape; soon they revised the figures up to 500,000, and then 700,000. Now they're looking at the possibility of breaking the one million mark. Originally it was thought that *The Red Sun* would be in heavy competition with *Goodbye*, the farewell tape of the "Little Tigers,"[2] but the Tigers have been routed. This is the first time in ages that a local [i.e., Mainland] recording has done so well. *The Red Sun* is no simple "phenomenon"; it has become a full-blown craze.

The reasons for this are complex. Although the "Little Tigers" are idols among teeny-boppers, people of all ages and from all walks of life have been buying *The Red Sun*.

He Ping: The element of nostalgia in the success of *The Red Sun*, especially among people who lived through the Cultural Revolution, cannot be ignored. For us, the Cultural Revolution was the most exciting period of our lives; you could say we grew up singing the songs that are reproduced in *The Red Sun*. Hearing them now brings back our lost youth, along with memories of a simpler and unsullied past.

Yan Bofei: I recall a few years back there was a period when there was a revival of Model Opera tunes and arias that led to something of a public debate. The opponents of the Model Opera revival won out in the end.[3] But not many years later, here we have all these Cultural Revolution–era songs blaring at us in the streets and no one is suggesting that they bring back bitter memories of the past or traumatize people so much that they can't get to sleep. This reflects a new type of tolerance and is proof that ideology is losing its grip on society. The songs on *The Red Sun* tape have been put to pop music; they are a form of pop culture now. There's none of that Cultural Revolution–style religiosity about any of it. They're just like all the books about Mao's personal life that show that Mao himself has been secularized.

Xu Jilin: When I first heard *The Red Sun* I thought it was sacrilegious. The songs did not feel the same at all, although by the end I was won over by the music. The tape secularizes what were originally pure, religious hymns. Once people sung them with fervor; now they are sung in a new type of arrangement and with a different sentiment. There is an effervescence in the singing that is made possible by distance. The original songs were heavily laden with a complex of signs and significance; now all that remains is a [version of the old] melody and rhythm. The actual ideological content, value, and psychological thrust of the songs has disappeared entirely and has been replaced by a totally different sensibility.

That we can accept these songs and see them in a new light is proof that we can now deconstruct the "time of suffering" and our memories of it. It is an era that has left us with an extremely complex legacy. Why do some people feel deeply touched by these songs? We cannot avoid the fact that some things about the past are worth valuing, like the sense of simplicity and purity people had, for example, their piety, a belief that great goodness was possible and that people were good; a belief that you should not become entrapped in your own inner world and you should throw yourself into things and thereby find a meaning in life. Today we lack all these things.

Hong Kong and Taiwan Canto Pop songs might be easy listening but the lyrics are pathetic. They are all self-indulgent ditties about minor personal tribulations; they reflect a sense of absurdity and meaninglessness; they show a desire for new social contacts and a position in life and give voice to the sense of constriction that comes from being isolated in a large city. In the mainland songs of the 1950s and 1960s, there is virtually no clear delineation between the individual and the collective. Everything was done communally and when you hear the songs of that age you feel the self-confidence, dignity, and enthusiasm that people enjoyed at the time. People have been exposed to so much Canto Pop that they know its inadequacies; they feel the need for a collective belief system, a means for the individual to relate to society, and they have discovered some meaning and fulfillment in the songs of *The Red Sun*. The popularity of the tape is significant in many ways and, although it will fall from favor before too long, I believe that a great deal can be said about it in terms of social and cultural psychology.

He Ping: Shen Rong wrote a story some time ago called "Ten Years Younger" and I'm sure that [like the characters in that story] all Chinese people from their forties up wish they could shed ten years.[4] Listening to *The Red Sun*, people aren't simply recalling Mao, they are reliving their lost youth. On one level, that decade simply doesn't exist. Be that as it may, we feel there are things about those years that are worth remembering, worth giving clear and positive expression to. [The famous literary historian and writer] Qian Zhongshu once said that "the media is the message."[5] Though the content of some of these songs may be fairly ridiculous, given a suitable treatment the melodies appeal to large numbers of people.

Yang Jianguo: In musical terms, quite a few paeans for Mao have appeared in recent years, like "The Sun Is So Red and Chairman Mao Is So Dear," "A Mile-High Skyscraper Shoots Out of the Ground." Old songs popular with rusticated youth and prison songs have also made an appearance.[6] None of these, however, have been as well-received as *The Red Sun*. One of the reasons for its success is that the new arrangement is entirely in keeping with the sentiments, musical tastes, and up-beat attitude of today's audiences. The songs make you feel good; they allow you to recall all the good things about your youth and relive the past in a new and positive way. Younger listeners enjoy the songs not simply because they are used to Canto Pop and a Euro-American style of singing, but also because *The Red Sun* exudes a romantic spirit that they crave. They might not know what the Eight-Word Constitution is,[7] but they can sense the exciting spirit of the past and don't simply dismiss it as absurd.

Yan Bofei: The popularity of *The Red Sun* is proof that the power of ideology has gradually waned in recent years. But it also reflects a sense of crisis. For a few generations, people believed that all they had to do was give themselves up entirely; in the present crisis people don't have the safety net of any belief system.

He Ping: You must admit that the songs in *The Red Sun* reflect a peasant civilization that is superficially very self-confident. But its success lies in the fact that the songs aren't sung as they were originally. If the originals were released, people would be repulsed. When some of the Model Operas were restaged, audiences felt that the movements of the characters were a burlesque; everything was too obvious and the operas weren't well received at all.

Xu Jilin: The reason I can enjoy *The Red Sun* is that the musical arrangement is very much in keeping with my present psychological state. In the past, this music would have incited me to get involved in things and I wouldn't have thought much of the actual aesthetic value of the songs; now I can enjoy them from a perspective of distance and on an aesthetic level. I saw a performance of "Sister Jiang" a while ago.[8] It was in the same style of the original [1960s version] and I thought it could become a classic if they only changed a few things. There are some really good arias in it, but if you stick too closely to the original [score] it feels unbearably drawn out. Shakespeare's plays have been adapted for every age and they are still popular. If they stuck with a Victorian interpretation of the plays, no one would want to watch them.

Yang Jianguo: The Japanese did a production of Mozart's *The Magic Flute* in which they used an astronaut and electronic music. It was reportedly very successful. Conceptually, we're just incredibly conservative.

He Ping: There are works that can live on beyond the age that gave them birth, but they need to be reworked so they can enter into a dialogue with contemporary audiences. Another thing that *The Red Sun* has done is to remind us of the extraordinary power of the media. Cassette tapes are a medium that is inexpensive to produce, easy to use, and quickly disseminated.

Xu Jilin: *The Red Sun* has led me to consider the question of the resources of popular culture. Pop culture can develop from highbrow culture. Take Richard Clayderman, for example. His piano music is adapted from classical works. It can also come from local culture, as in the case of so much American music—jazz, rock'n'roll, disco—which has been heavily influenced by black music. *The Red Sun* originated with historical songs. But I feel we should also add a note about self-awareness. You need to be completely clear about your original material and have a full understanding of and familiarity with the audience you are working for. The popularity of *The Red Sun* also reflects the paucity of contemporary pop music on the Mainland. It is obviously easier to enter into a dialogue either with the past [as in the case of the music of *The Red Sun*] or overseas [Hong Kong and Taiwan music] than with the rapidly changing realities of contemporary life. At best we are using outside cultural contact as an intermediary for establishing a dialogue with our own present. Given this creative deficit, South China is definitely lagging behind the North. At least the North has given us the "Northwest Wind."[9]

Yang Jianguo: The success of *The Red Sun* will lead to a fad for similar songs that will last for a while. Right at this moment a number of record companies are preparing to release other revolutionary songs, including quotation songs.[10] I'm not sure that this new deluge of music will be as much of a money-spinner as expected. The past has effectively acted as a massive form of presale advertising [for cassettes like *The Red Sun*]. Everyone's familiar with them so you don't need to spend any money on promoting them. But you can have too much of a good thing, and people can easily be turned off.

Notes

1. Many revolutionary leaders like Mao Zedong, Liu Shaoqi, Peng Dehuai, and even Hu Yaobang, hailed from Hunan Province.
2. *Xiaohu dui* was a teeny-bopper Taiwanese group of the early 1990s.

3. In late 1985, arias from a number of Cultural Revolution–period Modern Revolutionary Model Operas (*xiandai geming jingxi*, or *yangbanxi*), in particular "The Red Lantern" and "Taking Tiger Mountain by Strategy," were set to disco music and sold in cassette form as well as played on radio stations throughout the country. This led to a debate about the validity of reviving a widely reviled form of mass culture that was so closely associated with their patron, Jiang Qing. Outraged opponents of the operas like the Shanghai writer Wang Ruowang and the Beijing writer-bureaucrat Deng Youmei helped dampen the general enthusiasm for this tacky reprisal of the Cultural Revolutionary past. See Barmé, "Revolutionary opera arias sung to a new, disco beat."

4. In her comic late 1980s' story "*Jianqu shisui*" the novelist Shen Rong speculated as to what would happen if Party Central issued a document making everyone in China ten years younger enabling them to make up for time lost due to the Cultural Revolution.

5. Presumably, Qian was quoting Marshall McLuhan's famous line from the 1960s.

6. Songs of rusticated youth (*zhiqing gequ*) were popular with educated urban youth who were sent to the countryside in the late 1960s. Prison songs (*qiuge*) enjoyed a measure of popularity in 1987.

7. The Eight-Word Constitution or Eight-Point Charter for Agriculture (*Bazi xianfa*) was a Central Committee directive issued in 1958 as part of a socialist and communist education movement to increase production by paying attention to (and these are the eight words) "soil, fertilizer, water, seeds, close-planting, protection, tool improvement and field management" (*tu, fei, shui, zhong, mi, bao, guan, gong*).

8. For "Sister Jiang," see the note to Liu Xiaoqing, "A Star Reflects on the Sun" above.

9. The "Northwest Wind" (*Xibeifeng*) was a style of music combining local northwestern Chinese folk music troupes with Canto Pop that swept the nation in 1988. There are those who claim, however, that the first "Northwest Wind" songs came from Guangzhou and that much musical innovation spreads from the HK-Taiwan-influenced South.

10. Quotation songs (*yuluge*) were Mao quotes put to music. These generally tuneless and clumsy songs enjoyed considerable popularity in the early years of the Cultural Revolution. Twenty-two of these were published under the title "Wei Mao zhuxi yulu puqu." A recorded version of these songs was also produced, see *Wei Mao zhuxi yulu puqu*, Beijing: Zhongguo changpianshe, 1967. Some 365 Mao quotes were eventually put to music, the leading composer of such works being Jie Fu (Li Jiefu), who wrote over 70 tunes in a two-year period. See Lin Hongfa, " 'Wenge' zhong Mao zhuxi yuluge dansheng shimo." As in so many other areas of contemporary Chinese life, litigation has also marred the post-revolutionary fate of the quotation songs. The family of the late Li Jiefu successfully sued the Musical and Film Publishing House of the Beijing Film Academy for breach of copyright in their illegal use of Li's musical adaptations of Mao quotations, songs for the stage and the film version of the musical extravaganza "The East Is Red," released on cassette in 1977, and in music used in the *The Red Sun* tape discussed at this forum. See "Beijing Haidianqu renmin fayuan gongkai shenli Li Jiefu gequ qinquanan"; the cassette tape *Mao zhuxi yulu gequ/ Dahai hangxing kao duoshou*, Beijing: Beijing dianying xueyuan chubanshe, 1992; and, for a "rock'n'roll" version of the quotation songs, see *Mao zhuxi yuluge—yaogun lianchang*, Kunming: Yunnan yinxiang chubanshe (no date).

The Red Sun: Singing the Praises of Chairman Mao

China Record Company

The following translations are of songs on Side A of the cassette/CD The Red Sun *that became a MaoCraze hit in 1992. It is left to the reader's imagination to sense what these mindnumbingly simple but heartfelt Cultural Revolution paeans to Mao sound like when sung to a saccharine Canto Pop beat.[1]*

From the early 1990s many similar collections, imitations and sequels to the original The Red Sun *tape were produced[2] as were karaoke versions of the songs with such titles as* Sweet Sweet Red Sun.[3] *Karaoke adaptations produced on video and laser disk utilized documentary footage of Mao as well as MTV-like montages of young people who, among other things, wander around wistfully thinking of the late Chairman.*

In 1993, as part of the Mao centenary, tapes of speeches by Mao were also released. They featured such utterances as Mao's announcement of the founding of the People's Republic in 1949, as well as longer speeches made on such occasions as the Preparatory Meeting of the Chinese National People's Political Consultative Congress on 15 June 1949.[4]

The Red Sun

Odes to Mao Zedong Sung to a New Beat

> Singers: Li Lingyu, Sun Guoqing, Tu Honggang and Fan Linlin
> With Li Li, Jing Gangshan, Zhu Hua, Wu Ming, Zhao Li and Li
>   Xiaowen
> Music Conducted by Jin Wei[5]
> Accompaniment: Beijing Choral Orchestra
>
> China Record Corporation,
> Shanghai, China, 1992
> (Compact disc digital audio)

The Sunshine Is the Warmest, Chairman Mao the Dearest

The Sunshine is the warmest, Chairman Mao the dearest,
Your glorious Thought will forever shine in my heart.
The sun is the reddest, Chairman Mao the dearest,
Your glorious Thought will forever navigate my course.

The Bright Red Sun in the Sky

The Sun in the sky is red, burning burnished bright,
The sun in our hearts is Mao Zedong.
He led us to achieve Liberation,
The people stood up and became the masters.
Yi-ya-yi-zi-you-wei-ya-ya-zi-you-a.
The people stood up and became the masters.

The Red Sun Shines Over the Frontiers
(In the style of a "Korean minority" folk song)

The Red Sun shines over the frontiers,
The green mountains and clear waters are bathed in the morning
    light.
The fruit trees stand in rows at the foot of the Changbai Mountains,[6]
The rice on the banks of the Ganglan River is so fragrant.
Rend wide the mountains
and they will offer up their treasures.
Stop the rivers and build dams,
bringing the water up into the hills.
A-you . . .
The fighting spirit of the borderlands' people is high,
the army and the people on the frontiers are united to carry out
    construction.
Chairman Mao is leading us forward
in the direction of victory.

The Golden Sun in Beijing
(In the style of a Tibetan folk song)[7]

From that Golden Mountain in Beijing
the suns rays shoot out to illuminate the four directions.
And Chairman Mao is that Golden Sun.
How warm, how beatific,
bringing light to the hearts of the liberated serfs [of Tibet].
We are now walking on the great socialist highway of good
    fortune!

Eternal Life to Chairman Mao

Dearest Chairman Mao,
you are the sun in our hearts.
There are so many private thoughts that we would like to tell you.
There are so many songs of praise that we would like to sing to
you.
Millions of red hearts think only of Beijing.
Millions of smiling faces welcome the Red Sun.
We respectfully wish you, Chairman Mao, eternal life!

Notes

1. See Thomas B. Gold, "Go With Your Feelings: Hong Kong and Taiwan Popular Culture in Greater China." Orville Schell says the rearrangement turns them into "transvestite-like songs." See Schell, *Mandate of Heaven*, p. 288.

2. These include such titles as *Guoqude ge*, Guiyang: Guizhou dongfang yinxiang gongsi (no date); *Renmin wangbuliao Mao Zedong*, Yanbian yinxiang chubanshe (no date); *Zhongguo gechao Mao Zedong*, Guangdong yinxiang chubanshe (no date); and, *Hong taiyang OK*, Beijing yinxiang gongsi, 1992.

3. *Tiantian hong taiyang (xinshangban-OKban)*, Neimenggu yinxiang chubanshe, 1992.

4. Zhongyang dang'anguan/ Zhongyang wenxian yanjiushi, eds., *Juren zhi sheng: Mao Zedong jianghua yuanshi luyin*, Shenzhen: Shenzhenshi jiguang jiemu chuban faxing gongsi, 1993.

5. For details regarding Jin Wei's creative input, see Zhao Xiaoyuan, "Ta tuoqile 'Hong taiyang'."

6. Located in the southwest of Jilin Province, near the border with North Korea.

7. The original version of this song, along with a number of other popular nationalities' songs of the Cultural Revolution period, can be found on the LP record *Zhufu Mao zhuxi wanshou wujiang—gezu renmin gechang Mao zhuxi*, Beijing: Zhongguo changpianshe, 1967.

A Place in the Pantheon:
Mao and Folk Religion

Xin Yuan

Published under a pen name, the Beijing scholar Wang Yi has written on such diverse subjects as traditional Chinese gardens and elements of folk religion in the political culture of the Cultural Revolution. This article appeared in the Hong Kong press at the end of 1992.

From late last year [1991], China has experienced a craze that has involved the re-deification of Mao Zedong. It started in the South and has spread to the North. People have combined Mao's image with gold cash inscribed with the words "May This Attract Wealth"[1] or images of the eight hexagrams, and placed them in prominent places. Drivers throughout the country have Mao's picture hanging from their rear-view mirrors and claim that Mao can prevent car accidents. The cassette tape *The Red Sun: Odes to Mao Zedong Sung to a New Beat* has been a national best-seller. Mainlanders have variously called this the "Red Sun Phenomenon" or the "Mao Becomes a God Phenomenon." It has also given rise to numerous interpretations among political and cultural analysts.

Political conservatives are trying to dragoon this MaoCraze into the service of their efforts to "oppose peaceful evolution."[2] Deng Liqun has remarked "with the unprecedented international wave of revisionist thought coupled with the tide of Bourgeois Liberalism in China, we have indeed seen 'a miasmal mist once more rising.' "[3] But Deng has nothing to say on the subject of why the masses are now treating Mao Zedong like Zhao Gong or the Kitchen God.[4]

Intellectuals, on the other hand, see the MaoCraze as evidence that elements of the Cultural Revolution still hold sway and that there's been no rational attempt to understand the long-term damage wrought by that period on the people of China. But such views are all superficial and simplistic. No one has tried to discuss the question in terms of the psychology of folk religion. Therefore, it is obvious that further analysis of the phenomenon is necessary.

The present Mao cult is different from the past in that it constitutes a popular deification of Mao, not a politically orchestrated one. People now seek the protection of the Mao-God when they build houses, engage in business, and drive vehicles. Old ladies place images of Mao over their stoves and in niches built for statues of the Buddha and burn incense to him morning and night. Traditional folk religion provides the real basis for the present Red Sun Craze.

In Chinese culture, the power of the gods is always reliant upon the authority of the ruler. As early as the *Zuozhuan*, in the Record of the Fourteenth Year of Duke Xiang, we find the unequivocal statement: "The ruler is the host of the spirits and the hope of the people."[5] Politics and religion formed a mutually cooperative whole or, as [the late-Qing politician and military leader] Zeng Guofan put it, "The way of the kings rules in this world; the way of the gods in the other world." Both ways witnessed a plethora of rulers, however, with dynasties rising and falling in the human world and, in the other world, rulers like the Jade Emperor, Maitreya Buddha, and so on, gaining ascendancy at one time or another. The only thing that did not change was the immutable link between politics and religion.

With the communist takeover in 1949, popular religion in China underwent the most violent change in its history. First, in the 1950s, there was a movement to wipe out superstition, which was followed in the 1960s by the call to "eliminate the Four Olds"[6] and the suppression of virtually all forms of religious activity in the country. The effects were particularly devastating as both movements took place in tandem with the creation of grass-roots Party cells and nationwide Thought Reform. In traditional society, at the county level and lower, political life was ruled by popular clan bodies that also had responsibility for other activities including religious observances. The post-1949 organization of society, however, saw this traditional arrangement uprooted and the monopoly rule of Party committees at every level. Folk religion was deprived entirely of the social and organizational basis for its activities. Nonetheless, habits and practices that have weathered changes over the millennia and provided spiritual succor for people for so long are not so easily obliterated. Frustrated in its traditional form, it is only natural that popular religious sentiment would find new ways to express itself. In post-1949 China, the only sanctified form it could take was in worshipping the Red Sun, Mao Zedong.

The legacy of this intermingling of political and religious life is that the people tend to view divine providence and spiritual power in political terms. Not only were the sage-like figures of King Wen and Duke Zhou[7] respected and worshipped as religious personages, all other rulers with life-and-death power over individuals were cloaked in an aura of religiosity. Historical records show that from the time of [the legendary tyrant] Chi You, and in the case of [less than benevolent figures like] Qin Shihuang, Xiang Yu, Wang Mang, Dong Zhuo, Cao Cao, and Su Jun,[8] harsh rulers were treated with awe and commemorated in special temples with religious observances by later generations. Because of this venerable tradition Mao's actual sentiment for the people, or his munificence, or even his tyranny that was expressed so succinctly in his line that "for the 800 million Chinese, struggling is a way of life," is not really a major issue.[9] With the consolidation and expansion of his power it was inevitable that he become deified.

Mao's deification was synchronous with his political apotheosis. According to reports in the *Beijing Evening News*, Mao badges made an appearance in and around Yan'an as early as 1945. After 1949, Mao's transmogrification continued apace.

In 1950 the famous writer Lao She produced a play called "Fang Zhenzhu." It was a story about a performer of traditional theater who benefits from communist rule. Lao She was particularly pleased with the opening line: "A True Dragon and Son of Heaven has appeared in Yan'an; he's liberated Beijing and now sits on the Imperial Throne." Although the personality cult of the Cultural Revolution was dressed up in revolutionary garb, in essence its well-springs can only be found in traditional folk religious belief and practice. To speak of Mao [as in the lines of the song "Sailing the Seas Depends on the Helmsman"[10]] in terms of being "the Sun, sustainer of all things" is no different from the ancient belief in the nourishing powers of divinity.

Faith in the omnipresence of nonworldly power was reinforced during the Cultural Revolution. When everything else—all belief systems and cultural norms—was swept away and overthrown, Mao Zedong became the supreme and all-powerful super god, the "Sun that never sets." Mao was invested with a type of power equal, if not superior, to all other religious systems, expressed in such beliefs that he was the Sun, "sustainer of all things," a being who "turned the universe red." Because he was both omnipotent and omnipresent, people felt they could invest themselves with an "ever victorious" power through quasi-religious practices not dissimilar to shamanistic ritual and self-flagellation. They therefore paid homage to his image, sang Mao quotation songs, chanted his sayings, performed the Loyalty Dance, "struggled against self-interest and repudiated revisionism,"[11] and so on.

Faith in the power of the Red Sun in the Cultural Revolution was very much like ancient shamanistic belief. Both held that the power of the spirit could exorcise evil. In the past, people thought they were surrounded by malevolent forces that had to be subdued or expunged. Similarly, in the Cultural Revolution, there was a general belief that the world was full of evil subsumed under such rubrics as Imperialism and Revisionism, the Five Black Categories, as well as the grab-all expression Cow Demons and Snake Spirits.[12] People lived in constant fear that there could be "a restoration of capitalism," or that they would "have to suffer the bitterness of the past again," or that "millions would die" because of a disastrous counterrevolution. Since the Red Sun was a "Spiritual Atom Bomb" that could dispel all those evils, there is little wonder that the level of popular adoration and worship was so hysterical. The creation of a Red Sea (the ubiquitous displays of Mao's portrait, his quotations, slogans, and images that represented devotion to him) was a direct result of the "sweeping away of all Cow Demons and Snake Spirits" and "the rebellion against Class Enemies" that had seen the exorcizing of evil in the first place. More recently, Deng Liqun's attempts to use the new MaoCraze as a weapon to repel the "miasmal mist once more rising" is little more than a continuation of ancient shamanistic practice.

Another feature of shamanism is its proported power to subjugate nature and foster agriculture. Here again the Red Sun has an awesome power as evinced by the Movement to Learn from Dazhai.[13] One Party Secretary in a Shanxi commune issued the peasants with copies of the Three Standard Articles[14] with the words: "We don't need to rely on heaven or earth, all we need are these precious Red Booklets and we can dig through the mountains to irrigate our land." A member of a Tibetan commune even claimed that anyone armed with Mao Zedong Thought would become a Living Buddha.

Although such phenomena have disappeared since the Cultural Revolution, the cultural mechanisms that brought them into being in the first place are still influential. The habit of treating political leaders as spiritual guides is unchanged as witnessed in [the short-lived] praise for "the Wise Leader Hua Guofeng," or more recently in descriptions of Deng Xiaoping's [early 1992] trip to the south, an act that has been likened to manna falling from heaven to nourish the whole nation.[15]

Although popular beliefs have gone a long way to undermining political authority since the advent of the Reform era, none of the new cultural developments have anything more than a utilitarian value. "Crossing the river by feeling the stones"[16] can hardly be expected to provide the nation with a new belief system. Traditional deities live on and this is why we see people throughout the country, in particular in the countryside, erecting temples to the God of Wealth, Door Gods, Guan Gong, Boddhisattvas, the King of Death, and other ancient icons to cure illness, for the begetting of male children, for help in making money, finding the right marriage partner, and for scholastic achievement.

The speed with which temples are being restored or built is comparable to the rate at which they were closed and destroyed in the 1950s and 1960s. According to the television documentary, *A Record of Modern Superstitions: Incense Burning*, broadcast on Beijing TV on 9 February 1990, more than a million people travel to the Southern Peak[17] to burn incense each year and spend some 100 million *yuan* on incense alone. The *Guangming Daily* has also reported that in recent years many shamans have appeared in Fang County, Hubei Province. Some of these are state cadres or retired cadres. Similar reports abound. Things are more controlled in the cities where years of centralized education have meant that primitive beliefs have to find new forms for expression. Because Mao has been the only all-powerful figure for so long, he was the obvious choice for popular adulation during the recent religious revival in China. He has become the idol to which the revived worship of the God of Wealth, Guan Gong, Guanyin Boddhisattva, and other gods is married.

It would seem farcical that Mao, a man who led the assault on capitalism during his lifetime, should in death be put on a par with the God of Wealth and inscribed with traditional imagery. But the misprision and distortion of gods, their reinvention and reinterpretation, is a central element of popular religious activity. As was said long ago: "In a temple that has stood for five generations you can find all manner of strange things." The [Song dynasty literatus] Ouyang Xiu noted nearly a thousand years ago that people often misunderstand the spirits they worship when he wrote: "Of all distortions in the world those that one finds in a temple are the most extreme."

Notes

1. In Chinese, *zhaocai jinbao*.
2. "Peaceful evolution" (*heping yanbian*) was officially regarded by the Chinese authorities as being the greatest threat to the communist system. It was supposedly a Western stragegy that relied on peaceful rather than violent means—cultural, political and economic—to undermine communism and eventually replace it with a Western-style, free-market democratic government.
3. See Deng Liqun, "Permanently On Heat" above.
4. Zhao Gong (Zhao Xuantan, or *Zhao Gong yuanshuai*), the God of Wealth. The Kitchen God (*Zao jun, Zaoshen* or *Zaowang*), the spirit who rules over the hearth, was said to report back to Heaven every Chinese New Year's Eve.
5. The *Zuozhuan* is a Confucian historical text of considerable antiquity. For this quotation, see James Legge, *The Chinese Classics (The Chu'un Ts'ew with The Tso Chuen)*, p. 466, col. 2, and p. 462 for the Chinese original.

6. The Four Olds (*sijiu*) were: old ideas, old culture, old customs, and old habits, the elimination of which was formalized in the Party's 16 Articles on the Cultural Revolution promulgated in 1966.

7. Wen Wang and Zhou Gong were wise and righteous rulers honored in Confucian tradition.

8. Chi You, Qin Shihuang, Xiang Yu, Wang Mang, Dong Zhuo, Cao Cao and Su Jun were renowned as tyrannical rulers.

9. This Mao quote was published in a *People's Daily* editorial marking the tenth anniversary of the Cultural Revolution. See "Wenhua geming yongfang guangmang—jinian Zhonggong zhongyang 1966 nian 5 yue 16 ri 'Tongzhi' shizhounian."

10. In Chinese, the title of the song is *Dahai hangxing kao duoshou*. It was an alternative national anthem during the Cultural Revolution.

11. The Loyalty Dance (*zhongzi wu*) was a clumsy choreographic group dance designed to add rhythm to the adulation of Mao. To "struggle against self-interest and repudiate revisionism" (*dousi pixiu*) was a popular mantra that summed up the avowed aims of the Cultural Revolution.

12. The Five Black Categories (*hei wulei*) were: landlords, rich peasants, counter-revolutionaries, bad elements, and rightists. Cow Demons and Snake Spirits (*niugui sheshen*) was a classical Chinese expression reinterpreted for the denunciation of people in the early stages of the Cultural Revolution.

13. In Chinese, *nongye xue Dazhai*. In 1964, Mao called on the nation to emulate the vaunted socialist agricultural achievements of the Dazhai Commune in Xiyang County, Shanxi.

14. The Three Standard Articles—"Serve the People," "In Memory of Norman Bethune," and "The Foolish Old Man Who Removed the Mountains"—found in Mao's *The Selected Works* became prescribed devotional texts that were committed to memory and recited *ad nauseum*.

15. Deng's January-February 1992 "tour of the south" (*nanxun*) during which, among other things, he visited Shanghai and Special Economic Zones in Guangdong Province sparked off a new wave of economic reforms. It was reported by the national media with gaumless enthusiasm. See, for example, Zong Jun, *Zongshejishi*, pp. 3–26.

16. In Chinese, *mozhe shizi guo he*. This is Deng's much-lauded hit-and-miss approach to reforming socialism.

17. The Southern Peak (*Nanyue*), is Hengshan in Hunan Province, one of China's Five Sacred Mountains which feature in popular religious belief.

CultRev Relics

Zhou Jihou

By the mid 1980s, a small market for Mao-period memorabilia was developing. A taste for Cultural Revolution kitsch had been common among Sinologists and travelers to China from the early 1970s, and such objets d'art as clocks with Red Guards waving Red Books, Mao badges and Mao jackets were avidly collected.[1] Rare Cultural Revolution period stamps also attracted interest on the international market.

Mao badges, those ubiquitous relics of the Cultural Revolution, enjoyed a renewed popularity as a result of the Mao Cult. Private collectors, common in the past,[2] resurfaced to display massive caches of badges to the public. The more prominent of them had collections numbering in the thousands.[3] Of this group Zhou Jihou, a man from Guizhou with a passion for collecting Cultural Revolution memorabilia, wrote lovingly on the subject of Mao badges. In late 1991, his own collection stood at 19,000 badges, of which 10,350 were of different designs.[4]

Zhou Jihou makes a case for regarding Mao badges as bona fide cultural relics, although numerous post–Cultural Revolution imitations have been manufactured. Due to abiding political strictures on the Mainland, however, Zhou passes over the Cultural Revolution period badges that may really be classed as relics if for no other reason than their relative rarity. These include Liu Shaoqi badges, badges with the image of Lin Biao (or Mao and Lin), Lin's calligraphy and the 1976 limited-issue "classic" produced by supporters of Jiang Qing: imitation-silver badges made in the shape of the Japanese rohdea (wannianqing).[5] The Penny Black of Mao badges, however, include those produced in Inner Mongolia in 1967 which feature Mao looking to the right, as opposed to the standard revolutionary gaze to the left. The error, once discovered, led to the badges being recalled. Similarly rare "black Mao badges" produced accidently by a Beijing factory in 1966 as a result of silver plating (the silver surface of the badge gradually turned black upon exposure to air) were also highly valued, *as were multi-colored badges that resulted from failed experiments in Mao-badge manufacture that utilized various unorthodox materials.*

Overproduction of Mao badges was banned by Central order in June, 1969,[6] and only three factories in Beijing, Shaoshan and Shanghai respectively were allowed to continue their manufacture. By 1970, only limited quantities of the badges were being produced.

As the relics of an historical period, the value of Mao badges is by no means simply limited to their being craft objects. They are significant in that they embody the political, economic, and cultural values of the Cultural Revolution as a whole.

In Article 2 of the General Provisions of the "Law of the People's Republic of China on the Protection of Cultural Relics" adopted at the Twenty-fifth Meeting of the Standing Committee of the Fifth National People's Congress on 19 November 1982, it stipulates that:

"The state shall place under its protection, within the boundaries of the People's Republic of China, the following cultural relics of historical, artistic or scientific value:

"1) sites of ancient culture, ancient tombs, ancient architectural structures, cave temples, and stone carvings that are of historical, artistic or scientific value;

"2) buildings, memorial sites, and memorial objects related to major historical events, revolutionary movements or famous people that are highly memorable or are of great significance for education or for the preservation of historical data;

"3) valuable works of art and handicraft articles dating from various historical periods;

"4) important revolutionary documents as well as manuscripts and ancient or old books and materials, etc., that are of historical, artistic or scientific value; and,

"5) typical material objects reflecting the social system, social production or the life of various nationalities in different historical periods."[7]

According to the detailed rules governing the legal determination of cultural relics, and in light of China's particular national situation, as well as in consideration of the three standards for apprising the status of relics (that is, that they are of historical, cultural, and scientific value), Mao badges should be considered as relics. They are of historical, artistic, and scientific value; will not be produced again; and, they are typical material objects with a unique appearance and are a direct and concrete representation of an historical reality.

1. Mao badges are the product of the Cultural Revolution, a major his-

torical event and political movement. They are directly related to the ideology of the time, as well as to the [ideological] superstructure and the everyday lives of the Chinese people. On top of this, they have a unique value in that they commemorate a great man, Mao Zedong. At the same time, they constitute an "historical document" and are a means for the study of contemporary Chinese history and the Cultural Revolution. They are a firsthand record of the various incidents that occurred at the time. Mao badges are also representative works of contemporary Chinese industrial design that were produced using modern scientific methods and materials. They are typical of the then level of industrial design which is reflected in their range, immense number, and high quality. Without doubt they have significant historical, artistic, and scientific value.

2. On 12 June 1969, Party Central issued a document, "Concerning Certain Questions Deserving Consideration in Propagating the Image of Chairman Mao," which clearly stipulated that: "No further Chairman Mao badges are to be produced without the express authorization of the Centre."[8] The circulation of this document marked the beginning of the end of the mass production of Mao badges.

In the "CPC Party Central Directive on Questions Related to Pursuing the Policy on 'Cutting Back on Propagating Individuals' " of 30 July 1980, a further advance was made on this when it stated that: "Chairman Mao badges are to be recalled and recycled wherever possible so as to prevent the excessive waste of metal." Following this, a national-wide "cleaning out" and "handing over" of Mao badges was carried out in cities, the countryside, government organizations, factories, mines, companies, and the army all in the name of wiping out the negative influence of "the personality cult" and "contemporary superstition."[9] Based on the writer's own observations and estimates made over a period of many years, this purge resulted in 90 percent of Mao badges being recycled, lost or destroyed, leaving a mere 10 percent of the original number in circulation. That is to say, of the 4.8 billion Mao Zedong badges produced in the first years of the Cultural Revolution (1966–70), fewer than 500 million are still extant.

History has proved that the forms of commemoration related to Chairman Mao common during the Cultural Revolution, including the production of Mao badges, put too great an emphasis on the historical role of one individual. This resulted not only in considerable waste, but inferred that great men make history, something that was in direct conflict with Chairman Mao's statement that "the people create history." It is for this reason that Mao badges will not be produced in the future (although some badges have recently been manufactured for the Mao centenary, but their nature and significance is quite different from those made in the past).

3. Mao badges have a unique material quality. They are the concrete and physical embodiment of the political, economic, and cultural state, as well as of the social realities and spiritual mien of the people during the Cultural Revolution. They give people a physical sense—both visual and tactile—of an historical phenomenon.

Mao badges circulated widely and in great numbers. They were highly-crafted products made from numerous different materials, the result of both traditional craftsmanship and modern industrial design. They melded sculpture, painting, calligraphy, and design to produce something elemental and representative in Eastern art: works strong in imagery. Most Mao badges carry a portrait of Chairman Mao in relief with an effulgent red sun in the background. But many others represent Mao at various stages in his life with images of revolutionary holy places[10] or maps of revolutionary significance in the background. They provide a true and powerful record of Comrade Mao's outstanding achievements in relation to the Chinese revolution, as well as depicting numerous major historical incidents. They are of great value for the study of Mao Zedong Thought, Party history, and the revolution. They can be used as visual aids in carrying out education concerning the traditions of the Chinese revolution and patriotic education.

Moreover, on the back of many badges details of the place and date of various incidents of historical significance that occurred during the Cultural Revolution can be found. "The past is the teacher of the future." These details can fill in lacunæ found in other documents, as well as play an educative role for the young.

In his essay "A CultRev Museum" Ba Jin[11] wrote: "I suggest that they build a Cultural Revolution Museum. I firmly believe it is something we should do, something for which every Chinese should take responsibility."[12]

Further on he says: "None of us want to see another Cultural Revolution in China. Another disaster like that would signal the end of our nation. . . . It is extremely important that we build this Museum, for only in remembering the 'past' can we be masters of the 'future'."

Musées de France published a translation of Ba Jin's essay and the International Museum Association (with headquarters in Paris it is sponsored by UNESCO with 120 member states, including China, and 8,000 members) sent him a telegram which said: The Cultural Revolution was a unique Chinese product, and only China can build a Cultural Revolution Museum. Such a museum is not only of the greatest importance for the people of China, it would also be extremely significant for non-Chinese. Few outsiders understand the Cultural Revolution, but could hope to gain an accurate picture of this disaster through just such a museum. . . . They also expressed a wish that the Chinese Museum Association would jointly fund the museum with them!

In the spring of 1988, following lengthy deliberations, a group of concerned individuals decided to establish a committee that would call for plans for the building of a Cultural Revolution Museum. They would first construct a museum on paper. The committee consisted of the original board of directors of the Shanghai Museum Society, [and the writer] Ye Yonglie was made committee secretary.[13] In this way plans for the museum would be collected and [because he resided in Shanghai] Ba Jin's advice could constantly be sought.

Shortly thereafter, the committee issued an announcement to the media calling for draft plans for the museum that resulted in an overwhelming public response. The committee received 29,872 letters in the space of 23 days, as well as 367 visitors and 574 telephone calls related to the announcement. Over 99 percent of the letters supported Ba Jin's motion and many added their own proposals: that a new field of "CultRev studies" be established; that there be a "CultRev Research Institute," a "CultRev Research Association," a "CultRev Archive"; that a periodical be produced called *CultRev Researches*, and so on. . . .

Subsequently, Ye Yonglie was sent to Beijing to report back to his teacher, Comrade Zheng, a standing member of the Chinese Museum Association, on the progress of the proposal. [Ye told Zheng that:]

1. It was agreed that Ba Jin's essay "A CultRev Museum" summed up the aims and purposes of the museum;

2. Everyone who had submitted a plan felt that the museum should be in Beijing; and

3. There were conflicting opinions as to whether the museum should be red, black or white. Those in favour of red argued that during the Cultural Revolution people talked of turning the world into a "sea of red."[14] Others favoured black as a colour that represented the massive disaster of the period. Those who proposed white said it was to symbolize remembrance for those who died in the holocaust.

There were three proposals concerning the main entrance:

1. That a massive block of marble be set up engraved with Ba Jin's essay in gold;

2. That a stone bearing the inscription "16 May 1966–6 October 1976, an unprecedented holocaust in Chinese history";

3. That sixteen sculpted heads representing the sixteen ringleaders of the Lin Biao and Jiang Qing counterrevolutionary cliques be placed on a pillar of eternal shame. . . .[15]

The plans called for three exhibition halls. The Cultural Revolution was a period that revealed people's souls, therefore the most important exhibit would be just that.

The first hall would contain the upright spirits of those whose names will live on forever in history: Chen Yi, He Long, Peng Dehuai, Deng Tuo, Lao She, Fu Lei and Zhang Zhixin;[16]

The second hall would contain souls adept at turning things to their advantage, including the leaders of the Lin Biao and Jiang Qing counter-revolutionary cliques, as well as people like Nie Yuanzi and Xu Jingxian;[17]

The third hall would be for the survivors, those people who did not necessarily harm others, but nor did they oppose tyranny.

At the exit a large mirror for self-reflection would be set up with an exhibit of clubs, whips, letters of denunciation, handcuffs as well as the various caps like "capitalist roader" and "counterrevolutionary" used to denounce people. This mirror would reflect just what type of soul each individual had. . . .

Comrade Zheng supported Ye Yonglie's report and made some suggestions. . . .

The museum was to be a nonprofit organization and entry would be free. The International Museum Association wanted to send people to Beijing to carry out a feasibility study. The fact that they wanted to help finance the project was an indication of its importance.

But for various reasons, the project was buried under red tape and little further progress was made. . . .[18]

In Chinese history there are cases . . . of large amounts of relics being lost and historical records remaining incomplete leaving scholars nothing to work on. Later generations are thereby faced with many [historical] blanks.

It is necessary to build a Cultural Revolution Museum to prevent such an historical tragedy.

On 4 March 1989 Ye Yonglie wrote to Rao Guixiang, a collector of Mao badges, and told him that his badges would be an indispensible exhibit in the museum. . . . On 11 January 1991 Jin Chunming, a professor at the Central Party School and a famous Cultural Revolution historian, wrote to me that: "Some years ago, Ba Jin proposed that a CultRev Museum be established. Mao badges would have an important place in such a museum. I still have a collection of a few hundred badges myself. Unfortunately, Ba Jin's proposal was not accepted by the relevant authorities, and we still don't have a centre for research on the Cultural Revolution. It is a great pity that we lag behind overseas scholars in this respect." On 29 May that year he wrote again saying: "I fully support the museum, but Ba Jin's proposal has not been accepted by the leadership and, as you know, without approval from the leaders it would be very difficult to realize such a project. In the present circumstances I can only encourage you to work on by yourself and preserve the materials you have. . . ."

The spring [1992] edition of *New Culture* carried an article by Wang Zhuangling entitled "The Rising Tide of 'CultRev Relics.' "[19] . . . It was soon reprinted or excerpted in over 100 newspapers. . . . It wasn't long before everyone was familiar with the concept of "CultRev Relics" and, after having read it, many people hurriedly started going through their cupboards in search of relics that they could sell for a profit in the future. Some put their relics on display as works of art, others now treated them as antiques. . . .

The article "The Rising Tide of 'CultRev Relics' ". . . was so influential that I have chosen to reproduce it below in full:

> So-called "CultRev relics" are unique objects that reflect a specific historical period.
>
> "[Chairman Mao] Quotation songs" are one of the inventions of the Cultural Revolution. In those songs even conjunctions like "if," "therefore," and "so" were put to music. They were unique. The shortest line in those songs was "we must combat selfishness and repudiate revisionism" (*yao dousi pixiu*). Although there are only five words [in Chinese] it took three minutes to sing. . . . Records of these songs have sold in Hong Kong for as much as H.K.$2,500 each. The longest song can't simply be measured in words. At one evening performance called "The Effulgence of Mao Zedong Thought Will Shine Through the Ages," the "Three Standard Articles"[20] were put to music and it took a whole night to sing them.
>
> "The Precious Red Book"[21] has also become a commodified artifact that people both in China and overseas have started collecting. The book was produced in over 50 different languages and, during the Cultural Revolution, some 500 editions appeared with approximately 5 billion copies in circulation. If you add to that number the editions produced [informally] by various Red Guard groups and Revolutionary Commitees there would have been over 10 billion copies in print. But relatively few copies can be found in the cultural relics markets today and prices are constantly on the rise, especially for rare editions.
>
> The Mao badge, however, is the most widespread Cultural Revolution product. In the five-year period from the summer of 1966 to the summer of 1971, over 10,000 different designs appeared throughout China with 2 billion badges in circulation. Overseas Mao badges now sell for anything from U.S.$0.5 to $400. Not long ago, an American-born Chinese bought a Mao badge in the shape of a sunflower for U.S.$500.[22]
>
> But Cultural Revolution period stamps have seen the greatest price increase. . . . Take, for example, the 1968 stamp "The Mountains and Rivers of the Nation Are All Red," which was printed incorrectly.[23] In 1988, one of these stamps could fetch 6,000 *yuan* according to the median official price or 10,000 *yuan* on the open market.

All manner of Cultural Revolution relics—lecterns for the works of Chairman Mao, Mao statues, portraits, and various publications—have become the object of collectors' interest.

One can predict with considerable optimism that with the passage of time Mao badges will be appearing among the Chinese antiques sold at the best international auctions. Similarly, sooner or later Mao badges will find a well-deserved place in the British Museum, the Tokyo Kokuritsu Hakubutsukan, the Met in New York and the Musée Guimet in Paris. . . .

Notes

1. In 1982, I wrote an essay in Chinese for the Hong Kong *Ta Kung Pao* on the bright future of what I dubbed *Wenge wenwu* or "CultRev Relics." See Bai Jieming, *Zixingche wenji*, pp. 76–77.

2. Even Party leaders collected badges during the Cultural Revolution. Prominent among them was Zhou Enlai. See Zhou Jihou, *Mao Zedong xiangzhang zhi mi*, pp. 82–84.

3. There was Wang Anting from Sichuan, Rao Guixiang in Guangdong, who featured in numerous reports by overseas correspondents when the collectors first went public, as well as Huang Miaoxin from Shanghai and Xu Ren in Xi'an, originally a designer of Mao badges. See Hou Dangsheng, *Mao Zedong xiangzhang fengyunlu*, pp. 125–26; and, Zhou Jihou, *Mao Zedong xiangzhang zhi mi*, pp. 244–72. Xinhua News Agency reported that the largest collection of 101,688 badges of more that 4,000 different types belonged to an employee of the Zhuhai Department of Civil Affairs in Guangdong. See Schell, *Mandate of Heaven*, p. 281.

4. See Zhang Changlin, "Mao Zedong xiangzhang shoucangjia—Zhou Jihou."

5. The Japanese rohdea badge was inspired by the arrangement of flowers that Jiang Qing had placed at the foot of Mao's bier when his corpse was put on display in September 1976. For details, see the Xinhua News Agency report of 16 September 1976; and Qing Ye and Fang Lei, *Deng Xiaoping zai 1976: Huairentang shibian*, vol. 2, p. 119. The Japanese rohdea and the shiny-leaved yellowhorn flower (*wenguanguo* or *Xanthoceras sorbifolia*) which were central to the floral arrangement were supposedly Mao's favorite flowers. The badge, a small silver pin, appeared in the streets of Beijing for a short time before and even after Jiang Qing's demise in October 1976. Her detractors claimed that the name of the flower, *wannianqing*, literally "evergreen," was a counterrevolutionary code homophonous with the sentence "may [Jiang] Qing [rule for] ten thousand years." Similarly, the *wenguanguo* was taken to mean "civil officials [like Jiang and her followers as opposed to military men] can rule the nation." In 1977 a badge was minted to commemorate the building of the Chairman Mao Memorial Hall in Tiananmen. The legend on the badge was in Chairman Hua Guofeng's hand and it was decorated with a portrait of Mao, the Hall and a row of Japanese rohdea flowers.

6. "Guanyu xuanchuan Mao zhuxi xingxiang yinggai zhuyide jige wenti," Zhonggong zhongyang, 19 June 1969, in Beijing geming weiyuanhui chuban faxing gongzuo lingdao xiaozu, ed., *Zhonggong zhongyang wuchanjieji wenhua dageming wenxian xuanbian*, vol. 5, p. 17. This document also condemned hoarding badges and

instructed individuals with large collections to hand them over to the local authorities for redistribution to needy people in the borderlands.

7. See *The Laws of the People's Republic of China, 1979–1982*, compiled by the Legislative Affairs Commission of the Standing Committee of the National People's Congress of the People's Republic of China, pp. 313–14.

8. See note 6 above. Zhou gives the date for the document as 12 June. This was the day that Mao gave his approval for the document to be distributed, which was on 19 June.

9. Both "the personality cult" (*geren chongbai*) and "contemporary superstition" (*xiandai mixin*) are euphemistic shorthands for the Cultural Revolution period Mao cult and its continued post-1976 influence.

10. In regard to these holy places (*shengdi*), see Barmé, "Archeo-tainment: Fantasy at the Other End of History."

11. A May 4th period writer who, in a series of essays published first in Hong Kong and later on the Mainland, commented on the need for individuals to admit their complicity in the horrors of the CultRev period.

12. See Ba Jin "'Wenge' bowuguan," in Ba Jin, *Suixianglu*, "Diwuji: wutiji," pp. 134–38. For a translation of this essay, see Barmé and Minford, eds., *Seeds of Fire*, pp. 381–84.

13. Ye Yonglie, a writer of reportage, was one of the most prolific writers of popular Cultural Revolution–related semi-fictional literature. Born in Wenzhou, Zhejiang, in 1940 and a graduate of Beijing University, he published numerous biographical works of "faction" which he called "Party history literature" (*dangshi wenxue*). See Ye, Yonglie "Lishi xuanzele Mao Zedong," *Xinyuan (Jijian Mao Zedong zhuanhao)*, 1992: 4, p. 144. See also the inside cover of his book *Hu Qiaomu*.

14. The "red sea" (*hong haiyang*) policy was pursued by Red Guards. The result was that revolutionary slogans, Mao quotes and portraits were painted on all available surfaces and buildings.

15. The Lin Biao and Jiang Qing cliques consisted of: Jiang Qing, Zhang Chunqiao, Yao Wenyuan, Wang Hongwen, Chen Boda, Huang Yongsheng, Wu Faxian, Li Zuopeng, Qiu Huizuo, Jiang Tengjiao who were tried in 1980, and those who predeceased the trial: Lin Biao, Kang Sheng, Xie Fuzhi, Ye Qun, Lin Liguo, and Zhou Yuchi.

16. Before the Cultural Revolution, Chen Yi was Minister of Foreign Affairs, He Long was the head of the Sports Commission, Peng Dehuai a general purged in 1959 for criticizing the Great Leap Forward and attempts to rehabilitate him in the 1960s became the ostensible cause of the Cultural Revolution, Deng Tuo was an editor and writer whose satirical essays led to his demise, Lao She was a leading playwright and novelist who committed suicide after being denounced, Fu Lei was a famous translator of French literature who killed himself. Zhang Zhixin was a Party member who was executed in 1975 for denouncing the Cultural Revolution.

17. Nie Yuanzi, a teacher of philosophy at Beijing University, wrote the crucial first big character poster of the Cultural Revolution which Mao supported. Xu Jingxian was the Party Secretary of the Shanghai Revolutionary Committee at the end of the Cultural Revolution. Both were subsequently tried and jailed.

18. These details are all taken from a short story Ye Yonglie wrote and are, in fact, fictional. Ye discusses the story, "Ba Jinde meng," and well-intentioned misrepresentations of it like this in Jin Zhong, "Wenge yanjiu yu Zhonggong dang'an zhidu— fangwen Shanghai zuojia Ye Yonglie xiansheng," p. 57.

19. Wang Zhuangling, " 'Wenge wenwu' chao."

20. For the "Three Standard Articles," see "A Place in the Pantheon," note 14.

21. *Hong baoshu*, that is, *Quotations from Chairman Mao*.

22. In August 1995, it was reported that the largest porcelain Mao badge measuring 1 meter in diameter had been put on display by the Entertainment Company (*Yule gongsi*) of Xiamen, which had originally purchased it for 23,000 *yuan*. A recent offer of 280,000 *yuan* had been made for the badge. See "Juxing Mao xiangzhang."

23. "*Quanguo shanhe yipian hong*." In this stamp the whole of China was printed in red except for Taiwan. It was immediately withdrawn from circulation. A market in this and various other rare or important Mao-era stamps developed from the 1980s. The first Mao stamp was produced in Shandong in 1944. Illustrations of this and other Mao stamps can be found in Zhu Zuwei, Lin Xuan, et al., *Mao Zedong youpiao quanji*. For an illustration of "*Quanguo shanhe yipian hong*," see p. 91.

Hanging Mao

Hou Dangsheng

From 1991 laminated Mao portraits appeared hanging in the windscreens or set up on the dashboards of vehicles throughout China. The fad reportedly originated in Guangdong Province after a person or people miraculously avoided injury in a car accident because, it was said, their automobile was protected by a portrait of Mao. Like the door gods and lucky talismans that Chinese have traditionally used to adorn their dwellings, the Mao portrait was now recognized as a way to ensure safety and good fortune.

In Chinese, these laminated Mao mobiles are often simply called guawu, *literally "hangings." They were sold all over the country and by a range of outlets: from street-side stalls and temple stores to the Mao Memorial Hall itself.*

In design they varied widely. The more austere simply featured a picture of Mao, the most popular representations being of "the young Mao," that is, the retouched picture of Mao in a Red Army uniform taken by Edgar Snow in the 1930s, or the official portrait of the aged Mao, although Mao in a PLA uniform dating from the early Cultural Revolution was also common. More elaborate hangings had the Mao picture framed in mock-Chinese temples, or with gold ingots hanging from the picture with more traditional benedictions like "May the winds fill your sails" (yifan fengshun) or "May you make a fortune" (gongxi facai) on the reverse side.

So often these days when looking at the windscreen of a taxi cab I've noticed laminated pictures of Mao Zedong hanging from the rear-view mirror. Some drivers simply put a portrait of Mao on the dashboard. So the solemn figure of Chairman Mao travels in these cars around the city, dangling and bobbing with every jerk and movement of the vehicle, like an ever-present tutelary diety.

Car decorations directly reflect the attitudes of drivers. A few years back it was popular to display talismans with auspicious messages like "May you travel in safety," "May the wind fill your sails" or "May wealth come your way."[1] Back then no one ever imagined that these would be replaced by laminated pictures of Mao Zedong. What does it mean? It was this question that led me to observe drivers in the bustling heart of the cities as well as in the remote outskirts and I discovered many people hung pictures of Mao in their vehicles. My fascination in the subject led me to interview a number of drivers.

At Xi'an Train Station I came across a taxi driver whose beard really made him stand out from the crowd. He was in a red taxi reclining in his seat waiting for a fare. He was all alone, except for the Chairman who was hanging in front of him.

He jumped up when I tapped on the taxi window, got out and asked me whether I wanted a cab. I handed him a Red Pagoda Hill[2] cigarette and asked him whether he had time for a chat. He had me get into his car and wound up the window so as to shut out the distracting noises of the outside world.

It turned out that he used to work with a building company but he quit because business wasn't too good. He paid 3,000 *yuan* to go to a driving school and, with the help of some friends, bought his own taxi. He'd already paid off his debts and was making a pretty good living as a taxi driver. . . .

I asked him why he had a picture of Mao in his car. After a lot of hesitation he eventually said, "I'm just doing what everyone else does."

"But what do you really think of Mao?" I asked.

"I'm just an average guy. I don't understand the big picture or anything like that, but I reckon that since he sent Chiang Kai-shek packing off to Taiwan and founded the People's Republic of China, he must have been pretty amazing. There was something mystical about Mao Zedong. Whenever I get together with my other mates who drive taxis we always come to the same conclusion.

"Have you heard the story about the traffic accident in the south? There was this head-on collision between a truck and a taxi, see, and although the truck driver got hurt, the taxi driver came out of it without a scratch. They say he had a portrait of Chairman Mao in his car and that's what protected him. So now people reckon the Chairman's like a guardian god."

His story reminded me of something I'd heard: officials in a certain area not only inspected all the relevant documentation when a car came up for registration, they also checked to see if it had a Mao portrait hanging over the dash. If not, they fined the driver. . . .

It was warm and relaxing in the sun and not far away you could see part of the old Xi'an city walls that had not been repaired. They were replete with history. The taxi driver introduced me to some of his friends who were all hanging around on the lookout for fares.

This group started chatting and became very animated.

"You ask why I hang Chairman Mao. There's no particular reason, it's just that I still miss him.[3] He was victorious throughout China because he had the support of the people. He spoke on behalf of the people and was always thinking about them."

"If only cadres today could be a bit more like the Chairman."

"Corruption and dirty government is really undermining their prestige. If they don't do something about it there'll be hell to pay. . . . "

One morning I came across a woman taxi driver outside the Tang Dynasty Guest House [in Xi'an]. I got into her taxi and discovered that she too had a Mao picture hanging over the dashboard. It showed Mao as a young man in Baoan; the picture that was taken by Edgar Snow. . . . I really wanted to know why she had chosen to hang the young Mao.

"Where does your husband work and how old is your child?" I asked the usual questions.

She simply shook her head.

"Divorced?"

She still did nothing but shake her head. . . . Later I found out as we chatted that she drove a truck and was only helping out a friend by driving the taxi today.

"So you're still not married," I concluded.

She nodded.

"What type of partner are you looking for?"

"One just like him," she pointed at the portrait.

"You must be joking," I thought to myself. But I simply said, "You're being a bit romantic, aren't you?"

"I'll wait." She had her own view of things. She felt that there were too many materialistic people around, so she wanted to find someone with style like Mao Zedong.

What could I say? I recognized the fact that the charisma of Mao's personality has found a place in people's hearts. The image of Mao is not simply that of an individual; rather, he is the symbol of an incorruptible, practical Chinese communist who at all times and in all circumstances considered the welfare of the masses.

Quite by coincidence we came across a young man who had drawn a rope between two trees by the roadside and had hung Mao talismans from it for sale. I started chatting with him.

Q: Where did you get all of these?

A: Hunan and Guangzhou. They're common in the south.

Q: How many would you sell in a day?

A: Only a few dozen.

Q: Who are your customers?

A: Mostly drivers: people who drive taxis, trucks, as well as chauffeurs who work for cadres. Lots of different people.

Q: Do you know why they buy them?

A: Beats me. Maybe they just like 'em.

Q: Then why do you sell them?

A: To make money.

He was being completely frank and sold another seven or eight as we talked.

Notes

1. *Yilu ping'an, yifan fengshun* and *zhaocai jinbao* respectively.
2. *Hongtashan xiangyan*, a deluxe brand of cigarettes from Yunnan.
3. The expression used in Chinese is "*xiang ta lao renjia*," literally "I miss the venerable old boy."

The Imprisoned Heart: Consuming Mao

Li Xianting

Li Xianting is one of a number of rōnin art critics. Although he is based in Beijing, he now services the international art world, often acting as a guide to the arcana of China's nonofficial art world. An active writer and critic since the late 1970s Li has been witness to the evanescent fads and fashions of the Chinese art world. In the early 1990s he curated a number of major exhibitions of nonofficial art overseas, including soi-disant *works of "Political Pop," often featuring the reworking of Mao's image, which flourished as the Communist Party became increasingly mired in its own ideological confusion.*

Initially, it must have been liberating for younger artists to take the brush to the Chairman tongue firmly in cheek, but for the case of middle-aged painters the experience was more unsettling. As Zhang Hongtu, the New York–based artist wrote of his experience in 1989:

> *. . . the Mao image has a charisma of its own. It's still so powerful that the first time I cut up an official portrait of Mao for a collage I felt a pang of guilt, something gnawing away inside me. Other people, in particular other Chinese, may well feel the same. As long as this "power to intimidate" exists, I will continue to do Mao.[1]*

However, on Mainland China in an age when politics past is open to ironical abuse and every hallowed Party icon can be suffocated in air quotes, Political Pop found its greatest value as a commercial gimmick.

As I have written elsewhere: "It is not surprising that much of the cultural iconoclasm that plays with Chinese political symbols tempers its irony with a disturbing measure of validation: by turning orthodoxy on its head the heterodox engage in an act of self-affirmation while staking a claim in a future regime that can incorporate them. On this most sublime level Mao has become a consumer item.

"Mao and other dated icons of the militaristic phase of Chinese social-

ism can now safely be reinvented for popular and élite consumption. Madonna titillates her audiences with naughty evocations of Catholic symbols, ones that are culturally powerful and commercially exploitable. Political parody in China works in a similar fashion. Things might be very different—and dangerous—if Deng Xiaoping was the icon being given the Warhol treatment."[2]

Political Pop is a genre that developed and spread throughout the socialist world from the late 1970s through to the early 1990s. Combining the commercial dimension of Western Pop with the political icons of socialism, it resulted in works rich in a particular style of humor and absurdity. Political Pop can also be seen as emblematic of the late cold war period, a manifestation of the egregious absurdity artists felt as Western commercial culture infiltrated the socialist bloc.

In the late 1970s and early 1980s, the Czech artist Milán Kunc and the Soviet artists Alexander Kosolapov and Leonid Bohov began creating Political Pop at roughly the same time. In their works they utilized Western consumer icons like Coca Cola as part of a humorous representation of communist icons like Lenin, Stalin, and the hammer and sickle.[3]

It was not until the late 1980s and early 1990s, however, that Political Pop made its first appearance in China. Unlike the Soviet Union and Eastern Europe, Political Pop in China was not part of a movement aimed at desecrating political leaders; rather, it evolved at a time when a mass revival of the MaoCraze was sweeping the nation.

In 1991–92, numerous Cultural Revolution–period songs glorifying Mao were re-recorded and released, large numbers of books related to Mao were published, Mao badges made a reappearance, and Mao portraits were printed on T-shirts, and a range of other products. There was, I would argue, a more complex mass mentality at work in the history of Political Pop in China than we have seen in either the Soviet Union or Eastern Europe. The MaoCraze of the early 1990s reflected a "Mao obsession" that still haunted the popular psyche. It is an obsession that combined both a nostalgia for the simpler, less corrupt, and more self-assured period of Mao's rule with a desire to appropriate Mao Zedong, the paramount God of the past, in ventures satirizing life and politics in contemporary China. This satirical spirit was something that was also reflected in the Student Demonstrations of 1989, particularly notable when demonstrators surrounded the police and the army and sang revolutionary songs at them. Both instances, that is, of the students in 1989 and the popular appropriation of Mao thereafter, are an expression of a typical style of Chinese irony, a temper and form of expression that has evolved among people who have lived for so many years under extreme political pressure. It is a form of irony that takes as its basic strategy an inversion of Maoist language and symbolism.

Some people believe that the use of political images from the Cultural Revolution in contemporary Chinese art is representative of a type of mass cultural memory rather than being simply part of a critique of politics today. The important thing about the artistic use of the image of Mao Zedong in Mainland China, I maintain, is not its political significance, but the way in which the image is manipulated. After all, an image is altered by the very fact that it is incorporated into an artistic work. As Duchamp wrote in 1917: the crux of the matter is that an image, an everyday object, is selected and given both a new name and significance. It is thereby deprived of its original function and reveals a new meaning.

Whether it be Political Pop in art or the widespread reprisals of Mao during the MaoCraze of the early 1990s, what is significant is that Mao has now become a Pop icon in China. This represents a massive shift away from the days when Mao was a solemn and awe-inspiring god. Mao's aura of sanctity has been dissolved by these acts of commercialization and popularization.

For the artist, Political Pop is a creative endeavor, whereas the MaoCraze has been part of a larger trend toward commercialization in China and has lacked the self-conscious dimensions of the artists' work. This is what I mean in the above when I talk of the "consumption" of socialist ideology in China and in the Soviet Union and Eastern Europe before the end of the cold war. It is in this sense that the MaoCraze has been a fitting end to the post-Mao period of the 1980s. Mao made a reappearance at a time when the system of beliefs represented by him were being swept away by a tide of commercialism.

Looking at Political Pop from the perspective of modern art in China since the late 1970s, it is obvious that Pop art is a reaction to a number of earlier trends. The art of the 1980s was the product of China's open door, the impact of Western currents of thought, and the collapse of the Revolutionary Realist culture of the Maoist era. Western modernism provided the basic ideology for the evolution of a new Chinese culture during that decade and the "Modern Art Exhibition" held in Beijing in early 1989 was a retrospective of the work that had appeared during that decade. That exhibition marked the end of a particular stage in the development of contemporary art. More particularly, the shooting incident that occurred during the exhibition revealed not only the political sensitivity of contemporary Chinese art, it also led to the closure of the exhibition and marked (both in symbolic and actual terms) the end of 1980s' art.[4] The resulting expulsion of all those idealistic modern artists from the China Art Gallery, the leading state art gallery, forced them to go back underground and continue their wandering lives as opponents of official art.

It is this group of artists who had held on to their idealism despite everything, men and women who were hopeful that Western thought could be used to salvage and help rebuild Chinese culture. Now, in the early 1990s they were faced with a new collapse of values. This time they did not respond to their dilemma as they had in the late 1970s. Now many of them rebelled against their earlier heroism, idealism, and the quest for the metaphysical and sublime. They turned instead to the popular and to deconstructionist projects; they developed an interest in Political Pop.

More important, however, was the changing social scene in China that had resulted from the economic Reforms. Artists developed a Pop view of the rapid and confusing commercialization that was going on around them. They turned away from larger (and often vague and obtuse) cultural issues that had previously so occupied their thoughts and confronted social reality with a new and more practical means for self-expression. We should not forget that Chinese reality is suffused with politics. It is this ever-changing political landscape that forces all Chinese, in particular Chinese intellectuals, to adapt their position, consciously or unconsciously, to every modification in the political climate. To be a political chameleon is a rudimentary means of survival. It is part of an internalized habit, what is called "the captive mind."[5] By reprising political images in a new, unorthodox fashion, Political Pop found a nonheroic means for overcoming the predicament of the captive mind. At the same time, Political Pop became an ideal means for reflecting the social ambience of the post-1989 period.

The early 1990s marks the second period in which Pop has made an appearance in contemporary Chinese art. Following the 1985 exhibition of Robert Rauschenberg's work in Beijing, a fad for Pop swept the Chinese art scene. Artists were particularly interested in Rauschenberg's use of salvaged/found objects. This allowed them to escape for the first time from the easel and make an all-out assault on the accepted Chinese aesthetic.

The introduction of Pop on Mainland China led interestingly to a Dada-type artistic movement.[6] Although Pop art was a continuation of Dada art it was also the product of a highly commercialized environment. The attitudes of the artists engaging in Pop art were necessarily vastly different from those of the post–World War I Dadaists. In the mid 1980s in China, younger artists thought of themselves as revolutionaries united by a desire to overthrow the aesthetic and linguistic conventions of Chinese art. They were interested in how manufactured or found objects could have an impact on two-dimensional art. Dada had used objects to rebel against the aesthetic norms of the past, it is not surprising, then, that Chinese artists accepted the

Dadaist aspects of Pop art while generally ignoring its possibilities as a form of mass or popular art.

Five years later, in 1989, the modern art movement in China was repressed by the authorities while economic Reforms continued apace along with the wholesale commercialization of Chinese society. The mass, vulgar, and indeterminate aspects of commercialization had a particular influence on Chinese artists and they naturally came to utilize the language of Pop. In the context of the history of recent Chinese art, the "misreading" of Pop art in 1985 as a form of Dada had a revolutionary significance in China that fueled the trend toward Political Pop in the early 1990s.

In terms of modern art, China's Political Pop has been deeply influenced by American Pop, in particular the work of Andy Warhol. The differences between the two, however, are that Pop strengthens, even sanctifies popular icons, while Political Pop converts sacred political icons into Pop images. Where American Pop utilized recognized commercial and other icons, Political Pop draws more on the collective cultural memory, in particular those images that are most representative of the revolutionary age like Lenin, Mao, the symbols of the Communist Party, the red star, and so on, mixing these images with contemporary Pop icons.

This is evident, for example, in Alexander Kosolapov's "Lenin Coca Cola," or Wang Guangyi's "Great Denunciation Series," which combines the Cultural Revolution icons of the Worker, Peasant, and Soldier with commercial symbols such as Coca Cola. Similarly, Zhang Peili's "The Beauty Contest" combines the fireworks of the revolutionary past with the image of body building competitions. The Shanghai artist Yu Youhan has juxtaposed Mao with Whitney Houston, while Qi Zhilong has secreted Mao's image in a color photograph of contemporary stars. A more humorous interpretation of the Mao era is Feng Mengbo's "Endgame," where the artist has inserted characters from the Revolutionary Model Operas into a video game scenario, while Geng Jianyi's "Forever Effulgent" replaces the image of Mao familiar from Cultural Revolution propaganda iconography with the Panda and images taken from Chinese money.[7]

Other artists who have engaged in Political Pop create similar substitutions, juxtapositions, or collages. This genre, as in other (now former) socialist countries, is the product of a socialist cultural environment. The erratic nature of social development has meant that a range of cultures and mentalities coexist in the same space and time: the Cultural Revolution, post–Cultural Revolution, peasant society culture, and even postindustrial culture comingle in the China of today. Added to this is the general decay of values, and all these elements combine to create a confusion of cultural memory(ies) and their interrelationship. Tumbled together in the tidal wave of commodification, political fixations are deconstructed in a general mood of "instant consumption."

American Pop converted vulgar icons into something more elevated or highbrow, revealing an underlying seriousness in this style of art. In China, the sacrosanct has been vulgarized, epitomizing an attitude that is both playful and humorous.

Note

1. Quoted in Barmé and Jaivin, eds., *New Ghosts, Old Dreams*, p. xxvi.

2. See Barmé, "Export, Exploit, Expropriate: Artful Marketing from China, 1989–93," in Doran, *China's New Art, post-1989*, p. L.

3. For illustrations of these works, see Li's original article in *Art and AsiaPacific*.

4. See note 4 in "A Typology of the MaoCraze" above.

5. In Chinese *xinyu*, literally "the imprisoned heart." "The captive mind" is, of course, Milosz Czeslaw's term.

6. Such as the "Amoy Dadaist" (*Xiamen dadazhuyi*) movement led by Huang Yongping in the mid 1980s.

7. The Chinese titles of these paintings are *Da pipan, Jianmei, Youxi jiesu* and *Yongfang guangmang* respectively. See Doran, *China's New Art, post-1989*, for illustrations of the work mentioned here.

Drunk in the Rapeseed Patch

Li Jian

Of the many quaint retakes on the Mao age, Li Jian's 1980 short story "Drunk in the Rapeseed Patch" is one of the earliest. It is the tale of a Red Guard becalmed in an isolated village who gives herself in marriage and bondage to the poor-and-lower middle peasantry while keeping her spirit alive by living in a petit-bourgeois dreamworld.

In this story, Li Jian, an erstwhile staunch Maoist,[1] makes pointed use of Mao quotes in a way common in everyday life—in particular as part of Beijing banter—but with a more earnest literary purpose. Although predating the Mao Cult of the late 1980s by nearly a decade, an excerpt of the story is included here for its value as a literary artifact. The Mao quotes are printed in bold type out of respect for Cultural Revolution convention.

> "Good wine and coffee,
> I only want a glass,
> it reminds me of the past
> when I had one glass after another. . ."

She sang while walking. Her carefully-creased pants made her look neat and casual.

It was autumn and the willows that lined the road were changing colour. The wind was crisp and carried a few yellowing leaves in its wake.

There was a touch of red in the distance, not red flags but the kite of a young girl.

"I'm drunk. . ."

She leaned against a willow, her hands combing through her hair roughly.

"Am I drunk?"

She moved away from the tree and continued her way forward unsteadily.

"I . . . really . . . want to sleep some more. . . ."

She could vaguely make out a yellow field through the willows and realized it was rapeseed.

"I . . . really . . . want to sleep some more. . . ."

She started crying as she ran towards the field and fell into its embrace.

"I'm not drunk.
It's just that my heart is broken.
But why are you,
little rapeseed flowers,
weeping too?
If you are brokenhearted,
I'll join you in a glass . . . "

She lay there as though she was on a bed of yellow brocade.
She picked some rapeseed and flicked it against her breasts and sang:
"One glass after another . . .
one glass after another . . ."
The intoxicating effect of the wine hit her and she felt dizzy.

"What's wrong?"
A man who looked like a peasant with a hoe over his shoulder was
standing there.
She jumped with a start.
"I'm . . . a Red Guard."
She flicked her braided hair back and set her Red Guard armband straight.
"A Red Guard . . ."
He didn't seem to understand.
". . . but what are you doing in our mountains?"
"Revolution, rebellion, struggle, link-ups."
"All by yourself."
"No . . . but I've been cut off from my company."
He looked into the sky:
"It's getting dark. Stay here."
She went back to the village with him.
The village was called Eight Mile Ravine and consisted of about twenty
families scattered through the hills. Before Liberation it had been a Revolu-
tionary Base. Later, in particular after the communes, Party cadres virtually
never came here. There was no electricity and someone went to the com-
mune once a week to collect the papers.
"You're . . ."
That night she stayed at his place and asked him:
"How come all the women in the village are deaf, mute or crippled?"
"You don't understand," he said as he rolled himself a cigarette. "We're
so poor here and the weather's so bad—sand storms in the summer, snow in
the winter—and we survive just eating gruel made out of dried sweet pota-
toes, that no decent-looking girl would ever come here."
Her eyes lit up:

"So poverty has made you think of change. You want to act, to carry out revolution."

"Revolt against what? It's our lot to cut grass for our animals."

She slept on his heated *kang* bed.

She woke to find him kneeling beside her.

"What do you think you're doing?"

His face went bright red:

"I just wanted to kiss a girl from the city . . ."

"You hooligan."

She jumped up.

"Red Guard . . ."

He knelt and clasped her by the calf, tears flowing down his face.

"I'm 35 and I've never been with a woman. I was a hired labourer . . ."

Suddenly she recalled the Chairman's Highest Directive:

There would be no revolution without the poor peasants. If we negate them we are negating the revolution. If we reject them we are rejecting the revolution itself!

"We're class brothers."

She was so moved that she pulled him up.

"Just one kiss . . ."

He stood before her staring in a daze.

"The nation is our nation, the society our society. If we don't speak out who will. If we don't act who will?"

The Chairman's Highest Directive was like a revolutionary bomb that exploded in the depths of her soul:

The sufferings of the poor and lower middle peasants are our own sufferings. Their difficulties are our difficulties. We must fight against every selfish thought and concern ourselves with the cares of the poor and lower middle peasants.

She blushed.

He bundled her onto the bed in a mad frenzy, then blew out the light.

Her Red Guard armband was soon flecked with blood . . .

The East is Red, the Sun Rises. She greeted her first morning in Eight Mile Ravine. . . .

Notes

1. See Kam Louie, "Literary Double-Think in Post-Mao China: The Case of Li Jian," p. 30; and Beijingshi wenlian yanjiubu, ed., *Zhengming zuopin xuanbian*, vol. 2, pp. 69–87.

MaoSpeak

Wang Shuo

Many selections in this volume reek of MaoSpeak, or New China NewSpeak (Xinhua wenti), popularized on Mainland China as the political and social lingua franca from the 1940s. The Beijing novelist Wang Shuo utilized this language from the late 1980s in his satirical studies of life under socialism in its terminal phase.[1]

In the works of Wang Shuo the play on Maoist language was part of a sincere and at the same time ironic revival of Mao. In the early 1990s Wang's work created a fad of its own which encouraged a tongue-in-cheek recycling of Party language in the Chinese media, in particular TV. MaoSpeak did indeed repeat itself, first as tragedy then as farce.

Wang's nostalgia for the Cultural Revolution is real and vital. For him and many of his generation what was officially dubbed the "ten years of chaos" (shinian dongluan) had offered opportunities for sexual liberation, playing truant and the joys of gang warfare.[2] In 1990s' China, with the help of Deng's Reform policies, Wang and his fellows helped turn the rowdy youth culture of the Cultural Revolution into a pseudo-ethos of the Reform Age. Many of them also made a lot of money out of China's further social and cultural degradation. The anti-intellectualism evident in much of Wang's work—he consistently lambastes Chinese intellectuals—also antagonized some readers who saw in it a disturbing streak of chip-on-the-shoulder Maoist hooliganism. He defended himself by quoting Mao Zedong: "The lowly are the most intelligent; the élite are quite ignorant," and he claimed that only by overthrowing the intellectuals would people like him enjoy true freedom (fanshen).[3] Although one may appreciate Wang's dim view of intellectuals, to use satire, a weapon traditionally best employed against the powerful, to consistently denigrate the weak and powerless is not so much funny as vulgar.

Wang Shuo's novel Don't Treat Me As a Human Being (Qianwan bie ba wo dangren), *or* No Man's Land, *was serialized in 1989 and reprinted in*

1991 and 1992. It is Wang's satirical masterpiece, a loving and scarifying look at the dark side of the Chinese national character.[4] In a 'letter of appreciation' (ganxiexin) to the Party leadership read out by the grateful denizens of Tanzi Alley at the end of the novel, Wang Shuo creates an extreme parody of the logorrhea of Chinese political and commercial language, with some gratuitous references to traditional Chinese snake-oil remedies thrown in for good measure. The letter is read out as a tearful incantation by the mother of Tang Yuanbao, the novel's picaresque hero.

"Praise be to you, Lord Clear Sky! We the inhabitants of Tanzi Alley thank you for rescuing us from the bitter sea, from the flaming pit, from hell itself."

Tang Yuanbao, at the head of the inhabitants of Tanzi Alley, led everyone as they knelt down in the dirt in supplication. [The Party leader] Fatty approached on a horse, dismounted, helped the old lady [Tang's mother] to her feet and called out to the others:

"What is all this? Come on all of you, on your feet. This really is too much. After all, I'm one of you, your servant. All I've done is make some decisions on your behalf and give you my support. What need is there for thanks?"

At this point, Yuanbao's mother began mumbling. Crying and chanting, she praised Fatty:

"You have righted the wrong and crushed the bad in one fell swoop. Respected wise dear teacher leader helmsman pathfinder vanguard pioneer designer bright light torch devil-deflecting mirror dog-beating stick dad mum granddad grandma old ancestor primal ape Supreme Deity Jade Emperor Guanyin Boddhisattva commander-in-chief:

"You who are busy with ten thousand weighty matters each day, long-suffering one bad habits die hard and overworked to the point of illness done too often can be habit-forming shouldering heavy responsibilities speeding through the skies powerful and unconstrained staving off disaster and helping the poor dispelling the evil and ousting the heterodox, you who eliminate rheumatism cold sweats strengthen the *yang* and invigorate the spleen the brain who are good for the liver stomach pain relieving and cough repressing, and able to cure constipation.

"You personally yourself *in propria persona* have come deigned lowered yourself honoured us with your presence to investigate look over police search patrol pay a visit to ask about express solicitude and come to our alley. For our alley this is the most magnanimous expression of concern a massive encouragement a great impetus a considerable relief formidable expression of trust and care a great honor and really a nice thing to do. We are little people knaves the black haired scum your children grandchildren tufts of grass little dogs and cats a gang of *liumang* [hooligans] the cretinous crowds the great masses the hundred surnames and we feel ohsolucky extremely moved exceedingly uneasy terribly embarrassed so very pleased boundingly enthusiastic very very overwhelmed by our good fortune grateful as all get out tears o'fill our eyes our hearts swell like the seas and we're utterly and thoroughly lost for words. Ten thousand words a million songs endless mountains and seas ceaseless groans and grumbles mumbles and whispers expressions and phrases all combine into one sentiment which rends the very heavens an hysterical sound cracking through the universe circling the rafters for three days deafening reverberating through heaven and earth moving all who hear it mysterious and beautiful beyond compare making people drunk pissed completely out of it so they don't know the taste of meat for three days for it is the overriding chord of the age: longlife longlife longlonglife longlife longlife longlonglife!

Yuanbao's mother fainted dead away and Mother Li stood up to take her place, continuing in rapid fire:

"Without you we would still be lost in the darkness dimness greyness dustiness sootiness ashiness in a ditch a hole in the ground a cave a ravine a gully an abyss in a wok of boiling water in a firepit a vat of boiling oil in the bitter waters and we would be splashing gnashing crashing flashing flipping kicking. . . ."

She too went into a swoon and Yuanfeng took over:

"You are the light hope future ideal banner clarion wardrum victory success pride dignity triumph heaven Buddhaland wiseone shaman genius magician tuletary diety saviour sun moon stars effulgence splendour light ray beam brilliance. . . ."

She gave up the ghost and her place was taken by Blackie:

"Hercules hawk falcon lion tiger bronze-headed golden-faced steellegged iron-armed lightning-fisted cannon guided missile mainstay tombstone great wall mountain pass. Without you we would freeze to death starve to death be beaten berated argued to death die for being disorderly burn and drown to death die of hanging from falling and being treated really badly by others. . . ."

"Enough already," Fatty said with a benevolent smile. "If you go on you'll just keel over and faint too. In the past, I've heard my fill of respectful praiseful laudatory admiring speeches. You could go on until everyone in this alley died from exhaustion and you still wouldn't run out of things to say. It doesn't do a thing for me. I don't want you to run yourselves down like this. If you really want to make me happy then learn how to take care of yourselves. That's the best present you could give me."

"But you have to take us in hand, no matter what," Blackie said tearfully. "We can't survive without you. You are the clear skies, we are but tufts of grass. Without the sky how could the earth exist? Grass needs to be tended, watered, weeded and cut. We can't do it ourselves. Anyway, we're used to being kept in place. If you make us take over and leave us without anyone to cuss us kick us hit us and push us around we won't be able to eat drink sleep or shit. We'll lose control completely."

"No matter what, you can't leave us like this," the residents of Tanzi Alley chorused as they knelt. "We're happy to let you ride beat berate whip us. If it makes you happy order us around drive us and trample us under foot. If you're displeased feel free to punish humiliate and generally take it out on us. If anyone dares utter the slightest objection you won't have to lift a finger because we'll take care of them ourselves. Do what you will with us, but whatever you do don't say you're going to abandon us."

"Come on, get up," Fatty said with a heavy sigh. "How could I possibly leave you to your own devices?"

Notes

1. For a single-volume collection of these stories, see *Wang Shuo wenji (4): xiexue juan*.

2. See the depiction of this world in Wang's 1991 story "Dongwu xiongmeng," reprinted in *Wang Shuo wenji (1): chunqing juan*, pp. 406–93; and Jiang Wen's 1994 screen version of the story, *Yangguang canlande rizi*, which premièred in China in 1995.

3. See Wu Jiafeng, "Ping Wang Shuode yiduan hua," p. 144. During a tour of inspection of Dandong, Liaoning Province in 1958, Mao visited a tractor factory and wrote an inscription (*tici*) for the workers which read: "The lowly are the most intelligent; the élite are the most ignorant" (*beijianzhe zui congming, gaoguizhe zui yuchun*). Since the inscription was penned on 18 May (*5 yue 18 ri*), the factory changed its name to Factory No. 518. See also Ying Da, "Wang Shuode yuyan" in Liang Huan, ed., *Mingren yanzhongde Wang Shuo*, pp. 116–20.

4. For further details of this story, see Barmé, "Wang Shuo and *Liumang* ('hooligan') Culture," pp. 51–60.

Martial Mao

While the more studious might peruse books about Mao, the general read-ing public relied for their information on the tabloid press and magazines with eye-catching covers and headlines which were sold at bookstalls that dot the cities and at train and bus stations throughout the country.

Below is the editorial note and contents page of one such publication, a special issue of On and Off the Silver Screen (Yinmu neiwai), *published in Chengdu, Sichuan, in November 1993. Entitled* True Tales of the Adven-tures of Mao Zedong, *it was ostensibly produced "to commemorate the Mao Zedong Centenary."*

The prose used is the doggerel classical style favored by martial arts novelists, storytellers, writers of tales of court intrigue and popular Repub-lican-period histories further peppered with the revolutionary bravado of Party propaganda. This bastardized style can be contrasted with Wang Shuo's comic use of Party language (see "MaoSpeak" above).

The translation is literal and no attempt has been made to explain the numerous historical—and in some cases hysterical—references in the piece. The obsequious sincerity of the editors is in striking contrast to the sensa-tional contents of the actual magazine.[1]

Editorial Note [You Zhi]

One hundred years ago, in the land where the Emperor Shun heard the music of Shao,[2] a baby boy was born. Who would have thought that the peasant lad who left behind the hills of His homeland would be the Greatest Man of His generation, a man who initiated a new age?

Did history produce Him, or did He write history?

His name was—Mao Zedong!

Suddenly, seventeen years ago, Mao Zedong took His leave. However, His majestic body, His resonant Hunanese voice, like His name and the enterprise on which He embarked, are today still as lustrous as the sun and moon regardless of whether He is living or dead.

It is for this reason that we cherish His memory and commemorate Him.

We mourn Him with baneful songs and sorrowful tears. Not only because He is the Leader of the People, but even more so because He is the People's Son. He went from being a man to become a god, to return once more to the People as an outstanding individual.

The history of modern China was written for Him; the history of China's future will be possible because of Him.

His name was—Mao Zedong!

He was a man of flesh and blood, a man with a rich emotional life. He was a man of chivalry and honor, a man whose spirit filled the very heavens. He was a man of prodigious foresight, a man limited by neither time nor space.

Daring and wise, transparent and complex, a realist and an idealist, stubborn and creative, all of these things went to make up the unique spirit of Mao Zedong. His uniqueness informed the 83 years of His life and gave birth to the eternal legends of His greatness.

We have edited this special edition of our magazine on the eve of His centenary as an expression of our collective respect for His memory. Through our magazine we hope to offer the youth of today a paragon of revolutionary leadership from which they can learn.

Contents

The Autumn Harvest Uprising (film synopsis)/p. 52

Amazingly, this film is about the Great Man's military defeat in Hunan. It's a truthful account of how the Leader ignored the Committee's directives and sent the local despots packing. As the autumn harvest approached He took command and was alone possessed of wisdom at a time of violent tempests.

The Chongqing Negotiations (film synopsis)/p. 50

". . . if I, Mao Zedong, can spare China civil war by offering up my life and save the people from shedding blood, then I am willing to be taken prisoner by Chiang Kai-shek." The People's Leader faced disaster bearing the responsibility of the whole nation; facing down the enemy leader this Revolutionary Giant analysed history past and present.

Jinggang Mountains (film synopsis)/p. 88

After the failure of the Autumn Harvest Uprising the Great Man takes to the Jinggang Mountains. In re-organizing the army the Leader reveals a strategic genius upon which the one-thousand year enterprise will be built. Herein we see the storms surrounding the birth of the People's Leader and witness the struggles that led to the growth of the People's Army.

Mao Zedong's Pronouncements Amaze the World/ p. 4

A middle school girl student commits suicide and His fury knows no bounds! In the depths of agony He reflects deeply and produces one astounding article after another on suicide and young love. Each is like a spear aimed at the very heart of the boundlessly evil old society and feudal concepts.

Mao Zedong was a Casual Laborer/p. 21

The expression "casual laborer" is one that annoys people today and one would think it has nothing in common with the name of Mao Zedong. But, in reality, in His youth Mao Zedong had to make a living and this was an important way for Him to undertake an in-depth study of the society. Even more amazing is the fact that "casual laborer" is a term that is inextricably linked with Mao Zedong's young love and wife Yang Kaihui, as well as with the names of such famous modern figures as Li Dazhao and Cai Yuanpei.

Mao Zedong Causes an Uproar at Xinhua Gate/p. 32

Zhang Jingyao, the Hunan bandit warlord, was making mincemeat of the local populace, burning, butchering and pillaging. The homeless and destitute wandered the countryside. To punish and expel Zhang Jingyao, Mao Zedong led the Hunan students to Beijing and organized a protest of 70,000 people to create an uproar outside Xinhua Gate to force the Northern Government to deal with Zhang. The bureaucrats fled in terror. This was the first major act Mao Zedong initiated involving Himself in the affairs of state. It took the capital by surprise and shook the whole of China!

Mao Zedong Gives a Loutish Soldier a Knuckle Sandwich/p. 38

From His youth Mao Zedong admired the heroes of the past. He was outraged by injustice and fought for redress, His chivalry was known throughout the land. He throws the Mao Family Temple into uproar when He beats up a loutish soldier and local punk. . . . Time and again, delighting one and all, disheartening the vile troops and thugs in the area. From [1930 when He wrote the lines of poetry] "In June Heaven's armies chastise the corrupt and evil/ Seeking to bind roc and whale with a league-long cord"[3] right up to the time He founded New China, His whole life is a depiction of the sublime chivalrous spirit!

The Highest Military Rank Mao Zedong had was Company Commander/p. 44

Mao Zedong was the natural commander of the Party, the Nation and the

Army, but He never got beyond the rank of company commander. Believe it or not, it's the truth. Mao Zedong once remarked to Edgar Snow: "Now they call me the Great Commander. It's absurd! Frankly, the most I've been is company commander. . . ."

Mao Zedong's Strategic Invasion of the Temple of the Heavenly King/p. 48

Mao Zedong had a provocative personality: if He knew there was a tiger in the hills, He would still go marching forward. Large numbers of troops prepared an ambush around the Temple of the Heavenly King in the hope of taking Mao by surprise. But Mao Zedong, a man possessed of superior wisdom and courage, refused to take another route; He was determined to walk straight into the jaws of the tiger. . . . All of those who were with Him were in mortal fear for His safety!

Mao Zedong Established "The Republic of Hunan"/p. 66

"The Republic of Hunan" struck China like a thunderbolt. Mao declared that the only hope for China was for it to be divided into 27 countries. Mao Zedong and Peng Huang proposed establishing "The Republic of Hunan." It would have been the equivalent of an American state or a French *département*. Mao Zedong cried out: Oppose unity! Chen Duxiu lent Him support. Mao shouted out: "Long live the Republic of Hunan!" He was prepared to fight to the death for the republic!

The Inside Story of the Assassination Attempt on Mao's Life/p. 76

Mao Zedong survived numerous perils. This particular attempt on His life was neither a plot authored by the secret agents of the KMT, nor a scheme of the reactionary warlords. The plotters were traitors within the ranks of our own revolutionaries. The pitch-black muzzle of the gun, an evil assassin and Mao with His back turned. . . . At that crucial instant, another body appeared between Mao and the gunman. This article reveals in exact detail the inside story of this historical episode. It will terrify you and it will make you reflect!

Mao Zedong Loses Control Over the Army/p. 82

In the chronicles of Communist Party history, the Ningdu Conference is shrouded in mystery. That is because it was a time when all firepower was concentrated on criticizing Mao Zedong and stripping Him of His military command. This incident has always been off limits for historians. But in this article the whole truth is revealed in the hope that the original mien of history can be restored.

The Real Mystery of "8341" has Nothing to do with Superstition/p. 86

"8341," these four numbers are connected with Mao Zedong. But superstition has made a mystery of them, and for years they have confused and beguiled a great number of Chinese. Mao Zedong was a believer in materialism. "8341" had nothing to do with superstition. This article collates a large body of historical fact to reveal finally the truth of this mystery. . . . [4]

Other articles:

Originally Mao wanted to be a policeman/p. 7
The demonstrations that Mao organized and led/p. 26
Mao Zedong's first big character poster/p. 10
The first military campaign Mao led/p. 45
Mao Zedong's record of battles during the Xinhai Revolution/p. 13
Which martial hero did Mao Zedong admire most?/p. 54
The trouble Mao Zedong's "critical friend" got himself into/p. 18
The secret of the relationship between Mao Zedong and Zhou Zuoren/p. 58
Mao Zedong was a representative at the First Congress of the KMT/p. 19
Mao Zedong nearly became the Party Secretary of Sichuan Province/p. 64

Notes

1. See also, Scharping, "The Man, the Myth, the Message," p. 178.
2. According to legend, Emperor Shun heard the music of Shao in this area of Hunan during a tour of the South. Thereafter the place was called Shaoshan, "Mount Shao." Shaoshan was Mao's birthplace.
3. Mao Zedong, "Cong Dingzhou xiang Changsha," in *Mao zhuxi shici*, p. 37. For this English translation, see "March from Tingchow to Changsha," July 1930, Mao Tsetung, *Poems*, p. 9.
4. See "Mao, a Best-Seller" and note 5.

Who's Responsible?

Wei Jingsheng

This is reportedly the first article Wei Jingsheng had published in the Hong Kong press following his release from some fourteen years in jail in 1993. Although a powerful indictment of the Chinese government, the awkward style that is so common among China's dissidents—added to the fact that Wei had not written for publication for some time—weakens the piece considerably. Wei was spirited away once more by the authorities in early 1994 and sentenced to another long jail term in December 1995.

Can anyone have the final word on Mao Zedong? No, because he still has an influence. Put frankly, there are still people around who want to use his name for their own nefarious ends.

I think most people have had a pretty good idea about what type of man Mao really was for quite some time now. He cast virtually the whole of China into a state of violence, duplicity, and poverty. He was indirectly responsible for more than a 100 million people starving to death and for the destitution of a similar number who were forced to abandon their homes and become beggars. Another 100 million were subjected to direct or indirect political persecution and suffered years of spiritual and physical anguish. He was guilty of other heinous crimes that are too numerous to list.

He was an outstanding tyrant who outdid similar figures both in China and overseas. In this sense alone he can be called a "Great Man" or "unique." But to be fair, although he must be held chiefly responsible for the extreme poverty and backwardness the Chinese have had to put up with for some four decades, he is not the only guilty party. All the henchmen who helped him concoct those disastrous plots and plans must also be held culpable. As for the general mass of people who have tolerated their outrageous behavior and have even treated them as superior beings, giving them support and encouragement, they too cannot escape a certain amount of responsibility.

As a youth I too worshipped Mao Zedong. When I finally woke up to myself, I was overcome with remorse. Only later did I realize that remorse was not enough. It was necessary to see through him and the louts who assisted him and then fight back, for only then could we save ourselves and others who were experiencing the same suffering.

We cannot hold out any hope for a savior or upright official to deliver us. Nor can we rely too heavily on the help of friends. Only we can help ourselves, for only then will others be willing to help us. No one is going to help people who tolerate abuse without fighting back.

These are basic and pressing lessons that we Chinese cannot afford to forget. If we don't learn from the past the people who like to deploy the unprincipled "Great Men" to support their own actions will abuse us once more, just as Mao toyed with and denigrated us, while he expected people to treat him like a god. To an extent the viciousness of the rulers is the result of the weakness and compliance of the masses. Only when people learn how to defend their own rights will the rulers be forced to make concessions. The Chinese should never forget this lesson for it is a lesson written in blood.

3 November 1993

Publish and Perish

Central Department of Propaganda

By the early 1990s, the Mao Cult, in particular in publishing, had spawned an extremely lucrative industry. The tabloid press and local publishers who produced on-off "magazine-books" churned out articles and special editions devoted to Mao and various aspects of his life and career. Although nearly all of this material kept safely within the confines of PC taste as defined by the propaganda authorities the style of the publications attempted to be as sensational as possible. A number of liberal intellectuals in Beijing and Shanghai, however, attempted to produce books that examined Mao and the MaoCraze in a more critical light, but they were prevented from publication by the following Department of Propaganda order. Independent analysis and evaluation of the complex and disturbing legacy of Mao by nonspecialists was, for the time being, thwarted on the Mainland.

Meanwhile, numerous volumes of hagio-trash that made only passing acknowledgement to the po-faced stipulations of the following document were produced for the centenary, many of them published by supposed bastions of ideological rectitude like the Central Party School Publishing House in Beijing.

Central Department of Propaganda and News and Publishing Administration Circular Concerning Publication Work Related to the Commemoration of the Centenary of Comrade Mao Zedong's Birth (24 March 1992)

26 December 1993 is the centenary of the birth of Comrade Mao Zedong. Comrade Mao was a great Marxist, the founder and leader of the Communist Party of China, the People's Liberation Army and the People's Republic of China. The solemn commemoration of Comrade Mao's centenary is of the greatest significance in our pursuit of the Party's basic line of adhering to "one centre and two basic points"[1] and in the task of building socialism with Chinese characteristics. One of the important elements of the

commemorative activities is the publication of outstanding theoretical works related to the study and propagation of Mao Zedong Thought, as well as the publication of popular and other books. In order to carry out this task efficiently we hereby issue the following circular:

1. The effective publication of works in relation to Comrade Mao's centenary is an important and serious political duty. All propaganda departments and news and publishing organizations must give their full and earnest attention to energetically organizing this work, making careful arrangements, prioritizing tasks, ensuring the quality of publications and guarding against empty formalism;

2. Works to be published as part of the centenary, including the writings of Mao Zedong, selected writings, manuscripts, collections of letters, as well as biographies of Mao Zedong, memoirs, works of reportage, academic studies, reference books and picture albums, are to be strictly reviewed and approved according to the stipulations and guidelines that have been set out;

3. In accordance with the relevant rules, it is forbidden for any publisher without the appropriate authority to produce books of this kind. If plans have been made for such publications they are to be abandoned forthwith and any infraction of this regulation will be investigated and punished severely;

4. The writing and editing of all books in this category is only to be undertaken by specialized personnel. Manuscripts that, according to the regulations, have to be submitted to the relevant organs for review must be sent in. All manuscripts that deal with major historical issues must take as their standard Party Central's [1945] "Resolution on Certain Questions of History" and [the 1981 document] "On Questions of Party History—Resolution on Certain Questions in the History of Our Party Since the Founding of the People's Republic of China." As for matters pertaining to major Party secrets, publishers must comply with the relevant rules of Party Central without exception and ensure that no state secrets are disclosed;

5. In producing the above books all publishers must strictly enforce the system of the "three-tier editing" of manuscripts[2] so that the political content of all works can be carefully monitored. If there are any uncertainties advice should immediately be sought according to the relevant regulations. At the same time, it is vital that the quality of manuscripts is insured, as well as the quality of printing and binding; and

6. So as to enthusiastically and responsibly carry out this important work, all titles to be produced for the centenary are to be submitted by local publishers to the relevant provincial departments of propaganda and news and publishing bureaux for examination and approval. Central publishers

are to report to their relevant superiors.[3] All titles, both from local and central publishers, are to be collated and reported to the Publishing Bureau of the Department of Propaganda and the Book Department of the News and Publishing Administration by 15 April 1992 for filing. These two organizations are to carry out effectively the coordination and direction of the production of these titles.

Notes

1. "One center and two basic points" (*yige zhongxin, liangge jiben dian*) is the official shorthand for the Party's line during the "primary stage of socialism." In full, the line is "to take economic construction as the center, adhere to the Four Basic Principles and pursue Reform and the Open Door."

2. "Three-tier editing" (*sanshen*) refers to the process whereby a manuscript would be reviewed first by an editorial group, then by the head of the relevant editorial department and finally by the editor-in-chief of the magazine, journal or publishing house. See Zhongyang xuanchuanbu bangongting, ed., *Dangde xuanchuan gongzuo wenxian xuanbian*, p. 197.

3. Central publishers include such national publishers as the People's Publishing House, People's Literature Publishing House, Joint Publishers, Zhonghua Publishers, and so on. They would report directly to the Department of Propaganda and the National News and Publishing Administration.

The MaoCrazy West

Hai Feng

An employee of the Party School of the Hainan Provincial Party Commit-
tee, Hai Feng comments on the origins and significance of the long-term
"MaoCraze" among overseas scholars and analysts.

Why did people overseas start doing research on Mao Zedong? Why
does the MaoCraze continue? An American scholar gave the following
overview: "The reason we do research work on Mao and Mao Thought is so
that we can better understand China's past, present, and future." This man
has found the key with which to open the door of China. China gave birth to
and created Mao Zedong; Mao was born· for the sake of China and he
created New China. China and Mao Zedong are regarded as being one unit.
Only by studying and understanding Mao Zedong can you really know
China. This realization is the crucial basis for any work you want to do on
China. Therefore, there is a logical connection between the objective need
for the outside world to understand China and to study Mao Zedong and his
relationship with China. This is why Mao and his Thought have spread so
far internationally and there are in-depth studies of him. This is why we are
interested in the origins of the Mao fever overseas.

1. The Strategic Position of China Determines International Attention
and Demands That People take Mao Zedong into Account.
In the twentieth century China has undergone an enormous historical
transformation. It has gone from being a colonial and semi-colonial society
to one that has won national independence; it has developed from being a
poor and backward nation to becoming a prosperous one. Politically and
economically China has had a profound influence on the international
scene. Under the leadership of the Communist Party and Mao Zedong and,
following the founding of the People's Republic, the Chinese people have
been self-reliant and struggled hard and, up to the time of the Cultural

Revolution, achieved great victories in the socialist revolution. When Deng Xiaoping addressed the General Assembly of the United Nations [in 1972] it was a sign of the international recognition of China's political status and marked the defeat of attempts to keep China isolated from the rest of the world.

In the 1980s, each successive wave of China's reforms has sent a shock through the international community. China once more has displayed its heroic genius on the world stage. China is increasingly the object of international interest. Whoever ignores the existence of China will be making a serious tactical blunder. John King Fairbank, former chairman of the American Historical Society pointed out that the reason for America's repeated failures in Asia was a lack of understanding and incorrect policies. He emphasized that: The case of China is a unique one in the world scene that requires special treatment. It is important to apply the old Chinese adage that "victory will only be possible if you know both thyself and the other" to the modern world. It is important to work towards and achieve a peaceful coexistence with China. It was on the basis of such strategic thinking that foreign academic institutions, in particular Western academics, have paid great attention to the study of China from the 1950s. Mao Zedong and Mao Thought have been an important part of international China studies.

2. The Heroic Achievements of the Communist Party of China as well as the Daring and Success of the Open Door and Reform Policies in the New Era Have Had a Profound Influence on the World. Both Supporters and Critics Have Been Witness to the Extraordinary Path Along which the Chinese Communists Have Traveled and Pay Their Respects to the Heroic Leaders of the Party. Of course, of Those Leaders Mao Zedong Is the Most Preeminent.

The role that Mao Zedong played in the founding and development of the Party, in particular the theoretical and practical activities in which he engaged during various crucial stages of the Party's history, have been central to the research work of foreign scholars of Chinese Party history. From Edgar Snow's *Red Star Over China* to Harrison E. Salisbury's *The Long March: The Untold Story*, the depictions of Mao Zedong have brought this political leader and thinker to life. Snow was of the opinion that Mao's speeches on the Party's policies were worthy of serious attention since they would possibly be the basis for monumental changes in China in the future. It is fair to say that two thirds of the Party's history is a record of Mao Zedong's activities. Therefore, regardless of whether you want to understand the Party's past or present, its successes or failures, first and foremost you must study the entire corpus of Mao Zedong's life and thought. In particular, if you want to understand the Communist Party as it has developed after Mao, then you need to have an accurate appreciation of Mao Thought and its development in the New Era [since 1978] and view things in terms of historical continuity.

3. The Shimmering Intellectual and Cultural Treasures of the 5,000 Years of Chinese History Contain Within Them the Deep and Mysterious Character of the Oriental World and Its Vast and Rich Content. They Have an Irresistible Attraction to the Rest of the World.

Over the past decade the various fads among foreign academics for Sunzi's *Treatise on Warfare*, Confucius, the *Book of Changes*, and so on, are evidence that they are searching for the roots of Chinese thought and culture. This is not merely a case of nostalgia for their work has a practical dimension in that they are interested in achieving a clearer understanding of the background of contemporary Chinese thought and culture. There is a desire to study the history of the Chinese national spirit from Confucius to Mao Zedong. Mao Thought, in particular Mao's philosophical thought, has as one of its origins the rich world of traditional Chinese thought. This "lineage" has been crucial in establishing the abiding and important position of Mao Thought in the history of Chinese thought and has enabled it to have such a profound effect on the rest of the world. Edgar Snow was right when he said that Mao was not only a scholar steeped in traditional Chinese thought but that he was also a thinker and philosopher who could use the past to serve the present and find new meaning in old forms. Ross Terrill was even more perceptive when he said that Mao surpassed any other ruler in Chinese history, including Qin Shihuang, by formulating his own theories. Therefore, an in-depth study of Mao Thought and its relationship to traditional culture, a study of how Mao critically adopted and reformed classical and modern Chinese thought to create a new intellectual mainstream, is one area in which foreign academics have been concentrating their efforts. It is a field which will increasingly attract scholars of Chinese studies.

4. Mao Zedong Creatively Combined Marxism-Leninism with the Revolutionary Realities of China and Thereby Earned the Respect and Approval of the Comintern as well as Its Support.

Mao Thought was directly nourished by the propagation and development of Marxism-Leninism in China. However, the reason that Mao Thought could mature was that it was melded thoroughly with Chinese realities. It forged a path for revolution and construction that was uniquely Chinese. Mao's practical application of his theories made an outstanding contribution to the realization of Marxist-Leninist ideals in the twentieth century. And it is the living soul of Mao Thought that provides today the theoretical underpinnings for the building of socialism with Chinese characteristics.

All progressive Western academics and international Communist organizations recognize the fact that Mao Thought grew out of yet also contributed to the development of Marxism-Leninism. Be they the "heretics" of "liberalism" or those "leftists" who pursue "developmental theories," there is a common acceptance of the fact that Mao Thought is a revolutionary developmental strategy aimed at the realization of Marx's communism in China.

Internationally famous politicians, theoreticians, scientists and, in particular, China specialists agree that Mao Zedong was a major twentieth-century figure. They also affirm the important influence of Mao Zedong and his Thought on both China and the world. . . .

5. The Anti-Imperialist, Anti-Colonialist Patriotic and Democratic Revolutionary Movements of the Third World Countries of Asia, Africa and Latin America Need Mao Zedong Thought as Their Main Theoretical Weapon and Practical Guide.

Mao Zedong's strategic theory on "the three worlds" made him the spiritual leader of all Third World countries. Everyone, from presidents to the common man, were filled with admiration for him. They praised him as a leading light in the Third World, an inspiration to them all. It is through the Third World that Mao Thought became an international force. There are countless students of Mao's writing in the Third World. Mao Zedong's successful experience in applying his theory of using the countryside to surround the cities and his work in building socialism are a model for many countries with a similar history to that of China. The theory of the "Three Worlds" provided a basis for an international united front among developing countries and is a spiritual treasure in their struggle against violence and in the process of self-strengthening. Mao Zedong and China will forever be a source of inspiration and support for the Third World.

6. The Complex Developments Within the International Communist Movement and the Dissolution of the Socialist Bloc Have Led the World to Pay Particular Attention to the Fact That China Has Pursued a Path of Self-sufficiency and Implemented the Theory of Building Socialism with Chinese Characteristics.

At the end of the 1950s Stalinist dogmatism led to a political split between the Chinese and Soviet Communist Parties and then a heated theoretical debate. The capitalist West followed these developments closely and for international political and strategic reasons led them to turn their attention to the study of China and Asia. Add to this the impact of the Cultural Revolution in the 1960s, Mao Thought, in particular the universal discussion of his theory concerning the correct handling of contradictions among the people, were all major political factors in the growth of interest among academics in the study of Mao Thought. During this period, Mao Thought became the theoretical basis for a number of international communist organizations.

The significant developments that occurred in the Soviet Union and Eastern Europe in the late 1980s and early 1990s mark a low tide in the international communist movement and the balance of world power has undergone an historical transformation. Faced with the challenge of the future of socialism, the Communist Party of China as represented by Deng Xiaoping has continued to pursue the path of building socialism with Chinese characteristics and has diligently learnt the lessons of the "domino theory" as witnessed in the collapse of the former Soviet Union and Eastern Europe. China has availed itself of the opportunities that have presented themselves and concentrated on developing productive forces, accelerated the process of Reform and, in this unsettled world, revealed its possibilities for development and prosperity. In doing all of these things, "seeking truth from facts,"[1] the central element of Mao Thought, has played a key role. The successes of China's Reform and Open Door policies since the late 1970s have shaken the world once more. The economic take-off of the Chinese nation will alter the international balance of power once more. Perspicacious scholars throughout the world cannot fail to be interested. Following Deng Xiaoping's "tour of the south"[2] and the announcement at the Fourteenth Congress of the Communist Party [in 1992] that China would establish a socialist market economy, we have witnessed a renewed wave of Reform that has once more had an international impact.

For the above reasons, it is inevitable that research into Mao Zedong overseas will continue to develop and flourish. History has shown that it is because the world has recognized the value of Mao Zedong and his Thought, and because there has been such massive faith in Mao, the Communist Party of China and the People's Republic of China, that Mao and his Thought have been so widely disseminated and studied. As an historical giant Mao Zedong will only grow in international stature with the passing of time. Research into Mao Zedong both in China and overseas will become a rich topic with great historical significance. Mao Zedong is already an historical figure of international significance, his name will live forever in the chronicles of history.

Notes

1. "To seek truth from facts" (*shi shi qiu shi*), a classical Chinese expression, was reinterpreted for the Communist cause by Mao in his May 1941 speech "Gaizao womende xuexi" in which he said: ". . . seek truth from facts. 'Facts' are all the things that exist objectively, 'truth' means their internal relations, that is, the laws governing them, and 'to seek' means to study." See *Mao Zedong xuanji*, p. 759. Mao wrote the four characters *shi shi qiu shi* as an inscription for *Qinghai Daily* (Qinghai ribao) and it was published on 17 July 1961. After the Cultural Revolution, Deng Xiaoping claimed that "seeking truth from facts" was the central element of Mao Thought and he used it as the "philosophical basis" for his own pragmatic approach to China's problems. See, for example, Deng Xiaoping, "Gaoju Mao Zedong sixiang qizhi, jianchi shi shi qiu shide yuanze (1978 nian 9 yue 16 ri)," in *Deng Xiaoping wenxuan*, vol. 2, 2nd ed., pp. 126–28.

2. See "A Place in the Pantheon" note 15.

All That's Fit to Print

Joint Publishers

The following list of books appeared in the Joint Book News *produced by the Hong Kong branch of the Mainland publishing house Joint Publishers (Sanlian shudian) in late 1992. It is a partial record of the materials that appeared at the height of the Mao Cult. The books are listed in the order in which they appeared in* Joint Book News.[1]

Mao Zedong's Philosophy and Contemporary Chinese Philosophy, by Hu Weixiong, Beijing

Collected Annotations on Mao Zedong's Philosophy, ed. by the Central Documentary Research Institute, Beijing

An Overview of Researches into Mao Zedong's Philosophical Thought, Yang Huanzhang et al., Tianjin

Selected Works of Mao Zedong (4 vols.), 2nd edition, Beijing

A Draft History of Mao Zedong Thought, Beijing

Mao Zedong's Reading Habits, Beijing

Mao Zedong's Military Philosophy and Modern Business Warfare, Jiang Shui and Tie Zhu, Guangxi

An Outline of the Original Works of Mao Zedong Thought, Wu Minxian, Wu Zhenghong and Liang Fu, eds., Northeastern Normal University

Birth of a Giant—the Origins of the "Mao Zedong Phenomenon" and the Development of Modern Chinese Political Culture, Xiao Tingzhong, Beijing

A Dictionary for the New Edition of Selected Works of Mao Zedong, Zhang Zhanbin and Jiang Jiannong, Shanxi

A Great Dictionary for the Works of Mao Zedong, Zhou Enlai, Liu Shaoqi, Zhu De, Deng Xiaoping and Chen Yun (3 vols.), ed. by Gao Di, Liaoning

The Great Mao Zedong Dictionary, Liao Gailong et al., Guangxi

A Dictionary on the Mao Zedong Style, Liu Xueqi, et al, Beijing

A Dictionary of Mao Zedong Thought, ed. by the Chinese Mao Zedong Thought, Theory and Practice Research Institute, Central Party School, Beijing

A Great Dictionary on the Works of Mao Zedong, Beijing

A Students' Dictionary for the New Edition of Selected Works of Mao Zedong, Feng Lei, Tian Wen and Xing Bin, eds., Dalian

A Handbook for the Words and Idioms Found in Selected Works of Mao Zedong, He Gong et al., Beijing

Mao Zedong, Zhou Enlai, Liu Shaoqi, Zhu De, Deng Xiaoping and Chen Yun Discuss National Culture, ed. by the Materials Center for the Secretariat of the Office of the Central Committee, Beijing

Mao Zedong on Art and Culture (Revised Edition), Beijing

A History of Mao Zedong's Theories Regarding the Building of the Party (2 vols.), Zhang Weiping and Zhang Liejun, Jiangxi

In Search of Mao Zedong, Wu Fangze et al., Sichuan

A History of Mao Zedong Thought (vol. 1), Yang Chao and Bi Jianheng, eds., Sichuan

Researches on Mao Zedong's Economic Thought, Ni Daqi, Shanghai

Collected Annotations on the Classical Idioms in Mao Zedong's Works, Wang Yuzong and Lu Yuke, eds., Beijing

Collected Studies of Mao Zedong's Works, Zhu Guiyu and Zhao Dongli, Beijing

Mao Zedong and Deng Xiaoping on Seeking Truth from Facts, Party Building Group of the Policy Research Centre of the Central Committee, Central Party School

Classical Idioms in Selected Works of Mao Zedong, ed. by Chen Jun, Beijing

A Reader of Selected Works of Mao Zedong (New Edition), Cheng Min, Beijing

Mao Zedong's Legal Thought and Practice, Li Zhongda, Shaanxi

Specialized Researches on Mao Zedong Thought, Mao Shixin et al., Shaanxi

Mao Zedong's Revolutionary Path (1921–1935): A Tribute for the 70th Anniversary of the Founding of the Communist Party of China, Ma Yuqing and Zhang Wanlü, Shaanxi

A History of the Development of Mao Zedong Thought (2 vols.), Zheng Derong et al., Jilin

An Outline of Mao Zedong Thought, Zheng Derong et al., Northeastern Normal University

The Art of the Way of Mao Zedong Thought, Wang Yongsheng and Zhang Wei, eds., Shandong

The Works of Mao Zedong, Zhou Enlai, Liu Shaoqi, Zhu De and Deng Xiaoping Arranged Thematically, ed. by Yu Cheng, Liaoning

A Guided Reader for Selected Works of Mao Zedong (Second Edition), ed. by Shi Chongke, Beijing

Mao Zedong and Nixon in 1972, Chen Dunde, Beijing

Mao Zedong, Zhou Enlai, Liu Shaoqi, Zhu De, Deng Xiaoping, Chen Yun and Jiang Zemin Discuss Building the Party, ed. by the State Education Commission, Beijing

A New Study of Mao Zedong Thought, Peng Chengfu and Guan Wenhu, Beijing

Researches into Mao Zedong's Fiscal Thinking, Ma Wenrui and Yang Zhilin, eds., Beijing

Researches into Mao Zedong's Economic Thinking, Xiao Gongda, Southeastern University

The Military Art of Mao Zedong, Wang Yongsheng and Zhang Wei, eds., Shandong

The Theory of Democracy and Legality in Mao Zedong Thought, China Legal Association, Shaanxi

The Art of Mao Zedong's Calligraphy, Wang Yongsheng and Zhang Wei, eds., Shandong

The Great Dictionary of Mao Zedong's Calligraphy, Wang Yue and Li Guijun, eds., Hunan

Selected Calligraphic Inscriptions by Mao Zedong (traditional binding), ed. by the Central Documents Institute, Beijing

Mao Zedong's Poems in the Calligraphy of Guo Moruo, Guo Moruo, Beijing

A Calligraphic Copybook of Mao Zedong's Poems, Yan Jialong et al., Hunan

Mao Zedong's Poems in His Own Hand, Guangxi

Selected Paeans for Mao Zedong, Wen Yin, Sichuan

The Art of Mao Zedong's Language, Wang Yongsheng and Zhang Wei, Shandong

The Annotated Poems of Mao Zedong, Yi Mengchun, Hunan

Gazing Out at the Green Willows from the Walls of Yan'an—Collected Articles on Studying Comrade Mao Zedong's "Yan'an Talks on Literature and Art," ed. by Ai Keen, Beijing

The Art of Mao Zedong's Poetry, Wang Yongsheng and Zhang Wei, Shandong

The Classical Poems That Mao Zedong Appreciated, Hangzhou

An Appreciation of Mao Zedong's Poetry, Wang Zhenzhong and Zhong Zhenzhen, eds., Nanjing

Mao Zedong's March on the East (an historical novel), Dou Jiaxu, Henan

A Record of Mao Zedong's Contacts with Others—1915–1976, Jia Xiaohua, Lin Xingsi and Zeng Shannan, Jiangsu

A Veritable Account of Mao Zedong's Life—1946–1976, Zheng Yi and Jia Mei, eds., Jiangsu

Collected and Annotated Couplets Based on Mao Zedong's Poetry, Xiao Yongyi, Hunan

An Exploration of Mao Zedong's Poetry, Li Zijian, Hehai University

An Appreciation of Mao Zedong's Poetry, Zhang Jing, Shao Ruijuan and Xu Hongsheng, eds., Dalian

Mao Zedong's Early Student Years, Li Rui, Liaoning

The Emotional World of Mao Zedong, ed. by Bin Zi, Jilin

Mao: A Biography (Revised Edition), Ross Terrill, Hebei

Fifteen Years at the Side of Mao Zedong, Li Yinqiao, Hebei

The Emotional World of the Founder of the Republic, Quan Yanchi, Inner Mongolia

Liang Shuming and Mao Zedong, Wang Donglin, Jilin

Mao Zedong and Modern China, Li Junru, Fujian

The Origins of a Great Man: Mao Zedong, Cao Zhiwei et al., Zhejiang

Mao Zedong and the Great Revolution, Li Yongtai, Sichuan

Mao Zedong's Youth, Xiao San, Hunan

Mao Zedong's Cultural Character, Chen Jin, Beijing

China Brought Forth a Mao Zedong—Comments by Famous Chinese and Foreigners, Su Yang, PLA

Mao Zedong and His Secretary Tian Jiaying, Dong Bian, Tan Deshan and Zeng Zi, Central Document Publishers

Mao Zedong and Cultural Tradition, Chen Jin, Central Document Publishers

Mao Zedong and His Townsfolk, Zhao Zhichao, Hunan

Mao Zedong in Real Life, Hai Lude, Hualing Publishers

Mao Zedong's Reading Career, Gong Yuzhi, Pang Xianzhi and Shi Zhongquan, Beijing

Mao Zedong's Family Tree, ed. by Li Xiangwen, Guangdong

Approaching Mao Zedong—A Foreigner and His Contact with the Leader of New China, Jiang Jiannong and Cao Zhiwei, Beijing

Reverberations: A New Translation of the Complete Poems of Mao Zedong, Mao Zedong, Hong Kong

Mao Returns to Mankind, Quan Yanchi, Guangdong

Note

1. For further bibliographical material related to 1980s and 1990s' Mao books, see Scharping, "The Man, the Myth, the Message," p. 168, n. 1.

In the Footsteps of the Great

Beijing Evening News

Revolutionary tourism has been common in China since the founding of the People's Republic and in particular since the Cultural Revolution, when Red Guards roamed the country in search of the political highlights of Party history.

The following article from the Beijing Evening News, *the leading evening newspaper in the Chinese capital, appeared shortly before Mao's centenary. It introduces one of the methods being used by some schools to inculcate a love of the Chairman among his prepubescent revolutionary successors.*

One afternoon recently, some seven hundred students of the Xiaomachang Primary School in Xuanwu District [central Beijing] engaged in an unusual educational exercise. As part of their commemoration of the centenary of Chairman Mao Zedong's birth, they went in search of Mao Zedong's footsteps in Xuanwu District.

According to various studies, Xuanwu District is the area in which Chairman Mao spent a lot of time both working and as a resident [in his youth]. In order to encourage the students to be more aware of the Older Generation of Proletarian Revolutionaries, the school enlisted the services of Wang Kechang, a teacher who has been awarded a government citation as an outstanding district tutor in Party history.

Utilizing relevant visual materials, Teacher Wang informed the students that Mao Zedong had attended the wake for Yang Huaizhong, the father of [Mao's wife] Yang Kaihui, at the Fayuan Temple. At the Hunan Provincial Association Hall in Lanman Alley Mao Zedong organized a meeting of some one thousand people to denounce the warlord Zhang Jingyao. Mao Zedong made dumplings with his teacher Li Jinxi at Li's home in the Second Street of Xiangluying. . . .

When Wang had finished his lecture the students went by bus to the

Second Street of Xiangluying, the Open-Air Stadium at the Altar of Agriculture, the Taoran Pavilion, and three other spots to see for themselves where Chairman Mao had lived and worked.

To think that all this had happened around them and they were not even aware of it! Hearing all of these little-known but deeply moving stories, the primary school students recorded the information in various ways. Some used notebooks, others utilized tape recorders to capture the grand and glorious image of Chairman Mao that appeared before them. One sixth grader said: "My family used to live in Weiran Alley outside Xuanwu Gate. Not even my father knew that the pen factory that is there now was originally the headquarters of the famous newspaper *Jingbao*. Let alone did he know that Chairman Mao lived there!"

Praise Be to Mao

Various Hands

In March 1993, Zhongliu, an unabashedly pro-Mao monthly established after 4 June 1989, announced a poetry competition sponsored jointly with the "Three Star Industrial Group" as part of its commemoration of the Mao centenary. The "Three Star Cup" and various monetary prizes were awarded to poems that most successfully "sang the praises of Comrade Mao Zedong and Mao Thought, glorified patriotism, socialism, and the collective spirit and hailed the Chinese revolution and construction."[1] In May 1993, on the anniversary of Mao's "Yan'an Talks on Literature and Art," speeches he made in 1942 that subsequently formed the basis of Party cultural policy, a special issue of Zhongliu featured the first entrants in the competition. Subsequent issues of the journal printed dozens more. The following is a small sampling of this awesome body of poetry. "Mao Zedong, electrician extraordinaire" and "Mao Anqing" were both prize-winning entries.[2]

Mao Zedong, Electrician *Extraordinaire*
Da Wei

The Long March, 25,000 *li*,
was a mighty electrical cable

Mao Zedong, crouching in the smoke of battle
studied a field map while gunfire sounded all around
That red pen in his hand moved swiftly and
shot out a powerful current
that cut through the darkness of China

In the dim light
Mao Zedong stood on the Pagoda Hill [in Yan'an]

yet could make out that ravenous neighbour who,
under the guise of "coexistence and co-prosperity,"
was shamelessly stealing electricity from China
At this point, Mao Zedong stepped forward angrily
and with a right hook sent the Japanese reeling
and their boastful signature fell sprawling on that
pledge of surrender in 1945

As the ambassador of light
he often used his 1.83 meters in height
to act as a high-voltage pole
the fiery gaze of the people
providing him with energy

But, exhausted by overwork,
he fell one day
And now his vast and deep Thought
has become the energy source for all China

Mao Anying
Lu Ximing

> Bitter sacrifice strengthens bold resolve
> Which dares to make sun and moon shine in new skies.
> —Mao Zedong[3]

You were Mao Zedong's son
New China's "No. 1 Princeling"
But you did not care about your status
for you knew you were
    the child of a revolutionary
    the relative of martyrs
    a member of the Communist Party of China!

When you graduated university
your father sent you to the countryside to work
Those massive hands that had turned the world on its head
patted your tender and youthful shoulders
You knew you now bore the weight of true responsibility
You set off with a humble backpack filled
    with the pride of the son of the revolution

the deep love bestowed by a father
Like a seed planted in those vast fields of
    the revolutionary holy land of Yan'an
you now sprouted roots and flowered
    among the People

That year, our neighbours were in distress,
Your father sent you, just recently married,
    like a common bullet
to be used on the Korean front
And that was the end of you
for you were never to return home
In your 28 years you could not
experience all that life could offer
But you shone with the glory of
a solemn paean to internationalism

When your loving father recalled
his beloved eldest son
he would hold back tears of agony
But why couldn't Mao Zedong's son die?
Indeed, why not?
His only comfort
came from the fact that as a youth who had
gone hungry, suffered illness and grown up on the march
you had now, like all the People's children
who have sacrificed themselves for the cause of justice,
gone on to eternal life

Aaah, Comrade Anying
You were New China's
"No. 1 Princeling"
who became her highest ranking young martyr
Because of this you are
a classic work in the library of the Chinese nation

Mao Zedong in the Snow
Hai Xingxing

With hands behind his back
Mao Zedong set out from a stela of poems

and walked into the snow-bound history of China
The warmth of his every step
sent tremors of delight
through the frozen earth
So much emotion trapped in frustration
silently found release
How many seeds that had been dormant
now woke from sleep

This oak that grew in the soil by the Xiang River [of Hunan]
embued with the strength of its waters and its indomitable
    spirit
Mao Zedong's imposing figure bowed down
only to Truth and the People
He advanced slowly
and in a landscape of evening snow
he became the concrete symbol of the Chinese revolution

He used the spark on the prairie
to weld together hammer and sickle
raising them to become a new banner
Mao Zedong, that giant man,
always marched to the beat of a different drummer
and gave voice to a unique emotion
Every step he took was a solid beat
Every step he took left a deep impression
He buried the shadows of a dynasty
Every line of his poetry
was a Great Wall that stood solid against the storm

Towards the end of his poem
Mao Zedong turned around slowly
gave a nonchalant wave of his hand and said:
all are past and gone![4]
His shining forehead stands out on the horizon of the snow-
    lands
and is the shining glory of a new dawn for China.

Eternal Remembrance
Zhao Aimin

At Chairman Mao's Memorial Hall I gathered these blossoms
    . . .

If
A husband and wife in their seventies came from Guangzhou
and exclaimed: If it hadn't been for Chairman Mao, we
probably wouldn't be alive today.

If there was no sun in the skies
how would anything grow
If there was no dew on the earth
even the grass would wither

If he did not take the helm of the revolution
we may well still be wandering in the dark
If the nation hadn't produced this great son
the future of China would probably still be unclear

This old couple understand completely that: he was our saviour;
to remember Mao Zedong means that you will love the Communist Party . . .

Lest we forget
A mother brought her four year-old child from Liaoning to
see Chairman Mao. The mother said: I can't let my child
forget Mao Zedong.

Lying here is a one hundred year-old man
He is looking out at his motherland, land of hope
He has spent seventeen springs and autumns lying here
The tempests of the time still stir his breast

Generation after generation
bask in the effulgence of the Red Sun
May this child who is just learning to speak
take nourishment from the revolution

How can we forget, we will never forget
that the banner of Mao Zedong will always fly on high

He belongs to the world
A foreign student studying in China was in the long queue of
people waiting to go into the Hall. He was wearing a T-shirt

bearing a picture of Chairman Mao. He said: Mao is not China's alone, he belongs to the world.

He is not only China's sun
Mao Zedong is a star that dazzles all eyes
He is undoubtedly a giant of world stature
Shining forth in the constellation

His theories suit not only China
They express the wisdom of humanity, a treasure of civilization
His Thought is not only a weapon for revolution
for it holds out hope for the advancement of mankind

Because of this, he and his motherland
stand firm in the Orient like a giant . . . . . .

Dreaming of Chairman Mao
Gou Huaxian (doctor, No. 5 People's Hospital, Chengdu, Sichuan)

Night is so still
All the clamour of the day has disappeared
leaving only the ink-black vastness of the heavens
and the slumbering earth

I stand before the window
eyes closed
in a reverie recalling the dream I just had
for it was like a bolt of lightning piercing the cloak of darkness

My dear Leader
walked oh-so-naturally into the land of my dreams
and chatted with me
His laughter was relaxed,
so calming
He said something
very clearly
not obscure in any way
But, sadly,
at that instant I awoke . . .

I have left behind the age of many dreams
and thank the heavens for granting my wish
to dream of Chairman Mao on his centenary
I am so delighted
for although I am just a common person
we are both children of the Yellow Emperor
descendants of the Han and Tang Dynasties
The leader gave his all to overthrow the Old World
and I will do my utmost to serve New China[5]

Notes

1. *Zhongliu* zazhishe and Sanxing qiye jituan gongsi, "Jinian Mao Zedong tongzhi danchen 100 zhounian 'Sanxingbei' shige zhenggao pingxuan huodong qishi," p. 30.

2. See "Sanxingbei" shige zhenggao pingxuan huodong zuzhi weiyuanhui pingxuan weiyuanhui, "Jinian Mao Zedong tongzhi danchen 100 zhounian 'Sanxingbei' shige zhenggao pingxuan huodong banjiang tongbao," pp. 13–14. For the zealous speeches made at a seminar on the poems entered in this competition, see "Yu shidai tongbu he renmin tongxin—'Sanxingbei' shige zhenggao pingxuan huodong banjiang zuotan jiyao," pp. 18–33.

3. From Mao's poem "Qilü: dao Shaoshan," June 1959.

4. This is a quote from Mao's poem "Snow."

5. The good doctor was by no means the first person to dream of the Chairman. Lei Feng, the red samaritan canonized by Mao, dreamt of the Chairman as a kindly father who offered encouragement during a nocturnal visitation. See *Lei Feng riji*, 1968, p. 8, quoted in Yang, *Gifts, Favors, and Banquets*, p. 259. Dream visitations (*tuomeng*) are common in traditional Chinese literature and, in particular, works like Pu Songling's *Liaozhai zhiyi*. See also Liu Wenying, *Mengde mixin yu mengde tansuo*.

Sparing Mao a Thought

People's Daily

The People's Daily *editorial published on 26 December 1993, the centenary of Mao's birth, concentrated not on Mao the man, but Mao Zedong Thought. The first half of the front-page editorial was devoted to Mao Thought, the second to the innovative contributions that Deng Xiaoping, the "Grand Architect," has made to the ruling ideology of China. It concludes with a nod in the direction of Jiang Zemin, the new Party General Secretary, and head of the "third leadership collective" that was supposed to rule China into the twenty-first century following Deng's demise.*

Comrade Mao Zedong's most important contribution has been the creation of Mao Zedong Thought, that is, the uniting of the basic principles of Marxism-Leninism with the practical realities of the Chinese revolution. This is something he achieved in collaboration with his comrades-in-arms over a long period of revolutionary struggle. Comrade Mao Zedong creatively formulated a series of guiding principles for the Chinese revolution on the basis of the nature of China's status as a semifeudal, semicolonial oriental nation. The might of Mao Zedong Thought is self-evident. Time and again it has been proven that Mao Thought is a source of endless ideological strength in the work of both revolution and construction. The basic principles of Mao Thought still shine brilliant rays of light. . . .

Comrade Deng Xiaoping has pointed out: "In many respects we must still make reference to Comrade Mao Zedong. We must finish work that he started, correct his mistakes, and improve on his work."

Comrade Deng Xiaoping has applied the fundamental truths of Marxism-Leninism to China's present situation and has formulated answers to such urgent basic problems as how a country like China, which is relatively backward both economically and culturally, can build and consolidate socialism. In doing so he has developed the theory of socialism with Chinese characteristics. . . . The last fifteen years of the Reform and Open Door policies, coupled with socialist modernization, are proof that Comrade Deng's theory of building socialism with Chinese characteristics is a powerful weapon that can guide us to create a prosperous and powerful nation. This theory is contemporary Chinese Marxism.

Comrade Deng Xiaoping has set a shining example for us in how to sustain and develop Mao Zedong Thought.

The Last Ten-Thousand Words

Jiang Zemin

Party General Secretary Jiang Zemin, or the Core Leader as he is also known,[1] delivered the official eulogy at the mass meeting to commemorate Mao's centenary held in the Great Hall of the People in Beijing on 26 December 1993.

In the numbingly long-winded fashion common on such occasions (the speech takes up over a page in the People's Daily*), Jiang reiterated the Party line on Mao and praised the genius of his own benefactor, Deng Xiaoping, as well as the significance of the "socialist market economy."*

In death Mao continued to serve the cause by legitimating every shift in the Party line. A few tantalizing excerpts from the speech must suffice here.

As Comrade Deng Xiaoping has pointed out, Comrade Mao's achievements are of primary importance; the errors he made in his latter years are secondary. His errors came about because he ignored his own correct principles. His were the errors of a Great Revolutionary and Great Marxist. Comrade Deng has resolutely criticized all tendencies to negate entirely Comrade Mao and Mao Thought on the basis of the mistakes he made in his old age. He has said that only by following Mao Thought did the Chinese revolution achieve success. We cannot abandon the banner of Mao Thought. If we do not pursue Mao Thought we will be guilty of a grave historical error. Our central aim is to confirm Comrade Mao's historical position, as well as to maintain and develop Mao Thought. We will continue to hold high the banner of Mao Zedong Thought, not only today but in the future as well. . . .

Mao Zedong Thought is a science that changes with the times. Comrade Deng's theory concerning socialism with Chinese characteristics is an enrichment of Mao Thought and has allowed it to attain even greater heights. By following this path in the future and through the struggle of a number of generations [of Chinese] we will surely build a rich, democratic, and civilized modern, socialist country. No matter what difficulties we face we must pursue the basic Party line, and do so without wavering for a century. We must earnestly study Marxism-Leninism and Mao Zedong Thought in reference to the tasks raised by Reform and by the ever-changing objective situation. The central theme of our study must be the application of Comrade Deng's theory concerning socialism with Chinese characteristics and use it to arm the thinking of all comrades in the Party and all the peoples of China. . . .

Notes

1. Head, that is, of the "Third Core of Leadership" in the history of the Party. According to 1990s Party dogma, Mao was the First Core Leader and Deng the Second.

Galluping Mao: A 1993 Opinion Poll

Tang Can, Zhu Rui, Li Chunling and Shen Jie

In late 1993, the Beijing Youth News *published a survey conducted by scholars at the Chinese Academy of Social Sciences. They interviewed one hundred people about what they thought of Mao Zedong.*

Beijing Youth News *is a popular daily produced under the aegis of the Party Youth League. Most of its editors and writers were under 40 and the paper was widely read among Beijing youth. It was in the vanguard of commercialized Party propaganda.*

The tone of the report is factual and detailed. It frankly admits what everyone knows from their own experience: that official ideology had little impact on young people, especially those in their early 20s and under. Unfortunately, although it indicates that some of those questioned were highly critical of Mao, no details are given.

The poll was published with a lengthy commentary by Yang Ping, one of the paper's leading journalists who was also an active conservative involved with the journal Strategy *and* Management *(Zhanlüe yu guanli). Daresay because of the alarming ignorance about Mao and official ideology among the young that the survey reveals, Yang, a young man himself, wrote an editorial comment entitled "Confronting Mao Zedong":*

Young people today who have experienced the twists and turns of the 17 years since Mao's death understand all too well the negative influence of romantic and extremist approaches to China's Reform. We appreciate that the transformation of Chinese society cannot happen overnight. We need to develop a tireless spirit of long-term commitment. We are also painfully aware that nihilism, cynicism, and petit-bourgeois attitudes are corrupting the souls of our youth at this crucial juncture in our history. It is in this context that Mao Zedong's boldness of vision, his indomitable will, his approach that combined revolutionary realism with revolutionary romanticism allowing him to determine the way forward and then not stray off course, as well as his lofty desire to change both China and the world, offer our young people a shining example and a model for emulation.

Interviewees:
37 people under the age of 25
19 people between the ages of 26–35
24 people between the ages of 36–50
20 people over the age of 50

What does the average Chinese think of Mao Zedong today? How is the historical giant who determined the fate of modern China regarded now and how much influence does he still have? And what do today's young people know about him? These are the types of questions which interest us, as well as many others, as Mao Zedong's centenary approaches. To find some answers we carried out an opinion poll among 100 average Chinese.

Our investigation started 17 years after Mao's death. In that period his prestige has fallen and risen once more. Today, the majority of those questioned (61 people) still hold him in very high esteem, and over two thirds expressed their basic admiration, love, and worship of Mao.

Of the various groups interviewed those over 50 years old were the most enthusiastic and emotional about Mao. Of them, 80 percent said they definitely felt that Mao's achievements outweighed his errors.

When some older intellectuals spoke of Mao their admiration was evident: "Mao Zedong was a historical giant who initiated a new age. One can say without doubt that in terms of both his abilities and achievements he was, and remains, unique." "Mao was the man who really helped the Chinese to stand up."

Older workers and peasants put it more simply: "Chairman Mao put us in charge." "Without the Communist Party there would be no new China; without Chairman Mao there would be no Communist Party." One worker compared the achievements of Mao and Deng and summed it up as follows: "Chairman Mao founded the nation; Deng Xiaoping has let us enjoy a better life."

All the older cadres we interviewed expressed support for our poll because they felt it had "an educative value" for the society as a whole. One old man grabbed us by the hand as he said tearfully: "Usually we have no way of expressing our feelings about the Chairman!" Similar things were said to us many times. We got a very strong impression that although a lot of time has passed, Mao still occupies an unassailable position in the hearts of many Chinese.

When talking about the errors of Mao's later years most older people were forgiving and understanding. Despite the fact that many of them had suffered at the time, and they didn't shy from the issue, they saw their sufferings as being due to errors made by a collective leadership. One retired woman teacher said: "Chairman Mao may have made mistakes but at least he wasn't corrupt. His intentions were good, and no one can avoid making mistakes."

Most middle-aged people have a far more complex relationship with Mao. Over half of them admitted that they had mixed feelings about him and it was impossible to characterize their attitudes by saying that they either "loved" or "hated" him. The rest have considerable respect for Mao but they rarely used such terms as "adore" or "love" to express their feelings.[2] When asked to evaluate Mao's achievements and failures, however, they revealed a rational and dispassionate stance. Of this group, 67 percent gave Mao a fairly high score.

One man was born into a landlord's family and was branded a counter-revolutionary when he was 16. He suffered a great deal and was later refused university entrance a number of times. He said: "I feel very ambivalent towards Mao. In personal terms, the Mao era was one of suffering for me. But historically speaking, Mao was a remarkable giant. He managed to flow with the course of history and brought an end to decades of internecine strife and division. He unified China and for a time after 1949 he let the people enjoy a good life. These were all remarkable achievements."

A 45-year-old intellectual said: "Mao laid waste to my generation. By isolating China from the outside world he also delayed the development of our nation. But Mao did allow the Chinese people to stand up and achieve a sense of dignity. We have him to thank for that."

Many middle-aged people also showed considerable understanding of the mistakes Mao made in his later years. One man who spent a decade as a rusticated youth in northern Shaanxi and is now an employee in a small company said: "Being sent to the countryside destroyed my life. But that wasn't Mao's fault. It was caused by the system as a whole."

Another interviewee who has done research on Mao offered the following analysis: Mao tried throughout his life to find a developmental model for the East that was different from that of the West. He hoped thereby to put China in the centre of the international stage so that we would become the model for others. But he was not all that careful or mindful of just how each step should be taken or what consequences they might have. As he got older he became increasingly lost in a world of his own.

Middle-aged and older intellectuals, regardless of their profession, revealed two completely different attitudes in their evaluation of Mao: they were either very mild or very extreme. These groups were also the most thoughtful in their analysis and evaluation of Mao, whether it be positive or extremely critical.

We were completely unprepared for the discovery that younger people, that is the group from 25 to 35 years of age, generally praised Mao highly and in many cases openly worshipped him. They most often used words like "worship" to describe their attitude. Some 57 percent of those interviewed used the word "worship" in their responses.

Older people saw Mao in terms of his historical and political influence. Younger respondents tended to evaluate Mao in more personal terms. They often prefer to discuss their admiration for him in regard to his individuality, character, talents, courage, and political ability rather than in relation to concrete historical and political events.

Many young people said that they were deeply moved by books that depicted details of Mao's private life. Generally, they were very much impressed by the fact that he combined greatness with a common touch, that he was frugal and strict in his own life. They were also fascinated by his odyssey, to have started out as a peasant's son and end up as a major world figure.

Some were completely uninterested in discussing his political career. They had their own insights into the interior world of a man with whom "no normal mortal could compare" and had the deepest admiration for him.

A university graduate said: "Mao is one of the people I admire most." A book vendor said he was incredibly impressed by the man who hundreds of millions of Chinese had worshipped. A woman reporter said: "Mao was the type of leader who suits orientals. You need a figure like that, someone who will stand at the apex of the pyramid and keep everything together."

Although most of these people had little direct experience of Mao, or remembered the errors of his later years, most of them had heard a lot about that time. Apart from a few individuals who were still critical of Mao because their families had suffered under him, the majority felt that things like the Cultural Revolution, the Anti-Rightist Movement and the Great Leap Forward were very distant historical incidents. Some even expressed doubts about the suffering they'd heard people had gone through during the Cultural Revolution. They commented that malcontents were exaggerating things for personal reasons. Others were so enamoured of Mao that they said they wished they'd lived in the 1950s or 1960s.

Respondents under 25 provided a striking contrast to this slightly older group. Apart from a general respect and admiration for Mao among most university students, a considerable proportion of respondents in this group—some 40 percent—were virtually completely ignorant of Mao and the historical, social, and political developments that surrounded him. They were therefore unable to comment on him. Many middle school and primary school students responded to questions about why Mao's portrait hangs from Tiananmen and who founded the People's Republic of China by saying: "I don't know." Asked whether they were interested in knowing more about Mao, many of them said "not particularly," "don't have the time," or "not interested."

The majority of Chinese, however, hold Mao Zedong in the highest regard. This would have been unimaginable only a few years ago when Mao's prestige had hit rock bottom. There are complex socio-political reasons for the re-emergence of Mao Zedong. But the fact of the matter is that although there is widespread respect for Mao, things are very different from the past. For many younger Mao worshippers the Chairman is no longer an ideological or political symbol, rather he has a charisma that is related to outstanding personal qualities and his profound influence and authority. This is the essential difference between today's MaoCraze and the political fascination older people once had for Mao. A tendency for people to become divorced from history and politics has meant that young people can be free to admire Mao's personality. The complete ignorance [about the past] among people in their early 20s and adolescents is proof that this tendency is becoming more evident.

The survey indicated that people in the 25–35 age bracket were the main consumers of Mao-related popular publications with some 75 percent of them having read such books. Some 90 percent of university students under 25 as well as 43 percent of other young people in this age group were also readers of these books. Most young people got their information about Mao's personal life and his history from these books.

The American academic Ross Terrill's *Mao: A Biography*[3] was the most highly regarded of the Mao books among university students and other relatively well-educated people. Readers felt that Terrill's account was "accurate," "compelling," and "the most outstanding." We can therefore conclude that many young people have a view of Mao Zedong that is based on the perceptions and analyses of foreigners.[4]

Other books popular among young people include *Memoirs of a Bodyguard*, *China's First Man* and *Mao Zedong Quits the Altar*. But most surprising was that many young respondents mentioned having heard certain myths and superstitious tales about Mao. They claimed, for example, that at the time of his birth a flash of red light was seen in the sky; again, a comet fell from the heavens when he died ... many of the respondents half believed such stories. One Master's student said that he was completely convinced by the absurd tales found in *Mao Zedong and His Hometown*.[5]

In striking contrast to all of this was the fact that most of the people under the age of 35 were relatively unfamiliar with Mao's own writings. One third of young people (most of whom have had a tertiary education) claim to have read *Selected Works* and they can name a few articles like "On Protracted Warfare," "On Contradiction" and "On Practice." But on closer questioning most of them admitted that they had "only flicked through" or "read the opening lines of" these essays. Some didn't have a clue about the contents of these works, though they could name them. They certainly had not "studied" them. Others were not even sure whether Mao had authored "The Communist Manifesto" or *How to Be a Good Communist*.[6] Only 6 or 7 of the 56 young people interviewed had any concept of Mao Thought. Some university students said they felt Mao's ideas were so divorced from reality that they couldn't be bothered to read him. One young man who held forth on the subject of Mao admitted that he had never read anything by him but that "it didn't matter since Mao Thought has been so widely propagated that everyone knows what it's all about."

Do our young people have an adequate knowledge of the essence of Mao Thought? The answer to this question reveals whether the spiritual heritage of Mao Zedong is intact. According to our survey, over half of the young people questioned were completely ignorant of the detailed contents of Mao Zedong Thought. Some could readily spout abstract slogans like "Mao Thought is the crystallization of collective wisdom"[7] that they had learned by heart. The Master's student mentioned above remarked that: "The only Mao quotes I know are ones I saw written up on slogan boards. . . . I learned a few for my politics exam, but have forgotten the lot. The only one I remember is 'study hard and you'll improve every day'."[8] Surprisingly, five primary school students whom we interviewed had no idea where this quotation came from.

Because of a patchy understanding of Mao plus a general ignorance of politics and history, the adulation for Mao among young people often amounts to little more than blind worship. Furthermore, most young people draw a complete blank when it comes to Mao Thought itself. This is a clear indication that mainstream ideological propaganda, which has spared no effort in promoting Mao Thought, is in crisis.

Time does indeed march on. So what elements of Mao Thought have survived; which aspects of it are still relevant to the social and political realities of China today?

In response to these questions, 60 percent of middle-aged and older people said it was the concept of "serving the people."[9] Some were quite emphatic and added: "That's the main element [of Mao Thought]."

One old worker became quite animated as he spoke: "Chairman Mao said you have to 'serve the people wholeheartedly.' I might not be capable of wholehearted service, but even if you're half-hearted and don't serve yourself wholeheartedly then I think you've got a pretty good grasp of Mao Thought."

A middle-aged cadre who works for a state organization said: "Mao made 'serve the people' the central platform of the Communist Party, that's how they won popular support and came into power. If they still want the people to support them then they'd better stick with this policy."

A 45-year-old intellectual opined: "The best thing about Mao's theories was the line 'serve the people.' All that stuff about combining theory with practice has nothing to do with us. But 'serving the people,' that's a theory for the masses, everyone can arm themselves with it."

This wide-ranging survey left us with a very strong impression that 17 years after his death Mao Zedong still has a place in the hearts of the Chinese people. This is not only because of the massive impact he had on the development of China during his lifetime, and because of the power of his thought and personality, but also because he continues to exert an influence on Chinese life today. We were particularly struck by the fact that Mao led the Chinese out of internecine strife and forged unity in what was a poor and backward nation to achieve a sense of national dignity. These are the reasons why people now still have such a high regard for him.

It is evident that for the Chinese strength and unity, as well as national dignity, are extremely important factors in political life. These are and will remain central to the feelings and actions of the Chinese. From what we heard about Mao it is also obvious that the Chinese hold out expectations for a strong political leader and rely on such figures. Political strength and authority are still central features of life in China today.

Notes

1. Yang Ping, "Miandui Mao Zedong."
2. The terms in Chinese are *chongbai* and *reai*. *Reai*, literally "hot-love," is a term that has been used to describe popular adulation of Mao for many decades.
3. Ross Terrill, *Mao: A Biography.*
4. Not all university students were fans of Terrill's work, however. Mao Xinyu, Mao's grandson and a student in the Department of History at People's University in Beijing at the time, was highly critical of "the works of Americans regarding my granddad. Those books [he names Terrill and Schram's work] are biased and ridden with errors." He preferred the more "reliable" memoirs of Mao's bodyguard Li Yinqiao and the works of other Mainland writers like Quan Yanchi and Wang Hebin which all conform with official dogma on Mao. See Zhao Zhichao, "Yingmian zoulai Mao Xinyu," part 1, pp. 11–12.
5. For this material, see "Mao Zedong he tade xiangqinmen" in Liu Jianguo, *Shaoshande zuotian yu jintian: Mao Zedong zhi gen.*
6. This latter work, *Lun Gongchandangyuan xiuyang*, was written by Liu Shaoqi. See Liu Shao-ch'i, *How to Be a Good Communist.*
7. A Party formulation that kept the vehicle of Mao Thought intact while its dated contents were effectively jettisoned. See "Mao: The Body Corporate" above.

8. *Haohao xuexi, tiantian xiang shang*, also rakishly translated as "good good study study, day day up." This "Mao quote" was and is regularly written up at entrances to primary and middle schools. It is, in fact, a combination of two inscriptions by Mao. "*Haohao xuexi*" was penned in Beijing for the inaugural issue of *Zhongguo ertong* (China's Children) magazine that appeared in September 1949, while "*tiantian xiang shang*" was written nearly a decade earlier in Yan'an to commemorate Children's Day, then celebrated on 4 April, and published in *Xin Zhonghua bao*, 12 April 1940. Despite the disparity in calligraphic styles, the two lines were later combined into one "Mao quote." See *Mao zhuxi shoushu xuanji*, pp. 188 and 279.

9. *Wei renmin fuwu*. This line comes from "Serve the People," a speech Mao made at a memorial ceremony for Zhang Side on 8 September 1944 and one of the "Three Standard Articles." See *Mao Zedong xuanji, yijuanben*, pp. 905–7.

Chairman Mao Graffiti

Zhang Chengzhi

At the inception of the Cultural Revolution, Zhang Chengzhi was a student at Qinghua Middle School in Beijing. He was an activist and the first to call himself a "Red Guard" (hongweibing) when writing his own "small character posters." The term was subsequently adopted by his schoolmates and then by the Cultural Revolution student movement.[1] Like many of his generation Zhang was a fervent disciple of Mao and Mao Thought. Pictures of him studying Mao's works can be found in the pages of official propaganda publications of the time.

In the 1980s, Zhang became a prominent writer of "minority fiction" centered in Inner Mongolia,[2] where he had been sent as a youth after Mao terminated the Red Guard movement. In the early 1990s Zhang achieved fame as a proto-nationalist and was noted for his anti-Western stance. Other prominent ex–Red Guards enjoyed different career paths. Su Xiaokang and Zheng Yi, both writers, went into exile after 4 June 1989, while the four surviving "Five Great Leaders" of the Red Guard Movement had reportedly gone into business.[3] As a popular saying originating among former Red Guards put it: "Chairman Mao let us take control; Deng Xiaoping lets us make a bankroll."[4]

This following article, published in the Japanese journal Sekai, *consists of a series of loosely connected notes, or graffiti, as Zhang chooses to call them. It is one of the most interesting contributions a Mainland-based former Red Guard has made to discussions of the 1990s' Mao Cult.[5]*

In writing about Mao it is virtually impossible to avoid either praising or condemning him. When you think of those people who were sacrificed in that great wave of history you are overwhelmed by a premonition that by breaking this taboo I will be committing an historical crime.

There is no subject harder to deal with than this. But thinking Chinese are destined to suffer this fate. Faced with the harsh realities of China's future, especially as a Chinese author confronted with the injustices created by the New World Order of the Anglo-Saxons, it is a topic that for reasons of conscience and self-respect I am loathe to ignore.

The year 1993 marked the centenary of Mao Zedong's birth. One hundred years is too short a time in which to be able to say anything definitive about him. However, in order to express some views common among Chinese thinkers, and also to be released from an excessive personal responsibility in writing about Mao, I have decided to pen what I chose to call "Mao grafitti."

He was born on 26 December. Everyone referred to his birthday simply as 12.26. I vividly recall two different incidents that occurred on Mao's birthday in my youth.

The first was in 1966. Red Guards in Beijing middle schools announced they had formed a "United Action Committee" and they launched an attack on the Ministry of Public Security. It was the sixth time we'd attacked. It was the middle of winter and we marched in ranks along Chang'an Avenue wearing ridiculously large Red Guard armbands and faded PLA uniforms. In our excitement we kept looking around. We were too young to have any sense of fear. Confusion reigned and no troops or policemen were to be seen anywhere, but still our attack failed. The only thing we could do was mess around a bit. Our group was eventually dispersed by a mass demonstration on Chang'an. It had been a complete failure.

Only now it occurs to me: what were all those people doing on Chang'an in the dead of night? Were we really all there to celebrate the Chairman's birthday?

The other occasion was during the snow storms of the winter of 1971 when I was in Inner Mongolia. It was the only "white disaster," as the Mongolians call it, that I ever experienced. Everything came to a standstill. The plains on which the horses usually galloped were now lost in a deep sea of snow. Even the camels occasionally sunk into the snow drifts, crying mournfully as they struggled. And then the livestock, starting with the cows, the sheep and the Mongolian sheep, unable to get at the grass with their hooves, began to starve. Having run out of their supplies of tea and staple grains the lives of the nomads all but collapsed. I'll never forget the grim faces of everyone as they sat down to eat the same black mutton day after day. That's the first time I knew what it was like to be on the brink of death.

The PLA began airlifting flour and feed for the livestock by helicopter along the mountain ridges which weren't too deep in snow. The first time when people emptied the grain into their containers back in their yurts they placed them in front of a portrait of Mao with the words "grain of good fortune" written on them.

On the evening of 26 December, everyone enjoyed the first meal made with white flour in the yurts that were scattered in the darkness of the snow-covered plains. There was joyful singing and everyone got drunk on veterinarian alcohol used for the livestock, diluted with water.

It's been over ten years since he was repressed. I was completely untouched by the criticisms made of Mao by Chinese intellectuals—the most faddish group in the world—and those so-called "China experts" overseas. That's because those people are completely out of touch with the sentiments of China's broad masses.

However, the MaoCraze that started three years ago came as a complete shock. Calendars featuring Chairman Mao suddenly became all the rage while those with girlie pictures fell out of fashion. Books about him flooded the market, as did cassettes of songs from the Mao era making, in one case, 5 million *yuan* for the producer. China's a hard place to get moving. But just what it means when it does move is something I'd like to but still don't understand.

No matter how you look at it Mao remains an outstanding individual, a man with great charisma, as everyone says. And for reasons that no one really understands, the new MaoCraze began three years ago and has continued.

I don't care if people deride me for being the last Red Guard. I just never want to forget the principle Mao pursued in dealing with Red Guards and students. In 1966, before the student movement became violent, he issued a warning to high-level cadres in the Party. Quoting from memory it went something like this:

> No one who crushes a student movement will come to a good end. The northern warlords repressed the students and look what happened to them. So did the reactionaries of the KMT and you know it was useless. I advise you all: don't crush the student movement. No good will come of it. Heed my words.[6]

I don't know what people think today when they re-read this passage. It still moves me deeply. He may have been a hopeless politician, but he took students seriously and respected their demands as a matter of principle.

Mao spent his student days in his homeland of Hunan, an area that has a strong and ancient spiritual tradition. Those student years left a lasting impression on him and turned him into an eternal student. Youthful impulsiveness is a privilege students enjoy and it is something that became a basic political principle for Mao. Mao didn't repress students and this is proof that no one can deny his youthfulness, and those who do only prove that they have lost the edge of youth themselves.

His relationship with intellectuals was also significant. There is no denying the fact that under his rule Chinese intellectuals were in a difficult
position. But nor can we avoid asking just what type of role Chinese intellectuals (or as Lu Xun sarcastically called them, "the learned classes")
played in Chinese history after the Sino-Japanese War, in particular during
the first half of this century?

During a recent stay in Japan I've felt ashamed as I watched television
reports on the lawsuit being pursued by former comfort women from Korea.
A handful of courageous old Korean ladies began legal proceedings in
Shimonoseki against the Japanese government for crimes committed
throughout Asia during the War. Shimonoseki is the place where the Japanese government forced China—the mother of Japanese culture—to sign a
humiliating treaty initiating a process that led to a disastrous war. This is
where it all began. I have to admit that compared to these old Korean
women the Chinese intellectuals living in Japan have only made the weak-
est, dare I say, indulgent statements about this country.

The chorus of denunciations of Mao Zedong that was heard from the late
1970s was accompanied by equally loud praise for the bureaucratic system
of China. Although it is not without some fear that I say this, especially as I
will shortly be returning to China, but if only that praise for the system
hadn't been so clamorous then perhaps the finger that pulled the trigger four
years ago [on 4 June 1989] would have been more hesitant.

But now we are in the 1990s. Following the collapse of the Socialist
Bloc, and during the Gulf War the international powers led by America and
England set out to destroy the Islamic world which they perceived as being
a potential enemy. The infamous Monroe Doctrine, formulated to deal with
the forces of self-determination in Latin America, is an old weapon in the
U.S. arsenal. The most recent example of its application was the Panama
invasion. Next time it will be China's turn. China, not Communist China,
but the massive cultural entity of China, is next on the hit list of the New
World Order. Although we are confronted by this international situation
Chinese intellectuals (and here I include the majority of Chinese studying
overseas) are still unashamedly pro-American.

Of course, these are only the personal opinions of one Chinese writer.
But perhaps Mao Zedong was particularly aware of the defects of modern
Chinese intellectuals. Another person with a similar distaste for the Chinese
intelligentsia was Lu Xun. Why did both of these men choose a life that cut
themselves off from the intellectuals? Mao even went so far as to exile them

to the countryside. Shortly before his death Lu Xun wrote to the effect that: When facing death Europeans have a tradition of begging for forgiveness or forgiving others. But I will continue to let my enemies detest me and I will forgive none of them. It was a significant stance. . . .

Mao did leave behind one work that can be regarded as his last will and testament. It was a letter he wrote to his wife, Jiang Qing, dated 8 July 1966. The Politburo of the Party released an edited version of this letter in 1972. Many Chinese have thought of it as being the most important thing Mao ever wrote. The centenary of Mao's birth provides a perfect occasion for me to quote a few paragraphs from it:

> Ruan Ji of the Jin dynasty thought little of [the founder of the Han dynasty] Liu Bang and on his way from Luoyang to Cheng Hao [in Henan] he stopped at Guangwu to view the site of the battle between the states of Chu and Han [which led to Liu Bang's victory] and he sighed: "there were no true heroes that's why a minion [like Liu] could make a name for himself."[7] Lu Xun has made similar remarks in his essays. Lu Xun and I are like-minded men. I appreciate his frankness. He said that it is always much harder to dissect yourself than it is to analyse others. After slipping up a few times I feel very much the same. But other comrades won't accept this to be the case. I'm sure of myself but I also lack confidence. When I was a lad I said that: the confident live 200 years and can send the water flying for 3,000 *li*. See how cocky I was then. But I'm not all that sure. I always have the sense that since there are no lions in the mountains the monkey has crowned itself king. That's the type of king I am. I'm not being eclectic here but I do feel that I'm possessed of a tiger spirit, and it is the guiding force in my personality; the monkey spirit is secondary to it.
>
> In the past I've quoted some lines from a letter written by Li Gu of the Latter Han dynasty to Huang Qiong. He said: " 'that which is too high is easily found deficient just as that which is pure is easily sullied.' There are certain songs which few can join in chorus. Few great men can live up to their reputation."[8] This last line describes me perfectly. . . .
>
> But things always turn into their own opposite. The higher you climb the harder you'll fall. I'm prepared to be dashed to pieces in the fall. It's no big deal. Nothing is created or destroyed, only broken up. There are over 100 political parties in the world and the majority don't believe in Marxism-Leninism. People have pulverized Marxism-Leninism, so you can imagine what will happen to us. . . .
>
> I predict that if there is an anti-communist right-wing coup in China they won't have a day of peace; it may even be very short lived. That's because the Revolutionaries who represent the interests of over 90 percent of the people won't tolerate it. Then the Rightists may well use what I have said to keep in power for a time, but the Leftists will organize themselves around other things I have said and overthrow them. The Cultural Revolution is a full-scale exercise. . . .[9]

Due to the limitations of space I cannot quote the letter in full. This may lead to further misunderstandings about Mao, but there has already been so much confusion in regard to him it doesn't really matter. This quotation allows you to see into the workings of Mao's mind. If this isn't sufficient then perhaps nothing can make people really think about and understand him.

In fact, in relation to the evaluation of Mao, I believe that he can teach us something. This letter vibrates with a mordant brilliance; it is a powerful and rich text that presents us with a living image of Mao. No one else could possibly have written such a beautiful thing. I've read it twice: once in 1972 and again recently. Although I have savoured the letter I must confess that I still cannot claim to understand exactly what he means. It fills me with inexplicably complex emotions.

With his death China's age of great men came to an end. The masses felt a sense of loss. They have not yet found an alternative. That is to say that despite the passing of time, when the masses feel themselves discriminated against and oppressed they can think of no other leader than Mao Zedong.

Despite all the talk of international peace for our ancient motherland of China the New World Order is a pitiless killer and every Chinese will have to face its onslaught one day. In the future world justice will continue to be frustrated and there will be no such thing as compassion; nor will anyone stand up for the dispossessed.

The name Mao Zedong will remain eternally a symbol of rebellion against this new order. His prestige may well gradually rise among the masses once more. Of course, Mao Zedong must be criticized in human terms, but ironically, for Chinese like me who continue to oppose neo-colonialism, the international balance of power makes it necessary for us to look to him as a bastion of human dignity.

It is in this light, for the people of China and of the poor nations throughout the world who are confronted with the new international scene, it is possible that the influence and significance of Mao Zedong will gain a new lease of life.

When we were young we only ever called him "Chairman Mao." Everyone chanted "Long live Chairman Mao!" But later people got used to calling him simply Mao Zedong without an honorific, but that always sounded somewhat denigrating. However, now to call him "Chairman Mao" [as I have in the title of this article] seems to require a measure of courage.

The word "grafitti" has a connotation of playfulness, or at least it conveys a sense of something that is less than serious. I would have never thought of using such a word in connection with His name. By deliberately choosing such a title I thought I might be able to show how hard I have struggled to understand Mao.

Notes

1. Pu Dahua, a Red Guard leader at the same school, gave these details in his 1995 interview with Sang Ye. From Sang Ye, "Piandi yingxiong xia xiyan: Weidade 1966," unpublished interview transcript. The Qinghua Middle School students formally adopted the name "Red Guards" at what they called the "Yuanmingyuan Meeting" in the former Summer Palace near their school, on 29 May 1966. Mao expressed support for the students in a letter addressed to them in August that year.

2. See Zhang Chengzhi, *Huiminde huangtu gaoyuan: Zhang Chengzhi huizu xiaoshuo*; also Zhang Chengzhi, "Hanwula-haote," pp. 636–37, for further evidence of his devotion to Mao in the early 1970s.

3. See Yin Hongbiao, "Rendao zhongniande 'Hongweibing' shidai," p. 39. The Five Great Leaders (*wuda lingxiu*) were: Nie Yuanzi, Kuai Dafu, Han Aijing, Wang Dabin and Tan Houlan (deceased).

4. *Mao zhuxi rang women zhangquan; Deng Xiaoping rang women zhengqian.*

5. For another view by a famous ex–Red Guard writer in exile published about the same time as this essay, see Zheng Yi, "Miandui yidapian jingshen feixu," pp. 56–57.

6. This is a conflation of comments that Mao made to Central and Beijing municipal leaders in mid 1966.

7. See "Liezhuan di shijiu: Ruan Ji," in Fang Xuanlin, et. al, *Jin shu*, vol. 3, *juan* 49, p. 1361.

8. See "Zuo Zhou Huang liezhuan di wushiyi: Huang Qiong," in Fan Ye, *Houhan shu*, vol. 3, *juan* 61, p. 2031.

9. For the full Chinese text of this letter, see Mao Zedong, "Mao Zedong gei Jiang Qingde xin, 1966 nian 7 yue 8 ri," pp. 55–56.

The Specter of Mao Zedong

Liu Xiaobo

A social and political critic of no fixed abode, Liu Xiaobo, one of China's most outspoken dissidents, was, like so many of his fellows, banned from publishing in China after 4 June 1989. Jailed after the Beijing Massacre, Liu was released from police custody in 1991 and started writing occasional articles for the Hong Kong and Taiwan press. At about the same time that Li Jie undertook his lengthy critique of Mao on the Mainland, Liu Xiaobo wrote a denunciation of Mao published in Hong Kong in November 1988. In it he said:

> Seen solely within the context of Chinese history, Mao Zedong was undoubtedly the most successful individual of all. Nobody understood the Chinese better; no one was more skillful at factional politics within the autocratic structure; no one was more cruel and merciless; none more chameleon-like. Certainly, no one else would have portrayed himself as a brilliant and effulgent sun.[1]

Liu wrote the following essay about Mao and China's post-Deng scenario in late 1994 when speculation about the post-Deng era was rife.

Liu's analysis of post–4 June politics is somewhat simplistic, as are his comments on figures like He Xin. Nonetheless, his view of the MaoCraze and its popular appeal is representative of some of the more thoughtful public critics of the Party in China.

The specter of Mao Zedong has continually haunted Deng Xiaoping and his Open Door and Reform policies. The specter of Mao doesn't simply inform the attitudes of the Maoists[2] among the Party leadership, it also has a mass following among the people. On this issue those at the top and those at the bottom [of society] are united: they deploy Mao Zedong to oppose Deng's Reforms. The spirit of Mao is the most powerful weapon in the arsenal of Maoists in the upper echelon [of the Party]. Mao is also the symbol that the masses use to express their frustrations. It would appear that apart from the present policies pursued by the Mainland government there are no alternative, viable political resources for people to rely on apart from the heritage of Mao Zedong. This has been particularly evident since the Massacre of 4 June [1989]. Now most people feel that Western political models are, in the case of China, both impractical and dangerous. What we are presently seeing is the combination of nationalist currents of thought with a nostalgia for the Maoist past. We are being drawn back to the age of Mao Zedong.

Certainly, the Open Door and Reform policies of Deng Xiaoping took as their starting point a complete negation of the Cultural Revolution and a betrayal of the Maoist line. In the last decade or so China has experienced massive changes and the country's fast-track economic development has astounded the world. Consumerism and hedonism have made people feel richer. It seems as though nothing can stop the "peaceful evolution"[3] that is going on in China. But nobody can afford to forget the following facts: our economic takeoff has not changed the one-party dictatorship created by Mao Zedong; the improvement in the standard of living has not led to increased human rights; the market economy is not predicated on a legal structure based on private property; every political movement strikes terror in the hearts of the new rich; the popularity of karaoke bars and the flood of violent and pornographic literature has not enhanced the status of freedom of speech; industrial reform that has led to the separation of Party and industrial management and the conversion of state industries into companies has not given the masses any greater opportunities or rights to participate in the political life of the nation.... This is the true legacy of Mao Zedong.

Rapid economic development has exacerbated various social antagonisms and brought them to the fore. It has also led to greatly increased public dissatisfaction and frustration. Once Deng Xiaoping effectively blocked any attempts at democratic political reform people increasingly turned to nostalgia as a means of expressing their unhappiness with the state of affairs. People outraged by overt corruption and the activities of official speculators who have become wealthy overnight only too readily think of how Mao Zedong overthrew Capitalist Roaders in the Party and warned of the need to purge bureaucrats from the government. They recall fondly the incorruptible Party of the Maoist past. The people who have been cast to the bottom rung of the economic ladder as disparities in income increase, as well as those who have not benefited from the redistribution of wealth that has taken place, recall with longing the egalitarianism and social justice of the past. Although poverty was the hallmark of that age, at least everyone was equally impoverished. People did not feel as lost and disenfranchised then as they do today. Nor did they feel they were the victims of such social injustice. Unemployed or semi-employed people as well as workers in state enterprises who are no longer being paid will recall their former exalted position under Mao as the masters of society. They remember the iron ricebowl that assured them an income for life and the Party organization that took care of them from cradle to crypt. The people who witness in terror and disgust the flood of itinerant workers swelling the population of the cities will recall that under Mao there was a strict household registration system that kept the peasants bound to the land. As for the peasants who have been forced to abandon the land they look forward to another peasant leader like Mao Zedong who will lead them to overthrow the landlords and divide up their property just as Mao did. The former powerholders, from high to low, who have retired or who have been forced aside will remember how, under Mao, they were assured power for life. People dissatisfied with the increase in crime, the spread of pornography and prostitution and the production of shoddy and bogus goods think of the innocent and pure days of Mao. . . . In comparison to these very practical and utilitarian views, the dissidents who were purged after 4 June and who still oppose the government have little to offer the masses. Their manifestoes and petitions have little impact on the powerholders especially in comparison to workers' strikes, peasant riots, fluctuations in the stock market and violent crime. At the slightest hint of activity the organs of the proletarian dictatorship go into operation and crush all opposition. The dissidents have absolutely no impact on the society as a whole.

We are faced with an absurd social tableau: the poverty of the Mao age was emotionally satisfying and exciting, it made people sing with joy although the social ambience was stultifyingly pure. The wealth generated in the age of Deng, however, has made the Chinese feel impotent and disgruntled. The social scene is chaotic to the point of complete degradation. On one hand, we have a peasant leader who murdered tens of millions of people and turned hundreds of millions into pliant slaves, but he is still deeply missed. On the other, is the second generation leadership [Deng, et al.] which rehabilitated countless numbers of unjustly condemned people and which has given the Chinese unprecedented wealth. Yet these people are the object of mass discontent. In my opinion, the person chiefly responsible for this ridiculous situation is not Mao Zedong, nor even the Chinese, but none other than Deng Xiaoping himself.

Since coming to power Deng has been caught in a bind. The Maoists within the Party as well as the malcontents outside it have criticized him for taking the Capitalist Road. The Reformers in the Party (including people who called for political reform like Hu Yaobang and Zhao Ziyang) as well as the dissidents in the society at large have attacked him for upholding authoritarian rule and for being a dictator. Caught in a tussle between these two forces Deng has been powerless to respond to the attacks of the Maoists. He has constantly compromised with them and been forced to do so because his Four Basic Principles are used by the Maoists to bolster and protect themselves. No matter how outrageous they become they have never been treated like the dissidents. On the contrary, there has been an escalation of the pressure Deng has brought to bear on radical reformists. First, they were named in the media and criticized, then came expulsions from the Party and dismissal from office. Finally, he resorted to using tanks and mass jailings to silence them. As Deng upped the ante in regard to the Reformers, the Maoists took advantage of the situation to increase pressure on Deng.

The Anti-Spiritual Pollution Campaign in 1984 and the Anti-Liberalisation Campaign of 1987 resulted in the fall of [Party General Secretary] Hu Yaobang from power and the purging of a large part of the reformist élite.[4] Those purges were, for the Maoists, relatively moderate. The bloody massacre of 4 June sealed the fate of Zhao Ziyang and his plans for political reform as well as leading to the ouster of large numbers of élite intellectuals, not to mention the murder of pro-Reform citizens. What followed was a massive Maoist purge in all realms—political, economic, and ideological. People had to make self-criticisms before they could be let off the hook. China now pursued a policy of "preventing peaceful evolution" and propaganda about foreign imperialists plotting to overthrow the Party not heard for many years was trotted out once more.[5] A "neo-conservatism" led by He Xin spread throughout the nation. He Xin's sophistry even managed to fool many university students who had experienced 4 June.[6] The high-level Maoists within the Party now blamed 4 June on Deng's capitalist policies and said they had encouraged bourgeois liberal elements within the society.

Meanwhile, among the masses, Mao badges reappeared everywhere. Old songs in praise of Mao reverberated throughout the land and books, films and teleseries related to Mao became all the rage.... Suddenly the whole nation seemed to be possessed by a desire to return to the Maoist past. Deng's prestige was clearly under threat.

In early 1992, Deng Xiaoping responded to all of these pressures by going on his "tour of the south,"[7] reaffirming his policy that the Reform policies must continue for another century. This led to a new high tide of Reform. Although the Maoists were forced into retreat they kept up the pressure in both the political and ideological arenas. While consumerism and money making swept the nation, the Maoists still issued warnings against peaceful evolution. Although the authorities published the third volume of *Deng Xiaoping's Selected Works* at the time of the Mao centenary in an attempt to divert interest in Mao,[8] in the hearts and minds of the masses Mao remains the greatest modern leader of China.

In 1994 the various social tensions in China became more evident and violent. Party Central took measures to strengthen its power and control over local Party organizations. About this time the book *China Through the Third Eye* was published and in July a conference, "Socialism and the Modern World," was held in Beijing.[9] Both were highly critical of Deng's policies and expressed nostalgia for the Mao years. The popular impact of these two events goes without saying; but it is interesting to note that the authorities took them seriously as well. This is an indication that the types of views expressed [in both the book and at the conference] have a wide-spread appeal.

Deng's greatest achievement may well have been that he was able to break free of the Mao era and abandon "class struggle" in favour of eco-nomic development. But Deng's greatest dilemma has resulted from the fact that he persevered with Mao's political system and was unable to change fundamentally the nature of authoritarian rule in China. Nor could he ex-pose the disasters that Mao's rule created. On the contrary, by pursuing his Four Basic Principles, Deng maintained Mao as the ruling icon of the Party and the nation. Particularly, in his autumn years, Deng has re-enacted the tragedy of Mao himself.

It may well be that as a Party member who worked under Mao for decades Deng was congenitally incapable of cutting the umbilical cord to the Chairman. Despite his own suffering under Mao and the horrors wrought on the Chinese people by him Deng could not bring himself to betray him entirely. Deng's greatest tragedy has been his inability and unwillingness to develop a Reform strategy that could supersede Mao Zedong.

China has lived under Reform for sixteen years now; still the specter of Mao haunts the land. Those who are disgruntled with the present state of affairs find resources of confidence and strength in the legacy of Mao. Every time Reform suffers a setback, whenever social tensions are exacer-bated people from the highest echelons of the Party to the broad masses pay homage once more at the altar of Mao Zedong and seek to negate the policies of Deng Xiaoping. People ignore the fact that the social problems of today are, in essence, remnants of Mao's rule. They are oblivious to the fact that any sustainable effort to transform China must negate Mao's leg-acy. And still they worship him.

In reality, the reason that leftist thinking repeatedly resurfaces in China and finds support is that Deng Xiaoping has allowed it to do so. The Maoist system that he has continued to promote is the greatest enemy of the Reforms on which he embarked. The 4 June Massacre served only to entrench the contradiction between the Four Basic Principles and the Reform policies.

After Deng, it will be the banner of Mao Zedong that may be unfurled once more to stabilize China. Maoist socialist egalitarianism may well be used to pursue policies of social equality and clean government. For in these policies the authorities may find a way of dealing equitably with mass disaffection. But that will mean that China will fall back into the vicious cycle of history.

November 1994, Beijing

Notes

1. Liu Xiaobo, "Hunshi mowang Mao Zedong."
2. *Maopai* in Chinese. This is the common Hong Kong term for ideological conservatives in favor of monolithic Party power, the planned economy and limited reform.
3. See "A Place in the Pantheon" note 2.
4. The Anti-Spiritual Pollution Campaign was a short-lived cultural purge that began in late 1983. The Anti-Bourgeois Liberalisation Campaign of early 1987 was only marginally more effective, although it did result in the resignation of Hu Yaobang. For details, see Barmé and Minford, eds., *Seeds of Fire*, pp. 342–53.
5. Deng Xiaoping claimed that the activists who were supposedly behind the student demonstrations of 1989 were agents of enemy powers (that is, the U.S.) who were hoping to turn China into a bourgeois republic that would be a vassal state of the West.
6. He Xin was active in the first few years after 4 June and he reportedly impressed many university students when he spoke at campuses in Beijing presenting his avowedly conservative view of contemporary events. He Xin and Liu Xiaobo have been public enemies since the late 1980s. He Xin cannot be single-handedly held responsible for the neo-conservative wave of the early 1990s.
7. See "A Place in the Pantheon" note 15.
8. The third volume of Deng's works (*Dengxuan sanjuan* as it was called in Chinese) was published in 1993 in an obvious attempt to focus people's attention on Deng and his policies. The propaganda authorities directed that the book be used in obligatory political study sessions and as a result it was soon on the official best-seller list.
9. See Wang Shan (alias Luoyiningge'er), *Disan zhi yanjing kan Zhongguo*. This book created a sensation when it was published in the spring of 1994 and although it was eventually banned it was widely discussed. The conference, *Shehuizhuyi yu dangdai shijie*, was organized by Wu Qin (see "Mao More Than Ever") with the support of the Beijing Capital Steel Corporation. See Shao Yanfeng, "Shehuizhuyi shi guoqu geng shi weilai, shoudu xuezhe yantao 'shehuizhuyi zai dangdai shijie.'"

Musical Chairmen

Anonymous

Rather than leave the reader with the impression that the MaoCraze produced only hagiographic works related to the Great Leader, I choose to end this work with two punning rhymes and a quotation from an itinerant worker.

The first was common in China after 1989. In six lines it sums up the dilemmas of the Chinese leadership and the feeling among average Chinese people that, apart from occasional private satire, they are powerless in the face of the political musical chairs played by their rulers.

> Zhou sile esi zhu
> zhu sile meiyou mao
> mei mao hua yige
> hua buhao hu yige
> hu buxiang zhao yige
> zhao bucheng jiangjiuzhe

> 粥死了餓死豬
> 豬死了沒有毛
> 沒毛畫一個
> 畫不好糊一個
> 糊不好照一個
> 照不成將就著

> （粥：周；豬：朱；毛：毛；
> 畫：華；糊：胡；照：趙；將：江）

The congee [zhou = Zhou Enlai] goes and the pig [zhu = Zhu De] starves to death
With the pig dead its hair [mao = Mao Zedong] will go
[It's useless] without hair so draw [hua = Hua Guofeng] one instead
If that's no good, paste [hu = Hu Yaobang] one together
If it doesn't look right take a photo [zhao = Zhao Ziyang]
If the photograph doesn't come out, then you just have to put up with things as they are [jiang = Jiang Zemin].

***

The floating population, deracinated rural workers and beggars,
mangliu *in Chinese, became an increasingly major social problem as the*
economic Reforms continued in the 1980s and 1990s. Urban dwellers often
spoke of the masses of roving peasants (tens to hundreds of millions de-
pending on what sources you accepted) as being a major threat to social
stability and future prosperity. Some mangliu, *however, believed that it was*
from their ranks that a new strongman, someone perhaps with the stature of
Mao Zedong, would eventually appear to rule the nation.

Mao himself had an early career as a mangliu *of sorts, details of which*
are recorded in a book by his companion at the time, Siao-yu.[1] *In the 1990s*
China's floating population armed itself with the invincible weapon of Mao
Thought, or as a popular rhyming saying put it:

> Beijing kao zhongyang,
> Shanghai kao laoxiang,
> Guangzhou kao Xianggang,
> Mangliuzi kaode shi Mao Zedong sixiang.

> 北京靠中央，
> 上海靠老鄉，
> 廣州靠香港，
> 盲流子靠的是毛澤東思想。

> Beijing relies on the Center,
> Shanghai on its connections,[2]
> Guangzhou leans on Hong Kong,
> The drifting population lives by Mao Zedong Thought.[3]

***

In February 1995, the Australian-based Chinese journalist Sang Ye, co-author
with Zhang Xinxin of Chinese Lives: An Oral History of Contemporary China,[4]
was back in China working on a new volume of interviews. His subjects included
a mangliu *who spoke of the venerable pedigree of* mangliu *in Chinese history.*[5]

In fact, the founding emperors of all China's dynasties were *mangliu.*
Chairman Mao was a big *mangliu.* When he first came to Beijing from
Hunan, [the leader of the Communist Party] Chen Duxiu and [Mao's wife]
Yang Kaihui's father were well-known professors. They made hundreds of

dollars a month, but Mao couldn't even find a decent job. He ended up earning 8 *yuan* a month working in [Beijing University] library. Everyone treated him like a bumpkin and laughed at him for his [peasant] accent. But later Mao was Chairman and nobody else counted for shit.

The East is red, the sun comes up, the *mangliu* brought forth a Mao Zedong.[6] —Most people reckon it's gonna happen like that again. Lots of books have said so, too.

Notes

1. Siao-yu, *Mao Tse-tung and I Were Beggars. A Personal Memoir of the Early Years of Chairman Mao.*
2. Beijing relies on the power of Party Central to protect it and prosper; Shanghai on all the officials in Beijing of Shanghai provenance (the so-called "Shanghai Gang": Jiang Zemin, Zhu Rongji, Huang Ju, and so on).
3. In "Sailing the Seas Depends on the Helmsman" (*Dahai hangxing kao duoshou*), the unofficial anthem of the Cultural Revolution, there is a line that goes: "The Revolutionary Masses rely on Mao Zedong Thought" (*geming qunzhong kaode shi Mao Zedong sixiang*).
4. Zhang Xinxin and Sang Ye, *Chinese Lives: An Oral History of Contemporary China*, edited by W.J.F. Jenner and Delia Davin, New York: Pantheon Books, 1987.
5. For a history of the words and associations of the "floating population" in Chinese history, see Chen Baoliang, *Zhongguo liumangshi.*
6. The original line in the Maoist anthem "The East Is Red" (*Dongfang hong*) goes: "The East is red, the sun comes up, China has given birth to Mao Zedong. . . ." (*Dongfang hong, taiyang sheng, Zhongguo chulege Mao Zedong*).

Sources

Mao on Mao. From Richard M. Nixon, *The Memoirs of Richard Nixon*, New York: Grosset and Dunlap, 1978, p. 561.

The Mysterious Circle of Mao Zedong. From Liu Yazhou, *Guangchang—ouxiangde shentan*, Hong Kong: Tiandi tushu youxian gongsi, 1990, pp. 235–36. Originally translated in Barmé and Jaivin, eds., *New Ghosts, Old Dreams: Chinese Rebel Voices*, New York: Times Books, 1992, pp. 326–27.

Deng Xiaoping: Mao in Short. From Deng Xiaoping, "Dui qicao 'Guanyu jianguo yilai dangde ruogan lishi wentide jueyi' de yijian," in Deng, *Deng Xiaoping wenxuan (1975–1982)*, Beijing: Renmin chubanshe, 1983, pp. 262–63 and 266.

The Party on Mao. From "On Questions of Party History—Resolution on Certain Questions in the History Of Our Party Since the Founding of the People's Republic of China (Adopted by the Sixth Plenary Session of the Eleventh Central Committee of the Communist Party of China on June 27, 1981)," *Beijing Review*, no. 27 (July 6, 1981): 20, 23, 25, and 29.

A Specter Prowls Our Land. From Sun Jingxuan, "Yige youling zai Zhongguo dadi youdang," *Chang'an*, 1981: 1. This translation is taken from Barmé and Minford, eds., *Seeds of Fire: Chinese Voices of Conscience*, New York: Hill and Wang, 2nd ed., 1988, pp. 121–29.

Documenting the Demise. From "Zhongyang xuanchuanbu guanyu jinhou baozhi, kanwu, tushu, wenjian yinyong Ma, En, Lie, Si he Mao zhuxi yulu bu zai yong heitizide tongzhi, 1978 nian 3 yue 23 ri," in Zhongyang xuanchuanbu bangongting, ed., *Dangde xuanchuan gongzuo wenjian xuanbian (1976–1982)*, Beijing: Zhonggong zhongyang dangxiao chubanshe, 1994, vol. 2, restricted circulation, p. 595;

"Zhongyang xuanchuanbu guanyu chuli liucunde 'zhong' zipinde qingshi, Xuanqingzi (78) 36 hao, 1978 nian 7 yue 28 ri," in *Dangde xuanchuan gongzuo wenjian xuanbian (1976–1982)*, vol. 2, pp. 609–10;

"Zhongyang xuanchuanbu guanyu tingzhi faxing *Mao zhuxi yulu* de tongzhi, Zhongxuanfa [1979] 5 hao, 1979 nian 2 yue 12 ri," in *Dangde xuanchuan gongzuo wenjian xuanbian (1976–1982)*, vol. 2, p. 679;

"Zhongyang xuanchuanbu guanyu chuli gongzhong changsuo yulupai he biaoyu kouhao wentide tongzhi, Zhongxuanfa [1979] 14 hao, 1979 nian 9 yue 6 ri," in *Dangde xuanchuan gongzuo wenjian xuanbian (1976–1982)*, vol. 2, p. 682;

"Zhongyang xuanchuanbu guanyu chedi qingchudiao guoshi biaoyu kouhaode tongzhi, Zhongxuanfa [1980] 16 hao, 1980 nian 6 yue 2 ri," in *Dangde xuanchuan gongzuo wenjian xuanbian (1976–1982)*, vol. 2, p. 779;

""Zhonggong zhongyang bangongting guanyu Mao Zedong tongzhi suxiang wentide tongzhi, Zhongbanfa [1980] 73 hao, 1980 nian 11 yue 6 ri," in *Dangde xuanchuan gongzuo wenjian xuanbian (1976–1982)*, vol. 2, p. 720; and,

Zhongyang xuanchuanbu guanyu zai huichang he gonggong changsuo gua lingxiuxiang wentide tongzhi, Zhongxuanfa [1981] 13 hao, 1981 nian 7 yue 29 ri," in *Dangde xuanchuan gongzuo wenjian xuanbian (1976–1982)*, vol. 2, p. 909.

Mao, a Best-Seller. From Gao Jiangbo, "Tan qikanzhongde 'Mao Zedong re,'" *Zhongguo tushu pinglun* 4 (1989): 122–25 and 22.

The Mao Phenomenon: A Survivor's Critique. From Li Jie, "Lun Mao Zedong xianxiang—yige xingcunzhede pipan shouji, zhiwu," *Baijia* 3 (1989): 51–52, 53, 57, 58, 64–65, 65–66 and 66–67.

Crazed Critics: Two Views of Li Jie. From Meng Fei, "Mao Zedong yu Zhongguo geming—ping 'Lun Mao Zedong xianxiang,'" *Huadong shifan daxue xuebao (zhexue shehui kexue ban)* 4 (1991): 25; and, Ying Congying, "'Shangba' weihao mo 'wangteng'—du 'Lun Mao Zedong xianxiang' yougan," *Zhongliu* 3 (1991): 39.

From Sartre to Mao Zedong. From Hua Ming, "Cong 'Satere' dao 'Mao Zedongre,'" *Renmin ribao (haiwai ban)*, March 1, 1990. Originally translated in Barmé and Jaivin, *New Ghosts, Old Dreams*, pp. 406–7.

Permanently on Heat: An Interview with Comrade Deng Liqun. From "Guanyu 'Mao Zedong re'—Deng Liqun tongzhi da benkan jizhe," *Zhongliu* 12 (1991): 2–4.

A Fan from Way Back. From He Xin, "Lun Mao Zedong ji Zhongguo shehuizhuyi—da zhu Jing waiguo jizhe wen (zhiyi)," in He Xin, *Dongfangde fuxing—Zhongguo xiandaihuade mingti yu qiantu (dier juan, jingji fenxi yu zhanlüe yanjiu)*, Haerbin: Heilongjiang jiaoyu chubanshe, 1992, pp. 80–81.

The Sun Never Sets. From Su Ya and Jia Lusheng, *Buluode taiyang*, Zhengzhou: Zhongyuan nongmin chubanshe, 1992, pp. 1–5, 7 and 18–22.

A Typology of the MaoCraze. From Zhang Weihong, "Daxuesheng 'Mao Zedong' rede leixing fenxi," *Dangdai qingnian yanjiu* 5 (1990), restricted circulation, 24–27.

A Star Reflects on the Sun. From Liu Xiaoqing, "Wo zai Mao Zedong shidai," *Zhongguo zuojia* 5 (1992): 86, 88–89 and 96.

In a Glass Darkly: An Interview with Gu Yue. From Jin Zhong, "Zhuizong Mao Zedong—fangwen dalu yanyuan Gu Yue xiansheng," in Liu Xiaobo, et al, *Hunshi mowang Mao Zedong: mingjia ping Mao ji*, Hong Kong: Kaifang zazhi chubanshe, 1993, pp. 169–74.

Draco Volans est in Coelo. From Jiang Shui and Tie Zhu, "Xu: Heshi fuzhu canglong," *Mao Zedong junshi zhexue yu xiandai shangzhan*, Guilin: Guangxi minzu chubanshe, 1991, pp. 1–2.

Let the Red Sun Shine In (A Forum). From Yuan Youming and Xie Congcong, "Toushi 'Hong taiyang' rechao," *Qingnian bao* (Shanghai) 31 January 1992.

The Red Sun: Singing the Praises of Chairman Mao. From *Hong taiyang: Mao Zedong songge xinjiezou lianchang*, Zhongguo changpian gongsi, Shanghai gongsi, 1992.

A Place in the Pantheon: Mao and Folk Religion. From Xin Yuan, "'Mao Zedong re' yu Zhongguo minjian zongjiao," *Jingbao yuekan* 12 (1992): 86–88.

CultRev Relics. From Zhou Jihou, *Mao Zedong xiangzhang zhi mi—shijie dijiu da qiguan*, Taiyuan: Beiyue wenyi chubanshe, 1993, pp. 213–24.

Hanging Mao. From Hou Dangsheng, *Mao Zedong xiangzhang fengyunlu*, Beijing: Zhonggong zhongyang dangxiao chubanshe, 1993, pp. 131–38.

The Imprisoned Heart: Consuming Mao. From Li Xianting, "Zhengzhi bopu—bei 'xiaofei'zhede yishi xingtai." This English version, translated by Barmé, was originally pubished in *Art and AsiaPacific* (Sydney) 1, no. 2 (April 1994): 25–30.

Drunk in the Rapeseed Patch. From Li Jian, "Zuiru huacong," *Zhanjiang wenyi* 6 (1980): 29–31.

MaoSpeak. From Wang Shuo, "Qianwan bie ba wo dangren," *Zhongshan* 6 (1989): 41–42.

Martial Mao. From "Mao Zedong maoxian jishi," *Yinmu neiwai* 7 (1993): 88 and 2–3.

Who's Responsible? From Wei Jingsheng, "Shei yinggai fuze?—Mao Zedong gei womende zuihaode jiaoxun," *Kaifang zazhi* 11 (1993): 8.

Publish and Perish. From "Zhongyang xuanchuanbu xinwen chubanshe guanyu jinian Mao Zedong tongzhi danchen yibai zhounian tushu chuban gongzuode tongzhi, [92] Xinchu lianzi di 3 hao, 1992 nian 3 yue 24 ri," in *Dangde xuanchuan gongzuo wenjian xuanbian (1988–1992)*, vol. 4, pp. 2137–38.

The MaoCrazy West. From Hai Feng, "Haiwai Mao Zedongre tanyuan," *Xin dongfang* (Haikou) 5 (1993): 40–42.

All That's Fit to Print. From "Mao Zedong tushu da jianyue," *Sanlian tongxun*, 15 November 1992.

In the Footsteps of the Great. From Zhang Xiujiang, "Xunzhao weirende zuji," *Beijing wanbao*, 13 October 1993.

Praise Be to Mao. From Da Wei, "Youxiu diangong Mao Zedong," *Zhongliu* 5 (1993): 18; Lu Ximing, "Mao Anying," *Zhongliu* 5 (1993): 18; Hai Xingxing, "Mao Zedong ta xue," *Zhongliu* 12 (1993): 7; Zhao Aimin, "Yonghengde sinian," *Zhongliu* 2 (1994): 6–37; and from Gou Huaxian, "Mengli jian Mao zhuxi," *Zhongliu* 2 (1994): 37–38.

Sparing Mao a Thought. From "Jianchi he fazhan Mao Zedong sixiang—jinian Mao Zedong tongzhi yibai zhounian danchen," *Renmin ribao* (26 December 1993).

The Last Ten-Thousand Words. From Jiang Zemin, "Zai Mao Zedong tongzhi danchen yibai zhounian jinian dahuishangde jianghua (1993 nian 12 yue 26 ri)," *Renmin ribao* (27 December 1993).

Galluping Mao: A 1993 Opinion Poll. From Tang Can, Zhu Rui, Li Chunling and Shen Jie, "Dangdai renxinzhongde Mao Zedong—dui 100 ming putongrende zhuanti diaocha," *Beijing qingnianbao (Xinwen zhoukan)* (21 December 1993).

Chairman Mao Graffiti. From Zhang Chengzhi (Chō Shō-shi), "Mō shūseki gurafiti," *Sekai* 1 (1994): 210–16.

The Specter of Mao Zedong. From Liu Xiaobo, "Zhonggong Maopai yu Dengde kunjing—houDeng shidaide zhengju guancha," *Kaifang zazhi* 12 (1994): 22–24.

Musical Chairmen. From Barmé, "Culture at Large: Consuming T-shirts in Beijing," *China Information* 8, nos. 1/2 (Summer/Autumn 1993): 3; and, quotations from Sang Ye, "Chairman Mao's Ark" (*Mao zhuxide fangzhou*), unpublished interview, February 1995.

Glossary of Chinese Terms

baoan pixie　　保安辟邪

Bawanba　　八萬八

beilin　　碑林

budao Changcheng fei haohan　　不到長城非好漢

chi Mao　　吃毛

dadong bu?　　打洞不？

daxia qidu　　大俠氣度

Die lian hua　　蝶戀花

fa Mao zhuxide cai!　　發毛主席的財！

fanshen　　翻身

fumuguan　　父母官

ganxiexin　　感謝信

geren chongbai　　個人崇拜

gongxi facai　　恭喜發財

guawu　　掛物

huajiang chuli　　化漿處理

huan wo feiji　　還我飛機

huochaihe　　火柴盒

hushenfu　　護身符

jinqu　　禁區

lao sanpian　　老三篇

laoyidai wuchanjieji gemingjia
老一代無產階級革命家

liuli　　琉璃

mangliu　　氓流

Mao Xinyu　　毛新宇

Mao Zedong re; Maore　　毛澤東熱；　毛熱

Mao zhuxi rang women zhangquan; Deng Xiaoping rang women zhengqian
毛主席讓我們掌權；　鄧小平讓我們挣錢

Mao zhuxi yongyuan huo zai women xinzhong
毛主席永遠活在我們心中

Mao zhuxide erzi shang qianxian; Zhao Ziyangde erzi dao caidian; Deng Xiaopingde erzi gao mujuan; Renminde erzi dao dian'r guokuquan　毛主席的兒子上前綫；
趙紫陽的兒子倒彩電；　鄧小平的兒子搞募捐；
人民的兒子倒點兒國庫　券

Maojia fandian　　毛家飯店

mie zhuixingzu　　滅追星族

Paoda silingbu—wode yizhang dazibao
炮打司令部－－我的一張大字報

pixie　　辟邪

qiancengde buxie　　千層底布鞋

qing Mao zhuxi xiang jinwu　　請毛主席像進屋

Quan Yanchi　　權延赤

Sanyuansi　　三源寺

shinian dongluan   十年動亂

shisuhua   世俗化

shunkouliu'r   順口溜兒

sida tianwang   四大天王

tansuo   探索

texing yanyuan   特型演員

wannianqing   萬年青

wanshou wujiang   萬壽無疆

wenguanguo   文冠果

xiandai mixin   現代迷信

xianling   顯靈

xingxing zhi huo keiyi liao yuan   星星之火可以燎原

Ye Yonglie   葉永烈

yi bupa ku, er bupa si, ye bupa ni   一不怕苦，二不怕死，
也不怕你

yifan fengshun   一帆風順

yindao　　引導

Yu Gong yi shan　　愚公移山

zaoshen yundong　　造神運動

zhaocai jinbao　　招財進寶

zhong　　忠

Zhongliu　　中流

Zhongshan zhuang; Maoshi fuzhuang　　中山裝；毛式服裝

zhuixingzu　　追星族

zong shejishi　　總設計師

Bibliography

English Books and Articles

Anagnost, Ann. "The Nationscape: Movement in the Field of Vision." *Positions*, no. 3 (Winter 1993): 585–606.

Andrews, Julia F., and Gao Minglu. *Fragmented Memory: The Chinese Avant-Garde in Exile*. Columbus: Ohio State University, Wexner Center for the Arts, 1993.

Apter, David E., and Tony Saich. *Revolutionary Discourse in Mao's Republic*. Cambridge, MA: Harvard University Press, 1994.

Asia Watch, ed. *Detained in China and Tibet: A Directory of Political and Religious Prisoners*. New York: Human Rights Watch, 1994.

Barmé, Geremie R. "Archeo-tainment: Fantasy at the Other End of History." *Third Text* 30 (May 1995): 29–38.

———. "Critics Now Chip Away at China's Concrete Eyesores." *Far Eastern Economic Review* (17 November 1988): 54.

———. "Culture at Large: Consuming T-Shirts in Beijing." *China Information* 8, nos. 1–2 (Summer/Autumn 1993): 1–44.

———. "The Greying of Chinese Culture." In Kuan Hsin-chi and Maurice Brousseau, eds., *China Review 1992*. Hong Kong: Chinese University Press, 1992.

———. "Revolutionary Opera Arias Sung to a New, Disco Beat." *Far Eastern Economic Review* (5 February 1987): 36–38.

———. "'Road' versus 'River.'" *Far Eastern Economic Review* (25 October 1990): 32.

———. "Soft Porn, Packaged Dissent, and Nationalism: Notes on Chinese Culture in the 1990s." *Current History* (September 1994): 273–75.

———. "To Screw Foreigners Is Patriotic: China's Avant-Garde Nationalists." *The China Journal* 34 (July 1995): 209–34.

———. "Using the Past to Save the Present: Dai Qing's Historiographical Dissent." *East Asian History* 1 (July 1991): 141–81.

———. "Wang Shuo and *Liumang* ('Hooligan') Culture." *The Australian Journal of Chinese Affairs* 28 (July 1992): 23–64.

Barmé, Geremie R., and Linda Jaivin, eds. *New Ghosts, Old Dreams: Chinese Rebel Voices*. New York: Times Books, 1992.

Barmé, Geremie R., and John Minford, eds. *Seeds of Fire: Chinese Voices of Conscience*. New York: Hill and Wang, 1988.

Baum, Richard. *Burying Mao: Chinese Politics in the Age of Deng Xiaoping*. Princeton, NJ: Princeton University Press, 1994.

Bevan, Charlotte. "Making a Mint out of Mao." *Eastern Express* (25–26 February 1995).

Boym, Svetlana. *Common Places: Mythologies of Everyday Life in Russia*. Cambridge, MA: Harvard University Press, 1994.

Bracher, Paul Dietrich. *The German Dictatorship: The Origins, Structure and Consequences of National Socialism*, trans. Jean Skinberg. London: Penguin, 1991.

Calinescu, Matei. *Five Faces of Modernity: Modernism, Avant-Garde, Decadence, Kitsch, Postmodernism*. Durham, NC: Duke University Press, 1987.

"Chairman Mao Swims in the Yangtse." *China Pictorial* 10 (1966): 1–5.

Chan, Anita, Stanley Rosen, and Jonathan Unger. *On Socialist Democracy and the Chinese Legal System: The Li Yizhe Debates*. Armonk, NY: M.E. Sharpe, 1985.

Chan Wai-fong. "Mao Outstrips Deng in Popularity Poll." *South China Morning Post (Weekly)* (28–29 January 1995).

Chatwin, Bruce. Quotation from *Songlines* in "The Starn Twins: Christ (Stretched)." *Aperture* 110 (Spring 1988): 58–59.

Cheater, A.P. "Death Ritual as Political Trickster in the People's Republic of China." *The Australian Journal of Chinese Affairs* 26 (July 1991): 67–98.

Ch'en, Jerome. *Mao and the Chinese Revolution*. London: Oxford University Press, 1967.

———, ed. *Mao*. Englewood Cliffs, NJ: Prentice-Hall, 1969.

———. *Mao Papers: Anthology and Bibliography*. London: Oxford University Press, 1970.

Chenivesse, Sandrine. "For Us, Mao Was a First Love." *China Perspectives* 1 (September/October 1995): 70–74. Hong Kong: French Centre on Contemporary China.

China Study Group. "A Protest Against Random House's Fraudulent Memoirs of Mao's Physician, by Mao Zedong's Staff and Others." Distributed by C. Y. Tung, New York, 1995.

Ci Jiwei. *Dialectic of the Chinese Revolution: From Utopianism to Hedonism*. Stanford, CA: Stanford University Press, 1994.

Cohen, Joan Lebold. *The New Chinese Painting, 1949–1986*. New York: Harry N. Abrams, 1987.

Cohn, Don J., ed. *Liu Da Hong, Paintings 1986–92*. Hong Kong: Schoeni Fine Oriental Art, 1992.

"Collectible Edition of Deng's Writings Planned." Reuters (5 April 1995).

Condee, Nancy, and Vladimir Padunov. "Pair-a-Dice Lost: The Socialist Gamble, Market Determinism, and Compulsory Postmodernism." *New Formations: Postcommunism, Rethinking the Second World* 22 (Spring 1994): 72–94.

Conquest, Robert. "The Somber Monster." *The New York Review of Books* 42, no. 10 (8 June 1995): 8–12.

Core, Philip. *Camp: The Lie That Tells the Truth*. London: Plexus, 1984.

Crouch, Stanley. "Hooked: Michael Jackson, Moby Dick of Pop." *The New Republic* (21–28 August 1995): 18–20.

Dean, Kenneth, and Brian Massumi. *First and Last Emperors: The Absolute State and the Body of the Despot*. Brooklyn, NY: Autonomedia, 1992.

Deng Maomao. *Deng Xiaoping: My Father*. New York: Basic Books, 1995.

Doran, Valerie C., ed. *China's New Art, post-1989 (with a retrospective from 1979–1989)*. Hong Kong: Hanart TZ Gallery, 1993.

Elvin, Mark. "Tales of *Shen* and *Xin*: Body-Person and Heart-Mind in China During the Last 150 Years." In Thomas P. Kasulis, ed., with Roger T. Ames and

Wimal Dissanayake, *Self as Body in Asian Theory and Practice*. New York: State University of New York Press, 1993, pp. 213–91.

Eng, Victoria. "Vivienne Tam." *A. Magazine* (April/May 1995): 52–53.

Fowler, Peter J. *The Past in Contemporary Society Then, Now*. London: Routledge, 1992.

Friedman, Edward. "Democracy and 'Mao Fever.'" *The Journal of Contemporary China* 6 (Summer 1994): 84–95.

"Fun in the Magic Kingdom of Mao." *Eastern Express* (27–28 August 1994).

Geyl, Pieter. *Napoleon For and Against*, trans. by Olive Renier. London: Jonathan Cape, 1949.

Gill, Graeme, J. "The Cult of Personality and the Search for Legitimacy: The Cases of Mao and Stalin." M.A. thesis, Monash University (Clayton, Victoria), 1973.

Gold, Thomas B. "Go with Your Feelings: Hong Kong and Taiwan Popular Culture in Greater China." *The China Quarterly* (December 1993): 907–25.

Goldblatt, Howard, ed. *Chairman Mao Would Not Be Amused: Fiction from Today's China*. New York: Grove Press, 1995.

Gordon, Richard, and Carma Hinton, directors. "The Gate of Heavenly Peace." Boston: Long Bow Group, 1995 (3-hour documentary film).

Han Minzhu, ed. *Cries for Democracy: Writings and Speeches from the 1989 Chinese Democracy Movement*. Princeton, NJ: Princeton University Press, 1990.

He Di. "The Most Respected Enemy: Mao Zedong's Perception of the United States." *The China Quarterly* (March 1994): 144–58.

He, Xin. "A Word of Advice to the Politburo." *The Australian Journal of Chinese Affairs* 23 (January 1990): 49–76.

———. "A Letter from Beijing." *The Australian Journal of Chinese Affairs* 24 (July 1990): 337–45.

Higgins, Andrew. "Maoists Emerge from the Closet." *The Independent* (30 March 1990).

Hoberman, J. "The Fascist Guns in the West." *Aperture* 110 (Spring 1988): 64, 68–69.

Hochschild, Adam. *The Unquiet Ghost: Russians Remember Stalin*. London: Penguin Books, 1995.

Hutchings, Graham. "China's Anger with Leaders Bursts Out." *The Telegraph* (14 April 1995).

Jaivin, Linda. "Love All, Serve the People: Mao Blesses a New Hard Rock Cafe." *Rolling Stone* (Australian Edition) (July 1994): 28.

———. "Mao's Bigger—and Better—Than Ever." *Asian Wall Street Journal* (24–25 April 1992).

Jones, Andrew F. *Like a Knife: Ideology and Genre in Contemporary Chinese Popular Music*. Ithaca, NY: Cornell University Press, 1992.

Kadare, Ismail. *The Concert: A Novel*, written in Albanian and trans. from the French of Jusuf Vrioni by Barbara Bray. New York: William Morrow, 1994.

Katz, Jon. "Why Elvis Matters." *Wired* (April 1995): 100–105.

Kaye, Lincoln. "Against the Grain: A Maoist Village Puts Capitalism to Shame." *Far Eastern Economic Review* (17 November 1994).

———. "Mummy Dearest: The Expensive Art of Preserving a Great Leader." *Far Eastern Economic Review* (1 September 1994): 17.

Kinzer, Stephen. "'Love Letters' to Hitler, a Book and Play Shocking to Germans." *New York Times* (25 May 1995).

Koestenbaum, Wayne. *Jackie Under My Skin: Interpreting an Icon*. New York: Giroux, 1995.

Kraus, Richard C. *Brushes with Power: Modern Politics and the Chinese Art of Calligraphy*. Berkeley: University of California Press, 1991.

Ladany, Laszlo. *The Communist Party of China and Marxism, 1921–1985: A Self-Portrait*. London: C. Hurst & Co., 1988.

Laing, Ellen Johnston. *The Winking Owl: Art in the People's Republic of China*. Berkeley: University of California Press, 1988.

Lam, Willy Wo-lap. *China After Deng Xiaoping: The Power Struggle in Beijing Since Tiananmen*. Singapore: John Wiley & Sons, 1995.

Lawrance, Alan. *Mao Zedong: A Bibliography*. New York: Greenwood Press, 1991.

Legge, James. *The Chinese Classics (The Chu'un Ts'ew with The Tso Chuen)*, vol. 5. Hong Kong: Hong Kong University Press, 1960.

Legislative Affairs Commission of the Standing Committee of the National People's Congress of the People's Republic of China, comp. *The Laws of the People's Republic of China, 1979–1982*. 2 vols. Beijing: Foreign Languages Press, 1987.

Lewin, Moshe. *Russia/USSR/Russia: The Drive and Drift of a Superstate*. New York: The New Press, 1995.

Lewis, John Wilson, ed. *Party Leadership and Revolutionary Power in China*. Cambridge: Cambridge University Press, 1970.

Leys, Simon. *Broken Images*. New York: St. Martin's Press, 1980.

———. *The Burning Forest: Essays on Chinese Culture and Politics*. New York: Henry Holt, 1985.

Li Haibo. "A Journey Back to Mao's Birthplace." *Beijing Review* (6–12 December 1993): 22.

Li Tuo. "Resisting Writing." In Liu Kang and Xiaobing Tang, eds. *Politics, Ideology and Literary Discourse in Modern China: Theoretical Interventions and Cultural Critique*. Durham, NC: Duke University Press, 1993, pp. 273–77.

Li Xianting. "The Imprisoned Heart." *Art and Asia Pacific* (Sydney) (April 1994): 25–30.

Li Xianting, and Shan Fan. *Der Abschied von der Ideologie: Neue Kunst aus China*. Hamburg: Hamburg Kulturbehorde, 1995.

Li Yanchun. "Mao's Family Members Brought Out of the Shadow." *Beijing Review* (13–19 December 1993): 20–22.

Li, Zhisui. *The Private Life of Chairman Mao: The Memoirs of Mao's Personal Physician Dr. Zhisui Li*, trans. Tai Hung-chao. London: Chatto and Windus, 1994.

Lindesay, William. *Marching with Mao: A Biographical Journey*. London: Hodder and Stoughton, 1993.

Liu Shao-ch'i. *How to Be a Good Communist*, 4th ed., rev. Peking: Foreign Languages Press, 1964.

"Long Live the 'Three Most Read Articles'!" *China Pictorial* 5 (1967): 2–9; *China Pictorial* 6 (1967): 2–9; and *China Pictorial* 7 (1967): 1.

Louie, Kam. "Literary Double-Think in Post-Mao China: The Case of Li Jian." In Louie, *Between Fact and Fiction: Essays on Post-Mao Chinese Literature and Society*. Sydney: Wild Peony, 1989, pp. 21–37.

McHugh, Fionnuala. "How Cool Is Mao?" *Sunday Morning Post Magazine* (4 June 1995): 22, 24, 26.

McIlwraith, Hamish. "Raise the Red Emperor." *Guardian Weekly* (5 November 1995): 14.

Mao Tse-tung. *Poems*. Peking: Foreign Languages Press, 1976.

———. *Selected Works of Mao Tse-tung*. 4 vols. Peking: Foreign Languages Press, 1965.

"Mao's Birth Place" in "Signs of Disintegration." *China News Analysis*, no. 1218 (October 1981).

"Mao's Thoughts, Not Mao's" in "Freedom of the Spirit." *China News Analysis*, no. 1168 (23 November 1979).

"Mao Zedong Still Fresh in Memory." *Beijing Review* 36 (1986): 15–18.

Marcus, Greil. *Dead Elvis: A Chronicle of a Cultural Obsession*. New York: Doubleday, 1991.

Martin, Helmut. *Cult & Canon: The Origins and Development of State Maoism*. Armonk, NY: M.E. Sharpe, 1982.

Marks, Laurence. "Watching a Pile of Popcorn." *The Spectator* (3 June 1995): 49.

Marx, Karl. "The Eighteenth Brumaire of Louis Bonaparte." In Marx and Friederich Engels, *Selected Works*. Vol. 1. Moscow: Foreign Languages Press, 1950.

Meisner, Maurice. *Marxism, Maoism and Utopianism*. Madison: University of Wisconsin Press, 1982.

Metzger, Thomas A. *Escape from Predicament. Neo-Confucianism and China's Evolving Political Culture*. New York: Columbia University Press, 1977.

Mihalca, Matei. "The Pied Piper of Peking." *Far Eastern Economic Review* (30 September 1993): 54–55.

Miner, Steven Merritt. "Revelations, Secrets, Gossip and Lies: Sifting Warily Through the Soviet Archives." *The New York Times Book Review* (14 May 1995): 19–21.

Minford, John, and Joseph Lau, eds. *Classical Chinese Literature, Vol. 1: From Antiquity to the T'ang*. New York: Columbia University Press, forthcoming.

Montefiore, Simon Sebag. "History in a Pickle." *The Sunday Times*, repr. *The Australian, The Weekend Review* (15–16 April 1995).

Morris, Andrew. "Mastery Without Enmity: *Tiyu* (Athletics) in Early Republican China." Department of History, University of California, San Diego (unpublished paper), 1995.

Nickerson, Dierdre L. "Ge Xiaoguang: Painter Whose Job Is to Recreate Mao." *Far Eastern Economic Review* (15 April 1993): 74.

Nixon, Richard M. *The Memoirs of Richard Nixon*. New York: Grosset and Dunlap, 1978.

Noth, Jochen, et al., eds. *China Avant-Garde: Counter-Currents in Art and Culture*. Hong Kong: Oxford University Press, 1993.

"On Questions of Party History—Resolution on Certain Questions in the History of Our Party Since the Founding of the People's Republic of China (Adopted by the Sixth Plenary Session of the Eleventh Central Committee of the Communist Party of China on June 27, 1981)." *Beijing Review* (July 6, 1981).

Paglia, Camille. *Vamps and Tramps: New Essays*. New York: Vintage Books, 1994.

Pickowicz, Paul G. "Velvet Prisons and the Political Economy of Chinese Film-making." In Deborah S. Davis, Richard Kraus, Barry Naughton, and Elizabeth J. Perry, eds., *Urban Spaces: Autonomy and Community in Contemporary China*. New York: Cambridge University Press, 1995, pp. 193–220.

Pye, Lucian W. *Mao Tse-tung: The Man in the Leader*. New York: Basic Books, 1976.

Remnick, David. *Lenin's Tomb: The Last Days of the Soviet Empire*. New York: Vintage Books, 1994.

Reuter News Service. "Chinese Officials Ponder Temple to Mao Tsetung." (11 July 1995).

The Revival Handbook. London: *The Modern Review* (March 1994).

Rinden, Robert W. "The Cult of Mao Tse-tung." University of Colorado, Ph.D. diss., 1969.

Sammon, Paul M. *The King Is Dead: Tales of Elvis Postmortem*. New York: Delta, 1994.

Sang Ye. *The Year the Dragon Came*. Brisbane: Queensland University Press, 1996.

Scharping, Thomas. "The Man, the Myth, the Message—New Trends in Mao-Literature from China." *The China Quarterly* (March 1994): 168–79.

Schell, Orville. *Mandate of Heaven: A New Generation of Entrepreneurs, Dissidents, Bohemians, and Technocrats Lays Claim to China's Future*. New York: Simon and Schuster, 1994.

Schmetzer, Uli. "Cashing in on Mao's Name in Hunan Shaoshan." *Chicago Tribune* (24 November 1993).

Schoenhals, Michael. "The 1978 Truth Criterion Controversy." *The China Quarterly* (June 1991): 243–68.

———. *Doing Things with Words in Chinese Politics: Five Studies*. Berkeley: University of California, Institute of East Asian Studies, 1992.

Schram, Stuart R. "Mao Zedong a Hundred Years on: The Legacy of a Ruler." *The China Quarterly* (March 1994): 125–43.

———. "Party Leader or True Ruler? Foundations and Significance of Mao Zedong's Personal Power." In S. R. Schram, ed., *Foundations and Limits of State Power in China*. London: SOAS/Hong Kong: Chinese University Press, 1987, pp. 203–56.

———. *The Political Thought of Mao Tse-tung*. New York: Praeger, 1969.

———, ed. *Mao's Road to Power. Revolutionary Writings 1912–1949*, vol. 1: *The Pre-Marxist Period, 1912–1920*. Armonk, NY: M.E. Sharpe, 1992.

———, ed. *Mao Tse-tung Unrehearsed: Talks and Letters, 1956–1971*. London: Penguin Books, 1974.

Seymour, James D., ed. *The Fifth Modernization: China's Human Rights Movement, 1978–1979*. Stanfordville, NY: Human Rights Publishing Group, 1980.

Siao-yu. *Mao Tse-tung and I Were Beggars: A Personal Memoir of the Early Years of Chairman Mao*. Syracuse, NY: Syracuse University Press, 1959.

Snow, Edgar. *The Other Side of the River*. New York: Random House, 1962.

Solomon, Richard H. *Mao's Revolution and the Chinese Political Culture*. Berkeley: University of California Press, 1971.

Sontag, Susan. *Against Interpretation*. New York: Dell, 1969.

"Speculation Rife as Deng Believed Dying." *Sydney Morning Herald* (21 January 1995).

Spence, Jonathan D. *Chinese Roundabout: Essays in History and Culture*. New York: W.W. Norton, 1992.

Taylor, George E. "China as an Oriental Despotism." *Problems of Post-Communism* (January–February 1995): 25–28.

Teiwes, Frederick C., and Warren Sun. *The Tragedy of Lin Biao: Riding the Tiger During the Cultural Revolution, 1966–1971*. London: C. Hurst & Co., 1996.

Terrill, Ross. *Mao: A Biography*. New York: Harper and Row, 1980.

Tyler, Patrick E. "With Deng's Influence Waning, Privatizing of China's State Industries Stalls." *New York Times* (18 June 1995).

Unger, Jonathan, ed. *The Pro-Democracy Protests in China: Reports from the Provinces*. Armonk, NY: M.E. Sharpe, 1991.

————. *Using the Past to Serve the Present: Historiography and Politics in Contemporary China*. Armonk, NY: M.E. Sharpe, 1993.

Urban, George, ed. *The Miracles of Chairman Mao*. London: Tom Stacey, 1971.

Volkogonov, Dmitri. *Lenin: A New Biography*, trans. by Harold Shukman. New York: Free Press, 1994.

Wagner, Rudolf G. "Reading the Chairman Mao Memorial Hall in Peking: The Tribulations of the Implied Pilgrim." In Susan Naquin and Chün-fang Yü, eds., *Pilgrims and Sacred Sites in China*. Berkeley: University of California Press, 1992, pp. 378–423.

Wakeman, Frederic Jr. "Mao's Remains." In James L. Watson and Evelyn S. Rawski, eds., *Death Ritual in Late Imperial and Modern China*. Berkeley: University of California Press, 1988, pp. 254–88.

Ward, Peter. *Kitsch in Sync: A Consumer's Guide to Bad Taste*. London: Plexus, 1991.

Wasserstrom, Jeffrey N. "Mao Matters: A Review Essay." *China Review International* (Spring 1996).

Wasserstrom, Jeffrey N., and Elizabeth J. Perry, eds. *Popular Protest and Political Culture in Modern China*. 2d ed. Boulder, CO: Westview Press, 1994.

Wilson, Dick. *Mao Tse-tung in the Scales of History*. Cambridge, Eng.: Cambridge University Press, 1977.

Womack, Brantly. "Mao Zedong Thoughts." *The China Quarterly* (March 1994): 159–67.

Wong, Jan. "Around Mao's Centennial." *Toronto Globe and Mail* (24 December 1993).

Xinhua News Agency. "False Biographies Are Now Forbidden." *China Daily* (15 April 1993).

————. "Eulogy on the Glorious Life of Chen Yun." (16 April 1995).

Yampolsky, Mikhail. "The Shadow of Monuments: Notes on Iconoclasm and Time." In Nancy Condee, ed., *Soviet Hieroglyphics: Visual Culture in Late Twentieth-Century Russia*. Bloomington: Indiana University Press/London: BFI Publishing, 1995, pp. 93–112.

Yang, Mayfair Mei-hui. *Gifts, Favors, and Banquets: The Art of Social Relationships in China*. Ithaca, NY: Cornell University Press, 1994.

Yee, Lydia. *Zhang Hongtu: Material Mao*. New York: Bronx Museum of Fine Arts, 1995.

Young, Toby. "The End of Irony?" *The Modern Review* 1, no. 14 (April–May 1994).

Youngblood, Denise J. "*Repentance:* Stalinist Terror and the Realism of Surrealism." In Robert A. Rosenstone, ed., *Revisioning History: Film and the Construction of a New Past*. Princeton, NJ: Princeton University Press, 1995, pp. 139–54.

Yung, Danny. "Zuni Performance Worsening Day by Day." *Zuni Express* (20–21 January 1995).

Zaslavsky, Victor. *The Neo-Stalinist State: Class, Ethnicity, and Consensus in Soviet Society*. Armonk, NY: M. E. Sharpe, 1994.

Zha, Jianying. *China Pop: How Soap Operas, Tabloids, and Bestsellers Are Transforming a Culture*. New York: The New Press, 1995.

Zhang Hongtu. "Zhang Hongtu/Hongtu Zhang: An Interview." In John Hay, ed., *Boundaries in China*. London: Reaktion Books, 1994, pp. 280–98.

Zhu Wei. *Zhu Wei: The Story of Beijing*. Hong Kong: Plum Blossoms (International), 1994.

Chinese Books and Articles

A Yin and Ma Jian. *Mao Zedong zhi zi: Mao Anlong*. Neimenggu renmin chubanshe/Xianggang Xinshiji chubanshe, 1992. Published in Hong Kong as *Wo shi Mao Zedongde erzi*. Hong Kong: Dadi chubanshe, 1992.

Ba Jin. *Suixianglu*. Hong Kong: Sanlian shudian, 1988.

Bai Hua. "Bainian gudu—Mao Zedong bainian mingchen ji." *Kaifang zazhi* 11 (1993): 50–52.

Bai Jieming (Geremie R. Barmé). "Yangbanxide zai jueqi." *Jiushi niandai yuekan* 9 (1986): 144–45.

———. *Zixingche wenji*. Hong Kong: Tiandi tushu youxian gongsi, 1984.

Bai Meng. "Tiananmen shenpan." *Beijing zhi chun* 6 (1995): 37–44.

Bao Zunxin. "Huidao Mao Zedong, haishi chaoyue Mao Zedong—cong *Deng Xiaoping wenxuan* disan juan chuban tanqi." *Zhongguo shibao zhoukan* (12–18 December 1993): 16–18.

Beijing geming weiyuanhui chuban faxing gongzuo lingdao xiaozu, ed. *Zhonggong zhongyang wuchanjieji wenhua dageming wenxian xuanbian*, vol. 5. No publisher given, 1969.

"Beijing Haidianqu renmin fayuan gongkai shenli Li Jiefu gequ qinquanan." *Wenyi bao* (31 October 1992).

Beijingshi wenlian yanjiubu, ed. *Zhengming zuopin xuanbian*. Beijing: Beijingshi wenlian yanjiubu, 2 vols., 1981.

Bo Yibo. *Ruogan zhongda juece ji shijiande huigu*. Beijing: Zhonggong zhongyang dangxiao chubanshe, 1991 (vol. 1) and 1993 (vol. 2).

"Buzuo shengyi dang gexing; Maosun dasuan chu changpian." *Shijie ribao* (8 August 1995).

Cai Yongmei. "Maorede shangpinhua." *Kaifang zazhi* 11 (1993): 63–64.

Cao Weidong. *Hong bingli*. Taiyuan: Shanxi renmin chubanshe, 1993.

Chai Ling. "Qing zunzhong lishi." *Beijing zhi chun* 6 (1995): 31–33.

Chen Baoliang. *Zhongguo liumangshi*. Beijing: Zhongguo shehui kexue chubanshe, 1993.

Chen Mingyuan. *Jiehou shicun—Chen Mingyuan shixuan*. Beijing: Shijie zhishi chubanshe, 1988.

Cheng Jin. "Banren banshen, beiguan zimin—Mao Zedong wannian shenghuoju 'Buluode taiyang' zai Shenzhen shouyan." *Zhongguo shibao zhoukan* (2–8 January 1994): 82–83.

Cheng Lai. "Mao zhuxi taocan." *Hualian shibao* (21 April 1995).

Cheng Shi, Shan Chuan, et al., eds. *Wenge xiaoliao ji*. Chengdu: Xinan caijing daxue chubanshe, 1988.

Cheng Tong. "Zhongguo chulege Mao Zedong." *Wenhui dushu zhoubao* (25 July 1992).

Cheng Ying. "Dalu wenhua xuanchuande sanzhuang fenzheng." *Jiushi niandai yuekan* 11 (1991): 38.

Dai Qing. *Xiandai Zhongguo zhishifenzi qun: Liang Shuming, Wang Shiwei, Chu Anping*. Nanjing: Jiangsu wenyi chubanshe, 1989.

Deng Liqun. "Guanyu 'Mao Zedong re'—Deng Liqun tongzhi da benkan jizhe." *Zhongliu* 12 (1991): 2–4.

———. "Guanyu *Wuchanjieji gemingjia fengfan congshu* bianzhuan gongzuode jidian yijian." *Xinwen chuban bao* (28 October 1991).

———. "Xuexi 'Guanyu jianguo yilai dangde ruogan lishi wentide jueyi' de wenti he huida." In Quanguo dangshi ziliao zhengji gongzuo huiyi/Jinian Zhongguo gongchandang liushi zhounian xueshu taolunhui mishuchu, ed., *Dangshi huiyi baogao ji*. Beijing: Zhonggong zhongyang dangxiao chubanshe, 1982, pp. 74–174.

———. "Zhengque renshi shehuizhuyide maodun, zhangwo chuli maodunde zhudongquan." *Renmin ribao* (23 October 1991).

Deng Xiaoping. *Deng Xiaoping wenxuan (1975–1982)*. Beijing: Renmin chubanshe, 1983.

———. *Deng Xiaoping wenxuan*, vol. 3. Beijing: Renmin chubanshe, 1993.

———. *Deng Xiaoping wenxuan*, vol. 2, 2d ed. Beijing: Renmin chubanshe, 1994.

Dong Tai. "Dui 'wailun' de jingyan jiaoxun." *Renmin ribao* (9 March 1979).

"Duiwai jieshao yao zhuyi yige wenti." *Xuanchuan dongtai (xuanbian) 1979*. Beijing: Zhongguo shehui kexue chubanshe, 1980, pp. 258–59.

Er Yi. "Daxing lishi jilupian 'Mao Zedong' lüzao daoban." *Xiju dianying bao* (12 May 1995).

"Fabiao paoda silingbu." *Renmin ribao* (5 August 1967).

Fang Lixiong et al. *Zhongguoren zenmele?!—dangjin shehui redian datexie*. Beijing: Hongqi chubanshe, 1992.

Fang Zhou. "Huainian hu? Zichao hu?—toushi dalu 'Hong taiyang' yinyuedai changxiao shehui xinli." *Zhongguo shibao zhoukan* (15–21 March 1992): 73–74.

"Genzhe Mao zhuxi zai dafeng dalangzhong qianjin." *Renmin ribao* (25 July 1966).

Gong Yuzhi. "Deng Xiaoping lun Mao Zedong." *Renmin ribao* (25 December 1993).

Gong Yuzhi, Pang Xiangzhi, and Shi Zhongquan, eds. *Mao Zedongde dushu shenghuo*. Beijing: Sanlian shudian, 1986.

"Gonggu Jiang hexin, gaoju Deng Xiaoping qizhi." *Shijie ribao* (26 May 1995).

Guan Weixun. *Wo suo renshide Ye Qun*. Beijing: Renmin Zhongguo chubanshe, 1994.

"Guanyu 'Mao Zedongre' de sikao yu tantao—Beijing daxue bufen shisheng zuotanhui fayan." *Wenyi lilun yu piping* 11 (1993): 19–35.

Guo Jinrong. *Mao Zedongde huanghun suiyue*. Hong Kong: Tiandi tushu youxian gongsi, 1990.

Guo Tianyun. "Zhengshi zhuixingzu." *Beijing qingnian bao* (30 December 1993).

Guo Weijian. "Jinri Shaoshan 'ganhai' mang." *Fengliu yidai* 8 (1993): 24.

Guo Xiangxing. "Yingtan 'Mao Zedong' dengtanji—Gu Yue chudeng yingtan quwen." *Qingnian yuebao* 4 (1993): 22–24.

He Xin. *Dongfangde fuxing—Zhongguo xiandaihuade mingti yu qiantu (dier juan, jingji fenxi yu zhanlüe yanjiu)*. Haerbin: Heilongjiang jiaoyu chubanshe, 1992.

"Heihu buluo." *Shijie ribao* (24 May 1995).

Hou Dangsheng. *Mao Zedong xiangzhang fengyunlu*. Beijing: Zhonggong zhongyang dangxiao chubanshe, 1993.

Hu Qiaomu. *Hu Qiaomu huiyi Mao Zedong*. Beijing: Renmin chubanshe, 1994.

———. *Hu Qiaomu wenji*, 2 vols. Beijing: Renmin chubanshe, 1992, 1993.

Hu Sheng. "Dui 'Mao Zedong yisheng suozuode liangjian dashi' de jidian shuoming." *Zhonggong dangshi yanjiu* 2 (1994): 1–5.

———. "Mao Zedong yisheng suozuode liangjian dashi." *Renmin ribao* (17 December 1993).

Hu Sheng, ed. *Zhongguo gongchandangde qishi nian*. Beijing: Zhonggong dangshi chubanshe, 1991.

Hua Junxiong and Dong Qingyuan. "Guanyu *Mao Zedongde siren yisheng huiyilu* yishude gongkaixin," 17 February 1995, New York (manuscript version).

———. "*Mao Zedong siren yisheng huiyilu* yishu neirong zhenshixingde yanjiu baogao zhaiyao" (manuscript version, 1995).

Huangye Xianzi. "Neimenggu chulege 'Mao Zedong.'" *Qingnian yuebao* 12 (1993): 33.

Huigu yu fansi [Reminiscence and Reflections: Transcripts from the Conference on the History of the Democracy Movement of 1989]. Germany: Rhine Pen Club, 1993.

"Jianchi he fazhan Mao Zedong sixiang—jinian Mao Zedong tongzhi yibai zhounian danchen." *Renmin ribao* (26 December 1993).

"Jianchi Mao Zedong sixiang, fazhan Mao Zedong sixiang." *Renmin ribao* (2 July 1991).

Jiang Hui. "Wu Guanzhong zhuanggao Duoyunxuan." *Zhongguo shibao zhoukan* (3–9 March 1994): 54–55.

Jiang Zemin. "Zai Mao Zedong tongzhi danchen yibai zhounian jinian dahuishangde jianghua." *Renmin ribao* (27 December 1993).

"Jiannan chuan shiji, shui ling bainian fengsao? *Ershi shiji Zhongguo wenxue dashi wenku* wei 20 shiji Zhongguo wenxue dashi chongding zuoci." *Beijing tushu xinxibao* 208 (28 November 1994).

Jin Zhaojun. "Zai huishou huangran ru meng zai huishou wo xin yijiu—wo dui yindai 'Hong taiyang—Mao Zedong songge' de sikao." *Xinwen chuban bao* (24 February 1992).

———. "Zhi wei na gulaode cunzhuang, hai changzhe guoqude geyao—wo dui 'Hong taiyang—Mao Zedong songge xin jiezou lianchang' de zai sikao." *Xinwen chuban bao* (20 March 1992).

Jin Zhong. "Wenge yanjiu yu Zhonggong dang'an zhidu—fangwen Shanghai zuojia Ye Yonglie xiansheng." *Kaifang zazhi* 2 (1995): 57–59.

"Juxing Mao xiangzhang." AFP, in *Shijie ribao* (8 August 1995).

Li Honglin. *Lilun fengyun*. Beijing: Sanlian shudian, 1985.

Li Ping. *Wengezhongde Zhou Enlai*. Beijing: Beijing chubanshe, 1986.

Li Rui. *Mao Zedong zaonian dushu shenghuo*. Shenyang: Liaoning renmin chubanshe, 1992.

———. *Mao Zedongde zaonian yu wannian*. Guiyang: Guizhou renmin chubanshe, 1992.

Li Shuting. *Mao Zedong shufa yishu*. Wuhan: Hubei meishu chubanshe, 1989.

Li Weihai. *Weiren shenhoushi—Babaoshan geming gongmu jishi*. Taiyuan: Shanxi renmin chubanshe, 1993.

Li Yanchun. "Yeye bainian danchen sunzi zhuangzhong xuanshi: Mao Xinyu guangrong rudang." *Beijing qingnian bao* (26 December 1993).

"Li Yinqiao yu Quan Yanchi fenzhengde yuanqi." *Wenhui dushu zhoubao* (10 August 1991).

Li Yinqiao. *Zai Mao Zedong shenbian shiwu nian.* Shijiazhuang: Hebei renmin chubanshe, 1991.

Li Yong. "Zouguo yige lunhui zhan zai weiren shenhou." *Beijing qingnian bao* (26 December 1993).

Liang Huan, ed. *Mingren yanzhongde Wang Shuo.* Beijing: Huayi chubanshe, 1993.

Lin Hongfa. "'Wenge' zhong Mao zhuxi yuluge dansheng shimo." *Beijing qingnian bao* (22 February 1994).

Lin Jianhui and Dai Chixian. "Shaoshan jixing." *Zhongguo lüyou* 6 (1992): 22–27.

Liu Jianguo. *Shaoshande zuotian yu jintian: Mao Zedong zhi gen.* Changsha: Hunan wenyi chubanshe, 1993.

Liu Jintian and Wu Xiaomei. *Mao Zedong xuanji chubande qianqian houhou.* Beijing: Zhonggong dangshi chubanshe, 1993.

Liu Tao. "Mao Zedong yu shufa." *Dangde wenxian* 3 (1994): 59–61.

Liu Wenying. *Mengde mixin yu mengde tansuo.* Beijing: Zhongguo shehui kexue chubanshe, 1989.

Liu Xiaobo et al. *Hunshi mowang Mao Zedong: mingjia ping Mao ji.* Hong Kong: Kaifang zazhi chubanshe, 1993.

———. "Zhonggong Maopai yu Dengde kunjing—houDeng shidaide zhengju guancha." *Kaifang zazhi* 12 (1994): 22–24.

Liu Xiuming. "Cong yinzhi 'daziben' guji kan Mao Zedong wanniande sixiang he xintai." *Dangdai Zhongguoshi yanjiu* 2 (1994): 22–33.

Liu Xuesong. "Mao Zedong shaoxiang ke 'baoan pixie' ma?" *Jiushi niandai yuekan* 3 (1992): 96–97.

Liu Yazhou. *Guangchang—ouxiangde shentan.* Hong Kong: Tiandi tushu youxian gongsi, 1990.

Liu Yida et al. " 'Jinzhaopai' qidai qiangjiu—Laizi Jingcheng laozihaode baogao zhi er." *Beijing wanbao* (3 April 1994).

Lu Ding. *Hongdong quanguode "weizao Mao zhuxi shici" yuanan.* Changsha: Hunan wenyi chubanshe, 1986.

Lu Jia. "Wan-Qing zhengzhire ranshao quan Zhongguo." *Zhongguo shibao* (29 November 1994).

Lü Peng and Yi Dan. *Zhongguo xiandai yishu shi: 1979–1989.* Changsha: Hunan meishu chubanshe, 1992.

Luo Bing. "Jinian Mao mingshou zao feiyi." *Zhengming* 12 (1993): 8–10.

———. "Mao Zedong zhuzuo duo daibi." *Zhengming* 12 (1993): 11–12.

Luo Fu. "Mao Zedong xianshengde gushi." *Jiushi niandai yuekan* 3 (1994): 18–19.

Ma Linchuan. *"Mao zhuxi yulu* tanyuan." *Zhengming* 12 (1993:): 50–52.

"Mao Xinyu zouchu shufang rongru shehui." *Beijing qingnian bao* (30 September 1994).

Mao Zedong. "Zhonghua minzhongde dalianhede xingshi." *Xiangjiang pinglun* 4 (1919).

———. "Mao Zedong gei Jiang Qingde xin, 1966 nian 7 yue 8 ri." *"Wenhua da geming" yanjiu ziliao.* Beijing: Zhongguo renmin jiefangjun/Guofang daxue dangshi jingzhenggong jiaoyanshi, 1988, pp. 55–56.

————. *Mao Zedong xuanji,* 4 vols. Beijing: Renmin chubanshe, 1966.

————. *Mao Zedong xuanji,* vol. 5. Beijing: Renmin chubanshe, 1977.

————. *Mao Zedong xuanji (dier ban),* 4 vols. Beijing: Renmin chubanshe, 1991.

————. *Mao Zedong xuanji (yijuan ben).* Beijing: Renmin chubanshe, 1967.

————. *Mao zhuxi shici (zhushi).* Chengdu, 1968.

"Mao Zedong sixiang yongfang guangmang." *Renmin ribao* (26 December 1983).

Mao Zedong tongzhi shi dangdai zui weidade Makesi-Lieningzhuyizhe. Beijing, 1969.

Mao Zedong yiwenlu. Beijing: Falü chubanshe, 1989.

"Mao Zedong zui chongbaide xiake shi shei?" *Yinmu neiwai* 7 (November 1993): 54–57.

Mao zhuxi shoushu xuanji. Nanjing: Zhongguo renmin jiefangjun haijun zhengzhi xueyuan hongsiye chuban, n.d. (early Cultural Revolution).

Mou Qun. "Dangxiade chaoyue yu yiyide shengxian—jian ping Liang Mingyu 'Hongxing Mao Zedong xilie.'" *Yishu chaoliu* (Taipei) 6 (1994): 124–26.

Ni Yuxian. "Cong fouding Chai Ling dao fouding Minyun—jianping Ding Xueliang xianshengde jige guandian." *Beijing zhi chun* 6 (1995): 45–49.

Okura henshū keikaku, ed. *Mao zhuxi wenxuan, Mao Zedong sixiang wansui.* Saitama: Okura henshū keikaku, 1974.

Qijibu 519 Bingtuan. *519 zhanbao* (13 May 1969).

Qing Ye and Fang Lei. *Deng Xiaoping zai 1976,* 2 vols. Shenyang: Chunfeng wenyi chubanshe, 1993.

"Quanshen fa 'Mao.'" AFP, *Shijie ribao* (2 November 1994).

Ruan Ming. "Zenyang 'chonggu' lishi?" *Beijing zhi chun* 6 (1995): 34–36.

Sang Ye. "Mao zhuxide fangzhou." Unpublished interview transcript.

————. "Piandi yingxiong xia xiyan: Weidade 1966." Unpublished interview transcript.

————. "Zai Beijingde yitian." *Zhongguo shibao* (3 August 1991).

"Sanxingbei" shige zhenggao pingxuan huodong zuzhi weiyuanhui pingxuan weiyuanhui, "Jinian Mao Zedong tongzhi danchen 100 zhounian 'Sanxingbei' shige zhenggao pingxuan huodong banjiang tongbao," *Zhongliu* 5 (1994): 13–14.

Shao Yanfeng. "Shehuizhuyi shi guoqu geng shi weilai, shoudu xuezhe yantao 'shehuizhuyi zai dangdai shijie.'" *Beijing qingnian bao* (21 July 1994).

Shi Zhe, Ye Zilong, Wang Dongxing, et al. "Ruhua fangongde choue biaoyan— women dui Li Zhisui jiqi 'huiyilu' de kanfa," 22 July 1995, Beijing (manuscript version).

"Shishi qiushide xuanchuan Mao Zedong tongzhi." *Xuanchuan dongtai (xuanbian) 1980.* Beijing: Zhongguo shehui kexue chubanshe, 1981, pp. 92–95.

"Shizong weixing jiang 'za' xiang nali?" *Beijing wanbao* (21 December 1994).

Su Ya and Jia Lusheng. *Buluode taiyang.* Zhengzhou: Zhongyuan nongmin chubanshe, 1992.

————. *Baimao heimao—Zhongguo gaige xianzhuang toushi.* Changsha: Hunan wenyi chubanshe, 1992.

Sun Baoyi. *Mao Zedongde dushu shengya.* Beijing: Zhishi chubanshe, 1993.

"Suzao weiren." *Beijing qingnian bao* (30 September 1994).

Tang Can. "Qingchun ouxiangde bianqian: Cong Mao Zedong dao 'Sida tianwang.'" *Zhongguo qingnian* 9 (1993): 14–15.

Tang Wan'er. "Chongqing *Dagongbao* pi Mao yiwen—Mao Zedong yongxueci fengbo." *Kaifang zazhi* 7 (1994): 53–54.

Tao Kai et al. *Zouchu xiandai mixin—guanyu zhenli biaozhun wentide dabianlun.* Hong Kong: Sanlian shudian, 1989.

Tian Hao. "Ta shengwenle 'lingxiure.' " *Beijing qingnian bao* (8 November 1991).

"Tiananmenshangde Mao Zedong." *Beijing qingnian bao* (21 September 1994).

Tushu faxing gongzuo wenjian huibian (1979). Beijing: Xinhua shudian Beijing faxing suo, 1980.

Tushu faxing gongzuo wenjian, ziliao hui bian (shibianben). Beijing: Xinhua shudian Beijing faxing suo, January 1979.

Tushu faxing gongzuo wenjian huibian (1980). Beijing: Xinhua shudian Beijing faxing suo, March 1981.

Tushu faxing gongzuo wenjian huibian (1981). Beijing: Xinhua shudian Beijing faxing suo, June 1982.

Tushu faxing gongzuo wenjian huibian (1982). Beijing: Xinhua shudian Beijing faxing suo, March 1983.

Wang Dongxing. *Wang Dongxing riji.* Beijing: Zhongguo shehui kexue chubanshe, 1993.

Wang Hebin. *Xingcao shusheng Mao Zedong.* Beijing: Zhongguo renshi chubanshe, 1993.

Wang Ruoshui. "Mao Zedong wanniande daolu—ping Hu Sheng wei Mao Zedong kaituo zuize." *Kaifang zazhi* 7 (1994): 36–38.

Wang Shan (alias Luoyiningge'er). *Disan zhi yanjing kan Zhongguo.* Taiyuan: Shanxi renmin chubanshe, 1994.

Wang Shuo. *Wang Shuo wenji*, 4 vols. Beijing: Huayi chubanshe, 1992.

Wang Shuo, Feng Xiaogang, et al. *Bianjibude gushi—youmo dianshi gushi*, 2 vols. Shenyang: Shenyang chubanshe, 1992.

Wang Wangwang. "Huainian Mao Zedong ganji Deng Xiaoping 1994–1995." Shenzhen: Shenzhen Hongyu Dissemination Co. Ltd., 1993.

Wang Xingjuan. *He Zizhende lu.* Beijing: Zuojia chubanshe, 1985.

Wang Yue and Li Guijun, eds. *Mao Zedong moji dazidian.* Changsha: Hunan wenyi chubanshe, 1991.

Wang Zhuangling. " 'Wenge wenwu' chao." *Xin wenhua bao* 5 (1992).

Wei Wei. "Women, qidaizhe. . . ." *Zhongliu* 1 (1994): 3.

"Wei Mao zhuxi yuhu puqu." *Renmin ribao* (30 September, 12 October, and 25 October 1966).

"Wenhua geming yongfang guangmang—jinian Zhonggong zhongyang 1966 nian 5 yue 16 ri 'Tongzhi' shizhounian." *Renmin ribao* (16 May 1976).

Wu Fangze et al. *Xunzhao Mao Zedong.* Chengdu: Sichuan renmin chubanshe, 1991.

Wu Guanzhong. "Huangjin wanliang fu guansi." *Mingbao yuekan* 3 (1995): 57–63.

Wu Jiafeng. "Ping Wang Shuode yiduan hua." *Ershiyi shiji* 12 (1993): 144–45.

Wu Jiangguo et al., eds. *Dangdai Zhongguo yishi xingtai fengyunlu.* Beijing: Jingguan jiaoyu chubanshe, 1993.

Wu Mouren et al., eds. *Bajiu Zhongguo minyun jishi*, 2 vols. New York, 1990.

Xianggang Sanlian shudian, ed. *Aishuren yuebao* (15 September 1993).

———. "Mao Zedong tushu da jianyue." *Sanlian tongxun* (15 November 1992).

Xiao Fan. "Tamen wei Mao zhuxi hengdu Changjiang baobiao." *Qingnian yuebao* (Wuhan) 9 (1992).

Xiao Gongqin. "Gaige zhuanxingqi Zhongguo zhishifenzide xintai yu leixing fenhua." *Beijing qingnian bao* (2 February 1995).

Xin Ming. "Faxian Mao Zedong." *Zhongliu* 2 (1991): 18–21.

Xing Bensi. "Shehuizhuyiguanshangde zhongda tupo—du *Deng Xiaoping wenxuan disan juan*." *Zhongguo dangshi yanjiu* 2 (1994): 5–14.

Xinhua News Agency. "Jing Zhonggong zhongyang pizhun *Mao Zedong wenji* niannei chuban." *Jiefang ribao* (6 September 1993).

Xu Fei. "Yu sanbai xuesheng tong 'kan' gexing yu gemi." *Zhongguo qingnian yanjiu* 3 (1993): 12–16.

Xu Min. "Banyan Mao Zedongde diyi ren—fang Yu Shizhi." *Zhongguo guangbo yingshi* 12 (1993): 4–5.

Xu Weicheng. "'Zhonghua dajia chang (kala OK) jinku' xu." In *Yu Xinyan zawenxuan xubian*. Beijing: Beijing chubanshe, 1993, pp. 286–87.

Xue Yu. "Zhide pengMaozhe renzhen yidu." *Kaifang zazhi* 12 (1994): 38–40.

Yang Ping. "Disan zhong yanguang—ping *Disan zhi yanjing kan Zhongguo*." *Beijing qingnian bao* (25 June 1994).

———. "Lüelun 'xin zuoyi' de chuxian." *Beijing qingnian bao* (21 July 1994).

———. "Miandui Mao Zedong." *Beijing qingnianbao (Xinwen zhoukan)* (21 December 1993).

———. "*Zeng Guofan* xianxiangde qishi." *Beijing qingnian bao* (28 May 1994).

Ye Yonglie. *Lishi xuanzele Mao Zedong*. Shanghai: Shanghai renmin chubanshe, 1992.

———. *Hu Qiaomu*. Beijing: Zhonggong zhongyang dangxiao chubanshe, 1994.

Yi. "Xiandai pingju *Mao Zedong zai 1960* jinwan shangyan." *Beijing wanbao* (22 November 1994).

Yi Jun. "Furongguolide 'Mao Zedong re.'" *Zhengming* 12 (1993): 45–47.

Yin Hongbiao. "Rendao zhongniande 'Hongweibing' shidai." *Mingbao yuekan* 3 (1995): 37–39.

Yin Jindi. *Zhongguo wenhua getihu dasaomiao*. Chengdu: Sichuan renmin chubanshe, 1993.

Yin Zhao. "Weinisi yingzhan zuijia nü yanyuan Gong Li rongyao xiangei Shandong xiangqin." *Shijie ribao* (17 September 1992).

"Yu shidai tongbu he renmin tongxin—'Sanxingbei' shige zhenggao pingxuan huodong banjiang zuotan jiyao." *Zhongliu* 7 (1994): 18–33.

Yu Tian. "'Chaoxingzu—baozhuangshu' de qishi." *Zhongguo qingnian yanjiu* 2 (1994): 21–22.

Yu Xuejun. "Xiaoxiang xunji Mao Zedong." *Qingnian shidai* (Guizhou) 11–12 (1993): 2–4.

Yun Fei. "Cong 'Kaitian pidi' dao 'Qiushou qiyi'—ji qingnian Mao Zedong banyanzhe Wang Ying." *Zhongguo guangbo yingshi* 9 (1993): 8–9.

Zeng Ni. "Zhongguo Hunan jiancheng shouzuo Mao Zedong shenmiao, gedi xiangke dapi yongshi rida wuwan ren." *Donghua shibao* (Australian Edition) (6–12 July 1995).

Zhai Mowen. "Wu Guanzhong jiahua susongan zhuizong." *Zhongguo meishubao* (Taipei) 9 (1994).

Zhang Changlin. "Mao Zedong xiangzhang shoucangjia—Zhou Jihou." *Hunan ribao (Zhoumo zengkan)* (16 November 1991).

Zhang Chengzhi. "Hanwula-haote." In *Caoyan qishilu*. Beijing: Zhongguo gongren chubanshe, 1991, pp. 636–67.

———. *Huiminde huangtu gaoyuan: Zhang Chengzhi Huizu xiaoshuo.* Xining: Qinghai renmin chubanshe, 1993.

Zhang Chunqiao. "1967 nian 2 yue 21 ri Zhang Chunqiao zai Shanghai qunzhong dahuishangde jianghua." *Ziliao xuanbian,* a Red Guard publication (no date or place of publication).

Zhang Fan. "Zhongnanhai taiyi shouci pengji Li Zhisui." *Hualian shibao* (26 May 1995).

Zhang Peilin, ed. *Banquanxue anli.* Beijing: Beijing gongye daxue chubanshe, 1992.

Zhang Shulin. "Mao Zedong re, rechu yichang lianhuan guansi." *Zhongguo shibao zhoukan* (26 January–1 February 1992): 26–30.

Zhang Xiujiang. "Xunzhao weirende zuji." *Beijing wanbao* (13 October 1993).

Zhang Xixian. "Lüelun Zhongguo jin xiandaishishangde wuci xunzhao Mao Zedong." *Qinghua daxue yanjiusheng xuebao* 4 (1990): 89–95.

Zhang Yufeng. *Mao Zedong yishi.* Changsha: Hunan renmin chubanshe, 1989.

Zhang Zhanbin and Song Yifu. *Zhongguo: Mao Zedongre.* Taiyuan: Beiyue wenyi chubanshe, 1991.

Zhao Xiaoyuan. "Ta tuoqile *Hong taiyang.*" *Zhongguo qingnian* 11 (1992): 26–27.

Zhao Zhichao. "Yingmian zoulai Mao Xinyu." *Qingnian yuebao* 1 (1993): 11–13; 2 (1993): 14–16.

Zheng Wanlong and Li Xiaoming. *Kewang.* Beijing: Shiyue wenyi chubanshe, 1991.

Zheng Yi. "Miandui yidapian jingshen feixu." *Kaifang zazhi* 11 (1993): 56–57.

Zheng Youxian. "Shixi 'Mao Zedongre' xingcheng he fazhande yuanyin." *Qingnian tansuo* 5 (1992): 19–20.

"Zhezhong 'jinianshi' yinggai quxiao." In *Xuanchuan dongtai (xuanbian) 1979.* Beijing: Zhongguo shehui kexue chubanshe, 1980, pp. 135–36.

Zhonggong zhongyang wenxian bianji weiyuanhui, ed. *Mao Zedong zhuzuo xuandu.* Beijing: Renmin chubanshe, 1986.

Zhonggong zhongyang wenxian yanjiushi. *Guanyu jianguo yilai dangde ruogan lishi wentide jueyi, zhushiben (xiuding).* Beijing: Renmin chubanshe, 1985.

Zhonggong zhongyang wenxian yanjiushi, ed. *Mao Zedong du wenshi guji piyu ji.* Beijing: Zhongyang wenxian chubanshe, 1993.

Zhonggong zhongyang wenxian yanjiushi zonghezu, ed. *Lao yidai gemingjia lun dangshi yu dangshi yanjiu.* Xi'an: Shaanxi renmin chubanshe, 1993.

Zhonggong zhongyang xuanchuanbu, ed. *Dangde xuanchuan gongzuo wenxian xuanbian.* Beijing: Zhonggong zhongyang dangxiao chubanshe, 1989.

Zhongguo geming bowuguan, ed. *Jinian Mao Zedong.* Beijing: Wenwu chubanshe, 1986.

Zhongguo Mao Zedong sixiang lilun yu shijian yanjiuhui lishihui, ed. *Mao Zedong sixiang cidian.* Beijing: Zhonggong zhongyang dangxiao chubanshe, 1989.

Zhongguo zhaopian dang'anguan and Beijing Hangkong hangtian daxue, eds. *Huainian.* Beijing: Zhongyang wenxian chubanshe, 1992.

"Zhonghua renmin gongheguo guanggaofa (1994 nian 10 yue 27 ri dibajie quanguo renmin daibiao dahui changwu weiyuanhui dishici huiyi tongguo)." *Renmin ribao* (8 November 1994).

Zhongliu zazhishe and Sanxing qiye jituan gongsi. "Jinian Mao Zedong tongzhi danchen 100 zhounian 'Sanxingbei' shige zhenggao pingxuan huodong qishi." *Zhongliu* 3 (1993): 30.

Zhongnanhai huace bianji weiyuanhui, ed. *Pingfan yu weida—Mao Zedong Zhongnanhai yiwu yishi*. Beijing: Xiyuan chubanshe, 1993.

Zhongyang xuanchuanbu bangongting, ed. *Dangde xuanchuan gongzuo huiyi gaikuang he wenxian (1951–1992)*. Beijing: Zhonggong zhongyang dangxiao chubanshe, 1994.

———. *Dangde xuanchuan gongzuo wenjian xuanbian (1976–1992)*, 4 vols. Beijing: Zhonggong zhongyang dangxiao chubanshe, 1994.

Zhou Jihou. *Mao Zedong xiangzhang zhi mi—shijie dijiu da qiguan*. Taiyuan: Beiyue wenyi chubanshe, 1993.

———. "Mao Zedong xiangzhang xingshuailu." *Beijing qingnian bao* (27 August 1991).

Zhou Ming, ed. *Lishi zai zheli chensi*, 6 vols. Beijing: Huaxia chubanshe, 1986 and Taiyuan: Beiyue wenyi chubanshe, 1989.

Zhou Qun and Yao Xinrong. "Xinjiu Mao Zedong chongbai." *Ershiyi shiji* 12 (1993): 36–43.

Zhou Yongsheng. "Dangdai qingshaonian yingxiong chongbai yiqing qingxiang tantao—jianlun 'zhuixing' xianxiang." *Qingnian yanjiu* 6 (1994): 10–15.

"Zhouzhi luocheng Mao Zedong shoushu 'Changhenge' beilang." *Wenyi bao* (6 June 1992).

Zhu Yuan. "Mao Zedong zhenxiang qiaoqiao baoguang—dalu Maorezhongde zhongyao zixun xuan." *Kaifang zazhi* 11 (1993): 52–55.

Zhu Zuwei and Lin Xuan, et al. *Mao Zedong youpiao quanji*. Beijing: Beijing Yanshan chubanshe, 1991.

Zong Jun. *Zong shejishi*. Beijing: Zhonggong zhongyang dangxiao chubanshe, 1993.

Index

Geremie R. Barmé is a Fellow in Pacific and Asian History at the Australian National University in Canberra. He has published two collections of essays in Chinese and a number of books in English, including a translation of Yang Jiang's memoirs, *Lost in the Crowd; Seeds of Fire* (co-edited with John Minford); and *New Ghosts, Old Dreams* (co-edited with Linda Jaivin).